TRANSFORMATIVE ENCOUNTERS

BIBLICAL
INTERPRETATION
SERIES

VOLUME 43

TRANSFORMATIVE ENCOUNTERS

Jesus and Women Re-viewed

EDITED BY

INGRID ROSA KITZBERGER

BRILL
LEIDEN · BOSTON · KÖLN
2000

This book is printed on acid-free paper.

BT
590
.W6
T73
2000

Die Deutsche Bibliothek – CIP-Einheitsaufnahme

Transformative encounters: Jesus and women re-viewed / ed. by
Ingrid Rosa Kitzberger. - Leiden ; Boston ; Köln : Brill, 1999
 (Biblical interpretation series ; Vol. 43)
 ISBN 90-04-11311-8

Library of Congress Cataloging in Publication Data is also available

ISSN   0928-0731
ISBN   90 04 11311 8

PRINTED IN THE NETHERLANDS

In the beginning was the invitation,
and the invitation came from him.
All things came into being through him,
and without him nothing would have been.
In him was the idea,
and the idea was a spark of light.
The light shone into the dark,
where a host of ideas were in gestation.
And they were born of the will of a woman,
and of the will of men and women who joined her.
And the invitation became a book.
And it comes to you, dear readers,
and you are invited to receive it into your own locations.
And all who receive it,
who believe it is a challenge,
are given the power to become
transformed in the encounters.

CONTENTS

PART THREE

ACTUALIZATIONS

CONTRIBUTORS

Carmen Bernabé Ubieta
Universidad de Deusto
Facultad de Teologia
Bilbao
SPAIN

Musa W. Dube Shomanah
University of Botswana
Department of Theology
and Religious Studies
Gaborone
BOTSWANA

Séan Freyne
University of Dublin
Trinity College
Dublin
IRELAND

Leticia A. Guardiola-Sáenz
Vanderbilt University
The Divinity School
Nashville, Tennessee
U.S.A.

Tal Ilan
The Hebrew University
of Jerusalem
Jerusalem
ISRAEL

Hisako Kinukawa
International Christian
University
Tokyo
JAPAN

Ingrid Rosa Kitzberger
Universität Münster
Katholisch-Theologische
Fakultät
Münster
GERMANY

Amy-Jill Levine
Vanderbilt University
The Divinity School
Nashville, Tennessee
U.S.A.

Lilly Nortjé-Meyer
Rand Africaans University
Johannesburg
SOUTH AFRICA

Gerbern S. Oegema
Universität Tübingen
Institut für antikes Judentum
und hellenistische
Religionsgeschichte
Tübingen
GERMANY

Daniel Patte
Vanderbilt University
Department of Religious Studies
Nashville, Tennessee
U.S.A.

Victoria Phillips
West Virginia Wesleyan College
Buckhannon, West Virginia
U.S.A.

Marie-Eloise Rosenblatt
Graduate Theological Union
Berkeley, California
U.S.A.

Marianne Sawicki
Erasmus Institute
University of Notre Dame
Notre Dame, Indiana
U.S.A.

William R. Telford
University of Newcastle
Department of Religious Studies
Newcastle upon Tyne
ENGLAND

Elaine M. Wainwright
Catholic Theological College
Banyo, Brisbane
AUSTRALIA

ACKNOWLEDGEMENTS

This volume came into being through many encounters, which each had their particular and unique share in its making. It is, therefore, my sincere wish to extend my heartfelt gratitude to all those who contributed in their own individual ways.

David E. Orton invited me to do a volume on "Jesus and women." The timing for this challenge was perfect in terms of my own research and development. He accompanied my project with encouragement, patience, and good humour. Without him this volume would not be.

All those colleagues from all over the globe who joined me on this project and contributed their own creative ideas, made this volume possible in the first place. Without them this volume would not be. Besides that, I owe them innumerable challenging and enrichening encounters which have transformed my work as a biblical scholar as well as my personal life.

Many colleagues and friends who shared their interest in and enthusiasm about this project encouraged me to journey on through the more troubled times and waters.

Edgar McKnight, from Furman University (Greenville, SC), introduced me to cyberspace and thus made many lively encounters in virtual reality possible, which eventually led to a fuller realization of actual encounters between myself and all contributors around the globe. Without him, this project could not have been carried through so effectively.

Rosa Suiter supported and encouraged me with her unfailing love, concern, and interest through all the stages of the project and shared my enthusiasm about "the book." Encountering Jesus on the other side of life may be the reward she truly deserves, leaving her ultimately transformed.

Rosemary Brown has been an invaluable source of strength and vision throughout, until the last minute of the birthing process. Her expertise in reading papers and the stars has added much to the quality of the book and provided a glimpse of the deeper meanings behind both earthly and heavenly encounters. "Per aspera ad astra"— not without her.

Eugen Ruckstuhl (University of Lucerne, Switzerland) proclaimed, throughout his life and career, Jesus' special friendship with and advocacy for women, and acted accordingly. He has greatly shaped and influenced my own career and my work on Jesus and women, in particular in the Gospel of John. Encountering him at the well in the borderland shortly before his final departure has been like a beacon and lasting testament ever since.

Wolfgang Beilner (University of Salzburg, Austria), encouraged me, from early on, to encounter Jesus in the Scriptures, in spite of, or because of, being a woman. Knowing where I come from has empowered me to venture out into the unknown, and to cross borders in the process.

To all of you, THANK YOU!

INTRODUCTION

"But," she said. Resisting the resistance,
she re-defined the situation, turning the insult into a promise.
"Great," he said. Responding to her challenge,
he re-viewed his mission, turning its exclusivism into a global vision.

§ § §

"Jesus," she exclaimed. Touching his garment,
the gardener had turned into him.
His garment became glistening, intensely white,
as no fuller on earth could bleach it.
And her tears became
a stream of living water. Turning round,
she embarked on her first missionary journey.

~ ~ ~

Contacts between Jesus and women are transformative encounters, from the first moment when his mother Mary conceived him in her womb, according to the angel's message (Luke 1:26–38), until his last encounter with another Mary in the garden, after his final transformation (John 20:11–18). Jesus' life, as rendered in the Gospels, is marked throughout by his encounters with women, who he meets in the streets and in their houses (e.g. Luke 10:38–42; John 11:1–46; 12:1–8), and who, on the other hand, come to meet him, in the streets (e.g. Mark 5:24–35) and in other people's houses (e.g. Mark 14:3–9 par Matt.; Luke 7:36–50). Whether mentioned in passing or explored in more detail in a longer narrative, all these encounters bring about transformation. Women are healed and restored to their full integrity (e.g. Luke 13:10–17), or to life itself (e.g. Mark 5:21–24, 36–43); women follow him and leave behind their homes (Luke 8:1–3; Mark 15:40–41 parr), or remain in their homes, yet drastically changed (Mark 1:29–31; John 11/12). However, transformation happens also to Jesus, and this becomes most apparent in his encounter with the Syrophoenician/Canaanite woman (Mark 7:24–30; Matt. 15:21–28). Encounter, by its very nature, denotes a mutual process. Consequently, it affects both parties involved, even if Jesus transformed by a woman may not so easily be acceptable to some readers, starting with the author of Luke's Gospel, who decided to do away with this shocking story. To be sure, the potential in the Gospel stories dealing with encounters between Jesus and women is greater than its visible actualization in the text, however different the four Gospels are from each other also for that matter. Nevertheless, all Gospels also point to the reality behind the texts, that is, the transformative encounters between Jesus and women in first-century Palestine, and the formative impact of these encounters regarding the Jesus movement and the ensuing rise of Christianity in the context of its Jewish roots and heritage.

All this in view, "transformative encounters" were the lenses I programmatically chose and offered to colleagues when I started the project on "Jesus and women" in spring 1996. Besides pertaining to Jesus and women in the Gospel texts and in the historical reality behind them, as briefly sketched above, my concept, and hence my letter of invitation, referred to two further transformative encounters:

– between the biblical texts and the readers/interpreters,
– and between different interpreters applying different methods and working within different paradigms.

From the onset, the project was designed as multi-dimensional, global and post-colonial. It aimed at bringing together the widest possible range of colleagues, men and women, Jews and Christians, from all continents and very different social locations, to join on a topic of unwavering relevance and importance even 2000 years after its origin. Thereby, it aimed at inclusiveness regarding gender, race, ethnicity, class, and religious affiliation. Transformative encounters were en-visioned not only as referring to the subject, but also to the process of working on the project and to those involved in it. By joining together a variety of biblical scholars and the wide range of different methods employed all around the globe, I trusted that, eventually, the issue of "Jesus and women" would be re-viewed when asking new questions, addressing new issues, realizing new contexts, and challenging what has so far been taken for granted, including one's own stance in biblical scholarship. Thereby, the location of knowledge and its communal aspect was taken into account, and the transformative power of "reading with" others.

Sowing my programme of "transformative encounters," it fell into very good soil indeed, regardless of a few devouring birds, rocks and thorns (cf. Mark 4:3–8). It was, in fact, enthusiastically embraced by many colleagues who, in turn, came forth with their own creative ideas. Re-viewing Jesus and women started during the initial stages already, when discussing the project and deciding on the topics of the respective papers in the encounters between potential contributors and myself. It's been a pleasure to see many different and charming plants grow from the seed, in as many varieties as the soil they sprang from.

This present volume presents these plants, to you, dear readers. They have grown in a garden of transformative encounters, in virtual and real reality, in particular at the AAR/SBL Annual Meetings in New Orleans 1996, San Francisco 1997, and Orlando 1998, as well as at the SNTS Annual Meetings in Birmingham 1997 and Copenhagen 1998. Encountering each other has shaped the papers, and ourselves. All of them are original contributions, written specifically for this volume; some of them were "tested" with respective audiences at these and other meetings, and transformed in the process of the ensuing challenges.

The sixteenfold fruit of papers in this volume is arranged according to its three parts:

– literary approaches
– historical re-construction and contextualization
– actualizations.

Attribution is mainly due to the methodological approach and hermeneutical paradigm applied in them, and hence as pertaining to the three respective worlds of text interpretation: the world *in* the text, the world *behind* the text, and the world *in front of* the text. However, the borders and boundaries are not strict, as will become obvious very soon in reading the contributions. Each paper was engendered and strongly influenced by the worlds of the readers/interpreters in front of the texts, even when they focus on the worlds in or the worlds behind the texts. And vice versa, the worlds in the texts and those discovered behind the texts have strongly shaped and affected the worlds of the readers/interpreters in front of the texts. Thus, "the transformative power of reading"[1] as a border crossing experience has become apparent.

The *literary approaches*, as presented here, focus on the literary character and the narrative structure of the Gospel texts and their many

---

[1] W. Jeanrond, *Theological Hermeneutics. Development and Significance* (London: SCM, 1994), ch. 5 on "The Transformative Power of Reading," pp. 93–119.

dimensions regarding plot, characterization, and point of view. They offer new reading strategies based on narrative criticism, reader response criticism, and intertextuality.

Historical re-construction and contextualization, as presented in the second part, aims at situating Jesus and women in the context of first century Palestine and Mediterranean society. In addressing the Jewishness of both Jesus and his first followers, but also their embeddedness within a Hellenistic context, issues of gender, ethnicity, and class are raised. In so doing, historical-critical methods are employed, besides drawing on archaeology and social-scientific studies in cross-cultural perspective, including psychology and psychiatry, and medical anthropology.

Finally, *actualizations* comprise papers which concentrate on a variety of aspects of the same underlying core: the potential of biblical texts and their surplus of meaning. Actualization, consequently, refers to the realization of the many potentials of the texts in the readings of real readers, and it refers to readers reading readings, and hence to intercultural criticism.[2] Texts, as understood in this part, pertain to written texts, oral texts, and texts en-visioned on screen. The plurality of texts encountering each other testifies also to the interface of ordinary and critical readings.[3] Methods applied in this part are: cultural studies, with its focus on social location (and its questioning by a resisting reader); divination as an ethical method of reading; and literary and film theory, pertaining to intertextuality and "reversing the hermeneutical flow."[4]

All papers, regardless of point of departure and approach to the same goal, "Jesus and women," have one thing in common: they offer challenges and surprises, one way or another.

---

[2] F. F. Segovia, "Reading Readers of the Fourth Gospel and Their Readings: An Exercise in Intercultural Criticism," in idem (ed.), *"What is John?" Volume I: Readers and Readings of the Fourth Gospel* (SBL Symposium Series, 3; Atlanta, GA: Scholars, 1996), pp. 237–77, and idem, "Reading Readers Reading John: An Exercise in Intercultural Criticism," in idem (ed.), *"What is John?" Volume II: Literary and Social Readings of the Fourth Gospel* (SBL Symposium Series, 7; Atlanta, GA: Scholars, 1998), pp. 281–322.

[3] G. West and M. W. Dube (eds.), *"Reading With": An Exploration of the Interface Between Critical and Ordinary Readings of the Bible. African Overtures* (*Semeia*, 73; Atlanta, GA: Scholars, 1996); D. Patte, *Ethics of Biblical Interpretation: A Reevaluation* (Louisville, KY: Westminster John Knox, 1995), pp. 76–107.

[4] L. J. Kreitzer, *The New Testament in Fiction and Film. On Reversing the Hermeneutical Flow* (The Biblical Seminar, 17; Sheffield: Sheffield Academic Press, 1993), and idem, *The Old Testament in Fiction and Film. On Reversing the Hermeneutical Flow* (The Biblical Seminar, 24; Sheffield: Sheffield Academic Press, 1994).

In her contribution "Full Disclosure: Towards a Complete Characterization of the Women Who Followed Jesus in the Gospel according to Mark," Victoria Phillips challenges the characterization of the women followers in Mark, culminating in re-visioning their motivation for journeying to the tomb on Easter morning. Like the women themselves, the readers of this piece will meet with a surprise.

"Surprising Models of Discipleship" are revealed in Daniel Patte's reading of "The Canaanite Woman and Jesus" in Matt. 15:21–28, as "challenging our domesticated understanding of discipleship." Whether this be considered shocking or liberating, let the reader decide. Transformation is guaranteed in encountering a male European-American encountering the woman and Jesus at the cross-roads of text and readers.

Concentrating on "Gentile Female Characters in Matthew's Story," Lilly Nortjé-Meyer presents them as "An Illustration of Righteousness," thereby challenging and transcending the borders of ethnicity between a Jewish concept and its gentile appropriation. Informed by her social location as a white South African, righteousness is re-viewed in its post-apartheid perspective.

In my own contribution on "Synoptic Women in John. Interfigural Readings," I challenge the traditional views of the relationship between John and the Synoptics and show the presence of Synoptic female characters in John which are not visible at first sight. Surprising encounters are guaranteed, between men and women.

In her chapter "In the Footsteps of Jesus: Jewish Women in a Jewish Movement," Tal Ilan challenges many a Christian notion of its origins, in particular as it pertains to the female following of Jesus. Why were women attracted to the Jesus movement, over against other choices they had? The question invites and engenders a different view by stepping outside the ideological framework and by viewing sociological facts from a distance, thereby setting them in a new perspective.

Re-viewing the "Haemorrhaging Woman's Story Mark 5:25–34," Marie-Eloise Rosenblatt questions the commonly en-visioned ethnicity of the woman, thereby opening up new vistas of the story behind the story. Resisting the resistance is viewed in a striking new context of legal documents testifying to the transforming power of women going public. Rosenblatt's Christian-Jewish identity and her training and experience in law have informed this paper.

"Jesus the Wine-drinker: A Friend of Women" addresses a widely neglected vilification brought forward against Jesus. How do the two elements of the accusation of being a drunkard (besides a glutton) and his company of women relate, if at all, to each other? Séan Freyne, a lover of wine and women himself and an expert in archaeology, has brought forward challenging data and an equally challenging imagination in relating them to each other. He might well cheer you up in the process of reading.

Why were Joanna and Mary Magdalene paired in Luke's account of the women followers of Jesus? Starting with the question, Marianne Sawicki investigates the fascinating world of "Magdalenes and Tiberiennes" and consequently "City Women in the Entourage of Jesus." Drawing on rich archaeological evidence and on an equally rich imagination, available data are re-viewed within gendered archaeology and related to both hints and silences within Gospel texts. Issues of class and culture are raised in the process. A transformed view of the Jesus movement and its women results.

"Mary Magdalene and the Seven Demons in Social-scientific Perspective," as re-viewed by Carmen Bernabé Ubieta, addresses Mary Magdalene's illness in the context of cross-cultural studies in psychology and psychiatry. Drawing on the models of I. M. Lewis, Mary Douglas, and E. Dio-Bleichmar, the relation between women's physical bodies and society as body, in particular in its patriarchal shape, are analysed. Consequently, the healing of Mary Magdalene, and many other women, by Jesus has bearing not only on his relation to women, but also to the society of his time at large.

"Jesus, Women, and Healing in the Gospel of Matthew" are explored by Elaine M. Wainwright, starting with the impact of Jesus' confirming words addressed to women: "Your faith has made you well." Drawing on medical anthropology in cross-cultural perspective, the genderization of healing within the Jesus movement and in the Mediterranean challenges the traditional views of Jesus' healing powers and of the women healed by him.

Investigating the "Portrayals of Women in 1 and 2 Maccabees," Gerbern S. Oegema offers striking material, whose possible impact and bearing on women in the Jesus movement and the ensuing Christian churches facing persecution and martyrdom may be pondered. Besides that, the issue of class among the first followers of Jesus and their relations, if any, to the priestly dominated upper class in Jerusalem comes to the fore. Hasmonean names among the women followers of Jesus might offer equally new vistas. Evidence may activate the imagination.

Reading from her hybrid cultural identity as a Mexican-American woman from the borderlands living in the diaspora, Leticia Guardiola-Sáenz offers an unprecedented and unique reading of the story commonly entitled "the adulteress." The title of her paper is programmatic: "Border-crossing and Its Redemptive Power in John 7:53–8:11: A Cultural Reading of Jesus and *the Accused*." No reader will be able to resist the transformative power of this reading, whether he or she decides to remain within her/his borders, or crosses them as a consequence.

Presenting "An Interaction-centred Interpretation" of "The Miracle Story of the Bent-over Woman in Luke 13:10–17," Hisako Kinukawa approaches the story and the interaction of characters in it from her location as a Japanese woman dealing with the bending-over of Korean women. The encounter between the story world of the text and that of life in front of the text engenders a startling new reading for justice, liberation, and healing transformation.

In "Divining Texts for International Relations," Musa W. Dube Shomanah comes to the text Matt. 15:21–28 with the "other" text of her life and of the oral culture of her Batswana people. Starting from her oral text over against the written texts and regarding the latter as "bones-texts" for investigating international relations, she challenges, and possibly upsets, the notions of many a Western trained biblical scholar. By presenting an ethical method of reading biblical texts, which were previously used by the colonizers and have been re-appropriated by the ordinary, non-specialist readings of an oral culture and their "indigenized reading strategies," domesticated, traditional notions of biblical scholarship will be questioned fundamentally.

In "Lilies of the Field and Wandering Jews: Biblical Scholarship, Women's Roles, and Social Location," Amy-Jill Levine puts all social location readings, especially those of other feminists, on trial. The starting point for her resisting reading is her own social location as a Jewish woman confronted with the anti-Judaism permeating the numerous publications on "Jesus and women." Warning against the projection of present social locations into Jewish antiquity at the price of anti-Judaism, her chapter is a powerful wake-up call. Let anyone with ears to hear listen!

Last but not least, William R. Telford takes his readers into the fascinating world of media and their intertextual transformations of biblical texts in his chapter on "Jesus and Women in Fiction and Film." Drawing on L. J. Kreitzer's concept of "reversing the hermeneutical flow," new light is shed on the biblical texts themselves and on their portrayal of the transformative encounters between Jesus and women. Engendered by the rich imagination of its authors, the novels and films analysed here call forth the imagination of readers and spectators. This chapter implies the invitation to its readers to read the novels and watch the films addressed, and, in "reversing the hermeneutical flow," return to the Gospel texts with new lenses.

Each chapter makes up for the multi-facetted picture of Jesus and women presented here, which has resulted from the assembly of such diverse and colourful pieces. While each has its particular place in the overall project of "Transformative Encounters," they also interpret and influence each other in this context in a creative and challenging fashion. Many lines run through different pieces, linking them together in a way but different from the distribution chosen by the three parts of the volume. For example, the question of why women chose the Jesus movement in the first place, is an issue in the papers of Tal Ilan and of Séan Freyne, yet viewed from two different sides: Jewish sects on the one hand, Hellenistic mystery cults on the other hand. Interestingly enough, both make explicit that women had choices in the first place and could make decisions regarding their religious affiliations. Regarding the healing of women by Jesus, the chapters by Elaine M. Wainwright and Carmen Bernabé Ubieta, as well as the paper by Tal Ilan, shed new light on one another. Genderization of healing activities inside and outside the Jesus movement, and the relation of Jesus' healing women from illnesses and possession and being himself accused of possession and witchcraft as typical female transgressions, raise startling new questions. Furthermore, relating Marianne Sawicki's paper to that of Gerbern S. Oegema, the Hasmonean heritage within the Jesus movement may be re-viewed. Finally, ethnicity is raised as an issue *in* the text and *in front of* the text in the chapters by Marie-Eloise Rosenblatt, Leticia Guardiola-Sáenz, Musa W. Dube Shomanah, and Hisako Kinukawa. You, dear readers, are invited to discover more of the links between individual chapters which now make a challenging new text.

Border crossing is most welcome, in reading and as a consequence of it. Any interpretations, and those presented here in particular, are also texts, which have been created through the intertextuality of reader and focus text. Texts, however, are powerful, for better or for worse. They create new universes and propose worlds, according to Ricoeur. They shape and influence the realities of those who encounter them, whether in a resisting or an asserting manner. Thus, "the transformative power of reading" pertains also to the reading of these interpretations/texts. And hence, the ethics of interpretation,[5] which has been the concern of those involved in this project, implicit or explicit, is put also before you, our readers. Being accountable for our interpretations, you will be held accountable for what you do with them and for the worlds created out of them. Struggle and conflict are part of the process. Transformative encounters are born *from* them, not by avoiding them. Re-viewing Jesus and women from the many perspectives presented in this volume offers the chance of also re-viewing our present world and our relations, inside and outside academia. Awakening the imagination is strongly encouraged.

Ingrid Rosa Kitzberger
In the wake of Pentecost, 1999

---

[5] Patte, *Ethics of Biblical Interpretation*; E. Schüssler Fiorenza, "The Ethics of Reading: Decentering Biblical Scholarship," *JBL* 107 (1988), pp. 3–17; D. Nolan Fewell and G. A. Phillips (eds.), *Bible and Ethics of Reading* (*Semeia*, 77; Atlanta: GA, Scholars, 1997).

PART ONE

LITERARY APPROACHES

FULL DISCLOSURE: TOWARDS A COMPLETE CHARACTERIZATION OF THE WOMEN WHO FOLLOWED JESUS IN THE GOSPEL ACCORDING TO MARK

VICTORIA PHILLIPS

Introduction

One of the achievements of feminist biblical criticism has been establishing that Jesus included in his circle of disciples both men and women.[1] What to make of this discovery is still being pondered. The Gospel according to Mark is an apt text for considering the significance of women's discipleship, because the Gospel concludes with the actions of the women who followed Jesus, a focus that seems to underscore the absence of male disciples. No male disciples witness the crucifixion, whereas female disciples watch from afar (15:40). No male disciples observe Joseph's preparing the body for burial and its entombing, whereas female disciples do (15:47). No male disciples journey to the tomb three days later, but three female disciples go there with spices for anointing (16:1). The absent presence of the male disciples is invoked when the young man charges the women to "go and tell Peter and the disciples" that Jesus has gone before them to Galilee (16:7). The female disciples seem courageous, loyal, and loving; the male disciples cowardly, apostate, and selfish. But, whatever sense of the insufficiency of the men's discipleship a reader may have is quickly diverted to question the sufficiency of women's discipleship by the closing line of the Gospel. In response to the young man, the women flee the tomb and say nothing to anyone, silenced by their fear (16:8). Why the women are silenced by fear, what it signifies

---

[1] E. Schüssler Fiorenza, *In Memory of Her: A Feminist Theological Reconstruction of Christian Origins* (New York: Crossroad, 1983); W. Munro, "Women Disciples in Mark?," *CBQ* 44 (1982), pp. 225–41; and L. Schottroff, "Mary Magdalene and the Women at Jesus' Tomb," in *Let the Oppressed Go Free: Feminist Perspectives on the New Testament* (Gender and the Biblical Tradition; Louisville, KY: Westminster John Knox, 1991), pp. 168–203; and *idem*, "Women as Disciples of Jesus in New Testament Times," in *Let the Oppressed Go Free*, pp. 80–130.

about them as disciples, and its import for the absent male disciples are all critical questions whose answers require constructing a characterization of the women who followed Jesus.

Current characterizations of the Markan women who followed Jesus are unsatisfactory for several reasons. One, most characterizations replicate their absence from the Gospel until their sudden materialization 15:40; that is, they do not discuss the women who followed Jesus until after Jesus has died.[2] So doing perpetuates the deeply embedded perception that "the disciples" refers solely to the male disciples. Numerous interpretations of 16:7–8 rest on the false dichotomy of "the disciples" and "the women."[3] Critical reading of the androcentric language of the text would obviate these problems.

Two, the textual evidence for characterizations of the female disciples is limited to the scenes in which they explicitly appear: watching the crucifixion (15:40–41), watching the entombment of Jesus (15:46–47), and their encounter with the young man (16:1–8). Limiting the evidence to these passages means, with the exception of 16:8, that a reader must infer from the actions of the women their reasons for so acting. That is, the text gives no explanatory comment on why the women go to the cross, why they observe Joseph of Arimathea, and why they take spices for anointing to the tomb. Such suppression of motive is not unusual in androcentric and patriarchal

---

[2] For example, D. R. A. Hare, *Mark* (Westminster Bible Companion; Lousville, KY: Westminster John Knox, 1996), although he mentions them on p. 184; H. Kinukawa, *Women and Jesus in Mark: A Japanese Feminist Perspective* (Maryknoll, NY: Orbis Books, 1994); H. M. Humphrey, *He is Risen! A New Reading of Mark's Gospel* (New York and Mahwah, N.J.: Paulist, 1992); M. A. Tolbert, "Mark," in C. A. Newsom and Sh. H. Ringe (eds.), *The Women's Bible Commentary* (London: SPCK, and Louisville, KY: Westminster John Knox, 1992), pp. 263–74; H. C. Waetjen, *A Reordering of Power: A Socio-Political Reading of Mark's Gospel* (Minneapolis, MN: Augsburg Fortress, 1989), although he acknowledges on p. 103 that the circle of the disciples includes men and women.

[3] If the interpretation rests on whether or not the women convey the message to the absent disciples, then it collapses once it is realized that the women are themselves disciples; if the interpretation does not become incoherent, then it reveals that the focus of concern is not whether "disciples" get the message, but whether the *male* disciples do. See, among others, N. Perrin, *The Resurrection according to Matthew, Mark and Luke* (Philadelphia, PA: Fortress, 1977); T. J. Weeden, Sr., *Mark—Traditions in Conflict* (Philadelphia, PA: Fortress, 1979); N. Petersen, "When is the End Not the End? Literary Reflections on the Ending of Mark's Narrative," *Interpretation* 34 (1980), pp. 151–66; and W. Kelber, *The Oral and the Written Gospel: The Hermeneutics of Speaking and Writing in the Synoptic Tradition, Mark, Paul, and Q* (Philadelphia, PA: Fortress, 1983).

texts, and the challenge of a critical feminist interpretation is to recover—or supply—the unacknowledged motivation.[4]

Inferring from narrative action alone leads to the attribution of stereotypical gendered motives, such as women's love, devotion, and loyalty explaining their presence at the cross. Appeal is sometimes made to cultural practice: women's role in burial and bereavement.[5] Their presence at the cross is sometimes attributed in a general way to "their discipleship" or "their service,"[6] without specifying in what way witnessing Jesus' death or mourning his passing are connected with teachings about discipleship. In the Gospel according to Mark, Jesus does not encourage love or devotion toward himself, but imitation (cf. 8:34; 8:38; 10:18; 10:43–45).

The cumulative effect of such strategies and characterizations minimizes, if not obscures, the women's status as disciples, concomitantly transforming them into minor characters, despite acknowledged problems in defining them as minor,[7] or interpreting their presence as merely literary, demanded by the plot, or necessary for rhetorical effect.[8]

I propose that an adequate characterization of the women who followed Jesus must follow out the implications that they are disciples. That is, it will consider the women as having motives or reasons for their actions that are grounded in the expectations that the

---

[4] Having at its disposal more texts about women, feminist scholarship on the Hebrew Bible has explored the issue of suppressed motives. See E. Fuchs, "Who is Hiding the Truth? Deceptive Women and Biblical Androcentrism," in A. Yarbro Collins (ed.), *Feminist Perspectives on Biblical Scholarship* (SBL Centennial Publications, 10; Chico, CA: Scholars, 1985), pp. 136–44; A. Bach, "The Pleasure of Her Text," in A. Bach (ed.), *Ad Feminam. Union Seminary Quarterly Review* 43 (1989), pp. 41–58; and J. Ch. Exum, "Murder They Wrote: Ideology and the Manipulation of Female Presence in Biblical Narrative," in A. Bach (ed.), *Ad Feminam*, pp. 19–39.

[5] C. Osiek, "The Women at the Tomb: What Are They Doing There?," *Ex Auditu* 9 (1993), pp. 97–107.

[6] E. Struthers Malbon, "The Major Importance of the Minor Characters in Mark," in E. V. McKnight and E. Struthers Malbon (eds.), *The New Literary Criticism and the New Testament* (Valley Forge, PA: Trinity Press International, 1994), pp. 58–86, esp. 68–9; Osiek, "The Women at the Tomb," p. 106; Schottroff, "Mary Magdalene," p. 173.

[7] J. F. Williams, *Other Followers: Minor Characters as Major Figures in Mark's Gospel* (JSNT Supplement Series, 102; Sheffield: Sheffield Academic Press, 1994), p. 30; and Struthers Malbon, "Minor Characters," pp. 60–1.

[8] Petersen, "Ending," pp. 159–61; Tolbert, *Sowing the Gospel*, pp. 298–9; and J. Camery-Hoggatt, *Irony in Mark's Gospel* (Cambridge: Cambridge University Press, 1992), p. 177.

Gospel expresses for disciples. Of such expectations, Vernon Robbins emphasizes the disciples' preparation for remembering Jesus' teachings and acting on them in his absence.[9]

> The pattern of behavior exhibited by Jesus in the three-step progressions identifies him as a teacher whose goal is to transmit his system of thought and action to a group of disciple-companions who will perpetuate the system after his death. The death of the teacher tests the success of the effort. After this time there is no possibility for the disciples to return to the teacher to receive further instruction and encouragement. The disciple-companion goes on his [sic] own to embody the system of thought and action that his teacher attempted to transmit to him.[10]

Since the female disciples appear explicitly in scenes related to Jesus' death and resurrection, it will be necessary to determine what Jesus taught about responding to those events.[11] Then one can speculate on what the female disciples learned from Jesus' teachings. Attempting such reconstruction means facing the issue of the women's late entrance into the Gospel.

Having learned on a "first" reading that women number among Jesus' disciples, one could decide to re-read the Gospel in light of that knowledge. This proposes interpretive challenges—if there are no scenes in which the women who follow Jesus are represented, then it seems one is reduced to the less than ideal argument from silence. But this is only an apparent dilemma, which rests on assuming that "the disciples," an androcentric term, refers only to male disciples. Elisabeth Schüssler Fiorenza has argued that androcentric language should be critically interpreted as inclusive of men and women unless a specific case can be made for restricting the term to men or to women only.[12] Critically assessing the scenes in which "the disciples" may be construed as referring to men and women,

---

[9] V. K. Robbins, *Jesus the Teacher: A Socio-Rhetorical Interpretation of Mark* (Philadelphia, PA: Fortress, 1984), esp. pp. 19–51.

[10] Robbins, *Jesus the Teacher*, p. 48.

[11] M. Cotes asserts that the proper response is "faith," because "Knowing who Jesus is, is not a question of being told information. It is a question of looking again at the events of his earthly life, and making a response of faith" ("Women, Silence and Fear [Mark 16.9]," in G. J. Brooke (ed.), *Women in the Biblical Tradition* [Studies in Women and Religion, 31; Lewiston, N.Y.: Edwin Mellen, 1992], p. 165). However, such a view shifts the question of what the women as characters might be doing to the question of how we as readers are supposed to respond to Jesus.

[12] Schüssler Fiorenza, *In Memory of Her*, p. 44.

to men only, or to women only, will provide an alternative to the argument from silence.

Granting the rubric of "disciple" to both the men and women who followed Jesus will aid in comprehending the final episode of the Gospel. It will call for re-thinking Mark's teachings about discipleship, the resurrection, and life in the interlude before Jesus returns. In Jesus' absence, other than instances in which they are standing trial (for then they have the Holy Spirit speaking in them, 13:11), disciples have his teachings to rely on, which means they must remember them. "Heaven and earth will pass away, but my words will not pass away" (13:31). To make use of Jesus' words, disciples must remember them; Peter, for example, remembers too late, what Jesus taught about him (14:72b). To make use of Jesus' words, disciples must have heard them—the bewildering discovery the women make at the tomb is that they have not been told a key teaching. The reader knows that Jesus has said that he will go to Galilee after he is risen; the young man in white at the tomb knows that Jesus said that. Do the women? Or are they hearing it for the first time?

Who Are the Women Who Followed Jesus?

The women who followed Jesus are his female disciples. The key text for identifying female disciples in the Gospel according to Mark is 15:40–41:

> Now some women were observing this from a distance, among whom were Mary of Magdala, and Mary the mother of James the younger and Joses, and Salome. <These women> had regularly followed and assisted him when he was in Galilee, along with many other women who had come up to Jerusalem in his company. (*The Scholars Bible Version*)[13]

In the struggle to break the androcentric assumption that the disciples must be men, feminists developed strategies to show that women fit the criteria for discipleship. Since there are no call stories for the women who followed Jesus, nor is the feminine form of "disciple" used in the Gospels (the sole instance in the New Testament occurs

---

[13] D. D. Schmidt, *The Gospel of Mark* (The Scholars Bible; Sonoma, CA: Polebridge, 1990).

in Acts 9:36 for Tabitha), characterizing the women who followed
Jesus as disciples is based on their being described as "following"
and "assisting/serving" Jesus.[14]

Confirming, or more precisely, anticipating 15:41, the presence of
female disciples is implied by an earlier text, 3:33–35:

> In response he says to them: "My mother and my brothers—who ever
> are they? And looking right at those seated around him in a circle,
> he says, "Here are my mother and my sisters and my brothers. Whoever
> does God's will, that's my brother and sister and mother! (*The Scholars
> Bible Version*)

These texts are rarely brought together, but when they are they provide a starting point for developing a richer characterization of the
female disciples in the Markan Gospel. Set in its larger context of
Jesus' teaching, 3:33–35 reminds us that disciples are taught by Jesus
with the expectation that they will carry out his teaching.

Many feminist critics (and some mainstream scholars) make the
connection between the female disciples' presence at the cross with
Jesus' teaching the importance of taking up one's cross in 8:34 ("If
anyone wants to become my followers, let them deny themselves and
take up their cross and follow me," NRSV).[15] But, some scholars do
not interpret their presence at the cross as an act of discipleship,
but as establishing them as reliable witnesses for the events subsequent to Jesus' death.[16] They do serve as witnesses for those events
(after all, the male disciples are absent), but placing the emphasis on
their functioning as witnesses elides their being characters in a narrative who have motives that can be determined. Emphasis shifts
subtly to the evangelist who introduces them as witnesses rather than
to asking: do the women have a reason for thinking it is important
to view the crucifixion? It is one thing to go, because a given disciple has accepted to risk sharing Jesus' fate, another because she
has determined the importance of witnessing Jesus' fate.

The women who followed Jesus are not the only women present
observing the crucifixion. In addition, there "are many other women

---

[14] Munro ("Women Disciples," pp. 232–4) and Schottroff ("Mary Magdalene,"
pp. 176–8) offer two of the best treatments of the argument for women's discipleship on the basis of these two terms.
[15] For example, Schüssler Fiorenza, *In Memory of Her*, pp. 320ff.
[16] See, e.g., Waetjen, *Reordering*, p. 239.

who had come up with him to Jerusalem." Should these women also be considered disciples? Both Schüssler Fiorenza and Schottroff argue that they are, because they are present at the cross, a theological emphasis of Mark's, and because the verb "going up" (ἀναβαίνον-τες) is used both by the narrator and by Jesus to when Jesus explains that "going up" to Jerusalem means encountering suffering and death (10:32–34).[17] I do not agree, because "going up" to Jerusalem is ordinary discourse for travelling to Jerusalem. Since the text uses language of contrast ("many other women"), yet uses language of indefinite association ("came up with him") as opposed to relational terms ("followed and served him"), I conclude the other women may well be considered believers in Jesus as the Messiah, but they remain distinct from the female disciples.

If they are a group of women distinct from the female disciples, certain questions are opened: what is their relationship to the female disciples; why do they come to view the crucifixion; and why do they not re-appear in the remaining scenes of the Gospel, continuing their stand of solidarity or witness with the women who followed Jesus? Only two disciples watch the burial, and only three go to the tomb on the third day. Even if the "many other women" were rightly construed disciples, that would only increase the importance of questioning their not going with Mary Magdalene and the others on their two trips to the tomb.[18]

The reduction in the number of disciples taking action after the crucifixion is lightly skipped over by the habit of scholars' referring to the differing female characters after 15:40 as "the women." This practice can be partially justified in as much as contemporary scholars are impressed by the gender of the disciples specified in 15:40–41, 15:47, and 16:1–8.[19] Further grounds for using the indefinite plural form "the women" consists in the paucity of knowledge available

---

[17] Schottroff, "Mary Magdalene," pp. 178–9; Schüssler Fiorenza, *In Memory of Her*, pp. 320–1.

[18] One solution to the change from an indefinite number of female disciples to two or three is to consider the two sets of disciples as representative of the others. Just as Peter, James, and John stand as representative of the Twelve, so Mary Magdalene, Mary, the mother of James and Joses, and Salome stand for the female disciples; e.g., Schüssler Fiorenza, *In Memory of Her*, p. 320.

[19] Without demonstrating the point, Schottroff asserts that the evangelist, by contrast, placed no value on their gender ("Mary Magdalene," p. 173 and pp. 196–7, n. 16).

about the women named in the three final episodes of the Gospel. About Mary Magdalene, the authentic text of the Gospel tells only her name and her association with Jesus from the start of the Galilean ministry.[20] Concerning Salome, only her name is given. The third woman, Mary, the mother of James the younger and Joses,[21] or, if Mary, the mother of James differs from the Mary the mother of Joses,[22] the third and fourth disciples are identified in terms of family relationships. So little is known about these individuals that it seems clearer and more significant to stress the gender of the disciples by calling them "the women," or, if concerned to distinguish between the larger group of female disciples who watched the crucifixion and the specific women acting in 15:47 and 16:1–8, "the named women."[23]

But stressing the gender of these characters over their status as disciples—along with their late explicit entrance into the text—makes it difficult, if not impossible, to construe the women who followed Jesus as disciples. Joanna Dewey notes this problem as well:[24]

> The dilemma is that long before 15:41, we have interpreted Mark's androcentric perspective as narrative description and historical reality. We have created a mental picture of the Markan narrative world as one in which only men accompany Jesus. The mention of women in Mark 15 and 16 is too little and too late to modify our imaginative construction.[25]

---

[20] By contrast, the longer ending of Mark indicates that the risen Jesus appeared first to Mary Magdalene, from whom he had exorcized seven demons (16:9), a detail otherwise known from the Gospel according to Luke (8:2).

[21] Sometimes argued to be Mary, the mother of Jesus, because in Mark 6:3 Jesus' brothers are given as James and Joses.

[22] The lists of specific female disciples differ (15:40; 15:47; 16:1). At issue is whether "Μαρία ἡ Ἰακώβου τοῦ μικροῦ καὶ Ἰωσῆτος μήτηρ" refers to one person (15:40), Mary mother of Jacob the lesser and Joses, or to two people, namely "Mary, wife, daughter, or mother of Jacob" and "Mary, mother of Joses." Schottroff ("Mary Magdalene," pp. 173–4) and Schüssler Fiorenza (*In Memory of Her*, p. 320) opt for increasing the number of female disciples; most male scholars opt for the group of three.

[23] I find it ironic that scholarship can discuss "the named women" without using their names, whereas the names of the comparable triad of "named men," usually Peter, John and James, are usually spelled out or given that status of being "the inner circle" of the disciples. Tolbert (*Sowing the Gospel*, p. 293) at least discerns a rationale for why some women are named and some are not.

[24] J. Dewey, "The Gospel of Mark," in E. Schüssler Fiorenza (ed.), *Searching the Scriptures. Vol. 2: A Feminist Commentary* (New York: Crossroad, 1994), pp. 470–509.

[25] Dewey, "Gospel of Mark," p. 470.

Evidence supporting Dewey's contention is given by scholarly and popular works that focus their remarks about women following Jesus in the brief account of the Gospel of Luke (8:1–3) with little attention to the Markan text. In such cases, discussion of the Markan text about women following Jesus focuses on women's loyalty, faithfulness, or devotion by following Jesus to the cross, with little or no comment on the women's status as disciples.[26]

If the women who followed Jesus are his disciples, and if learning from and acting on his teachings is part of discipleship, two important consequences follow: first, the characterization of the women who followed Jesus, whether in its broader reference to the larger group of female disciples at the cross, or in its narrower reference to the two disciples who know the location of Jesus' tomb, or to the three disciples who return there on the third day, can be developed in terms of their discipleship, that is, in terms of what they learned from Jesus, and must not simply be generalized from their actions or cultural practice; second, the story of the women can be integrated into the preceding narrative, because their story is the story of "the disciples." Merging the neglected story of the female disciples into the story of "the disciples" will require re-reading the Gospel, knowing that the women who followed Jesus are present but not represented in the scenes of Jesus with his disciples. In other words, a critical reading of the androcentric language of the text is necessary.

Before taking up the methodological issues in re-reading an androcentric text, it will be helpful to work through an example of the resulting exegesis if one explores the possibility that the three female disciples not only were present in an earlier, significant scene, but also have learned something from what Jesus teaches in that scene. Since scholars often compare the women's going to the tomb with anointing oils to the unknown woman who anoints Jesus (14:3–9), usually to their detriment, this will be a good scene to examine.

---

[26] For example, C. Ricci focuses her admirable study on the Lucan passage, at times using the information from Mark to supplement it (*Mary Magdalene and Many Others: Women Who Followed Jesus* [Minneapolis, MN: Fortress, 1994], pp. 61–72). B. Witherington III, *Women in the Ministry of Jesus* (Cambridge: Cambridge University Press, 1984) treats the women who follow Jesus by discussing Luke 8:1–3 (p. 116) and the women's presence at the cross by discussing Mark 15:40 (p. 119). He does not interrelate the two texts.

Why Do Three Disciples Go to the Tomb with Spices?

Many scholars compare the three disciples' intention to anoint Jesus in 16:1 with the anonymous woman who anoints him in 14:3. In defending the woman against her detractors, Jesus interprets her action as anointing his body beforehand for burial (14:8b). The three female disciples are going to the site where Jesus' body has been entombed; hence scholars—appropriately—connect the two anointings. But, in contrast to the anonymous woman's correct and insightful action, scholars characterize the female disciples' intention as mistaken, ironic, or a sign of the inability of the human mind to comprehend the resurrection. For example, Robert M. Fowler concludes:

> Therefore, when three women come to his tomb expecting to anoint his body, the reader must have a strong suspicion that they will somehow fail to accomplish their goal. Their intentions may be good, but like so many in the story they have failed to understand what was happening without their knowing it. That the women would come to the tomb to anoint a body that has already been anointed must strike the reader as dramatic irony.[27]

Fowler assumes they have come to anoint Jesus' body, that they do not understand that in the interim the resurrection has occurred and that their effort is a repetition of an earlier, laudable action. Fowler does not imagine the women were present at the anointing, but he does not make their absence explicit. Daryl D. Schmidt does so: "These women are unaware of the earlier anointing that Jesus has interpreted as 'preparation for burial' (14:8)."[28] How does Schmidt know that they were unaware of the earlier anointing? Granted, the text that relates the episode of the anointing in Simon the Leper's house does not specify that female disciples were present. But is such specification necessary? Few readers doubt that male disciples were present with Jesus to observe this incident, even though the text does not make their presence explicit.

If the women who go to Jesus' tomb with anointing oils are properly construed as disciples, and if the disciples are present to observe the woman anoint Jesus, then we can infer that both male and female

---

[27] R. M. Fowler, *Let the Reader Understand: Reader-Response Criticism and the Gospel of Mark* (Minneapolis, MN: Fortress, 1991), p. 245.
[28] Schmidt, *The Gospel of Mark*, p. 150.

disciples observed the anointing and heard Jesus' response. Having learned that Jesus' body has been anointed for burial, the women may go to the tomb to perform a different anointing, a possibility which Grant R. Osborne dismisses casually even as he notes it: "The motive of the women in 16:1 was of course hardly messianic, but redactional purpose is evident in the literary connection between 14:3–9 and 16:1."[29] This dismissal ("hardly messianic") is surprising given Osborne's comments on the vocabulary used for "anointing" in the respective passages. In 14:8 the term μυρίσαι is used to refer to anointing for death; in 16:1 ἀλείψωσιν, the term for messianic anointing, is used![30]

Further, there is an issue of translation. The text states the three disciples ἠγόρασαν ἀρώματα ἵνα ἐλθοῦσαι ἀλείψωσιν αὐτόν (16:1). Did they buy spices to "anoint him" or "to anoint his body"? Translating literally, αὐτόν can be rendered as "him," Jesus, or "it," his body.[31] Those confidant that the women do not, or cannot, anticipate the event of the resurrection, or those who assume they are acting on cultural custom, can translate αὐτόν as "his body." Several scholars argue that the women cannot imagine the truth of the resurrection, because it is a mystery beyond human comprehension. "They only expected to see Jesus' body, and sought to render him posthumous homage. Confronted with the unexpected, the humanly inconceivable, confronted with what exceeded the too narrow confines of their hope—confronted with this, the supreme deed of God, they feel literally unhinged. . . ."[32]

The women's amazement becomes a figure for the limits of human

---

[29] G. R. Osborne, *The Resurrection Narratives: A Redactional Study* (Grand Rapids, MI: Baker Book House, 1984), p. 46.

[30] Osborne, *Resurrection Narratives*, p. 47.

[31] Matt. 28:1 states only that Mary Magdalene and the other Mary went to the tomb. Luke 23:55–24:1 states that the two went to the tomb with "spices they had prepared" (NRSV); Luke 24:3 states they did not find the body when they looked into the tomb. John 20:1 states that Mary Magdalene went to the tomb, but there is no mention of spices or companions. Translations of Mark 16:1 vary between acknowledging the ambiguity to solving it. For example, the NRSV and the REB have "anoint him;" whereas *The Scholars Bible* has "so that they could go and embalm him" and provides an explanatory note concerning "embalm." L. Hurtado agrees that "him" is the appropriate translation, "but the meaning is clearly Jesus' corpse, which the women expected to find in the tomb" (*Mark: A Good News Commentary* [San Francisco, CA: Harper & Row, 1983], p. 273).

[32] J. Cárdenas Pallares, *A Poor Man Called Jesus. Reflections on the Gospel of Mark* (Maryknoll, N.Y.: Orbis Books, 1986), p. 125.

understanding of divine activity. Whether the female disciples can
be imagined as anticipating a resurrected Jesus is also a question of
re-reading. According to Osborne, "Because these women were so
unprepared for the affirming revelation of Jesus' true nature, they
also totally failed to understand who the person was at the tomb."[33]
Eduard Schweizer is emphatic that the women act out of love, not
insight:

> It is clear again that the women are the only ones who are present
> to perform the necessary service of love (cf. 15:47). Of course, they
> are *merely* fulfilling a duty out of devotion and are *by no means* antici-
> pating the divine intervention which has already occurred (my italics).[34]

Why might the women be unprepared for the revelation? If the
women heard the predictions of the resurrection, then they might
come to the tomb expecting a risen Lord, not a body. In both these
examples, we are returned to the question of critically reading the
androcentric language to determine if the women who followed Jesus,
his female disciples, are present though not represented in previous
scenes.

Critically Interpreting Androcentric Language

Schüssler Fiorenza argues that androcentric language functions as
generic language.[35] That is, that androcentric terms are used even
when women perform the function named by the term. Her primary examples concern "brothers" when Paul addresses his churches,
and his use of the terms προστάτις and διάκονος of Phoebe (Rom
16:1–3), and ἀπόστολος of Junia (Rom 16:7). Even though the Gospel
according to Mark does not use the term "disciple" with explicit reference to women, since the women introduced in 15:40 are described
in terms of following and of serving, they can be considered disciples, because chapter 10 consistently links serving and discipleship.
Thus, the term "the disciples" should be taken to mean "male and
female disciples," unless the analysis of a specific passage indicates

---

[33] Osborne, *Resurrection Narratives*, p. 50.
[34] E. Schweizer, *The Good News according to Mark* (Atlanta, GA: John Knox, 1976),
p. 371.
[35] Schüssler Fiorenza, *In Memory of Her*, pp. 45–7.

that no women are present in the scene being considered. Only in such cases must "the disciples" refer to "the male disciples."

For example, male disciples constitute the Twelve. We know that because the names are given, and there are only male names (3:14–19).[36] Another example is Jesus taking only male disciples up to witness the transfiguration (9:2). The group of disciples left behind, who unsuccessfully attempt to exorcize the boy with a "mute spirit" (9:14, 17), can be read to include both male and female disciples.

Schüssler Fiorenza's principle also implies that the textual information used to construct a characterization of women in a given instance should not be restricted to texts that explicitly discuss women. Any text that uses the term "disciple" can be used to characterize female disciples unless an argument can be made that in a given instance the term is gender-specific.

Schottroff claims that the Gospel according to Mark uses androcentric language uncritically. Consequently, she interprets any reference to the disciples as inclusive of women disciples. Schottroff concludes that the female disciples as well as the male disciples abandoned Jesus at his arrest, because the text asserts "*all* fled" (14:50).[37] I am more cautious, and I believe that if Markan usage is uncritical, there is all the more reason for readers with feminist concerns to be critical in their evaluation of the text. Some examples will be useful, beginning with Schottroff's reading of 14:50.

The referent of "all" is clearly the disciples who were with Jesus at Gethsamene.[38] Who was with him? Jesus sent two disciples ahead to prepare the Passover (14:13). In the evening Jesus and the Twelve arrive (14:17). If the two disciples preparing the Passover are male, and the Twelve are male, then only male disciples are present for the Last Supper. The text uses an indefinite expression to describe their leaving the house and walking to Gethsamene: Καὶ ὑμνήσαντες ἐξῆλθον εἰς τὸ Ὄρος τῶν Ἐλαιῶν (14:26). "They" must refer to at least

---

[36] The significance of maleness to the identity of the Twelve and of the "apostles" is, of course, a controversial issue at the heart of the argument for restricting the ordained ministry to men. An important article on this is E. Schüssler Fiorenza, "The Apostleship of Women in Early Christianity," in L. Swidler and A. Swidler (eds.), *Women Priests: A Catholic Commentary on the Vatican Declaration* (New York: Paulist, 1977), pp. 135–40.

[37] Schottroff, "Mary Magdalene," p. 171.

[38] For a similar discussion, see Waetjen, *Reordering of Power*, pp. 216; and D. B. Taylor, *Mark's Gospel as Literature and History* (London: SCM, 1992), pp. 320–1.

Jesus and the Twelve. Should we include the two disciples who went
to prepare the meal? What is their gender? Once the group arrives
at Gethsamene (14:32), Jesus addresses himself to "his disciples" (τοῖς
μαθηταῖς αὐτοῦ). The group addressed as "his disciples" in 14:32
must be identical with the Twelve, or the Twelve in addition to the
two disciples who went ahead to prepare the Passover. These contextual clues indicate that no female disciples are present (unless the
two disciples who prepared the meal are female; a question I will
consider momentarily). Thus, the female disciples did not abandon
Jesus at his arrest, contra Schottroff. Their absence from the scene
precluded their participation in the abandonment.

Left unaddressed is the gender of the two disciples, δύο τῶν μαθητῶν
(14:13) and οἱ μαθηταί (14:16), who were sent to prepare the meal.
Schüssler Fiorenza's principle argues that androcentric terms are to
be read as inclusive unless a gender-specific argument can be made.
What would it mean to apply that argument here? The choices are:
both disciples are female; both disciples are male; Jesus sends a male
and a female disciple. There is no solution possible on grammatical
grounds alone.

Nor can we conclude that οἱ μαθηταί in this context must refer
to the women, because there is no reason to assume the only men
in Jesus' group of disciples are the ones who constitute the Twelve.
At the same time, as Schottroff observed, Mark uses androcentric
language uncritically. This could imply, contrary to our sensibilities,
that two women could be referred to by a masculine generic phrase.
Such usage would imply that their status as disciple is more significant
than their gendered identity. At the same time, I am wary of my
own desire that women to be present at all foundational Christian
events (the Last Supper functioning as the institution of the Lord's
Supper).[39]

For the moment, and for the sake of exploring the possibility of
a distinctive focus on the female disciples—in keeping with the text's
focus on them at the conclusion of the Gospel—I will follow out the
implications that the two disciples are male, and that consequently,
the female disciples do not know that Jesus told at least the Twelve
that after three days he would go before them to Galilee.

---

[39] On the dangers of "feminist apologetics," see L. Fatum, "Women, Symbolic
Universe and Structures of Silence. Challenges and Possibilities in Androcentric
Texts," *Studia Theologica* 43 (1989), pp. 61–80.

What Jesus Teaches about His Death and Resurrection

Scholars are happy to re-read the Gospel to relate the women's fear in 16:8 with earlier instances of fear. There is even the willingness, noted earlier, to relate the female disciples' presence at the cross with their understanding of Jesus' teachings about service and about suffering for the Gospel. Since the female disciples go to the cross and the entombment, and return again to the tomb on the third day, I propose that it is necessary to examine what Jesus teaches about his death and resurrection. It is conceivable that the female disciples take the actions that they do because they are thinking through what Jesus said about his death and resurrection.

The three passion predictions occur between chapters 8 and 10, chapters widely recognized to contain the core of Jesus' teachings about discipleship. Are the female disciples present but not represented in the scenes in which Jesus teaches about his passion and resurrection?

The first teaching is given in 8:31–32, in the context of Peter's confession, beginning at 8:27 and concluding at 8:33. There follows then Jesus' general call to discipleship and what "following him" will entail (8:34–9:1). The second teaching is given at 9:30–32; the third occurs at 10:32–34.

For the first two scenes, there is no reason to construe Jesus as instructing only male disciples or solely the Twelve. In 8:27, "Jesus and his disciples" are walking on the road; since the women followed him throughout his ministry, they must be present for this conversation as well. Moreover, after Jesus rebukes Peter (8:33), he instructs the crowd together with his disciples (8:34a) concerning how to follow him on this path of suffering and death (8:34–38). According to 9:31, Jesus was instructing τοὺς μαθητὰς αὐτοῦ, this time in Galilee, though clandestinely (9:30). Since "his disciples" is generic, both male and female disciples must be present. The narrowing of Jesus' audience is completed with the third teaching being extended to the Twelve alone: "He took the Twelve aside again and began to tell them what was to happen to him" (9:32). Thus, the Twelve hear three times what the others, the rest of the male and female disciples, hear twice.

Each teaching conveys that in Jerusalem Jesus will undergo suffering, be killed, and rise again on the third day. The text gives no indication of how his disciples responded to the first prediction of suffering and resurrection nor to the third. Concerning the second, the text says, "But they did not understand what he was saying and were afraid to ask him" (9:32). The theme of not understanding has appeared in the Gospel before, especially in the miraculous feedings (6:52; 8:17–21). Thus, it is easy to assume that they do not understand his prediction, as it says in 9:32. But, consider—Peter had no difficulty in understanding what Jesus meant when he rebuked him for teaching that the Son of Man must suffer, be killed and rise again (8:32–33).

The second prediction differs from the first in that Jesus introduces the element of betrayal. "The son of man is to be betrayed into human hands and they will kill him . . ." (9:31, NRSV). What the disciples do not understand is the indirect mention that Jesus will be betrayed. They could well understand that Jesus is implying that one—or all—of them will betray him. Understandably, no one presses for clarification. The situation is different at the supper with the Twelve. In the separate prediction to the Twelve (10:32–33), Jesus repeats that the Son of Man will be betrayed. Are they no more prepared when Jesus returns to the matter of betrayal at supper in the upper room? This time Jesus' direct statement that one of the Twelve will betray him is met with their equally direct question, each one of them, "Surely, not I?" (14:18–20).

From the two passion predictions that they heard, the female disciples, on whom I will concentrate since they are the ones who reappear in the scenes related to Jesus' death, know that Jesus will suffer, be killed, and rise on the third day. They know that they should take up their cross after him, not be ashamed of him, lest he be ashamed of them when he returns. Finally, from 9:1, they know that he has predicted these events will happen soon (before one of them tastes death). Jesus says nothing about witnessing his death, or about meeting with him afterward. As I argued earlier, the disciples who accompany Jesus to Gethsamene know something about meeting Jesus after his rising: they are told that he will go before them to Galilee (14:28). I also argued that the female disciples were not present to hear this. They learn it from a stranger at the tomb (16:7).

If the female disciples take actions, it must be as a result of other teachings.[40] That is, if the female disciples can be imagined as think-

---

[40] It is certainly plausible to imagine that once the female disciples experience Jesus' absence and death they lose faith in what he taught; but the text gives no hint in this direction. For example, the women at the cross are not described as mourning, nor as they watch Joseph at the tomb. Furthermore, women's will and

ing over and learning from what they see Jesus do and what they hear him say, then we readers can cast around for an incident narrated in the text that might have taught the female disciples how to respond to Jesus' death. I propose the episode of the woman who anoints Jesus (14:3–9) as a significant possibility for such an incident.

Commentators who assert that the women are coming to complete the burial by anointing, usually assert that the women are wrong to do so, because the unnamed woman already anointed Jesus for burial. They do not comprehend that Jesus will rise. My counter thought is, suppose they witnessed the anointing and heard Jesus describe it as for burial. They could be as capable as the reader is at realizing that the anointing for death is done; the anointing that is lacking is the one to recognize the risen lord as Messiah—especially if the woman's intention was to anoint Jesus as Messiah in the first place. Granted, Jesus doesn't say, after I rise anoint me. It is a conclusion that the women might have reached. However, given that Jesus claims in 9:1 "I tell you this: there are some of those standing here who will not taste death before they have seen the kingdom of God already come in power" (NEB), and that the female disciples were present to hear it, then they could have concluded that Jesus would come in power after rising on the third day.

Were the women present to observe the unnamed woman anoint Jesus' body for burial? The text does not specify that Jesus' disciples were present; it says only that "some of those present" criticized her (14:4). The opening line of the episode states "Jesus was at Bethany in the house of Simon the Leper" (14:3). Thus, it does not specify that his disciples accompanied him. But the presence of his disciples is not always stated.[41] For example, in 3:1 Jesus goes back into the synagogue. In the prior passage, he is talking with his disciples; in the subsequent passage, it states that he "went away to the lake-side with his disciples" (3:7, NEB). Are we to imagine the disciples were not present? I think it is reasonable to assume that they were. For whenever Jesus wishes to be alone, he says so (1:35;

---

theological capacity are frequently underestimated in favour of their well-developed affective powers. Thus, I resist such a characterization. I prefer to ponder what kind of resilience women on the road with Jesus might have developed that enabled them to respond to his crucifixion on the basis of what they had learned from him.

[41] Additional passages in which the presence of the disciples is not made explicit, but in which they are present are: 5:2 ("they" came to the other side of the lake [5:1], but do the disciples get out of the boat with Jesus?); 5:21, the scene with the haemorrhaging woman; and 7:31–37.

6:45–46; 14:35). Furthermore, Jesus asserts that her action should be recounted whenever the Gospel is proclaimed (14:9). Such an assertion makes the most sense if his disciples as well as the guests at dinner hear it. Lastly, the next event reported is that Judas departs to make his arrangements for betraying Jesus (14:10). If Judas is present, then the other disciples are as well.

If it is reasonable, or even plausible, that the female disciples knew about Jesus' interpretation of the anointing at Simon the Leper's house, then I contend there is no reason to argue that the women are mistakenly re-doing what has been done, or that they are going to the tomb expecting to find a dead body. If one thinks that the claim that "rising from the dead on the third day" is impossible for human minds to grasp, as many do, then one can appreciate their inconsistent behaviour—though they know Jesus will rise, such knowledge is abstract and remote, hardly a basis for action. But, consider—many people believe that John the Baptist rose from the dead (6:14–16; 8:28). Thus, it seems possible that the female disciples could hold such a belief and act on it.

A significant obstacle to imagining that some of the female disciples might have gone intentionally to greet their risen Lord is the implication that the women understood something the men did not. It seems to lead to—or rest upon—the assumption that women are "better" disciples or "better models" of faith, because they are women. I dislike ideologies of female superiority as much as I do of male superiority; each is equally ungrounded, and the former may well be a reaction to the latter. A way forward rests on acknowledging that the disciples who went to the tomb on the third day were women, but there were only three of them. Three disciples who act on a belief go to the tomb. Three disciples who were not present at the Last Supper learn that Jesus has gone to Galilee. One is less likely to generalize to "the disciples" as a class from the closing scene of the Gospel, because the reader knows that these disciples at the tomb differ from the other disciples. Some disciples never receive specific characterization in the Gospel—Philip for example (3:18). Others receive slight attention—Levi (3:14). A few, James and John, receive more extensive stage presence (1:19–20; 10:35–38; John alone in 9:38–39). Peter enters the narrative early and remains an important character until he denies Jesus (14:72). Mary Magdalene and her two companions belong as well on this continuum. They are disciples with varying capacities for insight and reflection. Since Mary

Magdalene's name is given in each list, it is likely that she took the initiative to bring her companions to the cross and, ultimately, to the tomb. Thinking that a woman cannot reach a conclusion that a man failed to make is simply sexist.

Conclusion

My intention has been to develop a more complete characterization of the women who followed Jesus, the characters that appear in the closing scenes of the Gospel. Since they are disciples, I argue that their characterization must draw on the teachings and expectations for discipleship expressed in the Gospel. Phrased negatively, I disallow characterization that relies on stereotypical views of women as more loyal by nature or by habit. Instead of arguing that the women go to the cross and then to the tomb from love or grief, I argue that they go because they learned from Jesus that he would rise on the third day. They remember this claim and they act upon it.

If the three disciples go to the tomb expecting to greet their risen Lord, then a different interpretation of the encounter with the young man at the tomb, as well as of their silence from fear, is possible. They are confronted with a stranger (to them, at least) who tells them vital information concerning the one they came to greet. Their silence from fear may indicate their dismay, confusion, and sense of abandonment.

Why would Mark end with such an emphasis? I propose that the evangelist is underscoring a point: in Jesus' absence the disciples and any others who become his followers will face abandonment, derision, and lack of security (reading together chapter 10 and chapter 13). The pressures of the last days will be so intense that they may not be able to rely on one another. "Those who hold out to the end will be saved" (13:13) implies some will not, for example. All that they have to rely on is what they remember of Jesus' teachings and his assurance that when they must testify in court, the Holy Spirit will speak for them (13:11). The importance of knowing what Jesus taught is a warrant for the writing of a Gospel in the first place.[42]

---

[42] Thus, I agree in general terms with W. H. Kelber's thesis that after Jesus' death and the death of those who knew him, writing down the Gospel becomes necessary (*The Oral and the Written Gospel*).

My intent is to awake the imagination. Commonly, the impact of the last line of the Gospel tilts against the women who followed Jesus and weighs in with their fallibility. I have leaned hard upon previous lines of the Gospel, especially the predictions of the passion and resurrection, by reading them with the expectation that the women as disciples are capable of reasoning and action. During the 1980s scholars began to break the grip of reading the Gospel according to Mark under the influence of the Gospel according to Matthew. I wish to break the grip of the androcentric presentation and continued assumption by readers that the phrase "the disciples" refers only to the men among Jesus' followers.

THE CANAANITE WOMAN AND JESUS: SURPRISING MODELS OF DISCIPLESHIP (MATT. 15:21–28)

DANIEL PATTE

Reading Matthew 15:21–28 for Its Teaching about Discipleship: An Androcritical Perspective

Matt. 15:21–28 has much to teach us about discipleship. Among its several potential teachings, in my judgement two are particularly helpful today: those which arise out of the readers' transformative encounters with the Canaanite woman and with Jesus. According to the readers and their situations, these encounters become invitations to imitate either Jesus or the Canaanite woman as models of discipleship. The question is: Which model is the most helpful in each of our particular situations?

With many,[1] my first inclination was to identify myself with the Canaanite woman. Who would not like to be praised for her or his "great faith"? But from an androcritical perspective,[2] as I *read with* persons who, like the Canaanite woman, have been marginalized because of their gender, race, culture, and/or religion, it becomes clear that it is not an appropriate choice for me in my present situation.

As I will argue below, it is both legitimate and plausible to conclude that Matt. 15:21–28 offers the Canaanite woman as a model of discipleship, even though this reading challenges traditional understandings of discipleship according to Matthew. With her "great faith" she models the relationship which disciples should have with Jesus

---

[1] Including Martin Luther, as noted by Kwok Pui-lan, *Discovering the Bible in the Non-Biblical World* (Maryknoll, N.Y.: Orbis Books, 1995), pp. 77–8.

[2] See D. Patte, *Ethics of Biblical Interpretation: A Reevaluation* (Louisville, KY: Westminster John Knox, 1995), pp. 113–29. From an androcritical perspective I assume a twofold ethical responsibility that involves, a) acknowledging and affirming the androcentrism and eurocentrism of my interpretations as a male European-American, and b) avoiding to coopt the readings of others. For this a crucial critical step is to *read with* other people, a process which involves, a) taking note of the differences between my interpretation and the interpretations of other readers, b) acknowledging the legitimacy and plausibility of our respective interpretations, and c) recognizing that my interpretation is the result of a value-laden choice, which can then be examined.

and with others. Contrary to the traditional expectations that, according to Matthew, discipleship involves meek submission to the authority of Jesus as Lord,[3] the Canaanite woman compels Jesus to do what she wishes. Contrary to the common understanding that Jesus defines the mission that disciples are to carry out,[4] the Canaanite woman deftly re-defines Jesus' mission. Contrary to our understanding that Jesus' role is to teach to disciples God's righteousness/justice,[5] out of the wisdom of her own culture the Canaanite woman teaches overabundant righteousness/justice[6] to Jesus. Then, who is the master? Who is the disciple? Who follows whom? In sum, what is discipleship? Certainly not passive submission. Rather, it is the relentless "struggle for the kingdom and God's justice"[7] exemplified by the Canaanite woman.

This teaching and its model of discipleship are very valuable. Many readers can unfortunately readily identify themselves with the Canaanite woman, because they are marginalized, ignored, insulted, oppressed.[8] In such cases, encountering the Canaanite woman as a model of discipleship has a welcome and empowering effect: it teaches readers that it is appropriate, and even a mark of great faith, to struggle for God's justice. Yet, for readers who do not perceive themselves as marginalized, encountering the Canaanite woman as a model of discipleship has an ambivalent effect: it invites readers to recognize their oppression or marginalization. This is a good conscientization in the case of actual victims of oppression who do not even have the strength to struggle for justice. But this is a destructive teaching when readers, who are not oppressed or marginalized as the Canaanite woman was, feel that they must see themselves as victims in order

---

[3] Then, 4:20; 4:22; 5:5; 7:21; 7:24 and similar passages need to be re-interpreted, which is possible. See D. Patte, *Discipleship According to the Sermon on the Mount: Four Legitimate Readings, Four Plausible Views of Discipleship, and Their Relative Values* (Valley Forge, PA: Trinity Press International, 1996).

[4] Then, 4:19; 5:13–16 and similar passages need to be re-interpreted.

[5] Then 3:15; 5:6; 5:20 and similar passages need to be re-interpreted.

[6] Then 5:20; 5:45–47 and similar passages need to be re-interpreted.

[7] A translation of 6:33, ζητεῖτε δὲ πρῶτον τὴν βασιλείαν [τοῦ θεοῦ] καὶ τὴν δικαιοσύνην αὐτοῦ, which is appropriate when it is read from the perspective of 15:21–28.

[8] Though there is always the possibility that someone who is marginalized and oppressed might herself or himself marginalize and oppress other people, as Kwok notes (*Discovering the Bible*, p. 82) referring to the privileged status of the Hellenized Syrophoenician woman in Mark's version of the story. See G. Theissen, *The Gospels in Context: Social and Political History in the Synoptic Tradition* [transl. by L. M. Maloney; Minneapolis, MN: Fortress, 1991), pp. 69–70.

to be recognized as having great faith. Then, instead of being empowered such readers end up artificially pitying themselves as victims
and denying the specificity of the marginalization and oppression of
those who are in situations truly comparable to the Canaanite woman.

This is why I believe the alternate reading is more helpful for me
and other male European-Americans. As we shall see below, it is
legitimate and plausible to conclude that Matt. 15:21–28 (as well as
the rest of the Gospel) offers Jesus as a model that disciples should
imitate. For many of us it is very easy to identify ourselves with
Jesus in this passage. His insensitivity, that might be shocking from
a high-christological perspective, makes him very human—one of us.
How typical of our own behaviour is Jesus' contemptuous refusal to
answer the Canaanite woman's plea! How typical to try to justify
this silence by adding insults to injury when he awkwardly explains
that "he was sent" by God for a specific mission which excludes her!
We European-American males—and many others with us!—can readily recognize that, more often than we care to admit, we similarly
ignore desperate cries for help, especially if they come from people
who are different from us, be it in terms of class, race, culture, religion, and/or gender.

When we acknowledge that we are like Jesus in 15:21–26, we
readily hear the teaching that the following verses have for us. As
Jesus recognizes and affirms the Canaanite woman's great faith and
allows her to transform the understanding he has of his mission
(15:28), so should we. Thus, as disciples we should recognize and
affirm the great faith of those we so easily despise, insult, marginalize and oppress; in the process we will allow them to re-define our
vocation as disciples. In sum, imitating Jesus as disciples means, a)
recognizing and affirming as persons of great faith those who, like
the Canaanite woman, obstinately importunate us by challenging our
domesticated understandings of discipleship, and b) allowing them to
re-define our vocation, so that we might recognize that all of us
struggle to feed our respective children with the same bread (15:27),
or, in other words, that all of us "struggle for the kingdom and
God's justice."

The Transformative Encounters that Led Me to These Conclusions

Such are the two kinds of conclusions about the teaching of Matt.
15:21–28 that I propose to hold in tension as I explain and justify

both of them—by showing how they are grounded in textual evidence and by making explicit the choices involved in each of these two interpretations. For this purpose, following Dr. Kitzberger's insightful challenge, I pay close attention to three kinds of transformative encounters involved in the interpretive process: (1) the transformative encounters of *the readers with the text*; (2) the transformative encounters *within the text*; (3) the transformative encounters *with other readers*. By making explicit the transformative encounters *within the text*, I show why both the Canaanite woman and Jesus can legitimately be read as models of discipleship. Similarly, by considering the transformative encounters of *the readers with the text*, I clarify why a diversity of teachings about discipleship is appropriately and plausibly found by readers in this text and its models of discipleship. Thus, as readers we can no longer hide that our choice of one or another of the legitimate and plausible teachings is based on a value judgement. By *reading with* others, and thus through transformative encounters *with other readers*, I can become aware of the value judgements involved in my own interpretation, and thus I can re-assess my choice of teaching, as I already suggested above when I briefly presented the two kinds of conclusions I keep in tension in my interpretation.

Before proceeding with this critical analysis of my interpretation, I need to explain how I conceive of the three types of transformative encounters we shall examine.

1. *Transformative Encounters within the Text*

This first kind of transformative encounter is self-evident as soon as one reads the text as a narrative. Three questions can be formulated regarding transformative encounters as expressed by narrative components of the story.[9] As we consider the characters: Who encounters whom? As we consider the narrative transformations: How are characters transformed as a result of their encounters with other

---

[9] This is proceeding to a systematic actantial analysis of the text (which could also be performed on a didactic discourse). See A.-J Greimas and J. Courtés, *Semiotics and Language: An Analytical Dictionary* (transl. by L. Crist, et al.; Bloomington, IN: Indiana University Press, 1982), pp. 5–6, 207–8, passim. D. Patte, *The Religious Dimensions of Biblical Texts: Greimas's Structural Semiotics and Biblical Exegesis* (Atlanta, GA: Scholars 1990), pp. 92–7, 173–215, 243–58. See also D. Patte, *Structural Exegesis for New Testament Critics* (Valley Forge, PA: Trinity Press International, 2nd printing 1996), pp. 23–45.

characters? As we consider the agent of each transformation: Who brought about the transformation? With the help of whom and/or of what? By overcoming the resistance of whom and/or what? In Matt. 15:21–28, a reading focused on transformative encounters calls our attention to the complex relationship among Jesus, the Canaanite woman, and the disciples.

2. *Transformative Encounters of the Readers with the Text: The Teaching of the Text for Readers*

It is very helpful to recognize that when we speak of the "teaching of a text for me or for us" we refer to a transformative encounter of one or several readers with the text. As a reader I am transformed by my encounter with this text. From it I learn something that I did *not know* before. Otherwise I would not have learned anything! The appropriate answer to the question "what is the teaching of this text for me/us?" would, therefore, underscore something which is *new* for me or for us.

Thus, one should not be surprised by the fact that the above conclusions about the teaching of Matt. 15:21–28 about discipleship are unexpected. This is as it should be.

What is transformed by my encounter with the text? Both a) my understanding of the subject-matter of the text and b) my perception of (some aspects of) my life and its concrete setting.

a) When I read a text, even if it is for the first time, I always come to it with a pre-understanding regarding the subject matter of this text.[10] I anticipate that the text will have something to teach me about a certain issue or theme. In the present case, I anticipated that Matt. 15:21–28 has something to say about discipleship. Of course, I quickly verified that there was at least some textual evidence that discipleship was a part of the textual content. The reference to Jesus' disciples in 15:23 provided me with a first confirmation. It remains that I came to the text with a view of "discipleship" much more complex than what the word "disciples" could have evoked by itself—I came to the text with the view of discipleship I presented

---

[10] In the case of a first time reading, the readers take their clues from the context in which the text is found, its title, its first few words, and often from what they heard about it. The point is that we do not read without at least some anticipation of what we would find in this text. Without such anticipation reading quickly becomes boring and stops.

in my monograph on this topic[11] and in my commentary.[12]

This theme and my conception of it provided me with an additional focus for my reading. Discipleship helped me make sense of the diverse features of the transformative encounters within the text.[13] It transformed my perception of the text and its significance. Yet, I did not simply "read into the text" my view of discipleship. Actually, the teaching of this text about discipleship challenged and thus transformed my original conception of discipleship. In sum, because of my encounter with this text my understanding of "discipleship" according to Matthew was significantly re-defined.

b) My encounter with the text also transformed my perception of my life and its concrete setting. This is directly apparent in the present case. Since discipleship is a practice, my encounter with this text transformed both the view of what I should do in my life setting and my perception of this situation. These *new* vistas upon my own practice of discipleship in the concrete situation in which I find myself also include a new perception of other people and of their eventual practices of discipleship. In sum, the *teaching* of the text *for me* (*pro me*) is necessarily contextual and thus *for us* (*pro nobis*).

Speaking of the way in which the text affects the readers' life is already discussing the pragmatic dimension of interpretation also foregrounded in the reading by Christian believers of the New Testament texts as Scripture. My contention is that this pragmatic dimension of the interpretative process is explicitly or implicitly present in *any* interpretation of biblical texts.[14] Whoever they might be, readers of the New Testament never fully ignore that this text is held as Scripture by Christian believers who live by it. Even if one is not a Christian believer and even if one exclusively reads this text in a "detached" scholarly way, it remains that one's descriptive conclusions about what the text is and says have pragmatic implications

---

[11] Patte, *Discipleship*.

[12] D. Patte, *The Gospel According to Matthew: A Structural Commentary on Matthew's Faith* (Minneapolis, MN: Fortress, 1987; Valley Forge, PA: Trinity Press International, 3rd printing 1996).

[13] In other words, discipleship became for me an epistemological category in terms of which I made sense of the text and its various features.

[14] As the intersection of the text and of the readers' views and life contexts this pragmatic dimension is what is at stake in the debates about pre-understandings in interpretation.

not only for Christian believers, but also for the interpreter. Even if the reading merely confirms and re-inforces the interpreter's view that living by this text as Scripture is non-sensical or dangerous, an aspect of the perception of his or her concrete life (possibly, his or her relationship with Christian believers) has been transformed by encountering this biblical text.

In sum, in the pragmatic dimension of interpretation we *"read"* *our life situations* and our views from the perspective of the text; our perceptions of our life situations and what we should do in them are transformed. By contrast, in the textual dimension of the same interpretation (which we discussed above), we *read the text* from the perspective of our contexts by choosing each time a theme (here, discipleship) which makes sense for us; our perceptions of the text and of its significance are transformed.

3. *Transformative Encounters with Other Readers of the Text: Reading with Others*

Transformative encounters in the process of *reading with* other interpreters cannot be over-emphasized. They play an essential role throughout the entire reading process, even though we often overlook this role, and as a consequence fail to benefit from these encounters.

Thus, it is only by *reading with* others that I can assume responsibility for my own interpretation. To begin with, after my first reading I would not learn anything from the text, if I did not read with others. (Remember that a teaching of the text *for me/us* is, by definition, something *new!*) Furthermore, without other interpreters who read the text differently, I would not recognize that all along my own interpretation I made many choices among equally plausible and legitimate options. Then, I have to reflect on my reasons for making such choices and assessing their relative value. In the present case, *reading* Matt. 15:21–28 *with* Dr. Kitzberger and other feminist scholars from various cultural contexts clarified for me that the Canaanite woman and Jesus as models of discipleship have been interpreted in very different ways, because each reading chose as its basis one of the options available in the transformative encounters within the texts, and/or because it chose to make sense of these data in terms of one of the several plausible conceptions of discipleship. Then, the teaching of this text has quite different pragmatic effects according to the chosen interpretation; lives are concretely affected.

In sum, it is only as I read with others that I can assess which teaching is the most appropriate for me and other European-American males in a given situation.

Transformative encounters *within* the text, transformative encounters of *the readers with the text*, transformative encounters *with other readers of the text*. We can consider them in this order, even though in the interpretive process as readers we move to and fro among these encounters.

Transformative Encounters within Matthew 15:21–28 and their Polyvalence: Who Is Transformed? By Whom? How?

The encounters in this text can easily be identified if we systematically read the text looking for the narrative transformations that result from encounters among characters. Besides the encounter between Jesus and the Canaanite woman (15:21–22), there is an encounter between the disciples and the Canaanite woman (15:23b), in which Jesus is also involved, since they are "his" disciples and since he apparently responds to them (15:24). Then, as we consider the transformations associated with these encounters, we note that they are more numerous and ambivalent than it appears at first.

1. *Transformations of the Canaanite Woman*

The clearest transformation related to the Canaanite woman is that of her daughter who was tormented by demons (15:22) and who is healed (15:28b). Already in this case several interpretations are plausible. The agent of transformation is indefinite, and thus can be interpreted in different ways. Since it is expressed by passive forms (γενηθήτω σοι . . . ἰάθη ἡ θυγάτηρ αὐτῆς, 15:28), the healing can be viewed as the result of God's intervention. Yet, Jesus can also be viewed as the agent performing the healing by means of divine powers, since he is the one uttering the imperative performative word ('Ιησοῦς εἶπεν . . . γενηθήτω σοι . . .). Furthermore, since Jesus utters these words in response to the woman's great faith (Ὦ γύναι, μεγάλη σου ἡ πίστις), she and her faith could also be viewed as the agent of the healing, with Jesus as mediator of divine powers.

The Canaanite woman is also transformed. By the end of the story, her status has changed as is expressed by Jesus' praise of her great faith in 15:28a. But the nature of this transformation is ambivalent: Is it the woman herself who is transformed? Or is it the perception of the woman by Jesus (and the disciples) which is transformed? Both interpretations are plausible.

One can conclude that through her encounter with Jesus *the woman herself is transformed*. At the beginning of the story, she was a worthless pagan woman (a Canaanite from the region of Tyre and Sidon, 15:21–22). As Meier notes, "the woman has three strikes against her before she even starts: She is a woman; she is the mother of a demoniac; and worst of all she is a pagan Canaanite, a member of the ancient enemy of Israel."[15] Nevertheless, from the start she has a glimmer of faith, since she addresses Jesus not simply as "Son of David" (as other marginalized and no-accounts do in Matthew as they recognize the Jewish Messiah) but also as "Lord" (a title used by true believers in Matthew). By the end of the story the woman's glimmer of faith is transformed into a genuine "great faith." Jesus brings about this transformation, as Meier says, through his "maieutic method" (his silent and verbal rebuffs) by deftly leading the woman to "the heights of faith, a faith that can transcend the barriers of race, religion, and even the set periods of salvation history."[16] These "heights of faith" include her humble submission to Jesus as "Lord" (15:22, 25, 27), a humility and meekness especially expressed by her acceptance and affirmation of her second level status as a Gentile (as her response in 15:27 is then interpreted, in terms of 5:5).

Alternatively one can conclude that it is *Jesus' way of perceiving the Canaanite woman which is transformed*. At first, Jesus and the disciples perceive the woman as a worthless and faithless person. By the end, they recognize her for the person she truly is, someone with great faith. In this case, it is Jesus' perception of the woman (and also possibly the disciples' perception of her) which is transformed. At first, Jesus and the disciples have an incorrect perception of the woman. In this case, one reads Jesus' silent treatment of the woman (15:23a) as a rebuff which is as contemptuous as the use of the ethnic slur "dogs" (15:26) to designate the Gentiles among whom she is.[17]

---

[15] J. P. Meier, "Matthew 15:21–28," *Interpretation 40* (1986), pp. 397–402, p. 398.
[16] Meier, "Matthew 15:21–28," p. 399.
[17] A.-J. Levine, *The Social and Ethnic Dimensions of Matthean Salvation History: "Go*

2. *Transformations of Jesus*

For many readers, the possibility that the text presents a transformation of the way in which the Canaanite woman is perceived by Jesus is most surprising, because it implies that *Jesus is the one who is transformed* by his encounter with her.[18] According to this reading, at first Jesus displays contempt for this Gentile woman by not responding to her, a contempt which is further made explicit by his use of the ethnic slur "dogs" to refer to Gentiles. By the end of the story, Jesus' view of the Canaanite woman is transformed.

For many, this is a shocking reading. "Matthew would not present Jesus as incorrect, rude, and thus imperfect, would he? From the very beginning of the Gospel, for Matthew Jesus is the omniscient and omnipotent Son of God, isn't he?"[19] Yet this objection holds only insofar as one reads the Gospel as a whole for its doctrines (about Christ, about discipleship, the continued election of Israel, etc.); then beginning, end, and centre of the Gospel are interpreted together, superimposed on each other. In effect, the entire Gospel is read in terms of its end. Throughout his ministry, Jesus is the resurrected *kyrios* who has "all authority in heaven and on earth" (28:18). This interpretation, and the foreknowledge that Jesus has of the great faith that the Canaanite woman will display if he

---

nowhere among the Gentiles . . ." (Matt. 10:5b) (Lampeter, Dyfed, UK: Edwin Mellen, 1988). At the end of a long discussion, which underscored that Jesus' original statement in 15:24 does not include any ethnic slur (pp. 142–3), she concludes: "Nevertheless, the association of gentiles with dogs, puppies or not, in Matt 15:26 is an ethnic insult" (p. 151).

[18] A reading found in several feminist interpretations, including those of: Sh. H. Ringe, "A Gentile Woman's Story," in L. M. Russell (ed.), *Feminist Interpretation of the Bible* (Philadelphia, PA: Westminster, 1985), pp. 70–2. H. Kinukawa, *Women and Jesus in Mark: A Japanese Feminist Perspective* (Maryknoll, N.Y.: Orbis Books, 1994), pp. 51–65 (though she exclusively focuses on Mark 7:24–30, her comments about the transformation of Jesus by the woman apply also to Matthew, *mutatis mutandis*), as well as Kwok, *Discovering the Bible*, p. 80 (where she refers to the preceding and other similar interpretations). This reading is also found in Patte, *The Gospel According to Matthew*, pp. 220–3.

[19] This is almost a paraphrase of Davies and Allison's reply to Beare's comments emphasizing the "incredible insolence" of Jesus in words which express "the worst kind of chauvinism" vis-a-vis the Canaanite woman. See W. D. Davies and D. C. Allison, Jr., *A Critical and Exegetical Commentary on the Gospel According to Saint Matthew* (ICC, Vol. 2; Edinburgh: T. & T. Clark, 1991), p. 552, n. 41, and F. W. Beare, *The Gospel According to Matthew* (San Francisco, CA: Harper & Row; Oxford: Blackwell, 1981), p. 342. For Davies and Allison, the entire focus of this text is the continuity of Jesus' ministry with Israel, and the importance of the election.

enables her to do so, is plausible, and therefore found in many commentaries.[20] After all, Matthew writes from a post-Easter perspective.[21]

But it is also plausible to read the Gospel according to Matthew as a narrative. Throughout the story, the character Jesus, as any other character, is constantly undergoing transformations; from his birth and throughout his ministry and passion, Jesus is progressively transformed in all the encounters depicted in the Gospel, the resurrection being the ultimate transformation when, at last, he receives all authority and power in heaven and on earth.[22] From the perspective of the unfolding of the plot this means that prior to the resurrection he was *not* the almighty (and omniscient) resurrected *kyrios*. (These observations should not be scandalous for any Christian believers. How could one conceive of the incarnation without acknowledging the humanity of Jesus during his ministry?)

From this narrative perspective another transformation of Jesus takes place: a transformation of his understanding of his own mission. Matt. 15:24 is read as an expression that, at this point in his ministry, Jesus understands his mission as exclusively devoted to Israel: "I was sent only to the lost sheep of the house of Israel." But as a result of his encounter with the Canaanite woman, by the end of the story he conceives of his ministry as at least partially open to Gentiles: it can both give priority to Israel and be open to Gentiles; it is now freed from its original ethnic and religious exclusivistic constraints.

The Canaanite woman is, therefore, the agent of transformation who brings about this radical change in Jesus' understanding of his

---

[20] For instance, in addition to J. P. Meier, *Matthew* (Wilmington, DE: Glazier, 1980), Davies and Allison, *A Critical and Exegetical Commentary*; R. H. Gundry, *Matthew: A Commentary on His Literary and Theological Art* (Grand Rapids, MI: Eerdmans, 1982); P. Bonnard, *L'évangile selon Saint Matthieu* (CNT, 1; Neuchâtel: Delachaux & Niestlé, 1963); E. Schweizer, *The Good News According to Matthew* (Atlanta, GA: John Knox, 1975). As the later suggests, the text sets in parallel to the miracle of healing the "miracle of faith"—that is, the miracle through which the woman's faith is produced by God through the intermediary of Jesus.

[21] As for instance Strecker and Kingsbury emphasize through their redaction-critical studies. See G. Strecker, *Der Weg der Gerechtigkeit: Untersuchung zur Theologie des Matthäus* (FRLANT, 82; Göttingen: Vandenhoeck & Ruprecht, 3rd edn, 1971, and "The Concept of History in Matthew," in G. Stanton, (ed.), *The Interpretation of Matthew* (Philadelphia, PA: Fortress, 1983), pp. 70–4, and J. D. Kingsbury, *Matthew: Structure, Christology, Kingdom.* (Minneapolis, MN: Fortress, 1975). See a detailed discussion of their approach in Patte, *Discipleship*, pp. 72–104 (concerning "Reading A").

[22] A point I developed in Patte, *Discipleship*, pp. 74–6 (and in all the comments throughout this book on "Reading B").

own ministry. She achieves this through her "great faith" which is manifested not only in her cry for help (both in 15:22 and 15:25), but also in her witty response to Jesus (15:27). Her faith is genuine and great, because it involves, a) an affirmation of revelations related to the Jewish Scripture (Jesus as the Son of David, the Messiah, and thus the Lord), b) her love and compassion for her daughter for whom she pleads at all costs, c) as well as her Gentile wisdom and wit. It is from the standpoint of her Gentile culture that she transforms Jesus' exclusive and cruel metaphors ("Gentiles are dogs," with the negative biblical and Jewish connotations that dogs have because they are impure scavenger animals to be kicked out of the house, already used in 7:6) into an inclusive metaphor ("Gentiles are indeed dogs," but with the *positive Gentile Hellenistic connotation* which dogs have as pets welcomed in the house).[23] There is no abject acceptance of Jesus' insult; through the hearing of the metaphor *from her own perspective*, the Canaanite woman perceives herself and presents herself as a faithful and welcome member of the household, without denying the priority of Israel. Her great faith is then comparable to the faith of all those presented by Matthew as models of overabundant righteousness since the beginning of his Gospel. As is exemplified by Joseph, the Magi, and other characters, and expressed in what the Sermon on the Mount says about overabundant righteousness, genuine faith and genuine righteousness involves bringing together the revelations of Scripture and those of extra-scriptural sources (angels, dreams, and Gentile wisdom).[24] The Canaanite woman's faith is great, because she does what Jesus preaches: she re-interprets for her situation the scriptural teaching about the election of Israel in terms of the Gentile wisdom of her own culture. In the process,

---

[23] See F. Dufton, "The Syrophoenician Woman and her Dogs," *Expository Times* 100 (1989), p. 417. By contrast with the biblical and early Jewish literature, where "dog" is predominantly used with negative connotations (according to the articles in the main Biblical dictionaries, including the TDNT, IDB, and Anchor Bible Dictionary), in the Hellenistic literature the connotations of "dog" are predominantly positive (faithfulness, watchful, etc., according to the numerous references cited in Bailly's unabridged Greek dictionary, see A. Bailly, *Dictionnaire Grec Francais* (Paris: Hachette, 1894). For this interpretation (together with many interpreters) we take Jesus' original use of the term κυνάρια as an ethnic insult, despite its diminutive form ("puppies").

[24] As noted in my commentary in many places, including the pages on 15:21–28 (Patte, *Matthew*, pp. 220–3) as well as in Patte, *Discipleship*, pp. 312–50 (regarding "Reading D").

she transforms Jesus' conception of his own ministry, which was limited by the cultural and religious context in which he exercised it.[25]

3. *Transformations of the Disciples*

Finally, another transformation occurs as a result of these encounters: that of the disciples. A narrative analysis shows it quite clearly.
At the beginning the disciples are associated with Jesus. They are
the interlocutors of Jesus, suggesting to Jesus what he should do as
they identify themselves with him; together with Jesus they are bothered by this woman because "she keeps shouting *after us*" (15:23).
But Jesus does not do what they ask him to do (15:23–24). At the
end of the story, the disciples have disappeared and are replaced by
the woman, who is now the interlocutor of Jesus and who suggests
to Jesus what he should do. She also associates herself with him and
his ministry (as one of the dogs who eat the crumbs, 15:27). And
Jesus does what she wishes. Why? What is the difference between
the disciples' (improper) relationship to Jesus and her proper relationship to him? It becomes clear when one notes that the disciples
are not successful in convincing Jesus to do what they want, because
they suggest to him *to overlook his sense of mission*. Their injunction in
15:23 means in this case: "Heal her child, then we will have peace."[26]
By contrast, the woman is successful, because *she affirms Jesus' sense
of mission while re-defining it in terms of the present situation*. As such, the
Canaanite woman assumes a role that disciples should perform. In
other words, in this story the role of a disciple has passed from the
male Jewish companions of Jesus to the Canaanite woman.

*Transformative Encounters of the Readers with Matthew 15:21–28:
Transformations of Our Conceptions of Discipleship*

In order to make sense of the multiple and polyvalent transformative encounters within the text, I focus my reading of Matt. 15:21–28
on what it says about discipleship.

---

[25] Note that, by contrast with its parallel in Mark 7:24, Matt. 15:21–22 can be
read as suggesting that Jesus has not departed Jewish territory, and that it is the
woman who came out of the Gentile territory into the Jewish territory—though
bringing with her Gentile wisdom.
[26] See Patte, *Matthew*, pp. 220–3; in agreement with Meier, "Matthew 15:21–28,"
p. 398.

In so doing I choose one among several themes in terms of which this passage can be read. Many other themes such as christology, Jewish-Gentile ethnic relations, the enduring election of Israel and the opening of the Gospel to the Gentiles have appropriately helped interpreters to hold together in a meaningful way the diverse features of this text. A review of the scholarly literature, such as the one found in Kwok's work,[27] readily makes this point. This brief remark is enough to underscore that my reading of Matt. 15:21–28 in terms of discipleship represents another choice among several plausible alternatives. As suggested above, this choice reflects my theoretical interest in elucidating the pragmatic dimension of interpretation and my ethical concerns related to my practice of discipleship as a Christian believer, including my pedagogical and scholarly activities.

Whoever reads Matt. 15:21–28 for its teaching about discipleship comes to the text with a specific conception of "discipleship" as practice of the Christian faith. In each case, implicitly or explicitly, we make a choice among several alternative conceptions of discipleship, which can be related to different ethical theories, as I have argued in my monograph on this topic.[28]

As is the case with any other thematic readings,[29] the conception of discipleship with which we came to the text is not that of the text, but ours. This is *appropriate*. In so doing we are not "reading into" the text something which is not there. In my quest for the teaching that the text offers to me about discipleship, that is, in my quest for *the way in which the biblical text should transform my view and practice of discipleship in a specific context*, I need to bring to the text my present view and experience of discipleship. Otherwise, how could these be transformed? Conversely, the fact that I come to the text with one or another view of discipleship focuses my attention on one or the other transformative encounters within the text. Therefore, I make sense of the text in a specific way. This is what I will now illustrate by briefly describing the transformative encounters between Matt. 15:21–28 and readers with three distinct views of discipleship.

---

[27] Kwok, *Discovering the Bible*, pp. 71–83, 115–17.

[28] In Patte, *Discipleship* (pp. 261–350), I have shown that studies of the Sermon on the Mount pre-supposed deontological, consequentialist (utilitarian), or diverse kinds of perfectionist pre-understandings of the moral life.

[29] In a sense all interpretations which strive to make sense of the text include a thematic reading.

1. *The Canaanite Woman as an Example of Faith: the First Step toward Discipleship as Doing God's Will Taught by the Authoritative Kyrios*

One might come to Matt. 15:21–28 with a deontological pre-understanding of the moral life and of discipleship.[30] In this case the text presents the way in which the Canaanite woman was transformed by Jesus into a disciple who fully submits to his authority (15:27). It is this acknowledgment of Jesus' authority and this total submission to it which constitutes "great faith." For readers, the Canaanite woman provides an example of the first necessary step toward discipleship; whether she becomes a full-fledged disciple is left unsaid.

The deontological views of such readers begin to be transformed as soon as they encounter the Gospel of Matthew. In summary, a deontological ethical theory underscores intersubjective relations as the structure of the moral life.[31] These relations are defined in terms of obligations toward others expressed in laws, codes, and regulations on the basis of "general principles and rules." For Immanuel Kant, these principles and rules are universal and foundational because they are those of *practical reason* and because they concern intersubjective relations with other rational beings. From the perspective of the Gospel according to Matthew, these principles and rules are universal because they are the Will of God revealed by Jesus, the Christ-Messiah and *Kyrios*.

From this perspective, as is expressed by Strecker and Kingsbury in their study of the Sermon on the Mount, discipleship is conceived of as "doing God's Will" revealed by Jesus as Lord. Disciples implement in their lives the general principles of God's Will by deriving from it laws and rules adapted for particular circumstances of their private and communal lives. In the "sphere of God's eschatological rule" (Kingsbury's phrase interpreting "kingdom of heaven"), disciples submit to God by submitting to Jesus' authoritative revelation of God's Will, and by submitting to the authoritative interpretation of it by the disciples/apostles—the "eleven" male disciples commissioned to make other disciples (28:16–20).

---

[30] This is the pre-understanding of moral life and of discipleship which is represented by the works of Strecker and Kingsbury, in Patte, *Discipleship*, pp. 269–311.

[31] For an excellent typology of pre-understandings of the moral life, see T. W. Ogletree, *The Use of the Bible in Christian Ethics: A Constructive Essay* (Philadelphia, PA: Fortress, 1983), pp. 15–45. My description of the deontological pre-understanding briefly summarizes his presentation of it—as will be the case below for the other pre-understandings.

From this perspective, all the attention is upon obeying God's Will as revealed by Jesus, and therefore upon the disciples' need to know God's Will, its basic principles, the way to implement it in specific circumstances, and thus, the hermeneutical principles to be used for its re-interpretation and to formulate clear rules for the disciples' lives in the "sphere of God's eschatological rule." In the process, the continuity of Jesus' ministry and of discipleship with Israel and the teaching of the Law and the Prophets is emphasized, but not much is said about the relationship with "secular" cultures, the role of faith, and the place of women in the community of disciples. Matt. 15:21–28 addresses these issues.

Seizing upon the possibility that *the woman herself is transformed* through her encounter with Jesus, her "great faith" in Jesus as authoritative "Son of David" and "Lord" is read as an example of the basic condition of discipleship: an acknowledgment of and submission to the authority of Jesus. Her grovelling acceptance of her status as a lowly dog is an exemplary implementation of the conditions for entrance into the kingdom/sphere of God's rule: recognizing oneself as a person "poor in spirit" and "meek" who is totally dependent upon what she will receive from the master and the children of the master; crumbs of "bread," a symbol of the word of God throughout this Gospel (as is explicit in 4:3–4). The transformation of the Canaanite woman in Matt. 15:21–28 shows that discipleship and faith are not something one can have without an intervention of Jesus in our lives. It also makes clear that becoming a disciple by having absolute faith in the authority of Jesus means renouncing any knowledge one might have had prior to one's encounter with Jesus and the community of disciples. The Canaanite woman accepts that her status as a Gentile is that of a dirty dog; accepting this ethnic slur she renounces her cultural heritage. Such is the "faith" that a disciple must have, as he or she abandons everything to submit to Jesus' authority.

2. *Jesus as a Model: Discipleship as Imitatio Christi*

Alternatively, one might come to Matt. 15:21–28 with a perfectionist pre-understanding of moral life and of discipleship.[32] Broadly

---

[32] This is the pre-understanding of the moral life and of discipleship which is represented in different ways by the works of Davies and Allison, Luz, and Patte (*Discipleship*, pp. 312–50).

speaking, perfectionist theories underscore that to be a moral agent is to have "character" (*êthos*), including moral discernment and practical wisdom (Aristotle). Practical wisdom is a matter of *practice*; moral discernment is something which one cultivates, as one acquires "culture" by learning to perform well one's function, as apprentices hone their wood-carving skills. A virtue (good wood-carving skill), and *a fortiori* practical wisdom as a series of virtues, cannot be gained by oneself. Apprentices need to learn in an actual workshop (with tools and benches) from a master cabinet-maker, and learning involves observing (discerning the useful gestures) and imitating the expert. From this perspective, disciples are people who have Christian virtues, learned in the concreteness of human experience by imitating the way in which "experts" perform them. The Gospel according to Matthew teaches discipleship to its readers by presenting persons who can serve as models for them. Of course, the primary model of discipleship is Jesus, so much so that discipleship is often conceived of as *imitatio Christi*.

As we seek to elucidate from this perspective the teaching about discipleship of Matt. 15:21–28, we find that our study of the transformative encounters has elucidated two potential roles of Jesus as model of discipleship: a) Jesus as the *one who transforms* the Canaanite woman, and b) Jesus as the *one who is transformed* by her. The former fits much better perfectionist pre-understandings: Jesus is the Lord and master whom humble apprentices should try to imitate, though without expecting to reach the same level of perfection. Yet, from beginning to end, the Gospel of Matthew resists such pre-understandings by also presenting Jesus as "poor in spirit," "meek," lowly "Son of Man," thus as one who is acted upon and thereby transformed. Furthermore, this second interpretation is demanded by a reading of the Sermon on the Mount as focused on "moral discernment" which shows that in his own teaching Jesus does not present himself as possessor of the truth about God's Will that he would impart to others. Rather, he posits as a characteristic of his own ministry and of that of the disciples a sharp moral discernment, a "sound eye," through which one can recognize expressions of God's Will in the words and deeds of other people as well as in oneself (see the Golden Rule and all the passages about "seeing" or "discerning" in the Sermon on the Mount). The "overabundant righteousness" (5:20, 46–47) required of disciples involves recognizing in the common teaching or behaviour of people (be they Pharisees, Gentiles, tax-collectors, parents) an expression of God's righteousness which, as such, disciples need to implement in all aspects of their lives.[33]

From this perspective, the only teaching about discipleship which makes sense in Matt. 15:21–28 is the one expressed in the transformation of Jesus by the Canaanite woman. Jesus is a model of discipleship in that he discovers in the Canaanite woman's deeds and words an expression of God's Will—or better, a manifestation of the kingdom—, affirms it and proclaims it as he exclaims: ᾿Ω γύναι, μεγάλη σου ἡ πίστις! By this exclamation through which "Jesus acknowledges the woman respectfully in contrast to the rejection that has characterized the story," "the particularist statements of vv. 24 and 26 are overturned, and it is the woman and those whose theological perspective she symbolizes who are acclaimed in the authoritative words of Jesus."[34] He accepts her re-definition of his mission which she *sees from her cross-cultural perspective*, and humbly renounces his earlier exclusivist and insensitive conception of his mission. Being a disciple involves imitating Jesus by recognizing a revelation of God's Will for us in the words or deeds of people who re-define our self-understanding and our sense of mission by helping us see our lives from a different contextual perspective. Affirming this manifestation of God's righteousness in others and applying it to our entire experience ("overabundant righteousness") is uncomfortable at times, because he demands from us to hear and to acknowledge that too often we display the shocking behaviour that involves ignoring and marginalizing those who are unlike us, be it because of gender, class, social, ethnic, cultural, and/or religious differences. Yet, it is also the exhilarating experience of discovering always anew the kingdom and what our participation in it as disciples involves.

3. *The Canaanite Woman as a Model of Discipleship as Struggle for the Kingdom and God's Justice*

Alternatively, one might come to Matt. 15:21–28 with a liberational pre-understanding of moral life and of discipleship.[35] In this case,

---

[33] See my discussion of "Reading D" in *Discipleship*, pp. 312–50.

[34] E. M. Wainwright, "The Gospel of Matthew," in E. Schüssler Fiorenza (ed.), *Searching the Scriptures, Vol. 2: A Feminist Commentary* (New York: Crossroad, 1994), pp. 672–3.

[35] This is the pre-understanding of moral life most clearly presented in E. Dussel, *Ethics and Community* (transl. by R. Barr; Maryknoll, N.Y.: Orbis Books, 1988). See also A. M. Isasi-Díaz and Y. Tarango, *Hispanic Women: Prophetic Voice in the Church*

the basic human predicament is that of "powerlessness," or better "lack of ability," because one is kept in bondage by supernatural or social evil powers which transcend individuals. The basic condition of moral life is, therefore, the empowerment of individuals and thus the liberation from oppressive forces. Conversely, the goal of moral life is justice, that is, life in a true "community," in contrast to life in a society of domination. From the perspective of this pre-understanding of moral life, the teaching about discipleship of the Sermon on the Mount is best summarized in the admonition of 6:33: "struggle for the kingdom and God's justice"—a translation which takes into account that throughout the Gospel of Matthew δικαιοσύνη can appropriately be translated as "justice," rather than as "righteousness." From this perspective, the Canaanite woman is a model of discipleship, not because of her meekness nor because she is transformed by Jesus, but rather because she relentlessly struggles for justice. In this quest, she crosses borders; she does not allow rebuffs to slow her down; she overcomes these obstacles by her wit and cultural wisdom.[36] She also has faith in Jesus as Son of David and as Lord, and thus as the one who is sent to empower the powerless, including her and her daughter who is possessed by an evil spirit. In all this, as suggested above, she replaces the male disciples as Jesus' true disciple. Unlike them, who are not particularly concerned with the pursuit of Jesus' mission, especially when it becomes bothersome or dangerous, the Canaanite woman seeks to maximize it, so that those who are empowered are not merely the "lost sheep of the house of Israel," but also all those who are victims of oppression. Furthermore, her role as a disciple is not so much to submit to the authoritative Jesus, but rather to confront him when his ministry becomes oppressive rather than liberative, and to help him redefine the scope of his ministry by bringing to him and showing him the situations of oppression which his ministry must address. Discipleship as struggling for God's justice includes joining in what God is

---

(San Francisco, CA: Harper & Row, 1988), especially pp. 77–93. For a study of New Testament ethics from the perspective of "lack of ability" as the primary human predicament, see J.-F. Collange, *De Jésus à Paul: l'éthique du Nouveau Testament* (Genève: Labor et Fides, 1980).

[36] As emphasized by L. A. Guardiola-Sáenz, "Borderless Women and Borderless Texts: A Cultural Reading of Matthew 15:21–28," in K. Doob Sakenfeld, Sh. H. Ringe, and Ph. A. Bird (eds.), *Reading the Bible as Women: Perspectives from Africa, Asia, and Latin America* (*Semeia, 78*; Atlanta, GA: Scholars, 1998), pp. 69–81.

already doing; this is "faith." But it also involves "great faith," becoming the point persons in the struggle for God's justice and calling the Lord, Son of David, to intervene in new areas beyond the borders.

Transformative Encounters with Other Readers of Matthew 15:21–28: Ongoing Readings

As I stated in the introduction, this latter interpretation is very attractive to me. I was tempted to adopt it, until I paid closer attention to other readings and remembered that I should self-consciously *read with others*. Reading with others reminded me of the many choices I made all along the interpretive process. The preceding pages present only a few of these choices. Reading Matt. 15:21–28 with still other people would help me see other dimensions of the text and thus other choices of interpretations. Transformative encounters with other readers of the text is an ongoing process which I need to pursue. But reading with others and recognizing the multiplicity of legitimate interpretations (i.e., of interpretations properly grounded in textual evidence) and of plausible interpretations (i.e., of interpretations which make sense in terms of diverse themes from the readers' conceptual worlds) opens for us the possibility to raise the ethical question: Why did I choose this interpretation rather than another one? What are the pragmatic implications of doing so?

The preceding pages have briefly described three legitimate and plausible interpretations. Why choose one rather than an other? There is no absolute, universal value judgement which applies. From the present religious, social, and cultural situation in which we find ourselves in North America at the end of the twentieth century, a situation in which colonialism, exclusivism, chauvinism, racism, and anti-Semitism are clear problems that we need to address, I believe the first reading, the Canaanite woman as model of submissive discipleship, to be quite dangerous as it ends up advocating a triumphalist view of discipleship and a hierarchical community of disciples which marginalizes many. By contrast, the last two readings are potentially helpful ones, provided that we carefully keep in mind the situation in which we are. These two readings can appropriately express the *teaching of the text for me or for us* (*pro me* or *pro nobis*), if we choose carefully between them. As I read Matt. 15:21–28 with Leticia Guardiola-Sáenz and other "borderless women," it is

clear that I, a male European-American, cannot and should not identify with the Canaanite woman as a model of discipleship. Unlike
Guardiola-Sáenz, I cannot approach this text "with a spirit of dispossession—the one . . . the Canaanite woman had when she approached
Jesus."[37] While I acknowledge her as a full-fledged disciple who carries out her discipleship in an exemplary way by challenging Jesus,
she is not a model of discipleship *for me*. This would be denying,
marginalizing, silencing the "spirit of dispossession" which is at the
centre of the discipleship of the Canaanite woman and all other
borderless and dispossessed women (and men). This is why, as I suggested in the introduction of this essay, for me as a male European-
American, Jesus is the most appropriate model of discipleship. Like him,
I need to speak with and read with borderless and border-crossing
women[38] and to allow them to transform my sense of discipleship.

---

[37] See Guardiola-Sáenz, "Borderless Women and Borderless Texts."
[38] See I. R. Kitzberger, "Border crossing and meeting Jesus at the well: An auto-
biographical re-reading of the Samaritan woman's story in John 4:1–44," in I. R.
Kitzberger (ed.), *The Personal Voice in Biblical Interpretation* (London and New York:
Routledge, 1999), pp. 111–27, and M. W. Dube Shomanah, "Divining Texts for
International Relations: Matt. 15:21–28" (in this volume).

GENTILE FEMALE CHARACTERS IN MATTHEW'S STORY: AN ILLUSTRATION OF RIGHTEOUSNESS

LILLY NORTJÉ-MEYER

1. *Introduction*

The position of women today and the position of women in ancient society have influenced the subject of this study. Today the world is increasingly being made aware of the rights of minority groups, oppressed people and the outsiders of society. I am a supporter of the rights of all people and therefore sensitive not to overemphasize the rights of one group of people at the expense of another. This only causes a vicious circle. To me, restoration of the balance in society is of importance.[1] The contribution of feminist criticism to restore this balance can be neither ignored nor underestimated.

In different ways, and from different points of view, feminist criticism attempts to shift the locus of biblical interpretation from predominant Western white male interpreters to marginal interpreters, who move the boundaries of race, sex and class to represent more interpreters in society than Western white males. This results in a shift in the perspective of biblical interpretation. Shifting the perspective does not automatically lead to a better reading of the text, but it extends the sphere of, and experience relative to, the debate.[2]

The contributors to feminist criticism share the view that the biblical text is predominantly patriarchal. Bird[3] summarizes this view by saying that the Bible is a thoroughly patriarchal document and that no biblical text escapes this influence, even though not conspicuously visible. Therefore, also the Gospel of Matthew is the product of a patriarchal society[4] and uses patriarchal models for religion and behaviour. It is also an androcentric document that views the

---

[1] Ph. B. Bird, "Authority and Context in the Interpretation of Biblical Texts," *Neotestamentica* 28 (1994), pp. 323–37.

[2] Bird, "Authority and Context," p. 332.

[3] Bird, "Authority and Context," p. 333.

[4] E. M. Wainwright, *Towards a Feminist Critical Reading of the Gospel According to Matthew* (Berlin: Walter de Gruyter, 1991).

world through the eyes of men and assumes the male experience to be the norm.[5] Men describe women and this does not allow unmediated access to the words of women or to the world of female experience.[6] This should be borne in mind when the gentile female characters in the story of Matthew are discussed. Feminist criticism reveals the androcentric character of the text and proves that the text is, therefore, an inadequate evidence of human and divine character and nature.[7]

2. *Methodological Approach*

To present a new interpretation of the themes in the New Testament and particularly of the theme of righteousness (δικαιοσύνη) in the Gospel of Matthew is hardly possible. Most aspects of biblical righteousness have already been comprehensively discussed. In this study, the significance and effect of gentile female characters on a Jewish religious notion, and specifically on the fundamental idea of righteousness, are discussed.

Matthew mentions only one encounter between Jesus and a gentile woman, i.e. the Canaanite woman, in 15:21–28. Another important, albeit indirect encounter, took place with Pilate's wife during Jesus' trial (27:19). However, these two women were not isolated from the other gentile female characters in the story, therefore the latter will also be reviewed for the sake of a general perspective.

For the topic addressed, it is important to emphasize the main aspects of narrative criticism. The reason for this is that, although Jesus encountered only the Canaanite woman, the function of gentile female characters and the theme of righteousness presented in Matthew's text are a unified and coherent whole. Thus, the focus will be on the function of the text as it is creating meaning and the way it affects readers, rather than on "its 'referential function' to serve as a source for historical knowledge."[8] The text is not used as

---

[5] In Matt. 8:5–13 Jesus consents to the request of the gentile officer without any resistance, but ignores the request of the Canaanite woman in 15:23.

[6] Bird, "Authority and Context," p. 333.

[7] Bird, "Authority and Context," p. 336.

[8] M. A. Powell, "Towards a Narrative-Critical Understanding of Matthew," *Interpretation* 46 (1992), pp. 341–6.

a window to historical reality, but for exploring the story world created in the text.[9]

3. Righteousness in the Gospel of Matthew

The topic considered does not allow for a complete discussion of
righteousness in the Gospel. Therefore, the focus will be on the most
important aspects related to the topic. The motif of righteousness in
the Gospel is related to other concepts. This interrelatedness is not
simple but nuanced. Loyalty and obedience to God and compassion
to people always form a key part in this nuance.[10]

Matthew's use of righteousness and faith shows that he does not
associate these two concepts, as Paul does.[11] Faith, as a soteriologi-
cal principle, plays almost no role in the Gospel. It concerns people's (mostly outsiders') belief in Jesus' ability to perform miracles on
request, in contrast to the unbelief of the Jewish religious leaders
(9:1–8). This is confirmed at the end of the narrative when Jesus
hangs "helpless" on the cross and the chief priests, scribes and elders
say that they will believe in him if he proves his power by coming
down from the cross (27:41–42).

The concept of righteousness in the Gospel represents the demand
of the law, namely, to do the will of God. The relationship between
the concepts of righteousness and law is important for this study.
The key to this relation is found in Matt. 5:17–20: the lasting validity of the law and the demand for something more than the righteousness of the Jewish leaders.

Matthew formulates the relation between righteousness and the
law in various ways. This is expressed, inter alia, in Matthew's way
of handling the Markan material. Whereas Mark portrays Jesus in
sharp contrast with the law, Matthew softens this severe difference
or else he colours it in such a way that the implication of the law
is no longer authoritative and binding.[12] On the contrary, Matthew

---

[9] F. J. Matera, "The Plot of Matthew's Gospel," *CBQ* 49 (1987), pp. 233–53.

[10] E. Engelbrecht, *Sending en Geregtigheid in die Matteusevangelie.* Unpublished Dissertation
(University of Pretoria, 1985), p. 157.

[11] G. Nebe, "Righteousness in Paul," in H. G. Reventlow and Y. Hoffman (eds.),
Justice and Righteousness. Biblical Themes and Their Influence (JSOT Supplement Series,
137, Sheffield: JSOT, 1992), pp. 131–53.

[12] Cf. Mark 1:23–28 and Matt. 12:1–50; Mark 7:19 and Matt. 15:20; Mark 10:12

presents Jesus' interpretation of the law as an "easy yoke" (11:21–30) in contrast with the legalistic tyranny of the Pharisees (23:3). The "easy yoke" focuses on grace, compassion and love. When a lawyer asks Jesus about the first of all the commandments, Jesus associates the demand of love with the entire law and the prophets (22:40). To Matthew this law is not only the law of Moses, but also God's word and commandment.[13]

One of the most prominent aspects of Matthew's use of δικαιοσύνη is its frequent appearance in a specific character context where he uses it to polarize his characters. For example, he alters Q in 3:15 and re-arranges the characters in such a way that the Jewish leaders become the object of John the Baptist's criticism (3:7). He also uses μετάνοιαν to put Jesus and John against the Jewish leaders. In 5:20 he places Jesus and the disciples in opposition to the Jewish leaders, and in 6:33 the disciples and the gentiles are contrasted with each other.

Matthew also gives prominence to righteousness by delimiting it against the hypocrisy of the Jewish leaders. In 21:23–32 he uses δικαιοσύνη to separate the Jewish leaders from the believers and this polarizing function becomes absolute in 5:10 when the disciples, and also the community, are persecuted for the sake of righteousness.[14]

Γίκαιος also plays a role in creating character context. In 10:17–42 δίκαιος is associated with "prophet" (10:41) and "disciple" (10:42). This contributes to the polarization of the community and the antagonists of the believers. This polarization concerns Jesus specifically. In 23:29–35 he uses δίκαιος to distinguish between the righteous and the Jewish leaders who were responsible for the death of the righteous. In 13:36–49 δίκαιος also causes polarization in an eschatological context: the people of the kingdom are contrasted with the followers of evil. The behaviour (13:41, 43) of these people determines the eventual separation of the good from the bad (13:49).

In order to understand Matthew's view of righteousness, it is important to note that he recognizes the work of the scribes (23:2–33), but he criticizes them for neglecting the most important demand of the law, and also for their hypocritical practices. Matthew's

---

and Matt. 19:3–9; R. Mohrlang, *Matthew and Paul. A Comparison of Ethical Perspectives* (Cambridge: Cambridge University Press, 1984), p. 10.

[13] Mohrlang, *Matthew and Paul*, p. 13.

[14] Engelbrecht, *Sending en Geregtigheid*, p. 160.

knowledge and use of the Old Testament prove that he himself stands in the tradition of exegetes. He uses the Old Testament not only to prove that Jesus fulfilled the prophecies, but also to justify Jesus' interpretation of the law wherever it differs from that of the Pharisees and scribes (9:13; 12:5–7).[15] He wants to portray Jesus particularly as a competent interpreter of the law, one whose life is perfect according to the will of God and who, therefore, conforms to a greater righteousness.

Matthew uses several themes to illustrate this demand for greater righteousness. The antithesis in 5:17–48 is intended for the deeper meaning of the law to be obeyed and to illustrate its extreme significance. The righteousness demanded by the law is more than legal conformity. 5:17–19 does not portray Jesus in conflict with the law, but as the one who demands radical obedience, in its most profound sense, to the extreme will of God.[16] This radical obedience leads to a greater righteousness, without which nobody can enter into the kingdom of God.[17] Whoever transgresses the most insignificant aspect of the law, or who teaches others to do so, will be the least in the kingdom of God. However, this does not mean that such a person will be cast out of the kingdom of God; it merely emphasizes the continuous importance of the law. This confirms the assumption that the antagonists of the Matthean community accused them and their leader (Jesus) of not keeping the law. Matthew answers that not only their leader lived according to the will of God, but also the members of his community. In accordance with the saints and the righteous of the Old Testament, they lived up to a greater righteousness than their hypocritical and legalistic accusers. Thus, Matthew encourages his community to conform to the demand of the greater righteousness.

Furthermore, Matthew particularly wants to show that the Jewish spiritual leaders and their legalism do not conform to the demand for a greater righteousness. On the other hand, especially the outsiders in society conform to this demand. He also urges the community not to become tired of practising righteousness; because, by acting righteously, they conform to the will of God.

---

[15] Mohrlang, *Matthew and Paul*, p. 16.
[16] Cf. Matt. 7:21; 12:50; 21:31.
[17] Mohrlang, *Matthew and Paul*, p. 19.

The relevant question now is: What is the relation of the gentile female characters to the concept of righteousness?

4. *Gentile Women as Characters*

In the narrative, the theme of the gentiles is not simple. For the purpose of this study, it is necessary to distinguish between several groups of gentile characters. Firstly, there are the gentiles who can be labelled as unbelievers and non-Jewish (e.g. 5:47; 6:7, 32). Secondly, there are the believers who were probably of gentile origin. This is supported by the debate on the identity of the author of this Gospel.[18] The sharp criticism of the Pharisees and the Jewish leaders some-times indicates that the believers could not have been Jews, but were mainly gentiles. Likewise, the rejection of Israel and the replacement of Israel by the gentiles (21:43) and the establishment of a new peo-ple of God, viz. the church, suggest this (ch. 18). Furthermore, the ultimate mission of the church is directed towards the gentiles (28:19).

A third group can be distinguished, viz. the gentile women. These characters do not fall in the above categories. From their original context they were unbelieving gentiles, but not in the way they func-tion in the story. The characterization of these female characters, as that of the other characters in the narrative, is done in relation to the protagonist, Jesus. As characters, they pose as the crowds, along two lines. As gentiles, they serve as foils for the disciples and form part of the antagonists (although they are never hostile towards Jesus), but their faith transforms them from supporters of the antagonists into followers and supporters of Jesus. However, they do not influence the plot or the flow of the narrative. The gentile characters are not developed in the story in spite of the fact that the story opens with the gentile women and closes with the mission to the gentiles.[19]

The gentile female characters do not merely serve as catalysts to provide other characters with the chance to exhibit their traits, nor do they fill up the scene. But, these characters serve to illustrate a certain point of view.

The narrator has a specific purpose for mentioning the genealogy at the beginning of the story. It contains important information for

---

[18] S. van Tilborg, *The Jewish Leaders in Matthew* (Leiden: Brill, 1972), pp. 171–2.
[19] J. D. Kingsbury, *Matthew as Story* (Philadelphia, PA: Fortress, 1988), p. 18.

the understanding and interpretation of the rest of the story. It is clear that he or she assumes that the readers have extensive knowledge of the Old Testament texts and traditions and that they are familiar with the Christian kerygma.[20] The introductory setting (1:1) seems to function as a heading for the whole story. When the reader comes across these titles for Jesus (Christ, son of David, son of Abraham) and the names (1:2–16) in the rest of the story, he or she will look for information and significance indicated in the genealogy. This can also serve as a key to unlock the narrator's message.

The genealogy serves as an introduction to place Jesus in the context of Jewish history and indicates the main events in Israel's history. The situation of the real readers imposes this setting. They know Jesus well, but they are in a crisis. They are accused by the antagonists for not keeping the law and the old traditions (15:1–2). Matthew writes to his community to ensure them that Jesus is the fulfilment of the Old Testament prophecies, that he lived according to the law, and that he was a competent interpreter of the law and the traditions. These indications are important for understanding the role of the gentile women in the story.

In the beginning of the Gospel, the readers find the names of certain women in the genealogy of Jesus. Besides, unaccustomed to the Jewish tradition, they are gentile women. Primarily, the focus is not on the inclusion of gentile women in the genealogy of Jesus, but on the descendants of Abraham and David, who are defiled by these gentile women. The narrator compiles the genealogy as an accusation against the religious leaders who are so concerned about their traditions and the correct conservation (15:1–20), while these traditions and their ancestors abound with unrighteousness (ch. 23).

However, Jesus, as the son of Abraham and in particular the son of David, is the one who has compassion for those despised by the religious leaders. That these women are included in his line of descent is, therefore, significant. It is noteworthy that also Jesus is included in the line of David by a deed of righteousness (1:19), because Joseph, who is not the biological father of Jesus (1:16), obeys the command of God and takes Mary as his wife (1:20–25).

Most scholars combine the roles of the four gentile women and associate them with the role of Mary. In this study they will be dis-

---

[20] I. R. Kitzberger, "Mary of Bethany and Mary of Magdala—Two Female Characters in the Johannine Passion Narrative," *NTS* 41 (1995), pp. 564–86.

cussed separately. Thus, the unique role of each will be emphasized and not only with respect to Mary.

The narrator does not give any information why these women are included in the genealogy. Therefore, by mentioning them, the narrator assumes that the readers are familiar with the characters and their significance. By mentioning them unexpectedly in the genealogy of Jesus, he is creating expectation. He also lets the readers fill in the scene with their knowledge of the women's actions and associations in their original context.

4.1 *The Narrative Role of Tamar (Matt. 1:3)*

The story of Tamar would not have attracted so much attention if the narrator had not included her in the genealogy of Jesus. From Gen. 38 it is not clear from what nation she originated. According to traditions in the Testament of the Twelve Patriarchs and the Book of Jubilees, she came from Aram, the land of Abraham, Rebecca, Leah and Rachel. The narrative in Genesis states clearly that, as a member of the family of Judah, she was treated unfairly. Judah chooses her as wife for Er, his eldest son and heir (Gen. 38:6). When Er dies as a result of his unrighteous life, Onan, the second son, is instructed to take Tamar as his wife. He humiliates her by having intercourse with her, but does not assume his responsibility with respect to her right of descendants. Judah also denies her this right by not allowing his youngest son to marry her. The Book of Jubilees and the Testament of the Twelve Patriarchs give her non-Canaanite descent as the reason why she is rejected by Judah's Canaanite wife and her sons.[21] Tamar is made an outcast by her in-laws (Lev. 22:14) and has to return to her father's house. This means that she becomes a burden and disgrace to her own family.

Abraham (Gen. 24:3–4) and Isaac (Gen. 28:1) instructed their sons not to marry Canaanite women. By obeying this order they would ensure that God's promise to Abraham and Isaac would be maintained.[22] As the substitute for Judah's Canaanite wife, Tamar restores the promises made to Abraham, because she is not a Canaanite as were Rebecca, Leah and Rachel.

---

[21] Cf. TJud. 10; Jub. 42:1–7.
[22] J. P. Heil, "The Narrative Roles of the Women in Matthew's Genealogy," *Biblica* 72 (1991), pp. 539–45, p. 539.

Ironically, Judah insists that she be burned to death because of
her adultery, until his own unrighteousness comes to light (Lev. 21:9;
Gen. 38:24). Tamar re-instates her dignity by demanding her rights
in a determined and systematic way. Thus, she reveals the unrighteousness of Judah and his sons and *her* son becomes part of the
Messiah's line of covenant. As a gentile woman, she maintains the
covenant when it was threatened by the conduct of the members of
the covenant. This is confirmed in Ruth 4:12 where the leaders at
the town gates bless the descendants of Ruth and Boaz and compare them to the descendants of Tamar and Judah. The descendants of Peres, son of Judah and Tamar, are mentioned in Ruth
4:18–22 as immediate ancestors of David. The narrator repeats this
phrasing precisely, but he or she adds the names of Tamar, Rahab,
Ruth and the wife of Uriah.

Tamar is the first woman mentioned in Matthew's story. Her conduct is characterized as a deed of righteousness. Through her per-
severance, she kept alive the promise made to Abraham when this
was threatened. The men mentioned in the genealogy represent the
line of David, but the gentile women preserve the promise made to
Abraham. The narrator reflects this information when he or she
announces that Jesus, son of Abraham, starts his mission in Galilee,
where the gentiles live (4:15).

4.2   *The Narrative Role of Rahab (Matt. 1:5)*

Rahab, a Canaanite prostitute, is the main character in the narrative in Josh. 2. She takes initiative and manipulates events; she hides
the spies and sends the men who were to arrest them on a wild
goose chase (2:5, 16). She bargains with the enemy to ensure her
own safety and survival, as well as that of her family (2:12–14).
Furthermore, she demands assurance from the spies that their promises
are not idle talk, but that they will honour their word with an oath
before God (2:12–13). Thus, she becomes the protector of her family. But, her action does not only ensure the safety of her family
and her entire household, it also ensures that she, as well as her
descendants, may live in the land of Israel. Even more, in this way,
she becomes part of the Messianic lineage and the great-grandmother
of king David.

In the genealogy of Matthew Rahab is the first example of a gentile who believes in the God of Israel. The Joshua narrative does

not state that she became the wife of Salmon.[23] There is no evidence that Rahab is the mother of Boaz and, according to estimation, she lived at least 200 years before Boaz. Therefore, one cannot conclude that she is listed in the genealogy because she was the mother of one of the male ancestors of the Messiah.[24]

She is mentioned by virtue of her deed of righteousness. The narrator suggests that this gentile Canaanite woman complies with the demand of righteousness, since her action is linked to God's redemption (Josh. 2:10). This leads to God's redemption through Jesus, the son of David, a redemption that is not intended exclusively for the Jews, but is also directed towards the gentiles (Matt. 28:19).

4.3 *The Narrative Role of Ruth (Matt. 1:5)*

It is remarkable that the Hebrew canon includes a book about a gentile woman, Ruth, and even bears her name as the title. This probably may be explained by the fact that she, as a Moabite woman, associates herself with Israel and the God of Israel. After the death of Ruth's Jewish husband, her mother-in-law advises her to return to her own country and her gods. Nevertheless, Ruth is determined to risk the unknown (Ruth 2:11) for the sake of her faith (1:18).

In this narrative Ruth is portrayed as the "good girl:" She is obedient, polite and diligent. She does not think only of herself, but also takes care of Naomi, her widowed mother-in-law (1:5; 2:18).

Yet, Ruth's actions are as intentional as were Rahab's. In the narrative, Ruth's character is developed from that of an obedient and polite woman to one who acts deliberately in order to reach her goal, to one who is blessed by the leaders of the nation, and finally she becomes the great-grandmother of king David. All this did not happen by chance. She had to experience many traumas before justice was done to her and her mother-in-law. Ruth faced the injustice that she, as a gentile woman, was not considered for a levirate marriage. This is illustrated by the first redeemer's willingness to buy the piece of land of Elimelech (cf. 4:4), but then by his unwillingness to take Ruth, the Moabitess, as his wife. When Boaz takes over the right to redeem, buys the land, and takes Ruth as his wife, righteousness is done. Ruth's action to leave her country and to bargain

---

[23] Cf. also Ruth 4:10 and 1 Chron. 2:11.
[24] Wainwright, *Feminist Critical Reading*, p. 166.

for her conjugal rights, was a deed of righteousness. Ruth, together with Rachel and Leah, built the house of Israel (4:11). Also the action of these women is associated with the action of God.[25]

The function of Ruth in the genealogy is not to emphasize her strong points, but because of the choices she made with respect to the God of Israel (Ruth 2:12). By following her mother-in-law, she claimed her rights as a childless widow. Thus, she overcame all obstacles and allowed righteousness to prevail.

Once again, this gentile woman is an example of someone who behaves according to the will of God, a woman whose deeds are associated with the deeds of God. Jesus says in Matt. 5:45 that the actions of the disciples should be so "that you may be sons of your Father in heaven," who acts righteously when "he causes his sun to rise on the evil and the good, and sends rain on the righteous and the unrighteous."[26] The particular accusation against the Pharisees is that they pay large tithes, but neglect the most important matters of the law of God: justice, mercy and faithfulness (23:23). Ruth, on the other hand, truly lived up to these requirements.

4.4 *The Narrative Role of the Wife of Uriah (Matt. 1:6)*

This woman is defined as the wife of Uriah. She is the only woman in the genealogy whose name is not mentioned, but is defined by her husband. From 2 Sam. 11:3 we learn that she is called Bathsheba. She is the daughter of Eliam and the wife of Uriah, the Hittite. In 2 Sam. 11–12 she is only referred to as the wife of Uriah, even after Uriah fell in battle and David took her as his wife (11:27). It is only after the death of her child, conceived in unrighteousness, that her name Bathsheba is mentioned (12:24). It is as Bathsheba, wife of David, that she becomes the mother of Solomon and thereby secures her position in the Davidic, and thus the messianic, lineage.

In 2 Sam. 11–12 she plays a passive role. Her own words are not recorded and her actions are not described. But, from 1 Kgs 1:11–13 and 1:28–31 it is clear that she acts deliberately. These texts refer to David's promise to her that her son Solomon will become king. By insisting that this promise is made true, she ensures a future for herself and her son: he as king and she as king-mother. Without this

---

[25] Wainwright, *Feminist Critical Reading*, p. 168.
[26] Bible quotations from NIV.

they probably would have been killed (1 Kgs 1:12). But this also ensures that the descendants of the sinful Saul do not obtain the kingship. In earlier rabbinical tradition an appreciation of Bathsheba occurs when she is associated with the "divine guidance of Israel's unfolding history and with the action of God."[27]

The narrator in Matthew's story deliberately does not mention her name because he wants to remind his readers of her specifically as the mother of Solomon. He or she focuses on the sin and un-righteousness of David. Although Uriah, the Hittite, is a gentile, the Lord is also the protector of *his* rights, and injustice done to Uriah will also be punished. In 2 Sam. 12:10 the Lord says to David: "Now, therefore, the sword shall never depart from your house, because you despised me and took the wife of Uriah, the Hittite, to be your own." The sin initiated by Judah and continued by David and his descendants culminated in the disastrous Babylonian exile (Matt. 1:11).[28]

The reference to the wife of Uriah recalls Nathan's judgement of David's sin when David despised God (2 Sam. 12:10). The impli-cation is that whoever despises God passes Nathan's judgement on him- or herself. The same judgement will be passed on those who call themselves children of Abraham and, by implication, children of David, and claim they do not need repentance while they are responsible for the death of the righteous and the innocent (Matt. 23:29–36).

However, it was Nathan who supported Bathsheba and her son in her struggle for their rights. He urged her to remind David of his promise to her. Therefore, Bathsheba ensured that the oracle of Nathan was fulfilled. The narrator discloses that Jesus as the son of David was indeed born out of this promise.

4.5 *The Narrative Role of Herodias (Matt. 14:1–12)*

It is noteworthy to recall the background against which this story is told. The narrator refers briefly in Matt. 14:3–5 to the event. Herod Antipas and his relatives were Edomites who converted to Judaism. They were half-Jewish. The reports on this family state clearly that

---

[27] Wainwright, *Feminist Critical Reading*, p. 169. Possible indications of this are found in b.Sanh. 101a; Midr. Ps. 3:5; b.Sanh. 107a.

[28] Heil, "Narrative Roles," pp. 541–2.

they were careless about keeping the law. Herod the Great, however, built the Temple according to the specifications of the law and Antipas attended the Passover on occasion (Luke 23:6–12).[29]

According to Josephus, Herodias was the daughter of Aristobulus, brother of Philip and half-brother of Antipas. Consequently, she was married to her uncle, Philip. Antipas visited Philip and robbed him of his wife. Antipas and Herodias then lived together as husband and wife. He rejected his own wife, the daughter of Aretas, king of Arabia Petrea, and therefore his father-in-law's hostility led to great misery for the Jews.[30] Intermarriage was a common practice among the Roman Emperors, but was strictly prohibited by the Torah (Lev. 18:16; 20:21–22). Consequently, John the Baptist took Antipas to task (Matt. 14:4).

John had many followers amongst the people. Josephus mentions that Antipas feared that John would initiate a rebellion against him, probably because of his poor political relationship with Aretas, and therefore he sends someone to behead John.[31] Matthew's story is close to Josephus's account of the event. Herodias's role is also limited, but it is still at her request that John the Baptist is imprisoned and beheaded (Matt. 14:8).

This narrative illustrates the possible consequences of the demand for righteousness. In the previous pericope, Jesus received resistance in his hometown. Consequently, he identified himself as a prophet because it is only in his hometown and in his own house that a prophet is without honour (13:57). In the opening scene of the narrative, Herod Antipas learns about the miracles Jesus is performing. His reaction to this proves that he is aware of the demand for righteousness, because he thinks that Jesus is John who was raised from the dead—the reward for righteousness. Although John's preaching in 3:1–12 characterizes him as righteous, he is portrayed as a prophet, and even more than a prophet (11:9; 14:5). The narrator probably intended to emphasize the prophetic status of Jesus. John is his forerunner, and what happened to the righteous John will also happen to Jesus. Furthermore, this illustrates what might await the followers of Jesus when seeking righteousness (24:9).

---

[29] P. J. du Plessis and B. C. Lategan, *Agtergrond en Geskiedenis van die Nuwe Testament* (Pretoria: Academia, 1987), pp. 36–8.

[30] *Ant.* 18:5, 1–2; W. Whiston, *The Complete Works of Josephus* (Grand Rapids, MI: Kregel, 1981), p. 382.

[31] Whiston, *Josephus*, p. 382.

Herodias is perceived to be one of the evil women of the Bible. Her character relates to that of Jezebel in 1 Kgs 19. She is an adulteress, a deliberate murderer, a poor mother and an abuser of people. She does not commit the murder herself, but allows others to do her dirty work. However, her actual sin and disgrace lies in her initiating the execution of a righteous man, a prophet.

Her role in the narrative is to act out unrighteousness. She is seen to be responsible for the death of a prophet, and therefore is in line with the scribes and Pharisees whom Jesus condemned, because they too were responsible for the death of the righteous and the prophets (23:29–36). Her actions are destructive and in contrast to the roles of the other gentile women in the story of Matthew.

4.6 *The Narrative Role of the Canaanite Woman (Matt. 15:21–28)*

The dialogue between Jesus and the Canaanite woman is the most comprehensive of all the miracle stories described in the Gospel of Matthew. This is the first account of a woman openly addressing Jesus. Distinctive lines for the national and spiritual boundaries between Israel and the gentiles are drawn here. That it is particularly a gentile woman who crosses these boundaries is significant. She does so on her own initiative and ignores any resistance.[32] Thus, the woman is charaterized as demonstrating initiative and being determined.

However, this is not the first encounter between Jesus and a gentile in the narrative. In 8:5–13 a gentile officer approaches Jesus with the request to heal his slave. Jesus consents without any resistance, rejection or refusal. But the Canaanite woman's plea for her daughter to be healed is ignored by Jesus, rejected by his disciples, and even rejected by Jesus when he refers to the gentiles as "dogs."[33] This is discrimination at its worst.

The narrator uses the Greek word for *withdraw* or *leave* (15:21) to indicate the increasing resistance and antagonism from the political and religious leaders against Jesus, and his periodical withdrawal to fulfil his mission. The immediate context of this pericope indicates this withdrawal in particular. In 12:9–13 Jesus withdraws after the

---

[32] R. A. Culpepper, *Anatomy of the Fourth Gospel. A Study in Literary Design* (Philadelphia, PA: Fortress, 1983), p. 137.

[33] Wainwright, *Feminist Critical Reading*, p. 115.

discussion with the Pharisees about the sabbath. Jesus also withdraws
to a desert place after he has heard of the death of John the Baptist
(14:13). After Jesus' debate with the Pharisees and the scribes on
cleanness and uncleanness, he seeks solitude outside the borders of
Israel in the regions of Tyre and Sidon (15:21). Jesus' withdrawal
indicates the increasing alienation between him and the religious
leaders.

The debate on cleanness and uncleanness (15:1–20) is of particular importance for the understanding of the encounter between Jesus
and the Canaanite woman. The Pharisees and scribes are portrayed
as characters with no faith or understanding.[34] They are supposed
to understand the Scripture and its meaning.[35] However, Jesus blames
them for disregarding the command of God and refers to their
unrighteousness with respect to their failure to fulfil their responsibilities towards their families. To them, the traditions of people are
more important than the word of God. In 15:11 Jesus calls the people and says: "What goes into a man's mouth does not make him
'unclean', but what comes out of his mouth, that is what makes him
'unclean'." Secondly, Jesus also reproaches his disciples for their ignorance and inability to understand his words (15:16). These narratives prepare the reader for Jesus' encounter with the gentile woman,
which is significant "for it was by way of women that the Gentiles
were considered unclean since their women were considered 'menstruants from the cradle'."[36]

It is noteworthy that Matthew changes Mark's identification of the
woman from Syrophoenician to Canaanite. The motive for this change
is unclear. Wainwright[37] refers to several scholars who are of the
opinion that when the Christian literature originated, it was common practice to refer to "outsiders whether by way of race, creed
or trade." If this interpretation holds true for "Canaanite," then this
woman is portrayed in contrast to the lost sheep of the house of
Israel in 15:24. Therefore, this conclusion simply does not hold.

From the analysis of the narrative it appears that the story of the
Canaanite woman is linked to two other stories in Matthew: the

---

[34] J. Capel Anderson, *Matthew's Narrative Web. Over, and Over, and Over Again* (JSNT
Supplement Series, 19; Sheffield: Sheffield Academie Press, 1994), p. 122.
[35] Cf. Ezra 7:10–11; Neh. 8:9–10, 14.
[36] Cf. m.Nid. 4:1. Wainwright, *Feminist Critical Reading*, p. 225.
[37] Wainwright, *Feminist Critical Reading*, p. 225.

story of Rahab, the Canaanite woman in the genealogy of Jesus (1:5), and that of Jesus' command to his disciples to a world mission in 28:19.

Different sections of the narrative can be identified and explained. In the first instance, this narrative is an example of the compassion of Jesus as the son of David, not only for the blind (9:27; 20:30), but also for a gentile woman. The Canaanite woman calls him "son of David" (15:22). This is unusual for a gentile woman, not familiar with Jewish traditions. However, this puts her into the framework of the other healing stories. It is significant that she uses the same words, ἐλέησόν με, as the two blind men in 9:27 (cf. also 20:30) But she adds something important, viz. κύριε. Also in the second plea for mercy, Jesus is called κύριε. Therefore, the narrator places her with the disciples and the other followers of Jesus, who exclusively call him κύριε. His enemies and strangers exclusively call him διδάσκαλη and ῥαββί, but never κύριε. The narrator prepares the reader for an important aspect of the discussion which follows.

Important rhetorical elements in the dialogue indicate the meaning and coherence of the underlying parts. Firstly, the woman pleads with Jesus by using ἐλέησόν με (v. 22) and a second time she asks βοήθει μοι (v. 25). However, the lack of understanding of the disciples is indicated by ἀπόλυσον αὐτήν (v. 23). This is in direct contrast with the words of the woman: she asks for mercy and help, while they demand that she must be sent away.[38] An interesting development takes place when the narrator uses alliteration to link two concepts: ἀπολωλότα to refer to the lost sheep of the house of Israel, and ἀπόλυσον to indicate the sending away of the woman.

This can have a twofold meaning. Firstly, one can reason that Jesus refers to the lost sheep of Israel, and includes the disciples, on account of their lack of understanding and inability to understand the situation. This view is supported by the extended theme of the lack of understanding of the disciples in the Gospel (cf. 15:16). Secondly, the lost sheep of the house of Israel may include the woman (cf. ἀπόλυσον αὐτήν, v. 23). Furthermore, Matthew calls her a Canaanite. This links her to Rahab, who is mentioned in the genealogy of Jesus, son of David. As a matter of fact, Rahab is the

---

[38] Cf. Ezra 10:2–3; Neh. 13:25–31.

grandmother of king David. Thus, by implication, the narrator links the Canaanite woman to the lost sheep of Israel (cf. also 9:36).

This interpretation is confirmed in the next part of the discussion. When Jesus reacts to her second plea, he uses the metaphor of the puppies (15:26). This metaphor was frequently used in Orthodox Judaism to refer to gentiles. Wainwright comments about the issue as follows:

> Many commentators consider this saying to be a mashal or wisdom saying, but its enigmatic nature leaves its meaning unclear. The commonly accepted position is that 'dogs' was a derogatory term used by the Jews to speak of Gentiles. There is no doubt that it was intended as insulting or degrading, as the use of the term in scripture suggests, but whether its referent was necessarily or solely the Gentiles is difficult to determine from scripture although there are such specific references in later rabbinic writings.[39]

Here Jesus uses the metaphor of the "dogs" to refer to the woman, but he softens it by using the diminutive form. Even this reference to the gentiles is used to describe the woman as part of the lost sheep of the house of Israel, since she does not interpret the reference to the dogs as street dogs, but as house pets. They are part of the household, and in this case the household is Israel. The dogs and the children are part of the same household but they differ in status. This image forms a link between the children and the dogs. By her response, the woman acknowledges that the children are the masters of the dogs. However, an interesting ambiguity characterizes the proper meaning of these metaphors. The analogy in the ambiguity of κύριε and κυρίων indicates that Jesus actually is the master of the children *and* the dogs. This is what the woman is able to understand, but neither the disciples nor the Pharisees and the scribes are able to understand. Jesus reacts to the woman's insight when he says that she has great faith (v. 28).

It is of significance that a gentile woman, who is regarded by the political and spiritual leaders as unclean, complies with the demand for righteousness. Her gentile origin does not make her unclean. By recognizing Jesus as the son of David and as the κύριος, and by pleading for her daughter, she shows more understanding of the command of God than the scribes and the disciples. She does not

---

[39] Wainwright, *Feminist Critical Reading*, p. 238.

retreat when she is faced with opposition or being rejected. She is an example of one who exerts her strength to lay hold of the kingdom of Heaven (11:12).

She accepts the fact that Jesus came to save Israel and, by implication, claims to be part of Israel.[40] Thus, she obtains the right to the lordship of Jesus. This is not an illegal act. As a Canaanite, she shares in the right that Rahab gained and, as part of the house of David, she belongs to the lost sheep of the house of Israel. On account of her faith, she becomes part of the "redeemed" house of Israel, viz. the church. The action and faith of the unknown Canaanite woman is an example of one whose righteousness exceeded that of the scribes and Pharisees (7:20; 15:1).

The initial resistance and rejection that the woman experiences form a sharp contrast with the closing of the story when Jesus grants her request. What was a faint reminiscence of Rahab in 1:5, and a prophetic promise of Isa. 42:1–4 in Matt. 12:18–21, turns into reality for the Canaanite woman in 15:27. She succeeds in influencing Jesus to include the gentiles in his and his disciples' mission. This mission was originally directed only at Israel. Thus, not only is *her* life changed, but she also influences the life of Jesus. When he returns to the Sea of Galilee, he continues his activities with renewed enthusiasm (15:29–31).

4.7 *The Narrative Role of the Wife of Pilate (Matt. 27:19)*

The Gospel of Matthew is the only Gospel which mentions the wife of Pilate. However, little is known about her, or the incident. Subsequent apocryphal literature[41] refers to her as Claudia Procula and describes her as God-fearing, and Jewish-orientated. However, this cannot be verified historically. The Greek and Ethiopian churches declared her to be a saint, possibly because she supported Jesus and recognized him to be a righteous man.[42]

---

[40] M. Davies, *Matthew* (Sheffield: JSOT, 1993), p. 115.

[41] H. Ridderbos refers to the wife of Pilate as Claudia Procula, but with no reference to the source of his information. Cf. *Het Evangelie naar Mattheüs II* (Kampen: Kok, s.a.), p. 224. In the English translation of "The Letters of Pilate to Herod," Pilate refers to her as 'my wife Procula'. Cf. "The Acts of Nicodemus or Acts of Pilate," in J. K. Elliott, *The Apocryphal New Testament. A Collection of Apocryphal Christian Literature in an English Translation* (Oxford: Clarendon, 1993), pp. 220–4, p. 223.

[42] Ridderbos, *Het Evangelie naar Mattheüs*, p. 224.

The story about the crucifixion and resurrection of Jesus is the heart of the Christian faith. Pilate's ill-considered sentence of Jesus continually serves to remind the reader that Jesus was crucified while innocent. This has two implications, viz. that Jesus' innocence, as well as the unrighteousness of humankind (represented by Pilate), is emphasized. The tragedy concerning Pilate is not that he misjudged Jesus, but that he knew that Jesus was innocent and, furthermore, he knew that it was out of envy that the chief priests and elders handed Jesus over to him (27:18).

There are three important issues. Firstly, Pilate had already occupied the judge's seat to sentence Jesus and was ready to meet the demands of the Jews. Secondly, his wife had a dream or received a warning in a dream. Nothing is said about the content of this awful dream. But because she warns Pilate not to have anything to do with this man, it is implied that she suspects the dreadful consequences. And thirdly, she is aware of the fact that this is a righteous and innocent man.

Twice the narrator uses dreams as warnings to avert imminent danger. Both dreams serve a similar purpose: to ward off a threat to Jesus' life. The story of Jesus' birth mentions that Joseph received a divine command to flee to Egypt (2:13, 14), which he obeyed and Jesus' life was saved. In 27:19 the wife of Pilate also receives a warning by means of a dream. This dream is not as clear and detailed as the dreams of the birth story. It creates a vague foreboding and was not presented directly to the woman. She, however, presents it to Pilate with an explanation.[43] This dream does not protect Jesus and he is handed over to be crucified. This dream was not recorded as a divine warning, but serves a divine purpose because the death of Jesus is God's will.

A remarkable feature of this story is that a superstitious, gentile woman recognizes Jesus as a righteous man, while the people of God want to execute him. She tries to convince Pilate not to have anything to do with his case. It is noteworthy that she does not try to persuade him to set Jesus free. She acts according to the will of God and proves to be more understanding than Peter in 16:21–23, who rebukes Jesus when he tells the disciples about his forthcoming death (16:22–23).[44] This woman does not want to prevent the death

---

[43] Anderson, *Matthew's Narrative Web*, p. 122.
[44] Cf. Matt. 15:15.

of Jesus, but her story emphasizes Israel's rejection of Jesus and the spreading of the Gospel to the gentiles.

In a legal system in which women have no right to testify, the futile testimony of this gentile woman becomes the evidence of Jesus as the "righteous one."[45]

5. Conclusion

It does not require a close analysis of the Gospel to notice that the narrative is conveyed in androcentric language, concepts and traditions. Female characters are seldom referred to and then they are mentioned mostly as wives of certain men. A woman has no identity of her own, but is identified solely by her association with her husband. Matthew uses the female characters to highlight certain aspects of his story. Here, the gentile female characters are of special importance. I cannot change Matthew's story. I also cannot change its patriarchal and androcentric context. But I can make use of the glimpse into the female world and experiences that the Gospel provides, to force open a wider perspective of my own female world and experience.

The encounter between Jesus and the Canaanite woman is the focal point of the gentile female characters in Matthew's story. Analysis of the encounter of Jesus with the Canaanite woman in 15:21–28 suggests two connections in the narrative: firstly, with the gentile females in the genealogy at the beginning and secondly, with Jesus' command to his disciples for a world mission at the end. This links the Canaanite woman to the other gentile female characters and Jesus' encounter with her is reflected in the other gentile female characters.

When Jesus and the Canaanite woman meet, she already believes in his power to perform miracles, which the Jewish religious leaders are never capable of, right to the end. She is the only person whom he seems to be unwilling to help, because he and the disciples were sent only to Israel. Her plea persuades Jesus to direct his mission also to her and the gentiles. Jesus not only changes his attitude towards her, he even changes the scope of his divine mission.

---

[45] L. Nortjé, "The 'Behind the scenes'-influence of women: A case study in the Gospel of Matthew," *Ekklesiastikos Pharos* 43 (1997), pp. 46–53.

The narrator prepares the community's antagonists for the inclusion of the gentiles into the new people of God, viz. the church.

The determination of the Canaanite woman to claim her right as part of the lost sheep of the house of Israel is reflected in the behaviour of the other gentile female characters. The gentile females mentioned in the genealogy acted deliberately and determined to let righteousness prevail so as to ensure the promise of God to Abraham and David. The actions of these women comply with the demand for greater righteousness. In the same way that the narrator uses δικαιοσύνη to emphasize the contrast between the believers and the unbelievers, he or she uses the gentile female characters to reveal the unrighteousness of the Jewish leaders. Even the wife of Pilate recognizes Jesus as a righteous man, in contrast to the Jewish leaders, who were intent upon crucifying him.

However, it is not their gentile descent or their characteristics as a woman, prostitute or adulteress, that is of importance, but their actions. Thus, the destructive behaviour of Herodias is an example of those who murder the righteous and the prophets, because they do not comply with the demand of righteousness and disregard the command of God.

The gentile female characters do not play a prominent role in Matthew's story, but they are used in a clever and skilful way as part of the portrayal of what the demand for righteousness is—even if this results in Jesus changing the scope of his mission. In a previous study,[46] I have shown that Matthew tells the story of Judas' suicide in such a way that the unrighteousness of the Jewish leaders is emphasized. Not only are they responsible for Jesus' death, but also for the death of Judas, because they had to punish him for the false testimony he gave, but neglected it (cf. Matt. 27:4 and Deut. 19:18–19). Thus, Matthew uses outsiders (e.g. Judas, tax collectors, prostitutes and gentile females) to show that *they*, rather than the Jewish religious leaders, enter into the kingdom of God (21:31–32).

Van Aarde's[47] description of the character of Jesus and the role that he plays, emphasizes this motive:

---

[46] L. Nortjé, "Matthew's motive for the composition of the story of Judas's suicide in Matthew 27:3–10," *Neotestamentica* 28 (1994), pp. 41–52.

[47] A. G. Van Aarde, *God-with-us. The Dominant Perspective in Matthew's Story and Other Essays* (HTS Supplementum Series, 5; Pretoria: University of Pretoria, 1994), p. 42.

Jesus is the embodiment of the behavior and attitude that is characterized by absolute obedience to the will of the Father in heaven. And,
since the 'fulfilment' of the will of the Father (= the 'law and the
prophets') is compassion, Jesus' dikaiosune is manifested, inter alia, in
his didactic approach to (e.g. Mt 5–7) and healing activities among
(e.g. Mt 8–9) the Jewish multitude in particular, as well as the Gentiles,
driven by the motivation of love. This same dikaiosune is expected of
the disciples. And it is a dikaiosune that testifies to something 'more'
than the dikaiosune of the Jewish leaders (cf. Mt 5:20). The Jewish
leaders' dikaiosune is of a formalistic nature and lacks the deep-seated
attitude of love towards the multitude and the gentiles. The Jewish
leaders are 'two-faced', 'murderers of the prophets', Satan's henchmen.

Matthew was quite audacious to use gentile female characters in an
androcentric story from an androcentric tradition, to illustrate such
a fundamental topic as righteousness. Furthermore, to describe the
behaviour of these women in contrast with that of the religious leaders of the people of God, will most certainly have been unaccept-
able to the Jewish antagonists of the Matthean community. With
Jesus' instruction to the disciples at the end of the narrative, Matthew
leaves a window open to the universal destination of the Christian
community and the community's communication with the universal
context in which women are in the process of occupying their legitimate position.

In what way does the text relate to our world and experiences?
Firstly, I must specify what I mean by "our world" and "our experience." "Our world" is the South African world and "our experience" is living in a society that is destabilized by a previous unfair
political and social system, *apartheid*.[48] The balance in society is disturbed. Most of the people of the society were, for that matter, marginalized. Not only the issue of race was involved, but also the
position and place of women.

Since the election in 1994, when black people came to power, the
South African society is in a process of transformation and affirmative
action. White people gave over their political power and now they
share their economical welfare with black, coloured and Indian people. This transformation is not without anxiety. The traditional identity of white people in South Africa is chauvinistic in nature. Therefore,

---

[48] Cf. H. P. P. Lötter, *Justice for an Unjust Society* (Unpublished Dissertation;
Johannesburg: Rand Afrikaans University, 1989).

many have a bias and chauvinistic attitude towards the transformation process. To them, the current situation is also destroying their cultural heritage. Concepts like "sharing" and "diversity" equal the idea of total loss of control and the road to the restoration of balance in society is long and steep.

For the first time in fifty years, black people are not foreigners in their country of birth, but citizens with human rights. Our Bill of Rights states clearly that in this country there is no more discrimination against people by way of race, sex, faith, sexual preference, etc. After a period in which white South Africans were privileged and guilty of being unjust, it is time we conform to the demand for righteousness. What nowadays are understood and defined as human rights, is what Matthew calls the demand for a greater righteousness. There is not a one-to-one identification between the Matthean narrative and the South African society, but Matthew illustrates that it was not the political and church leaders and the privileged people who conformed to the demand for a greater righteousness, but those who were considered outsiders and marginal people. This is absolutely true about the South African society.

The limited view that Matthew presents of women's involvement in changing society or male domination is not enough. He only introduces the abilities of women to restore righteousness in society. Feminist criticism enforces this process of restoration. Only after that restoration will adequate evidence be given of human and divine character and nature.[49]

---

[49] Bird, "Authority and Context," p. 336.

SYNOPTIC WOMEN IN JOHN. INTERFIGURAL READINGS

INGRID ROSA KITZBERGER

Interpersonal Fragments

"How can this be?," the old man wondered and looked up into the sky above whence he was supposed to be born again. It was a bright, starry night, recalling the promise given to his ancestor who became father of so many, starting with a miracle when he and his wife were already about his own age. But being re-born seemed a pure impossibility to the old man who felt closer to death than birth. Besides, his mother was lying buried in her tomb. A womb of no return.

"How can this be?," he finally addressed the man who was talking in such riddles. "Rabbi," he called him, though he was so much younger and—unlike himself—no real, trained rabbi, rather a self-made sort of rabbi. "With God, nothing is impossible," the young rabbi responded. And he began to relate a story his mother had once told him when he had asked her about his birth. It was a strange story about a miracle engendered by the spirit. And he was the miracle. "How can this be?," his mother had asked the angel who had communicated the unbelievable.

Talking with each other all through the night the old man and the young man got bonded deeply with one another, almost like father and son, a new experience for both of them, transforming their lives. When the new day dawned on them they parted, each going their separate ways. And the old man treasured every word and pondered them in his heart. There was a spark of light piercing his innermost self, the birth of something as yet unknown. But he would not tell anybody until all things were fulfilled.

*

"Do not weep," he whispered to the woman standing down below, together with the other women and a young man. "This is your son," he said to his mother, looking at the beloved man who was about his own age. "And you will be his mother," he added, "because

I am on my way to my father where I belong." And he looked up into the sky. It was a bright, sunny day. Then, crying out loud, he was pushed into the new life. The spirit's gentle breeze enfolded him when blood and water flowed forth from his wounded body. And a sword pierced his mother's heart.

*

"Let *us* do it," the two old men said to the three young women when they started their preparations to at least give their beloved master a decent burial. So it happened that the men brought a mixture of myrrh and aloes, about a hundred pounds, took the bloodstained body of the young rabbi and tenderly wrapped it into white linen, together with their spices. And he was laid into a new tomb, finally at rest like a baby in the womb. Angels were watching from on high, and peace was on earth in the hearts of the good-willed. "It's finished," the men said, and they returned home, together with the women. And they didn't say a word to anyone.

*

My Personal Encounters with Gospel Women and Men.
An Intertextual Journey

"How can this be?" The question was on my mind, and haunted me day and night whilst preparing a paper for the Johannine Literature Section at the AAR/SBL Annual Meeting in New Orleans in November 1996.[1]

For about a decade and a half I had been concerned primarily with women in the New Testament and had worked within a framework of feminist hermeneutics. Since 1993, when preparing a paper for the seminar on "Hermeneutics and the Biblical Text" at the SNTS Annual Meeting in Chicago, I had been concentrating on women in John. The primary focus on Mary of Bethany and Mary of Magdala[2] was like a stone cast into the water, creating ever wider

---

[1] I. R. Kitzberger, "How Can This Be?" (John 3:9): A Feminist-Theological Re-Reading of the Gospel of John," in F. F. Segovia (ed.), *"What is John?" Volume II: Literary and Social Readings of the Fourth Gospel* (SBL Symposium Series, 7; Atlanta, GA: Scholars, 1998), pp. 19–41.

[2] I. R. Kitzberger, "Mary of Bethany and Mary of Magdala—Two Female Characters in the Johannine Passion Narrative. A Feminist, Narrative-Critical Reader Response," *NTS* 41 (1995), pp. 564–86.

ripples. All the women in this Gospel soon caught my attention and I have approached them in ever new ways since then. In the beginning, I was fascinated with their importance in John and I advocated a *reading with the grain*. Relating the women to each other, but also to men in the Gospel of John as well as relating them to women in the Synoptic Gospels, widened the horizon of my research; it made room again for Synoptic women I had already encountered during my pre-Johannine period and also made room for men, with whom I had journeyed the greater part of my life when nobody as yet spoke of women, neither in the Gospels nor in Jesus' life.

Asking the question "How can this be?" whilst preparing for New Orleans marked a turning point in my research. The question of how a feminist *and* theological interpretation of the Gospel of John can be possible opened my eyes to text dimensions I had not realized until that moment. Hence I came to see that, regarding women in John, both a *reading with the grain* and also a *reading against the grain* is called for, and the Gospel as a happy paradise for feminists[3] was lost forever. I came to see that women in John can be viewed in both a positive way and a negative way, depending on which meaning dimensions[4] of the texts are chosen and activated in the reading process. Thus, the constructive character of interpretation and the ethical dimension of interpretation[5] were emphasized. Encountering Gospel women as well as men turned out to be a very dynamic process, depending on the reader or interpreter. Consequently, also my own encounters with the women and men I had journeyed with for some time changed drastically. Transformation happened in the reading process and in actual life, permeating one another in an interpersonal and intertextual fashion.[6] Over the years, focusing on

---

[3] On "de-constructing John's feminist paradise," see Kitzberger, "How Can This Be?," pp. 35–8.

[4] On "meaning-producing dimensions" and the multi-dimensionality of biblical texts, see D. Patte, *Ethics of Biblical Interpretation: A Reevaluation* (Louisville, KY: Westminster John Knox, 1995), and idem, *Discipleship According to the Sermon on the Mount: Four Legitimate Readings, Four Plausible Views of Discipleship, and Their Relative Values* (Valley Forge, PA: Trinity Press International, 1996).

[5] Cf. Patte, *Ethics of Biblical Interpretation*; D. Nolan Fewell and G. A. Phillips (eds.), *Bible and Ethics of Reading* (*Semeia*, 77; Atlanta, GA: Scholars, 1997); E. Schüssler Fiorenza, "The Ethics of Interpretation: Decentering Biblical Scholarship," *JBL* 107 (1988), pp. 3–17.

[6] On the intertextual relation between the biblical text and the reader as text, between the biblical story world and the reader's story world, see I. R. Kitzberger (ed.), *The Personal Voice in Biblical Interpretation* (London and New York: Routledge,

certain Gospel characters and reading them in a different light has
been greatly influenced by my own life story. Reading the Gospels
and in particular the Gospel of John has thereby become a very
personal way of encountering women and men and voicing them as
well as myself. Thus, after having journeyed a long way especially
with Mary Magdalene,[7] the Samaritan woman became another important companion and dialogue partner.[8]

Since taking up Nicodemus' question in 1996 I have journeyed
with him and his unanswered question, and we are still underway.
"How can this be?" has been my guiding question in many contexts, and living with the question has become more important than
finding answers. In 1997 I encountered another man who had had
his own personal adventure with Nicodemus, and still has.[9] After
about a decade and a half of concentrating on women in the New
Testament and especially in the Gospels this one particular man,
Nicodemus, has caught my attention and kindled my compassion.
He was soon to be followed by another Johannine male character,
Lazarus, the brother of Martha and Mary.[10]

Thanks to encountering these Gospel men, and others in due
course, my encounters with Gospel women have changed and under-
gone fundamental transformation with far-reaching consequences for
my research and personal life. As I head towards a post-feminist
hermeneutics[11] of biblical interpretation, I struggle for a gender anti-
apartheid community of believers and biblical scholars alike. This struggle for true liberation and justice has been greatly nourished by

---

1999). Cf. also J. Capel Anderson and J. L. Staley (eds.), *Taking It Personally:
Autobiographical Biblical Criticism* (*Semeia*, 72; Atlanta, GA: Scholars, 1995), and J. L.
Staley, *Reading with a Passion. Rhetoric, Autobiography, and the American West in the Gospel
of John* (New York: Continuum, 1996).

[7] I am working on a project on Mary Magdalene.

[8] I. R. Kitzberger, "Border crossing and meeting Jesus at the well: An autobiographical re-reading of the Samaritan woman's story in John 4:1–44," in idem
(ed.), *The Personal Voice in Biblical Interpretation*, pp. 111–27.

[9] F. J. Moloney, "An adventure with Nicodemus," in Kitzberger (ed.), *The Personal
Voice in Biblical Interpretation*, pp. 97–110.

[10] I. R. Kitzberger, "Untying Lazarus—A Sisters' Task? Re-visioning Gender and
Characterization in John 11." Paper presented in the Johannine Literature Section
at the AAR/SBL Annual Meeting in Orlando, FL, on Nov. 22, 1998.

[11] A post-feminist hermeneutics pre-supposes a feminist hermeneutics and is not
possible where feminism has not yet taken roots and where the liberation of women
from patriarchal structures has not yet taken place. A post-feminist hermeneutics,
however, goes a step further and transcends gender boundaries. It implies the voicing of women without the silencing of men.

reading and re-reading[12] the Gospel of John and by its portrayal of female and male characters, as well as the gender related ethics of equality conveyed in this Gospel.[13]

Thus, this present paper is both the result of and a part of that process of re-viewing the gender relations in the Gospel story world and in our present story world. My focus on Synoptic women in John was initiated and inspired by a process of re-reading all four Gospels, a process in which new and hitherto invisible text dimensions were gradually revealed to me. Therefore, I want to share part of my journey[14] with you, dear reader, and invite you on your own unique journey with women and men, both Synoptic and Johannine.

Women in John and the Synoptics—Part of the Never-Ending Riddle

The importance of women in John and their pivotal role in John's story of Jesus[15] has been widely acknowledged, however different the concrete interpretations may be.[16] Likewise, the importance of women in the Jesus tradition, as reflected in all of the Gospels, is beyond

---

[12] For the difference between first time reading and re-reading, see I. R. Kitzberger, "How Can This Be?," pp. 22–4; M. Calinescu, *Rereading* (New Haven and London: Yale University Press, 1993).

[13] I. R. Kitzberger, "Grenzüberschreitungen. Perspektiven neutestamentlicher Hermeneutik und Praxis aus dem Johannesevangelium." Lecture presented at the University of Salzburg, Austria, on Dec. 3, 1998.

[14] Note that the motif of the journey is essential for the plot of John's story. See F. F. Segovia, "Journey(s) of the Word: A Reading of the Plot of the Fourth Gospel," in R. A. Culpepper and F. F. Segovia (eds.), *The Fourth Gospel from a Literary Perspective* (*Semeia*, 53; Atlanta, GA: Scholars, 1991), pp. 23–54.

[15] R. Kysar, *John's Story of Jesus* (Philadelphia, PA: Fortress, 1984).

[16] R. E. Brown, "Roles of Women in the Fourth Gospel," *TS* 36 (1975), pp. 688–99; S. M. Schneiders, "Women in the Fourth Gospel and the Role of Women in the Contemporary Church," *BTB* 12 (1982), pp. 35–45; T. Karlsen Seim, "Roles of Women in the Gospel of John," in L. Hartmann and B. Olsson (eds.), *Aspects of the Johannine Literature* (CB.NT, 18; Uppsala: University Press, 1987), pp. 56–73; M. C. Boer, "John 4:27—Women (and Men) in the Gospel and Community of John," in G. J. Brooke (ed.), *Women in the Biblical Tradition* (Studies in Women and Religion, 31; Lewiston, N.Y.: Edwin Mellen, 1992), pp. 208–30; E. Schüssler Fiorenza, *In Memory of Her. A Feminist Theological Reconstruction of Christian Origins* (London: SCM, 1983), chap. on "Women as Paradigms of True Discipleship" in the Gospel of John, pp. 323–42; S. van Tilborg, *Imaginative Love in John* (Biblical Interpretation Series, 2; Leiden—New York—Köln: E. J. Brill, 1993), esp. ch. 4 on "Loving Women." R. G. Maccini, *Her Testimony is True. Women as Witnesses according to John* (JSNT Supplement Series, 125; Sheffield: Sheffield Academic Press, 1996); A. Fehribach, *The Women in the Life of the Bridegroom. A Feminist Historical-Literary Analysis of the Female Characters in the Fourth Gospel* (Collegeville, MN: The Liturgical Press, 1998).

doubt. However, when viewed in more detail, the question of which women and how they are presented in the Synoptic Gospels and in the Gospel of John respectively cause considerable problems and raise further questions, which have not been answered once and for all even 2000 years later. Thus, the question of women in the Gospels shares in the never-ending riddle of the relation between John and the Synoptics, which has troubled not only modern scholars but has been recognized as a problem from earliest times,[17] in fact ever since the four Gospel canon[18] came into existence. Therefore, the issue of Synoptic women in John, as addressed in this paper, may also serve as a test model for the relation of the Gospels and may open up new perspectives in search of an answer.

Compared to the women mentioned in the Synoptic Gospels, whether named or unnamed, the list of women in John's Gospel seems rather short: Jesus' mother (2:1–11; 19:25–27), the Samaritan woman (4:1–44), Mary and Martha of Bethany (11:1–46; 12:1–8), the sister of Jesus' mother, Mary, the wife of Clopas (19:25), and Mary Magdalene (19:25; 20:1, 11–18). In addition, though added later on, there is the unnamed woman accused[19] of adultery (7:53–8:11). Of these, only Jesus' mother, Mary and Martha of Bethany, and Mary Magdalene are known from the Synoptic Gospels, while the other women are characters unique to John's Gospel. However, though small in number compared to the women in the Synoptic Gospels, the importance of the women in John, in particular for the christology[20] of the Gospel, outweighs their small number. Besides that, no other Gospel presents such long narratives in which women feature prominently; John 4 and John 11/12 as well as John 20 are, for that matter, without parallel.

And yet, any informed reader familiar with the Synoptic traditions will still ask somewhat bewilderedly, "Where have all the women gone?" Apart from a possible slight reference in John 20:2 there is no trace of women followers of Jesus as mentioned in the Synoptic Gospels, no matter how different the lists are, with the exception of

---

[17] D. M. Smith, *John Among the Gospels. The Relationship in Twentieth-Century Research* (Minneapolis, MN: Fortress, 1992).

[18] Cf. G. N. Stanton, "The Fourfold Gospel," *NTS* 43 (1997), pp. 317–46.

[19] For the designation of the woman as the "accused" instead of the "adulterous," see the contribution of Leticia Guardiola-Sáenz in this volume.

[20] On the "christological internet of women in John," see Kitzberger, "How Can This Be?," pp. 24–8.

Mary Magdalene, who is always mentioned first (Mark 15:40–41; 15:47; 16:1–8 parr). Neither Susanna, Joanna, Salome, Mary of James and Joses/Joseph, nor the (unnamed) mother of Zebedee's sons, nor all the other women whom Luke knows to have been cured of their illnesses and who provided for Jesus (Luke 8:2–3) are present in John's Gospel. Besides that, the healing of women, which is a major part of the Synoptic Jesus tradition, is totally absent from the Fourth Gospel which, however, knows of the healing of men. There is no haemorrhaging or bent-over woman (Mark 5:25–34 parr; Luke 13:10–17), no girl of Jairus (Mark 5:21–24, 35–43 parr). Even Simon/Peter's mother-in-law (Mark 1:29–31 parr) is missing, and so are the Syrophoenician/Canaanite woman and her daughter (Mark 7:24–30 par Matt. 15:21–28), to name but a few. The more one looks for Synoptic women missing in John, the more one is at a loss how to explain such fundamental differences. "How can this be?," the question must indeed be haunting and daunting for every alert reader searching the Gospels for women.

But things get even worse when one pays closer attention to how the women known to both the Synoptics and John are portrayed respectively. In fact, they are hardly recognizable as one and the same person. Jesus' mother, who is never named Mary in John, enters the stage only very late on in Jesus' life, when he performs his first sign at the wedding of Cana, a story unique to John (2:1–11). She does not actually give birth to Jesus, as in the Matthean and Lukan infancy narratives (Matt. 1–2; Luke 1–2). On the other hand, the negative portrayal of Mary searching for her supposedly crazy son and trying to get him back home (Mark 3:20–21; 3:31–35 parr) is unknown to John. She is faithful unto the end, standing at the foot of the cross, a scene also unique to John (19:25–27).

Apart from any mention of a brother called Lazarus, the characterization of Mary and Martha in Luke's narrative (10:38–42) differs considerably from their portrayal in John (11:1–46; 12:1–8). There, they live rather happily and unanimously together, without any conflicts about housework or more or less important things. They share in hosting their special guest Jesus and serve him in equally important ways: Martha serves food and drink, while Mary offers her service of love by anointing him (12:1–8). Prior to any details of characterization, the very location of the sisters causes bewilderment when comparing the Synoptics and John. While they live in Bethany, near Jerusalem, in John's Gospel and Jesus encounters them towards the end of his life (11:1; 12:1), they live in a village in Galilee according to Luke's Gospel (10:38) and Jesus encounters them during his Galilean ministry. If they are the same Mary and Martha they cannot have lived in two different places, can they? So, while some agreement with regards to their characterization can be arrived at, as has so often been done in the history of interpretation, there are definite limits to this endeavour.

Finally, Mary Magdalene seems to be the most important female character in John's Gospel, even more important than Jesus' mother. Though she is not mentioned as following Jesus on his path of earthly ministry, as in the Synoptics (Mark 15:40–41 parr), this is taken for granted when she is depicted standing at the foot of the cross (19:25), without needing to be introduced to the reader. Yet, how and when she came to encounter Jesus in the first place is not so much as hinted at, unlike Luke's account, which mentions seven demons expelled from her by Jesus (Luke 8:2). In John, her only designation is according to her place of origin, Magdala. However, only in John's Gospel is she given the importance of a real character who features prominently within the narrative, and even more so at such an outstanding point both in time and place. She is the one who first encounters the risen Jesus and is commissioned by him to pass on the Easter message (20:11–18). Thus, the continuation of the Jesus movement is mainly due to this woman's role and her unique relation to her Rabbi (20:16). Thereby, she is characterized as Jesus' disciple in a much more pointed fashion than in the Synoptic Gospels.

Being confronted with all the differences, and only a few similarities, between the women, named and unnamed, in the Synoptics and in John, all the solutions that have been proposed over the past 2000 years regarding the never-ending riddle of the relation between John and the Synoptics could be applied here as well. The main starting point in each case is the question of whether or not John knew and was dependent on the Synoptics. Accordingly, the answers vary considerably. Yet, no matter to what solution one adheres, the uneasy feeling of "How can this be?" remains an open question.

In my present paper I shall not concentrate on the question of how and why many Synoptic women got missed out, or how and why other women are portrayed so differently. My concern is to trace the presence of Synoptic women in John who are not visible at first sight and who I myself have come to see only in a long process of reading and re-reading the Gospels and of encountering women and men at various stages in my research and personal life.

In approaching the Gospel characters I shall apply an intertextual approach which implies re-viewing female and male Johannine characters and which also aims at a re-visioning of the relation between John and the Synoptics.

Interfigural Characterization

Concentrating on characterization I am starting from a reader response[21] approach in which characterization is viewed as being achieved by a dynamic process of creative interaction of the reader or interpreter with the text. Thus, characterization implies the reconstruction of a text by the reader[22] and is hence a very individual endeavour, depending on the choices one makes within the reading process. In fact, one and the same text signal can be interpreted in very different ways due to the actualization and contextualization of meaning dimensions within the closer narrative and the story at large. Besides that, gaps, discontinuity, and ambiguity of the texts and how these problems are solved by the reader[23] have far-reaching consequences for the evaluation of a character. What is said in a text as well as what is not said shapes the perception of a character by the reader. By concentrating on the rhetoric and discourse[24] of the text the gradual unfolding of a narrative and hence

---

[21] On reader response criticism, see J. P. Tompkins (ed.), *Reader-Response Criticism. From Formalism to Post-Structuralism* (Baltimore and London: Johns Hopkins University Press, 1980); E. V. McKnight, *Post-Modern Use of the Bible. The Emergence of Reader-Oriented Criticism* (Nashville, TN: Abingdon, 2nd edn, 1990); idem, *The Bible and the Reader. An Introduction to Literary Criticism* (Philadelphia, PA: Fortress, 1985); R. M. Fowler, *Let the Reader Understand. Reader-Response Criticism and the Gospel of Mark* (Minneapolis, MN: Fortress, 1991); F. F. Segovia (ed.), *"What is John?" Volume I: Readers and Readings of the Fourth Gospel* (SBL Symposium Series, 3; Atlanta, GA: Scholars, 1996); *"What is John?" Volume II: Literary and Social Readings of the Fourth Gospel* (SBL Symposium Series, 7; Atlanta, GA: Scholars, 1998).

[22] Cf. J. Darr, *On Character Building: The Reader and the Rhetoric of Characterization in Luke-Acts* (Louisville, KY: Westminster John Knox, 1992); E. Struthers Malbon and A. Berlin (ed.), *Characterization in Biblical Literature* (*Semeia* 63; Atlanta, GA: Scholars, 1993).

[23] Cf. W. Iser, "The Reading Process: A Phenomenological Approach," in Tompkins (ed.), *Reader-Response Criticism*, pp. 50–69, here p. 55; McKnight, *Post-Modern Use*, pp. 223–41; R. Alter, *The Pleasures of Reading in an Ideological Age* (New York: Simon and Schuster, 1989), pp. 206–38.

[24] For the difference between story and discourse, see S. Chatman, *Story and Discourse: Narrative Structure in Fiction and Film* (Ithaca, N.Y.: Cornell University Press, 1978). See also G. Genette, *Narrative Discourse: An Essay in Method* (Ithaca, N.Y.: Cornell University Press, 1980).

the gradual unfolding of a character within the narrative is seriously taken into account, compared with an analysis aiming at some "content" as abstracted from the narrative ebb and flow.[25]

My character analysis in this paper is based on an "open view of character" as advocated by Seymour Chatman,[26] in which characters are not only evaluated by the functions of their actions in relation to the plot but are treated as autonomous beings and are assessed in the way we evaluate real people. Therefore, every detail in the text which provides a clue for characterization is taken into account, that is, what a character says or does, what the narrator says about him or her, and how she or he is related to other characters in the story.[27] In this paper, the focus is on further dimensions of characterization which are added by an intertextual approach and more concretely by an interfigural view of a character. The term "interfigurality," which was coined by Wolfgang G. Müller, refers to "interrelations that exist between characters of different texts" and it represents "one of the most important dimensions of intertextuality."[28] Thus, it is different from "configuration," which refers to the relation of characters within a given text.[29]

In the paper presented in Chicago in 1993 I applied the concept of interfigurality for the first time and showed how Mary of Bethany and Mary of Magdala are not only related to each other within the Johannine story world, but are also related to female characters of the Synoptic story worlds. Thereby, I suggested that the author of

---

[25] For the "content" as embedded in the form, see also G. O'Day, *Revelation in the Fourth Gospel. Narrative Mode and Theological Claim* (Minneapolis, MN: Fortress, 1986).

[26] Chatman, *Story and Discourse*, pp. 107–38.

[27] Cf. D. Rhoads, "Narrative Criticism and the Gospel of Mark," *JAAR* 50 (1982), pp. 411–34. W. C. Booth (*The Rhetoric of Fiction* [Chicago, IL: Chicago University Press, 2nd edn, 1983]) distinguishes between two techniques of characterization, telling and showing (pp. 3–20); Sh. Bar-Efrat (*Narrative Art in the Bible* [BiLeSe, 17; Sheffield: Sheffield Academic Press, 1989]) speaks of direct and indirect shaping of characters (pp. 47–92, esp. p. 64). In both cases, the latter categories demand more activity on the part of the reader. See also R. A. Culpepper, *Anatomy of the Fourth Gospel: A Study in Literary Design* (Philadelphia, PA: Fortress, 1983). On the relationship between language use and characterization, see N. R. Petersen, *The Gospel of John and the Sociology of Light. Language and Characterization in the Fourth Gospel* (Valley Forge, PA: Trinity Press International, 1993).

[28] W. G. Müller, "Interfigurality. A Study on the Interdependence of Literary Figures," in H. E. Plett (ed.), *Intertextuality* (Research in Text Theory, 15; Berlin and New York: Walter de Gruyter, 1991), pp. 101–21, here p. 101.

[29] Cf. Müller, "Interfigurality," p. 117.

John knew the Synoptic Gospels and transformed their characters in a very creative way. At the same time, the readers of the Gospel of John—at least those familiar with the Synoptic Gospels—were encouraged and invited to remember Synoptic characters and to link them to characters in the present Gospel. Thus, Mary and Martha of Bethany and Mary of Magdala were not only linked to the same characters in the Synoptics, but the two Marys were also linked to the women anointing Jesus as rendered in Mark 14:3–9, Matt. 26:6–13, and Luke 7:36–50. In my paper on "Love and Footwashing. John 13.1–20 and Luke 7.36–50 Read Intertextually," presented at the SNTS Annual Meeting in Madrid in 1992 in the seminar "The Role of the Reader in the Interpretation of the New Testament,"[30] I had already touched on the issue of interfigurality, without yet knowing and using that term. Since attending the Colloquium Lovaniense on "John and the Synoptics" in 1990,[31] the question of the relation between John and the Synoptics has become one of my main concerns in New Testament interpretation.

In this present paper, therefore, I shall push the issue of interfigurality and the relation between John and the Synoptics further by concentrating on the characterization of Nicodemus and the mother of Jesus in John and on their interfigural relations to Synoptic women. Thereby, new dimensions will also be added to gender as one important aspect of characterization. Gender, as a social construct and as relating to a literary character, is established by the roles attributed to a character within the narrative and by the context in which a character is drawn. Besides that, gender is also constructed by the relation of a character to other characters, both female and male, of the same text and of other texts, and hence by configuration and by interfigurality. As with any other aspect of characterization, also gender is established both by the construction of the text and by its re-construction on the part of the reader. Therefore, even the gendered characterization is a very individual issue, for both female and male readers.[32]

---

[30] Published in *Biblical Interpretation* 2 (1994), pp. 190–206.

[31] A. Denaux (ed.), *John and the Synoptics* (BETL, 101; Leuven: Leuven University Press and Peeters, 1992).

[32] Cf. I. N. Rashkow, "In Our Image We Create Him, Male and Female We Create Them: The E/Affect of Biblical Characterization," in Struthers Malbon and Berlin (eds.), *Characterization in Biblical Literature*, pp. 105–13.

While I imagined a first (female) reader in my early reader response papers, I have come to realize how much any reader construct or reading construct is shaped by one's own personality and will therefore always be the voice of a present real reader.[33] Because of this insight, the interfigural readings as presented in this paper are basically my own personal readings, based on the text dimensions I activated in the reading process. How much the author of John as well as the first readers of the Gospel did or could establish the same or similar intertextual connections will be left as an open question, though it will be taken into consideration. At the same time this paper is an exercise in ideological criticism[34] and in intercultural criticism[35] as it analyses the ideology embedded in the texts and as reconstructed in readings of the text, including my own readings of the characters.

The Characterization of Nicodemus

Nicodemus is one of the characters unique to John's Gospel. He enters stage explicitly three times within the Gospel story: In chapter 3 he comes to Jesus and they engage in a nightly conversation about re-birth from above; in chapter 7 he advocates Jesus when he is put on trial by the other Jewish leaders, and finally in chapter 19 he, together with Joseph of Arimathea, buries the body of Jesus in the garden tomb near the place where he was crucified.

---

[33] For real readers, as different from reader constructs, see Segovia (ed.), *"What is John?" Volume I*, especially the contribution by Segovia "Reading Readers of the Fourth Gospel and Their Readings: An Exercise in Intercultural Criticism," pp. 237–77. On the importance of real readers, see also F. F. Segovia and M. A. Tolbert (eds.), *Reading from This Place. Volume 1: Social Location and Biblical Interpretation in the United States* (Minneapolis, MN: Fortress, 1995), and *Reading from This Place. Volume 2: Social Location and Biblical Interpretation in Global Perspective* (Minneapolis, MN: Fortress, 1995); G. West and M. W. Dube (eds.), *"Reading With": An Exploration of the Interface Between Critical and Ordinary Readings of the Bible. African Overtures* (*Semeia*, 73; Atlanta, GA: Scholars, 1996).

[34] Cf. F. F. Segovia, "Cultural Studies and Contemporary Biblical Criticism: Ideological Criticism as a Mode of Discourse," in Segovia and Tolbert (eds.), *Reading from This Place, Volume 2*, pp. 1–17; F. Inglis, *Ideology and the Imagination* (London: Cambridge University Press, 1975).

[35] Cf. Segovia, "Reading Readers of the Fourth Gospel and Their Readings: An Exercise in Intercultural Criticism," in idem (ed.), *"What is John?" Volume I*, pp. 237–77; idem, "Reading Readers Reading John: An Exercise in Intercultural Criticism," in idem (ed.), *"What is John?" Volume II*, pp. 281–322.

These are the simple facts and there is no doubt about them. But when it comes to the evaluation of the character of Nicodemus, opinions about him differ widely. While some acknowledge his partial faith, others opt for his full faith in Jesus and argue for his becoming a true disciple of Jesus at the end of the narrative. Others, however, deny that Nicodemus made any progress or showed any growth in the course of the narrative; on the contrary, so they argue, he demonstrated the same lack of insight when burying Jesus as he did when he first came to him at night. Whatever an interpreter argues, his or her evaluation is based on certain choices of meaning dimensions over against others. In particular it's the long narrative about the nightly encounter in 3:1–21 and the narrative about the burial in 19:38–42 which have brought forth many different interpretations and hence very different pictures of Nicodemus. "How can this be?," we could also ask when comparing such different portrayals, based as they are on the same texts.

In chapter 3[36] Nicodemus turns up for the first time and is introduced to the reader as a Pharisee and "a ruler of the Jews" (v. 1). He comes to Jesus by night and addresses him as "rabbi" and confesses him as a teacher who has come from God, a belief based on the signs he has done (v. 2). Jesus, however, does not respond to Nicodemus' words but starts talking about the necessity of re-birth from above[37] in order to enter the kingdom of God[38] (v. 3), further specified as a re-birth of water and the Spirit (v. 5).[39] In good Johannine fashion Nicodemus, like other characters in John's story, understands on the material level what is meant to be understood

---

[36] For a reader response interpretation of this chapter, see R. Kysar, "The Making of Metaphor. Another Reading of John 3:1–15," in Segovia (ed.), *"What is John?" Volume I*, pp. 21–41. His view is that Nicodemus "remains . . . a thoroughly ambiguous character in the whole of the Gospel" (p. 32, n. 16).

[37] The Greek *anothen* can mean both, "again" and "from above." I translate it as "re-birth from above" because, in fact, both meanings are inherent at the same time in the Johannine use of the expression.

[38] The expression "kingdom of God," which is unique in John's Gospel and recalls Synoptic terminology, is, according to Francis J. Moloney, transformed here and refers to the Johannine community, and the re-birth of water and the Spirit refers to baptism and entering into this community, see F. J. Moloney, *Belief in the Word. Reading John 1–4* (Minneapolis, MN: Fortress, 1993), pp. 112–13. For his interpretation of 3:1–21, see pp. 106–21.

[39] On "birth from water and the Spirit," and the references to baptism, see C. R. Koester, *Symbolism in the Fourth Gospel. Meaning, Mystery, Community* (Minneapolis, MN: Fortress, 1995), pp. 163–7.

on the symbolical level. "How can a man be born when he is old? Can he enter a second time into his mother's womb and be born?,"[40] is his first response to Jesus' talk in riddles (v. 4). And when Jesus further develops his subject (vv. 5–8) Nicodemus again asks, "How can this be?" (v. 9). Twice Nicodemus asks Jesus about the "How" of the re-birth, but in neither case does he get an answer from Jesus. On the contrary, in the end he is even rebuked for his lack of under-standing; being a "teacher of Israel" he should know (v. 10). When Jesus starts on his long monologue, thereby merging with the voice of the narrator,[41] Nicodemus is left with his unanswered question and the rebuke. The narrative thus remains open-ended; there is no mention of how he responded to Jesus' further explorations (in case they are still addressed to him), nor do we get any hint at when they parted company again that night. Nicodemus seems to disap-pear silently into the night out of which he had come. He enters the stage again a few chapters later. On the last day of the feast of Tabernacles he defends Jesus against the accusations of his fellow Pharisees (7:50–51) and, in turn, he is once again met with a rebuke (v. 52). Also this scene remains open-ended, we do not get to know how Nicodemus responds nor what happens thereafter. We encounter him again only at the end of John's story, after Jesus' crucifixion, when he joins Joseph of Arimathea in burying Jesus' body and bring-ing along a huge amount of spices for that purpose (19:38–42).

The narrator does not give a definite evaluation of Nicodemus' character, rather, he characterizes him just by what he says, and what others say to him, by what he does, and by his relation to other characters in the story. Thus, characterization is constructed in the text by showing, not by telling, which therefore demands much more activity on the part of the reader and his or her imagination as to how to connect text signals and consequently how to evaluate the character. Features that function prominently in the various inter-pretations are the timing of Nicodemus' first visit to Jesus and his questions in chapter 3, as well as his spices in chapter 19.

---

[40] All quotations in this paper are from the RSV. I have decided on the English translation, rather than the original Greek text, because of the wide spectrum of intended readers in mind, among them many who do not read Greek.

[41] Cf. the chapter "From Teller-Character to Reflection-Character: The Narrative Dynamics in John 3," in D. Tovey, *Narrative Art and Act in the Fourth Gospel* (JSNT Supplement Series, 151; Sheffield: Sheffield Academic Press, 1997), pp. 148–67.

Because Nicodemus comes by night, many interpreters have related that to the dualism between night and day, darkness and light,[42] which permeates the whole Gospel and which is to be viewed in ontological and ethical terms. Consequently, his questions are also interpreted as demonstrating his lack of understanding and insight, and hence his belonging to the night. For sure, there is the contrast between darkness and light in the Gospel, starting with the prologue and its fundamental statements that the Word was the light (1:1–4), and, "The light shines in the darkness, and the darkness has not overcome it" (v. 5).[43] However, whether any statements concerning light and darkness in the story following the encounter between Jesus and Nicodemus are related to the latter depends on whether or not the reader establishes such connections. In Jesus' reflection mono-logue after the actual encounter he announces: "And this is the judg-ment, that the light has come into the world, and men loved darkness rather than light, because their deeds were evil. For every one who does evil hates the light, and does not come to the light, lest his deeds should be exposed. But he who does what is true comes to the light, that it may be clearly seen that his deeds have been wrought in God" (3:19–21). Some interpreters thought these words referred to Nicodemus and consequently regarded his coming by night as a clear sign of his love of darkness and his hatred of light, and hence his fear of his deeds being exposed. However, such interpretations simply do not pay attention to the very fact that Nicodemus *did* come to the light, that is, Jesus (cf. v. 21; 1:4–5). On the other hand, if the focus is put on this second part of Jesus' statement, then the reader's expectation is nourished so as to see any deeds of Nicodemus that have been wrought in God (v. 21).

When Nicodemus re-enters the stage in chapter 7, speaking for Jesus before the chief priests and his fellow Pharisees (who had sent the temple police to arrest Jesus, yet returned without him, vv. 45–46), this happens exactly in the context where the subject of the light re-appears. On the last day of the feast of Tabernacles Jesus speaks

---

[42] On light and darkness in the Gospel of John and in 1 John, see Koester, *Symbolism in the Fourth Gospel*, pp. 123–54.

[43] On light and darkness as John's anti-language, see Petersen, *The Gospel of John and the Sociology of Light*; for the relations between the prologue and chapter 3, see pp. 41–9.

about the rivers of living water flowing out of the believer's heart and which he gives to drink in the first place (vv. 37–39), and he speaks of himself as the light: "I am the light of the world; he who follows me will not walk in darkness, but will have the light of life" (8:12).[44] This is a statement but also an invitation, both to the characters addressed in the story and to the readers reading the scene.[45] As is obvious from the immediate context, those addressed in the first instance are the Pharisees (8:13). Therefore, we can imagine Nicodemus as being present and being addressed. With the Pharisees' question of 7:48 "Have any of the authorities or of the Pharisees believed in him?" and Nicodemus' subsequent defense of Jesus still ringing in our ears, we can consider Jesus' invitation to follow him (8:12) as a further effort to draw Nicodemus to him. When in 8:30 the narrator reports that "many believed in him," it leaves space to imagine Nicodemus being one of them.

The image of the light as well as the Pharisees come to the fore again in chapter 9 in the context of Jesus' healing the man born blind (9:1–41). Before healing the man, Jesus muses once again about night and day: "We must work the works of him who sent me, while it is day; night comes, when no one can work. As long as I am in the world, I am the light of the world" (vv. 4–5). The present moment of healing the blind man is, therefore, characterized as day, while the night belongs to the future. Being brought before the Pharisees, the healing of the man on the sabbath causes a split among them concerning Jesus. While some claim that he cannot be from God because he violated the sabbath, others say: "How can a man who is a sinner do such signs?" (v. 16). "There was a division among them," so the narrator concludes (v. 16). The question is reminiscent of Nicodemus' questions in chapter 3 and his love of asking about the "How?" As in chapter 3, this question is connected to Jesus' signs (3:2), which encourages the reader to imagine Nicodemus as being among the speakers who are in favour of Jesus. When the

---

[44] 7:52 continues with 8:11, as the narrative about the woman accused of adultery in 7:53–8:11 was inserted into the Gospel text at a later stage.

[45] Cf. Brodie's evocative note regarding the end of the scene in chapter 3: "Thus, as the episode closes, there is placed before Nicodemus, or at least before the reader, an implicit challenge: 'I place before you ... darkness ... and light ...'" (Th. L. Brodie, *The Gospel According to John. A Literary and Theological Commentary* [New York and Oxford: Oxford University Press, 1993], p. 200).

formerly blind man is questioned over and over again about his gaining sight, he asks, "Why do you want to hear it again? Do you too want to become his disciples?" (v. 27). And though they are reported as claiming to be disciples of Moses (v. 28), we as readers are confronted for the first time with discipleship as a possibility for the Pharisees. When later on the Pharisees are, once again, depicted as a divided group ("some," v. 40) and thus as not acting in unison, the possibility of Nicodemus' progress toward discipleship is at least made possible in the imagination of the reader, who still lives with the open end and the unanswered questions of the encounter in chapter 3.

Finally, both the Pharisees and the image of light and darkness turn up again in the context of the raising of Lazarus from the dead in chapter 11. In spite of the threat of his death (10:40; 11:8, 16), Jesus comes to Bethany when called by Lazarus' sisters Mary and Martha. Being confronted with the threat of his death by his disciples Jesus responds: "Are there not twelve hours in the day? If any one walks in the day, he does not stumble, because he sees the light of this world. But if any one walks in the night, he stumbles, because the light is not in him" (vv. 9–10). To be sure, this talk is to be understood on the metaphorical level and refers to the enemies of Jesus, who are stumbling in the dark while he is "the light." Is there any reason to link this scene to Nicodemus and hence interpret his coming by night as not having the light and therefore as stumbling? There is certainly no hint at all in chapter 3 that Nicodemus *stumbled* through the night, he just *came* to Jesus; hence there is no necessity to link these two scenes together. Yet, some ambivalence remains, and it might be weighted towards the negative side by the negative portrayal of the Pharisees in chapter 11 (vv. 46–53, 57). And yet, they are actually depicted as being rather helpless when faced with the crowd going after Jesus (12:19). When Jesus speaks about himself as "the light" for the last time he speaks about his forthcoming death: "The light is with you for a little longer. Walk while you have the light, lest the darkness overtake you; he who walks in the darkness does not know where he goes. While you have the light, believe in the light, that you may become sons of light" (12:35–36). The previous invitation to come to the light is re-inforced: "I have come as light into the world, that whoever believes in me may not remain in darkness. If any one hears my sayings and does not keep them, I do not judge him; for I did not come to judge the world but to save the world" (12:46–47). Although these words are not directed to the Pharisees but to the crowd (v. 29), the theme of judgement (vv. 31, 47–48) and of light and darkness (vv. 35–36, 46) relate this text to Nicodemus' encounter with Jesus in chapter 3 (cf. vv. 16–21, esp. v. 19). Walking in the darkness, one does not know where one is going, so Jesus says, and thus gives the reader some clue as to how to interpret his encounter with Nicodemus in chapter 3: He came by night, but he *knew* where he was going! Besides that, there is also Jesus' promise: "and I, when I am lifted up from the earth, will draw all men to myself" (12:32). Back in chapter 3, during his encounter with Nicodemus, Jesus had spoken about his being lifted up and had added, "that whoever believes in him [the Son of Man] may have eternal life" (3:14). Now, as Jesus enters the last chapter of his life, before his farewell dinner with his disciples, his promise and invitation to all those who will come to believe in him, remains in the air. And who would not keep pondering over Nicodemus and what will become of him? Having journeyed that far with him we have expectations that the mixed signals[46] surrounding him will result in clarity and in his decision for Jesus.

Thus, when we encounter Nicodemus after Jesus' crucifixion, that is, his being lifted up from the earth, we expect to get a final answer and arrive at a solution to the riddle of his charaterization. When he buries Jesus, together with Joseph of Arimathea (19:38–42), we find him acting publicly,[47] no longer in secret coming as he did by night. The reference to his first encounter with Jesus (v. 39) marks the contrast. *Then* it was night. *Now* it is day,[48] both on the material and the symbolical level.[49] But there is no happy end yet. Interpreters

---

[46] Cf. J. M. Bassler, "Mixed Signals: Nicodemus in the Fourth Gospel," *JBL* 108 (1989), pp. 635–46.

[47] Referring to Nicodemus and Joseph of Arimathea, Moloney makes this clear: "Both of these *secret* disciples of Jesus now become *public*." (F. J. Moloney, *Glory not Dishonor. Reading John 13–21* [Minneapolis, MN: Fortress, 1998], p. 149).

[48] In John, Jesus is buried while it is still day; in the Synoptics, the burial takes place in the evening, after sunset, cf. Mark 14:42 par Matt. 27:57; Luke 23:54. See also Koester (*Symbolism in the Fourth Gospel*, p. 205): ". . . on Good Friday Nicodemus acted before nightfall, while it was still the Day of Preparation (19:42) . . ."

[49] Note the difference to 13:30. When Judas went out, "it was night," which is definitely to be understood on the metaphorical level, even more so as this note is inserted in the midst of the story, not at the beginning when setting the scene, as in 3:2. Besides that, while Nicodemus *came* by night, Judas *went out* when it was

are around blaming Nicodemus for the huge amount of spices which only shows how ignorant he remained. He should have known better, so they say. He should have expected Jesus' resurrection, and hence there being no need to spend all that money on either the spices or the linen cloths to cover Jesus' body. Being rebuked and accused once again (cf. 3:10; 7:52), this time not by characters in the story but by the readers, Nicodemus is left without a voice of his own. As demonstrated all along, various dimensions in the text can be interpreted in very different ways, depending on the choices one makes, and Nicodemus cannot influence these choices.

To sum up: The mention of Nicodemus' coming by night can be interpreted in a negative way, but also in a positive[50] way, and the unfolding of the narrative leaves enough room for Nicodemus' conversion and his gradually being drawn to Jesus, finally at his death (cf. 12:32). His questions, unanswered by Jesus during their first encounter, can be viewed as a literary device for the readers to live with these questions and to remain as open as Nicodemus to what might happen, for the wind blows where it wills (3:8). Nicodemus' encounter with Synoptic women may also come as a surprise.

Nicodemus Encounters Synoptic Women

Re-viewing Nicodemus' encounter with Jesus during his first visit and during his paying his last respect to Jesus' body, we may become aware of some text signals which open up these texts to Synoptic intertexts and hence relate Nicodemus to Synoptic women. Thus, his characterization will be enriched by important new dimensions

---

night. Therefore, rather than linking the encounter of chapter 3 to the scene in chapter 13, it should be viewed in the light of chapter 20: Mary Magdalene arrived at the tomb when it was still dark (v. 1), yet the new day dawned when she met the resurrected Christ.

[50] A positive evaluation of the night is also suggested by the intertextuality between John 3 and the narratives in Gen 15–18, and thus by the interfigurality between Nicodemus and Abram/Abraham, but also Sarai/Sarah. Both narratives, in John and in Genesis, deal with the issue of (re-)birth. God's promise to Abram to become the father of a nation happens at night; the uncountable number of stars symbolize the descendents (Gen 15:5). In Gen 17, in a variation of the scene, Abraham responds to God's promise of a son by Sarah: "Shall a child be born to a man who is a hundred years old? Shall Sarah, who is ninety years old, bear a child?" (v. 17). And finally in Gen 18, focussing on Sarah's point of view, the response reads like this: "After I have grown old, and my husband is old, shall I have pleasure?" (v. 12) and, "Shall I indeed bear a child, now that I am old?" (v. 13).

achieved by interfigurality which subsequently will have an impact on the evaluation of Nicodemus' character.

"How can this be?" An (un)answered question

"How can this be?," Nicodemus asks Jesus when he is talking in such riddles about re-birth from above, further defined as a re-birth of water and the Spirit. Any informed first reader familiar with the Synoptic Gospels and for sure any present real reader of all canonical Gospels might be reminded of Mary's question "How shall this be?,"[51] when the angel Gabriel announced to her Jesus' conception and birth, of the Spirit as it were. Thus, Nicodemus' questions of "How," which are left unanswered in the course of the narrative in chapter 3 and in fact also in the the the whole of John's story, open up this text John 3:1–21 to the Synoptic intertext of Luke 1:26–38. Hence, interfigurality will be established between the man Nicodemus and the woman Mary, who is to become the mother of Jesus.

The encounter between Nicodemus and Jesus parallels the encounter between the angel Gabriel and Mary. "Hail, o favoured one, the Lord is with you!," is how the angel addresses Mary (Luke 1:28). "Rabbi, we know that you are a teacher come from God; for no one can do these signs that you do, unless God is with him," is how Nicodemus addresses Jesus (John 3:2). In both cases, the visitor comes along with a *captatio benevolentiae*, confirming that God is with the person being addressed. Mary, being troubled about such a greeting, gets reassured by the angel that she has found favour with God, and the angel explains that she will conceive in her womb and bear a son to be named Jesus, who will be the Son of the Most High (Luke 1:30–33). "How shall this be, since I have no husband?," Mary asks the angel, and he most willingly provides a detailed answer: "The Holy Spirit will come upon you, and the power of the Most High will overshadow you; therefore the child to be born will be called holy, the Son of God" (vv. 34–35). And she even gets a sign in the form of her cousin Elizabeth, who is six months pregnant, despite her old age, "for with God nothing will be impossible" (vv. 36–37).

---

[51] After being pregnant with the interfigural relation between Nicodemus and Mary for a couple of years, I was delighted when I recently came across Brodie's notice that Nicodemus' question "How can this be?" "Has something of Mary's 'How shall this be?' . . .," though Brodie does not develop this any further (Brodie, *The Gospel According to John*, p. 198).

Mary's answer follows right away: "Behold, I am the handmaid of the Lord; let it be to me according to your word" (v. 38). "And the angel departed from her," so the narrator closes (v. 38). This is a nicely arranged scene, with a beginning and an end, with a question and an answer. But what about Nicodemus? Viewed in the light of Luke 1:26–38, we become aware of the deficiencies and shortcomings in his story. He addresses the same question to Jesus of how that could be, after being informed about the necessity of a re-birth of water and the Spirit,[52] and yet he does not get an answer. On the contrary, he is rebuked by Jesus for asking that question in the first place. Being a "teacher of Israel" he should know, is the message which Jesus conveys, and hence this influences the reader to think alike and to thereby evaluate Nicodemus in a negative way. Mary, on the other hand, is depicted as worthy of an answer by the angel. Is it because she is an illiterate woman, not knowing the Scriptures and not being anybody's teacher? She gets all the information she needs in order to finally agree to the angel's message. For quite a while I have been pondering the question of what would have happened to Nicodemus had Jesus given him a proper answer, just like Gabriel, and explained to him how he, the old man, could be re-born of the Spirit, in spite of his age or rather, no matter what his age. He might have answered right away: "Behold, I am your disciple!"[53] But nothing like this happened in the course of the Johannine narrative, and Nicodemus is left with the unanswered question and Jesus' rebuke, and he is left exposed to the readers who could do many things with him, as the history of interpretation has so amply shown. He is left at the mercy of his readers and dependent on how they establish meaning in their encounter with the fragmentary text and the fragmented character.[54] Viewing Nico-demus in the light of Luke's Mary, mother of Jesus, we become

---

[52] There is a noteworthy inversion regarding the sequence of questions and state-ments/answers. Mary asks about the "How" and *then* receives the angel's explana-tion concerning the agency of the Spirit. Nicodemus, on the other hand, poses the question of "How" *after* Jesus' talk about the re-birth of the Spirit.

[53] Note that in John the process of becoming a disciple is expressed in terms of birth, cf. F. F. Segovia, *The Farewell of the Word: The Johannine Call to Abide* (Minneapolis, MN: Fortress, 1991), p. 254.

[54] Nicodemus is, in fact, a fragmented man, like many fragmented women, and hence a *reading against the grain* is called for. See J. Ch. Exum, *Fragmented Women. Feminist (Sub)versions of Biblical Narratives* (JSOT Supplement Series, 163; Sheffield: JSOT, 1993).

aware of his being marginalized,[55] by Jesus, by his fellow Pharisees,[56] and by readers throughout the history of interpretation. Hence, a *reading against the grain* of the story framework and the reader constructions is called for, that is, rescuing Nicodemus from the dark of the night and letting him come out of his tomb in order to free himself from the bondage of suppressive and colonialistic readers who have dared to speak for[57] and against him. Reading Nicodemus in the light of the Lukan Mary, we are, on the other hand, encouraged to opt for his becoming a disciple[58] in the end, just as Mary became the maid of the Lord. What happened within just one scene in Luke, can be considered to have happened in the course of the whole story of John's Gospel, from chapter 3 through to chapter 19.[59] When Nicodemus entombs Jesus, he says "yes" to being re-born of the Spirit, and hence the tomb and the womb become one. While he, for sure, cannot enter into his mother's womb and be born again, he is born again as a child of God when placing Jesus' bloodstained body into the tomb. Hence, the promise of the prologue turns into reality for him: "But all who received him, who believed in his name, he gave the power to become children of God; who were born, not of blood nor of the will of the flesh nor of the will of man, but of God" (1:12–13). Both, the young girl and virgin Mary and the old man Nicodemus responded to their call and to the promise of a (re-)birth, in the womb and out of the tomb.

---

[55] According to R. J. Karris (*Jesus and the Marginalized in John's Gospel* [Zacchaeus Studies: New Testament; Collegeville, MN: The Liturgical Press, 1990]) Nicodemus, being a religious leader, was a marginalizer who joined the community of the marginalized (cf. pp. 96–101). This statement is made in historical and sociological terms. My point in seeing Nicodemus as being marginalized refers to the literary level and pertains to the author/narrator of the story and to the readers.

[56] Cf. Moloney's strong comment on 7:52, that "'The Jews' . . . attempt to escape from Nicodemus's accusations by heaping abuse on him" (F. J. Moloney, *Signs and Shadows. Reading John 5–12* [Minneapolis, MN: Fortress, 1996], p. 92). Moloney holds that "throughout chaps. 7–8, 'the Jews' and the Pharisees are the same group" (p. 97, n. 108).

[57] Cf. L. Alcoff, "The Problem of Speaking for Others," *Cultural Critique* 1991–2, pp. 5–32.

[58] So Karris (*Jesus and the Marginalized*) in his chapter programmatically entitled "Nicodemus the Marginalizer Becomes a Disciple" (pp. 96–101).

[59] Likewise, Nicodemus' progress can be compared to Mary Magdalene's progress in just one scene: coming out of the darkness into the daylight on Easter morning, she is fully recognized as a disciple when she addresses the resurrected Christ as "Rabbouni" (20:16).

Thus, by realizing the interfigurality between Nicodemus and Mary, mother of Jesus, the first can be viewed in a much more positive light, and hence the ambivalence about his character can be resolved in a positive way.

Nicodemus and his spices

While Joseph of Arimathea is known from the Synoptic Gospels as the (secret) disciple of Jesus (cf. Matt. 27:57) who finally publicly claimed Jesus' body back from Pilate and buried it in his[60] garden tomb (Mark 15:42–47 parr), Nicodemus joins him only in the Gospel of John. There, his main function is to provide the huge amount of spices, in fact a mixture of about a hundred pounds in weight of myrrh and aloes (John 19:39). While all interpreters have taken note of this luxury, the consequences deduced from it differ widely. As stated above, some have viewed the incredible amount of spices spent on Jesus' burial as a lack of faith, that is, in Jesus' forthcoming resurrection.[61] However, viewing the spices as denoting the royal burial[62] provided for Jesus, cannot be neglected. But the ambivalence concerning the interpretation of the spices remains. One clue for a positive interpretation is offered by the configuration with Mary of Bethany within the Gospel story. Like Nicodemus, she spent quite a large sum on anointing Jesus' feet, in fact a pound of costly ointment of pure nard, which is valued as being worth three hundred denarii (12:3–5). Jesus defends Mary when Judas reproaches her for her lavishness: "Let her alone, let her keep it for the day of my burial" (12:7). Thus, Jesus himself can be imagined as also telling Nicodemus' past or present critics:[63] "Leave him alone!" On the other hand, by relating Nicodemus to the anointing Mary of Bethany,

---

[60] It's interesting to note that in John, as different from the Synoptics, the garden tomb is not defined as Joseph's tomb. I owe this insight to Karris (*Jesus and the Marginalized*, p. 101).

[61] So D. D. Sylva, "Nicodemus and His Spices," *NTS* 34 (1988), pp. 148–51.

[62] See Karris, *Jesus and the Marginalized*, pp. 98, 100. Karris recalls the funeral of "king" Herod the Great, as rendered in Josephus, *Jewish Antiquities* 17:198–99, where five hundred servants were carrying spices (pp. 98, 59). Throughout the Johannine passion narrative, Jesus is portrayed as a king (cf. 18:33–40; 19:1–5, 14–16, 19–22).

[63] See Sylva's evocative knowledge: "By shedding the garments in which he was wrapped, the resurrected Jesus dissociates himself from this action of Nicodemus and Joseph" ("Nicodemus and His Spices," p. 149).

the Johannine text is opened up to intertextuality with the Synoptic stories of the women who anointed or intended to anoint Jesus.[64]

Except for the anointing of Jesus' feet by the great lover in Luke 7:36–50, all Synoptic stories which render the achieved or intended anointing of Jesus are related to his death. The anointing of Jesus' head by the unknown woman in Bethany (Mark 14:3–9 par Matt. 26:3–16) is to be interpreted as the confession of the suffering Messiah,[65] different from Peter's confession (cf. Mark 8:29–33 par). Within the anointment scene, Jesus himself interprets the woman's action as an anointing of his body beforehand for burying (Mark 14:8 par). Jesus defends the woman and her lavishly using such a huge amount of precious spices (worth more than three hundred denarii, Mark 14:4) against her accusers (some, according to Mark; the disciples, according to Matt.)

The motif of anointing is also relevant in the Easter morning stories.[66] In Mark (16:1–8) and Luke (24:1–10) Mary Magdalene and other women followers of Jesus (Mary of James and Salome in Mark; Joanna, Mary of James, and others in Luke) come to Jesus' tomb early in the morning of the first day in order to anoint Jesus' body, but finding the tomb empty their intention to anoint him becomes superfluous. Matthew, on the other hand, does not mention any intended anointing; the women—Mary of Magdala and the other Mary—come just to *see* the tomb (Matt. 28:1). Thus, Matthew seems to take seriously what the unnamed woman had already done in Bethany, that is, anoint Jesus' body beforehand for burying, and hence there is no need to anoint him after his entombment.

In both Mark's and Matthew's Gospel Jesus was anointed by an unknown woman *beforehand* for burying, and Mark and Luke tell of the women intending to anoint Jesus *afterwards*. Yet, no Synoptic Gospel knows of any anointing of Jesus' body *at* his actual burial. It was left to John to fill this gap. Nicodemus comes out of the night

---

[64] See my paper presented at the SBL International Meeting in Münster in 1993, entitled "The (Intended) Anointing of Jesus by Women. The Interrelationship Between the Anointing Stories (Mark 14:3–9/Matt. 26:6–13/Luke 7:36–50/John 12:1–8) and the Easter Morning Stories (Mark 16:1–8 parr)."

[65] To my knowledge, E. Schüssler Fiorenza was the first to recognize this meaning (*In Memory of Her*, p. xiv).

[66] I have come to name them "Easter morning stories," instead of the widely used term "empty tomb stories," to denote that the focus is *not* on the tomb but on what happens *beyond* it.

to fulfill the task left undone by the Synoptic women. And he shows no less generosity. While the unknown woman spent more than three hundred denarii of pure nard (Mark 14:3; very expensive ointment, Matt. 26:6), Nicodemus came along, bringing about a hundred pounds in weight of myrrh and aloes (John 19:39). In all the Gospels, lavishness denotes the anointing of Jesus. And there's to be no objection to this, because—while the poor are always there—Jesus will soon be gone (Mark 14:7; Matt. 26:11; cf. John 12:8). Jesus himself is the competent interpreter of the women's actions in the Synoptics—and in John—and his words can be applied also to Nicodemus' generous gift and action. Therefore, wherever the Gospel is proclaimed in the whole world, what he has done should also be told in memory of him (cf. Mark 14:8 par). Furthermore, relating Nicodemus to the women who intended to anoint Jesus on Easter morning does not give rise either to any negative evaluation of his using the huge amount of spices on Jesus' body, which is to be resurrected and hence does not need to be anointed, as Nicodemus' critics have argued. For one thing, giving a decent burial to a beloved dead person is not only in accordance with Jewish burial customs, but in fact a general human need. After all, where and how should Jesus' body have been kept between the crucifixion and his resurrection? Besides that, in both Mark and Luke, who render an intended anointing of Jesus by his women followers, there is no trace of any negative evaluation of their plans. None of the angels speaking to the women reproaches them for bringing along the ointments, nor does the narrator add any such evaluation. The women simply don't need their gifts any longer, and their intended action of anointing Jesus is transformed into announcing him as the resurrected.

Therefore, when Nicodemus' interfigural relationship to the Synoptic anointing women is realized, the way is open to a positive evaluation of his character. While he was characterized by what he said or what others said to him in all instances discussed so far, it is here, at the end of the Gospel, that he is characterized by what he does. There's no longer any need of words; silently he and Joseph do what they have to do. They do what is true and their deeds turn out to have been wrought in God; they have finally come to the light (cf. John 3:21). This promise of the first encounter by night becomes reality in the last encounter between Jesus and Nicodemus.

On Easter morning the tomb is empty and Simon Peter and the beloved disciple find the linen cloths and the napkin placed neatly, denoting where Jesus' body had lain (20:5, 7). They were left behind as signs[67] for the male disciples to make possible their belief in the resurrection (20:8). But it is left to the female disciple, Mary Magdalene, to encounter the risen Christ personally[68] (20:14–17), and we are encouraged to imagine that there was no odour (11:39), but a smell of myrrh and aloes still clinging to his body and filling the air in the garden (cf. 12:3).

Nicodemus is left transformed after his encounter with the Synoptic women, and so is any reader, past or present, who left the confines of the Johannine text and read intertextually. After encountering Mary, the mother of Jesus, and the women who anointed or intended to anoint Jesus' head, feet, or whole body, Nicodemus moved out of the shadows of ambivalence inherent in the Johannine story world and entered into the daylight, with no fear of his deeds being exposed (cf. 3:20). By relating this male character to female characters, gender boundaries are also transcended. In fact, Nicodemus is portrayed as carrying out a female task, that of preparing a dead body for burial. And it is striking to find him portrayed in the context of Jesus' speaking about re-birth of water and the Spirit. Confronting the old man with the issue of birth adds to his characterization. As noted above, gender as a construct and as relating to a literary figure depends also on the roles attributed to a character and to the subjects in whose contexts a character is set. To be sure, the issue of re-birth could have been developed within a scene featuring a female character, for example the Samaritan woman at the well (4:1–44). Thus, choosing the old man is as striking and evocative as choosing a virgin to become a mother. For with God—or the author of a Gospel—nothing is impossible.

The Characterization of the Mother of Jesus

In John, the mother of Jesus, who is never named Mary, features prominently within two narratives. First, at the wedding of Cana

---

[67] See S. M. Schneiders, "The Face Veil: A Johannine Sign," *BTB* 13 (1983), pp. 76–92.

[68] It is significant to note that when Mary Magdalene looks into the tomb she does not see the cloths and the face veil. Instead she sees the angels sitting there (20:11–12).

(2:1–11), and again at the foot of the cross, together with the other women and the beloved disciple (19:25–27). She is portrayed as being present at the very beginning of Jesus' ministry, when he performs his first sign and where she acts as mediator for this sign, and as being present again at the end of Jesus' ministry, when "his hour" has finally come (16:32; 2:4). It is perplexing to note her total absence from John's story in the long intervening period, and also her absence after Jesus' resurrection. In fact the narrative in chapter 2 is, as so many other narratives in the Gospel, open-ended. Though the faith of Jesus' mother can be regarded as implicit[69] in her initiating Jesus' first sign, even if not stated explicitly like the faith of his disciples (2:11), she disappears into the dark after going down to Capernaum together with Jesus and the disciples and staying there for a few days (2:12). She is not depicted as accompanying Jesus during his ministry in Galilee and his journeys to Jerusalem, nor does the narrator give us readers any clue as to where she remained and lived during that period. So it comes as quite a surprise to encounter her again standing at the foot of the cross, together with three other women we have not met so far in John's Gospel, that is, her sister and Mary, the wife of Clopas, and Mary Magdalene (19:25–27).[70] Amongst the company at the cross, only the beloved disciple had, like Jesus' mother, turned up in a previous scene; he had first been mentioned during the last supper and the footwashing in chapter 13 (vv. 23–25). But not only through that common feature do they become related to each other in a special way. Of the company depicted at the foot of the cross, only they become characters in this short scene. As he is lifted up, the dying Jesus entrusts them to each other, and in so doing performs the last act of his ministry. "Woman, behold your son," he addresses his mother, and "Behold, your mother," he addresses his disciple. "And from that hour the disciple

---

[69] Her acting as mediator in Jesus' first sign can certainly be seen as a demonstration of her deep faith in him, so e.g. Moloney (*Glory not Dishonor*, p. 144): ". . . the woman who was the first to commit herself unconditionally to his word (see 2:3–5)." However, this is not the only possible reading.

[70] It has been debated whether there are three or four women mentioned at the cross, that is, whether or not the sister of Jesus' mother is identical with Mary, wife of Clopas. There are two main reasons to identify them as two different women: first, it's rather unlikely that two sisters of the same family should have been called Mary, and second, the four women would contrast with the four soldiers in the crucifixion scene (19:23). However, it remains strange that only the sister of the mother (besides the mother herself, of course) is not mentioned by name.

took her to his own house,"[71] the narrator concludes the scene. This, however, does not imply that they left right away, but have to be imagined as still being present when Jesus gives[72] his spirit (19:30). Giving his spirit does not only denote the moment of his physical death but also, on the symbolical and spiritual level of the Gospel, the giving of the Spirit which Jesus promised to his own for the time after his departure (14:16–17, 25; 16:7, 12). The four women and the beloved disciple are also to be considered as being present when blood and water[73] flow out of Jesus' wounded side (19:34), which, again, refers not only to the physical aspect of Jesus' death but also, and more importantly so, to his promise of the Spirit which Jesus previously, at the feast of Tabernacles, described as streams of living water (7:38–39). Of those standing at the cross, it is only two who explicitly re-appear on the scene after Jesus' resurrection: Mary Magdalene and the beloved disciple, who subsequently come to the tomb on Easter morning (20:1–18). Mary Magdalene comes to the tomb first and later on is also the first to encounter the risen Jesus (20:1,11–18), but it is the beloved disciple who is portrayed as the first to come to believe in the resurrection because of the signs of the linen cloths and napkin in the empty tomb (v. 8). But again, as already in chapter 2, we might ask, "Where has Jesus' mother gone?" While the narrator comments that the beloved disciple took her to his home (19:27), the very act of so doing and of leaving the scene at the cross is not described. We as readers can only conclude that they went home together later on, probably about the same time as Nicodemus, together with Joseph of Arimathea, prepared the hasty though decent burial for Jesus. However, there is one last, though implicit, trace of Jesus' mother after the resurrection. After their race to the tomb on Easter morning, Simon Peter and the beloved disciple are recorded as having returned to their homes (20:10). Remembering that the latter had previously taken Jesus' mother home, we

---

[71] The Greek *eis ta idia* is reminiscent of the prologue. See Moloney's comment: "The situation described in the prologue, where the Word came *eis ta idia* but was not received (*ou parelabon*), has now been reversed. Because of the cross, and from the moment of the cross, a new family of Jesus has been created." (Moloney, *Glory not Dishonor*, p. 145).

[72] The RSV is wrong here in translating "gave up his spirit" for the Greek *paredoken to pneuma*. See also Moloney, *Glory not Dishonor*, p. 146.

[73] On the flow of water and blood, see Koester, *Symbolism in the Fourth Gospel*, pp. 181–3, 203–4.

can imagine her as still being there, in a house somewhere in Jerusalem. And perhaps Mary Magdalene spent some time with her after going there to inform the disciples of the empty tomb (v. 2). The gap in the narrative created by not describing how and when Mary Magdalene returned to the tomb, allows for such imagination. But in any case, it is surprising that John, like the Synoptics, does not know of any post-resurrection appearance of Jesus to his mother. However, there is another encounter which may shed fresh light on Jesus' mother and her characterization in John's Gospel.

Returning to the scene at the cross, it has been widely accepted that in entrusting Jesus' mother and the beloved disciple to one another, the formula for adoption is applied and thus a new relation between mother and son is established. The very fact of that act is striking, however, because it presupposes that not only was the beloved son a motherless child, but even more puzzling, Jesus' mother appears to have been without any other male relatives to care for her after Jesus' departure. Though Jesus is referred to as the "son of Joseph" in the Gospel story (1:45; 6:42), Joseph never turns up as a character, not even early on at the wedding of Cana. On the other hand, Jesus' brothers are mentioned (7:3–10), but the narrator informs us that they did not believe in him (v. 5). Therefore, when standing at the cross, Jesus' mother is portrayed as a woman without a husband, probably a widow, and without any other sons to care for her. So while Jesus' brothers were most likely still alive, they, due to their unbelief, were no longer regarded as his real brothers, but were replaced by his disciples[74] (20:17). Seeing Jesus' mother as a widow and Jesus as her only son, any alert and informed reader familiar with the Synoptic Gospels will think of one particular story, that of the widow of Nain and the raising of her only son in Luke's Gospel (Luke 7:11–17). The possibility of an intertextual and interfigural relation is opened up.[75]

---

[74] The "brothers"—and hence also the disciples—may be inclusive of women, if the androcentric language is taken into account. Consequently, also the physical brothers (7:3–10) may have included Jesus' sisters, who are mentioned in the Synoptics (Mark 3:32 vl, 6:3 parr), but not in John.

[75] Such an intertextual/interfigural reading is also backed up by the quote of Zech. 12:10 in John 19:37: ". . . when they look on him whom they have pierced, they shall mourn for him, as one mourns for an only child, and weep bitterly over him, as one weeps over a first-born."

The Mother of Jesus Encounters the Widow of Nain

The narrative about the raising of the young man of Nain is unique to Luke's Gospel and is one of only three Gospel narratives of the raising of a dead person by Jesus (cf. Mark 5:21–43 parr; John 11:1–46). During his Galilean ministry, Jesus and his disciples, followed by a great crowd, come near the city gate just as a dead man is being carried out. The narrator informs us that he was the only son of his mother and that she is a widow (Luke 7:12). Jesus, filled with compassion, says to the woman, "Do not weep" (v. 13). Then, touching the bier, Jesus brings the bearers to a halt, and he addresses the dead man: "Young man, I say to you, arise" (v. 14). Immediately "the dead man sat up, and began to speak" (v. 15). "And he gave him to his mother," the narrator concludes the quick resurrection (v. 15). A comment on the enthusiastic reaction of the crowd and the spreading of this news follows (vv. 16–17).

Jesus meets a woman and her only son when she is faced with death. She is a widow, implying the death of her husband, and her son has just died. Within only seconds, or so it seems, death is transformed into new life by Jesus' action, or rather, just by his words. Communication seems all important in this scene. Jesus' words correspond with the words of the man raised from the dead; and it is only here that a person speaks after his return to life. Unfortunately, the content of his speech is not revealed and thus is left to the imagination of the readers, and so is the sequence of the narrative. We don't know whether Jesus and his disciples returned home with the woman and her son and had a resurrection celebration.[76] However fragmentary the whole scene is, the fact that Jesus gives the young man to his mother (v. 15) is most striking. By so doing, the original relationship between mother and son, which was cut off through death, is re-established.[77]

The parallels between the scene near the city gate of Cana, as described in Luke's Gospel, and the scene outside the city gate of Jerusalem, as reported in John's Gospel, are evocative. However, the

---

[76] Eating and sharing meals is all important after resurrections—see Mark 5:43; Luke 24:30; John 21:9–14.

[77] It's interesting to note that Lazarus is *not* given back to his sisters. On the contrary, Jesus gives orders to "unbind him and let him go" (11:44).

inversions are striking as well. Whilst in Luke Jesus restores life to the only son of a mother, who is a widow, and re-establishes their relationship, in John it is the dying only son of a mother, who also appears to be a widow,[78] who establishes a new relation between his mother and another young man. "Behold, your son," the Lukan Jesus might have addressed the mother. "Behold, your son," the Johannine Jesus addresses his own mother. Thus, the moment of death becomes also the moment of new life. As a mother is losing her son, another son is born to her, though without entering into her womb. Furthermore, in the context of the whole Gospel, the scene at the cross can also be viewed as a birthing[79] scene as it were, in which, however, also the mother is born, re-born from above, where her son has been lifted up on the cross. As he gives his Spirit to those who witness his crucifixion, they are re-born of the Spirit (cf. 3:5) and thus become "children of God" (1:12–13). Jesus' mother, who is not portrayed as actually giving birth to Jesus in John's Gospel, unlike in the Lukan (and Matthean) infancy narratives, is here viewed within the (implicit) image of birth in a spiritual sense.[80] And Jesus, who at the cross appears to be the only son of his mother, is actually the only son of his Father; he is born from him (1:18) and is now about to return to his Father, back into his womb.[81] This also denotes a re-vision of female and male roles.

---

[78] Reading Jesus' mother interfigurally with the widow of Nain also adds to the characterization of Joseph in John. That is, Joseph is considered dead and therefore does not function as a character in the story.

[79] The blood and water flowing out of Jesus' body (19:34) may also be reminiscent of an actual birth, where the water would refer to the amniotic fluid ("Fruchtwasser" in German). Judith M. Lieu, who relates the crucifixion scene, and in particular the mother of Jesus, to the parable in 16:21, notes: "So is this a birthing or a dying? [. . .]; we meet birth here only when we encounter death. Indeed, the birth, which is not narrated in this Gospel, becomes through 16:21 a death, or is the death a birth?" ("The Mother of the Son in the Fourth Gospel," *JBL* 117 [1998], pp. 61–77, here p. 73).

[80] Featuring Jesus' mother at the cross, intertextuality is also established to Mark's crucifixion scene. There, Jesus is portrayed as quoting the first verse of Ps. 22: "My God, my God, why hast thou forsaken me?" Any reader familiar with the Hebrew Bible, including members of John's community, knows that the lament is followed by belief in God's unfailing presence, thereby evoking the mother: "Yet thou art he who took me from the womb; thou didst keep me safe upon my mother's breasts. Upon thee I was cast from my birth, and since my mother bore me thou hast been my God" (Ps. 22:9–10). Thus, Jesus' mother was also invoked in Mark's Gospel, though implicitly. Besides the presence of Jesus' mother, the mention of Jesus' garment in John 19:24, quoting Ps. 22:18, opens up this intertextuality.

It's also an interesting detail to note that, different from the widow of Nain, Jesus' mother is not portrayed as weeping; the weeping is left to Mary Magdalene when visiting the tomb on Easter morning, and it is to her that Jesus addresses the question "Why do you weep?" (20:13).

To sum up: Opening up the Johannine text (John 19:25–27) to the Lukan intertext (Luke 7:11–17) and viewing the characters in the crucifixion scene, in particular the mother of Jesus, interfigurally, adds important dimensions to characterization. Reading the Johannine crucifixion in the light of raising the young man of Nain from the dead,[82] allows readers to also regard the moment of Jesus' death as the moment of his resurrection. And indeed, in John Jesus' death is at the same time his glorification (12:28; 16:14; 17:1–5). Death is transformed into new life already on the cross. And returning to his Father, Jesus does not leave his mother orphaned (14:18).

Interfigural Encounters and the Transformation of Gender in John

Nicodemus encountering Mary and the anointing women, and Jesus' mother encountering the widow of Nain, have left them transformed. But the characters they encountered, the Synoptic women, have also been transformed. Whenever reading the Johannine story of Jesus we shall, from now on, also think of them; and vice versa, when reading the Synoptic stories we shall always think of Nicodemus and Jesus' mother. Thus, we as readers, have been transformed in the process of encountering Johannine characters encountering Synoptic characters. Interfigural encounters create a network of relationships, between characters in different texts, and between characters and

---

[81] The Greek *kolpos* can mean both, "bosom" and "womb;" most translations, however, have "bosom" (RSV), or alternatively, "heart" (NRSV). Obviously, it's difficult for most to imagine a father with a womb, yet normally one is born from a womb ("born of God," 1:13). This is only one instance of many others in John's Gospel where gender boundaries are transcended. Lieu ("The Mother of the Son in the Fourth Gospel," p. 76) draws attention to the tradition of the maternal God of prophecy and psalmody in the Hebrew Bible (Hos 11:1–4; Isa. 42:14; Ps 139:13) and considers Deut. 32:10 as closest to our passage in John. God is the one who has carried from the womb and has given birth.

[82] The story in Luke is based on 1 Kings 17, where the prophet Elijah raises the son of the widow of Zarephath from the dead (vv. 17–24). Therefore, intertextuality and interfigurality is also established between the Johannine narrative and 1 Kings 17.

readers reading characters. It's a very dynamic process of vacillating between the story worlds of the texts and our own story worlds. Thereby, borders and boundaries are transcended. Texts are no longer fixed and closed entities; they are open to other texts, and they are open to readers to enter into them and transform them.

Reading Nicodemus and the mother of Jesus intertextually, their configuration within John's Gospel also comes to the fore in a more pointed fashion. Both feature at the beginning of the story, in open-ended narratives, which leave the readers with ambiguity about their faith; and they return at the end of the story, at Jesus' death, and show their faith by what they do. Though they are not portrayed as actually meeting one another within the story, they meet in the readers who are encouraged to link them together. Since Nicodemus' encounter with the Lukan Mary, his relation to Jesus' mother in John can also be viewed in a different light. It's particularly striking that in John birth is not related to Jesus' mother but to males throughout the Gospel, except for the parable in 16:20–22. And it's the old man Nicodemus, in particular, who is faced with the issue of re-birth. By relating Nicodemus to the Lukan Mary, the reversal of gender roles in John becomes even more obvious. In fact, gender boundaries are overcome, and gender as a social construct is transformed.[83] It seems that, since birth is primarily a spiritual experience in John (re-birth from above/of water and the Spirit), referring as it does to the coming to believe, gender roles among the community of believers have to be re-viewed and re-defined, or rather, the gender split has to be overcome altogether.

The interfigural readings as presented above have shown that these readings are not confined either to gender boundaries. Synoptic women become visible in Johannine men, but Synoptic women also become visible in Johannine women. Besides the interfigural relations mentioned in this paper, there are others. For example, the

---

[83] The portrayal of Jesus as Sophia in John has to be considered in that context too, as presented in more detail in my paper "Grenzüberschreitungen. Perspektiven neutestamentlicher Hermeneutik und Praxis aus dem Johannesevangelium." See also M. Scott, *Sophia and the Johannine Jesus* (JSNT Supplement Series, 71; Sheffield: JSOT, 1992); J. E. McKinlay, *Gendering Wisdom the Host. Biblical Invitations to Eat and Drink* (JSNT Supplement Series, 216; Gender, Culture, Theory, 4; Sheffield: Sheffield Academic Press, 1996); J. Lieu, "Scripture and the Feminine in John," in A. Brenner (ed.), *A Feminist Companion to the Hebrew Bible in the New Testament* (The Feminist Companion to the Bible, 10; Sheffield: Sheffield Academic Press, 1996), pp. 225–40.

"sinner" woman of Luke 7:36–50 has been the role model for Jesus' footwashing in John 13, and hence interfigurality between Jesus and her can be established.[84] The same woman also shines through in Mary of Bethany's anointing of Jesus' feet (John 12:1–8). Furthermore, the Synoptic anointing women become visible in John's Easter morning stories; the mention of Jesus' head and feet (20:12) invites readers to remember the women who anointed Jesus' head (Mark 14:3–9; Matt. 26:6–13) and Jesus' feet (Luke 7:36–50). Besides these and other Synoptic women in John, there are also Synoptic men in both Johannine women and men. But that needs to be left to another time and place.

To be sure, none of the interfigural readings are compulsory. The Johannine text has meaning in its own right. Yet, when opened to other texts and especially to the Synoptic texts, meaning changes fundamentally, and consequently characters appear in a very different light. The readings presented here are, as mentioned in the beginning, my own personal readings, and I offer them to you, my readers, as a starting point for your own journeys through the Gospels. I assume that intertextual and interfigural readings were a vital part of Gospel readings from early on, for certain as soon as the Gospel canon came into being, and thus since readers were confronted with four different Gospels.

Returning to the question of the relation between John and the Synoptics, there are good reasons to assume that John knew the Synoptic Gospels and used them in a very creative way, thus very different from the relation of Luke and Matthew to Mark. Whilst the latter relation can be approached in the traditional manner of literary/source criticism and redaction criticism within the historical-critical paradigm, this won't work the same way when applied to John and its relation to the Synoptics.[85] Therefore, approaching the

---

[84] Cf. Kitzberger, "Love and Footwashing. John 13.1–20 and Luke 7.36–50 Read Intertextually."

[85] That it *can* work, though it needs a different optic to start with, demonstrates the evocative work of Maurits Sabbe. For our particular subject here, see especially, "The Anointing of Jesus in John 12,1–8 and Its Synoptic Parallels," in F. Van Segbroek/C. M. Tuckett/G. Van Belle/J. Verheyden (eds.), *The Four Gospels 1992. FS Frans Neirynck* (BETL, 100; Leuven: Leuven University Press and Peeters, 1992), pp. 2051–82, and "The Johannine Account of the Death of Jesus and Its Synoptic Parallels (Jn 19,16b–42)," *ETL* 70 (1994), pp. 34–64. Sabbe advocates direct literary dependence of John on the Synoptics.

issue with the more dynamic paradigm of reader response criticism and intertextuality, as suggested in this paper, a fundamental shift of perspective and consequently a re-viewing of an old question becomes possible. Though we shall never be able to say for sure what the author of a Gospel really thought or knew or intended, it seems that John transcended the borders and boundaries of the texts presented by the Synoptics and used them in a very creative way. And even gender boundaries seem to have been no problem for John, or rather, he deliberately transcended them. We can assume that, besides the author of John, at least part of the Johannine community was familiar with the Synoptic Gospels and could, therefore, activate certain meaning dimensions of the text which open it up to intertexts.

Asking the question "How can this be?" regarding Synoptic women in John, a new optics is called for. When the issue is approached in the traditional way, we only see what is *not* there, that is, the Synoptic women who missed out in John, or, on the other hand, we only see what is so different about the women common to John and the Synoptics. Applying the interfigural lenses we come to see, however, that there *are* Synoptic women in John whom we could not see at first glance and when only looking at the the texts superficially. We need to dive deeper to search for these women and to eventually find them. It's more than worthwhile to bring them out of the darkness into the light, and to let them be re-born, in both men and women.

PART TWO

HISTORICAL RE-CONSTRUCTION
AND CONTEXTUALIZATION

IN THE FOOTSTEPS OF JESUS: JEWISH WOMEN IN A JEWISH MOVEMENT*

TAL ILAN

From early on in the feminist study of the New Testament it has been noted that women are not infrequently mentioned on the pages of the Gospels, and also as members of the movement that Jesus called into being.[1] Even cautious scholars who would point out that there are no women named among the "Twelve," or that a concrete statement about women who followed Jesus is found only in the Third Gospel (Luke 8:2–3), have to contend with bits of data which cannot be explained in any other way but as evidence that in Jesus' entourage or at the stations he frequented along the way were to be found women who were his devout followers and who participated in a lively fashion in the Jesus movement.[2]

Thus, it is of great interest that the sisters Mary and Martha are mentioned as having housed and supported Jesus on his way both in the Gospel of Luke (10:38–42) and in the Gospel of John (11:1–46; 12:1–8), although the traditions these two Gospels relate are distinctly different. No less fascinating is the description of several women's roles at the crucifixion, burial and resurrection of Jesus. Prominent among these was Mary Magdalene. When the rest of the disciples deserted Jesus, they remained to view his crucifixion (Mark 15:40–41; Matt. 27:55–56; Luke 23:49; John 19:25–27), and then

---

* Parts of this essay were presented in a paper at a conference on Christianity at Tel Aviv University in November 1996. An abridged version of it will be published in the proceedings of that conference.

[1] E.g. C. F. Parvey, "The Theology and Leadership of Women in the New Testament," in R. R. Ruether (ed.), *Religion and Sexism: Images of Women in the Jewish and Christian Tradition* (New York: Simon and Schuster, 1974), pp. 117–49; E. and F. Stagg, *Women in the World of Jesus* (Philadelphia, PA: Westminster, 1978), pp. 101–60; E. Moltmann-Wendel, *The Women Around Jesus* (New York: Crossroad, 1982); E. Schüssler Fiorenza, *In Memory of Her: A Feminist Theological Reconstruction of Christian Origins* (New York: Crossroad, 1983), pp. 105–59.

[2] E.g. E. Schüssler Fiorenza, "Der Beitrag der Frau zur urchristlichen Bewegung," in W. Schottroff and W. Stegemann (eds.), *Traditionen der Befreiung II: Frauen in der Bibel* (München: Kaiser, 1980), pp. 60–89; B. Witherington III, *Women and the Genesis of Christianity* (Cambridge: Cambridge University Press, 1990), pp. 88–120.

they attended to his corpse (Mark 15:47; Matt. 27:61; Luke 23:55–56) and visited his tomb, being consequently the first witnesses to the resurrection (Mark 16:1–8; Matt. 28:1–10; Luke 24:1–12; John 20:1–18). In fact, a thorough analysis of the passion stories strongly suggests that the most central doctrine of Christianity, that of Jesus' resurrection, was conjured up by women. These women, who believed they had witnessed an empty tomb and met the resurrected Christ, went on to tell their experience to the other disciples. Their position in the Jesus movement was strong enough for them to be believed and taken seriously. Thus, women were extremely instrumental at the most critical moment of Christian history. With the death of the leader of a messianic movement, the movement usually dies with him, but in the case of Christianity something happened which changed the local Jewish movement into the universal world religion, Christianity. Obviously, many factors contributed to this development, but the initial momentum seems to have begun with the people who interpreted the events following Jesus' death as a resurrection. The Gospels unanimously agree that these people were women. Thus, the basic creed of Christianity, namely that Jesus after his death had come back to life, is in fact a woman's idea. Such a claim had indeed been put forward by Celsus in the second century in his refutation of Christianity, and in his attempt to discredit it: "Who saw this [i.e. the empty tomb and the risen Christ]?," Celsus asks and immediately answers, "A hysterical female, as you say."[3] To him the gender of the witnesses makes their testimony doubtful. But in the Jesus movement it did not, which makes it unlikely that these women were hangers-on with a secondary status.

This brief description I have just suggested promotes a rather positivist approach to the words of the Gospels, taking them more as historical descriptions than is usually merited today. In fact, this approach could be viewed as naive and unsophisticated. I would, therefore, like to devote the following lines to an incorporation of my approach and conclusions within a wider historical perspective. I would like to bring into the discussion methods used in Synoptic, Pauline and feminist research in order to expose the sources to a closer literary and then "post-literary" scrutiny. By "post-literary" I mean identifying the residue left in the sources after their literary

---

[3] Origen, *Contra Celsum*, 55.

faculties have been exhausted. Then I would like to use the results of this study in order to demonstrate how all this fits into Second Temple Jewish Palestinian history. The aim of this paper is to show that there were women in the Jesus movement, and that this fact is interesting but not altogether unique or alien to the Jewish background from which it sprang.

Procuring Historical Data

1. *Choosing the Sources*

There are quite a few women found on the pages of the Gospels. Most of them are healed by Jesus. He heals Peter's mother-in-law, who then rises and ministers to him and to his disciples (Mark 1:29–31; Matt. 8:14–15; Luke 4:38–39); he raises from the dead a daughter of the head of the synagogue and cures a woman of a twelve year blood flow (Mark 5:21–43; Matt. 9:18–26; Luke 8:41–56); he exorcizes the daughter of a pagan woman (Mark 7:24–30; Matt. 15:21–28); and he makes well the woman who is bent over (Luke 13:10–17). All these actions are associated with Jesus' most prominent activity, healing. These women, however, cannot, in my opinion, prove that there were women members to his movement. Jesus also forgives a sinner (Luke 7:36–50) and sets free an adulteress who was to be stoned (John 7:53–8:11). These actions too (which are probably not historical) should be viewed more in the context of Jesus' general attitude to sinners, including those whose sins are sexual, than to any actual female following he was attempting to raise. All these stories speak clearly about the Gospels' attitude to some gender issues but are of little importance for the question of historical women in the Jesus movement.

   The sources that should be considered for the issue of the female following of Jesus are those which tell of women associated with Jesus on a more intimate level. These women are usually named, indicating their importance for the sectarian literature which sprang up in the circles which they frequented. The two sets of stories which conform best to these criteria are, as stated above, those about Mary and Martha and those about Mary Magdalene. These two sets of stories are of a clearly different quality, and therefore their historical value should be deduced with the application of different methods. Let us begin with the Mary and Martha collection.

1.1 Mary and Martha

The sisters Mary and Martha are only mentioned in the Gospels of
Luke (10:38–42) and John (11:1–46; 12:1–8). This suggests that the
source of information about them which Luke had was neither Mark,
nor Q (which he shared with Matthew), but some other tradition.
That he did not share this source with John becomes obvious when
we compare what John has to say about these women to what Luke
has. The two stories are not connected at all.[4] In John, Jesus encounters the two women as part of the Passion story. In Luke, the story
is dissociated from any specific event. In John, the house of Mary
and Martha is located in the environs of Jerusalem. In Luke, it is
most likely located in Galilee. Furthermore, the very story told of
Mary and Martha in Luke is significantly different from that in John.
In Luke, Martha ministered to Jesus at the table, while Mary learned
at his feet. In John, however, the visit with the sisters is associated
with the death of their brother, Lazarus, whom Jesus brings back to
life. Next, Mary is credited for anointing Jesus in anticipation of his
death, an action assigned in Mark and Matthew to an anonymous
woman. Obviously this was a pre-Markan tradition known also to
John. He chose to assign the action to a named heroine. This literary technique of assigning actions of nameless characters to more
prominent ones is a well known literary technique.[5] Obviously John's
tradition of the woman who anointed Jesus was no more associated
with Mary than Mark's. Thus, the only thing that emerges as a common premise from a conflation of the sources on Mary and Martha
in both Luke and John is that both knew of two sisters who were
devout disciples of Jesus. This would suggest that both stories cannot really be taken as telling anything of historical value. They can

---

[4] This paper is not concerned with developing new methods of Gospel analysis.
It takes as its starting point the traditional view that Mark is the source of Luke
and Matthew, who had also known another source, Q. It assumes John was conceived from another tradition and its author did not know the earlier Gospels, and
thus tradition shared by them all should be understood as "pre-Markan." In this I
follow E. Schüssler Fiorenza, "A Feminist Interpretation for Liberation," *Religion and
Theological Life* 3 (1980), pp. 21–36, and disagree with I. R. Kitzberger, "Mary of
Bethany and Mary of Magdala—Two Female Characters in the Johannine Passion
Narrative. A Feminist, Narrative-Critical Reader Response," *NTS* 41 (1995), pp.
564–86.

[5] See my *Mine and Yours are Hers: Retrieving Women's History from Rabbinic Literature*
(Leiden: Brill, 1997).

only be taken as remembering two sisters who were known to have been followers of Jesus. The women, not the stories, are historical.[6]

1.2 The Women at the Tomb

The stories about the women present at Jesus' crucifixion, burial and resurrection are well known. We are told that women who had followed Jesus from Galilee (Mark 15:40–41; Matt. 27:55–56; Luke 23:49) were present when Jesus died on the cross. Since in Mark and Matthew it is here we first hear of women followers of Jesus, although in all four Gospels we have already travelled with him far and wide, this detail may have prompted Luke, the most historically minded of the evangelists, to insert the list found early in his Gospel about the women who followed Jesus on his travels: Mary Magdalene, Joanna, Susanna, and many others (Luke 8:2–3). This list is strikingly similar to the one Luke produces of the women present at the empty tomb (Luke 24:10).

The Passion narrative then goes on to relate that these women also saw the place where Jesus' body was placed after it was taken down from the cross and before it was laid into the tomb (Mark 15:47; Matt. 27:61; Luke 23:55). Two days latter, when the women came to visit the tomb, they found it empty. Two Gospels (John and Matthew) then tell of the women's encounter with the risen Christ. Mark and Luke, who do not tell of a direct encounter, both agree, nevertheless, that Jesus' empty tomb was discovered by women. The identity of these women is disputed among the Gospels, but they all agree that the most prominent among them was Mary Magdalene.

The death and resurrection stories pose source-critical problems of another sort.[7] The stories are told, in general lines, quite similarly in all four Gospels, thus suggesting a pre-Markan tradition. Indeed, if there is one passage in the Gospels which is universally considered very old, it is this one. The resurrection is often mentioned in

---

[6] On Mary and Martha, see also A. Reinhartz, "From Narrative to History: The Resurrection of Mary and Martha," in A.-J. Levine (ed.), *"Women Like This." New Perspectives on Jewish Women in the Greco-Roman World* (Atlanta, GA: Scholars, 1991), pp. 161–84; M. R. D'Angelo, "Women Partners in the New Testament," *JFSR* 6 (1990), pp. 65–86.

[7] For an old but still excellent discussion of most of these problems, see M. Hengel, "Maria Magdalena und die Frauen als Zeugen," in O. Betz, M. Hengel and P. Schmidt (eds.), *Abraham Unser Vater: Juden und Christen im Gespräch über die Bibel* (Festschrift für Otto Michel zum 60. Geburtstag; Leiden: Brill, 1963), pp. 243–56.

the Pauline epistles, which predate the earliest Gospel by several decades. But there we encounter another problem. In 1 Cor. 15:5–8 Paul tells the new Christians of Corinth the order in which the risen Christ appeared to disciples after his crucifixion: "He appeared to Cephas, then to the Twelve, then he appeared to more than five hundred brethren at one time, most of whom are still alive, though some have fallen asleep. Then he appeared to James, then to all the apostles. Last of all, as to one untimely born, he appeared also to me."[8] In light of the Gospels, this list contains one striking omission: before he appeared to Cephas, Jesus had appeared to a number of women, foremost among them Mary Magdalene.

New Testament scholarship maintains that even though Paul's mission took place after the events related in the Gospels, the epistles of Paul are considerably earlier than the Gospels and therefore superior as a historical source. Following this strict formal approach, we would have to conclude that Paul is relating the historical sequence of events, and the women mentioned in the Gospels are a later editorial, perhaps even anti-Pauline, polemic addition. In the study of the history of women, however, such a method overlooks other no less formidable difficulties. In the words of Ross Shepard Kraemer, "the traditions of women as the earliest witnesses of the resurrection and of Mary of Magdala as the first to see the risen Christ are so problematic that they would surely have been omitted had they not been firmly believed to be true by tradents or transmitters of the Gospel tradition."[9] As suggested by Antoinette Clark Wire, the women's absence in Paul's list is better understood as a silencing of this tradition, as an usurpation of women's major role in the onset of Christianity and, in fact, as an act of attempted censorship.[10] If in later Christian circles somebody like Paul went into the trouble of censoring out the women in the original tradition, this suggests to me that the Gospel women were real people who had to be reckoned with.

---

[8] This and all other translations are from the RSV.

[9] R. Shepard Kraemer, *Her Share of the Blessings: Women's Religions among the Pagans, Jews and Christians in the Greco-Roman World* (New York: Oxford University Press, 1992), p. 130.

[10] A. Clark Wire, *The Corinthian Women Prophets: A Reconstruction through Paul's Rhetoric* (Minneapolis, MN: Fortress, 1990), pp. 161–3.

This then is the corpus of sources which, in my opinion, indicates that the Jesus movement had a substantial following of women. In what follows I would like to inquire who these women were and why they were attracted to the Jesus movement.

2. The Names

Another way of demonstrating the historicity of these women is an examination of their names. As I have previously said, these women associated with Jesus, as opposed to those mentioned in the healing stories, are named. Obviously they are named because they were well known. I think, however, that on closer scrutiny their names will reveal the historical milieu in which they were embedded and show clearly that, were they historical creations, the names given would hardly have been these.

Let us begin with the most baffling phenomenon of all. The name Mary (Miriam) appears in the Gospels and in chapters 1–12 of Acts (which still relate events associated with the Jesus movement) with five or six women: (1) Jesus' mother, (2) Mary Magdalene, (3) Mary, the sister of Martha, (4) Mary, the mother of James and Joses (Mark 15:40) (who is perhaps not identical with), (5) Mary, wife of Clopas (John 19:25), and finally, (6) Mary, mother of John Mark (Acts 12:12). Except for the last one, all these Marys are associated either with the Mary/Martha tradition or with the Passion narrative, and even the last Mary is mentioned in connection with the post-Passion events in Jerusalem. This plethora of Marys has often confused New Testament scholars, who have tended to reduce their number as far as possible. This has resulted in the famous historical fallacy according to which Mary Magdalene, Jesus' most important female follower, is identified as a prostitute. In the Gospel of Luke we are told of a woman sinner who approached Jesus in Galilee, wept at his feet and anointed him with expensive perfumes (Luke 7:36–50). This is the only story we hear about Jesus having contact with a woman sinner, and it is only assumed by the reader that her sin was sexual, perhaps because elsewhere Jesus mentions prostitutes as belonging to the population that will be saved in the kingdom of heaven (Matt. 21:31). The story of this sinner woman is unique to Luke, but in the other Synoptic Gospels another anointing story is told of an unnamed woman in Bethany, near Jerusalem, whose actions are perceived as part of the train of events that led to Jesus'

crucifixion and death (Mark 14:3–9; Matt. 26:6–13). John, as mentioned above, identifies this woman with Mary, the sister of Martha
(John 12:3–8). Although neither Luke nor John, the only Gospels
who mention this Mary, ever suggest anything of the sort, later Christian commentators identified her with Mary Magdalene. Thus, Mary
Magdalene was Mary, the sister of Martha, was the woman who
anointed Jesus, was the sinner, was a prostitute.[11]

Although this identification has been universally rejected by modern critical scholars as fanciful and going way beyond the mere facts,
even in the most "serious" academic writings Mary, the mother of
James and Joses, who, together with two other women, according
to Mark (15:40) and Matthew (27:56), saw Jesus die on the cross, is
still identified with Mary, Jesus' mother. This identification is grounded
on the latter being mentioned in a similar position in the Gospel of
John (19:25), and we know from elsewhere (Mark 6:3; Matt. 13:55),
that two of Jesus' brothers were called James and Joses.[12] This
identification, however, is methodologically wrong because, if Mary,
the mother of James and Joses, was the mother of Jesus himself,
why would the author refrain from stating the obvious? And if he
did not know she was, it is hardly likely that we may know it now.

Why has all this fanciful theorizing been going on for so long?
Simply because it had seemed to the readers that in a good story
the author does his best to name his characters by different, unique
names in order for the reader to identify each clearly and distinguish him/her from another. If the authors of the Gospels have not
done this, it is perhaps because they are actually referring to the
same woman, so we might argue. Such an approach is strictly literary. A historical approach, however, should explore other possibilities. In this case it turns out that the name Mary (Miriam) was
extremely popular in Palestine at the time of Jesus. It was by far
the most popular female name available and was borne by over 25
per cent of the female population.[13]

---

[11] For this identification see M. Warner, *Alone of All Her Sex: The Myth of the Virgin Mary* (New York: Knopf, 1976), pp. 225–9, see also pp. 344–5.
[12] For a discussion of the problem, see R. E. Brown, K. P. Donfried, J. A. Fitzmyer, and J. Reumann, *Mary in the New Testament* (Philadelphia, PA: Fortress, 1978), pp. 68–9.
[13] See my "Notes on the Distribution of Women's Names in Palestine in the Second Temple and Mishnaic Period," *Journal of Jewish Studies* 40 (1989), pp. 186–200.

But the historical onomastic setting against which the women of the Jesus movement can be re-viewed tells us more than that. The names of other women in the Jesus movement only further confirm this picture. There was one Salome, the second most popular name at the time, one Martha, the third most popular name, and one Joanna, the fifth on the list. The fourth most popular name—Saphire (שפירה)—is represented in a female character of the early Christian movement in Palestine after the death of Jesus (Acts 5:1). The only woman in the Jesus movement mentioned in the Gospels whose name was not extremely popular for women at the time is Susanna (Luke 8:3). This, however, is also useful in identifying the historical nature of the list. It consists, like any community of people, of the usual and of the unusual. Thus, it appears that if the distribution of names of the female followers of Jesus fails to meet any acceptable literary criteria, it certainly fits into a very specific historical situation. Obviously the names commemorate real women.

Thus, with the application of some source criticism and some onomastic methodology I hope I have been able to place the women of the Jesus movement in a strong historical framework. Regardless of the question whether the stories told about them reflect any historical facts, these women were real women. They lived in Jesus' time, they were impressed by his theological and ideological message, and they joined his movement. It is, therefore, appropriate to inquire at this point whether, on the one hand, their action should be considered outrageous or commonplace and, on the other hand, what it was in the Jesus movement that had attracted them.

Jewish Sectarianism, the Jesus Movement and Women

Second Temple Judaism was undoubtedly characterized by a strong schismatic tendency. Sects abounded, each with its own unique interpretation of Scripture and each with its own theology. Their Jewishness was demonstrated by their adherence to a more or less similar corpus of holy books, of which the five books of Moses constituted the least disputed section, and by a profession of monotheism. Otherwise, they were mutually exclusive, each claiming to represent the only correct Judaism, while denying its sister a similar claim. Thus, the Pharisees denied heretics who rejected the resurrection of the dead (probably the Sadducees) a part in the messianic future (*m.Sanh.* 10:1), the Dead Sea Sect prophesied for the Seekers of Smooth Things (probably the Pharisees) a doom of desertion and fall from grace (4QpNah 2:10–3:8; cf. 4QpIsa^c 23:2,10–19), and the Samaritans claimed that they alone were the true Israel, and anyone who upheld any book beyond the Pentateuch as holy was a heretic. These are perhaps only the most notable examples, but the times knew of more schisms and even worse enmities.

Thus, the Jesus movement was just one other option in the colourful array of religious, social and political affiliation options available to the Palestinian Jew during the first century C.E. Post-Easter Christianity, of course, changed all this completely. Once the Hebrew Bible and monotheism ceased to define Judaism as an exclusive type of religious affiliation, it had to be further defined. The emergence of Rabbinic Judaism after the destruction of the Temple in 70 C.E. meant two things: one, the victory of the Pharisee variant of Judaism over other manifestations which had flourished earlier; the other, the addition of another corpus of Holy Scriptures, the Mishnah (and later the Talmud) to the Jewish Canon. Adherence to the Hebrew Bible (or parts of it) was no longer enough for the identification of a Jewish group. All this, however, came later. At the time of Jesus, the movement described in the New Testament certainly met with the criteria for a Jewish sect.

We do not know, of course, what exactly was meant by an affiliation to one of the Jewish groups mentioned above. Some of them, like the Dead Sea Sect, seem to have required a total relinquishing of one's previous mode of life, and perhaps a physical transition to the sect's abode by the Dead Sea. On the other hand, compositions such as the Damascus Document suggest that such a total commitment was only undertaken by a few extremely devout members of the sects. Others continued to live among the rest of the population and had dealings with them (e.g. CD 7:6–7). In other cases it is even harder to understand what an affiliation meant. For example, do the laws found in the Mishnah requiring people with the unique title of *haverim* to take special precautions with their food and with the company they eat in (*m.Demai* 2:3; cf. *t.Demai* 2:2–3) refer to the membership demands in the Pharisee sect? When Josephus mentions 6000 Pharisees who refused to swear an oath of allegiance to Herod,[14]

---

[14] Jos., *Ant.* 17:42.

does he mean that these people carried some kind of membership card that identified them as Pharisees? We simply do not know.

In the absence of any clear understanding of these issues, it is equally unclear what a membership in the Jesus movement entailed. It is true that Jesus is recorded telling his disciples that he who does not leave behind his/her family members,[15] is not a true disciple (Mark 10:29; Matt. 19:29; Luke 18:29), but it has been suggested that this describes membership in the post-Easter missionary movement, and should not perhaps be assigned to Jesus himself. The two traditions about women disciples of Jesus certainly suggest two types of followers. Mary and Martha are sedentary adherents, who welcome Jesus and other members of the movement into their home, while Mary Magdalene and the other women at the crucifixion are described as having travelled with Jesus from Galilee (Mark 15:40–41). We may easily assume that both forms of discipleship were acceptable. Membership in the Jesus movement was obviously defined rather loosely.

This discussion is important in order to inquire whether the participation of women in the Jesus movement was particularly revolutionary or unusual in the Jewish society Jesus came from. Were they initiating something not found elsewhere, or was this female following merely another manifestation of a feature quite common at the time? In order to answer this question we must look into some other sources of information.

1. *Women in Jewish Sectarian Associations*

The most obvious place to begin this search would be among the Therapeutai, a Jewish sect that flourished in Central Egypt at the time. This sect of ascetics, described by Philo of Alexandria,[16] resembled in many ways the Palestinian Essenes, described in detail both by the former[17] and by Josephus.[18] Both sects upheld a rigorous schedule, ate little and were celibate. The most striking difference between the two sects was that while the Essenes were an all-male society, the Therapeutai included members of both sexes, who led

---

[15] See E. Schüssler Fiorenza's reading of this text in *In Memory of Her*, pp. 145–7.
[16] *De Vita Contemplativa.*
[17] *Hypothetica* 11:1–18.
[18] Jos., *War* 2:120–61.

a life of equality but segregation between them.[19] The membership
of women in this sect is such a fundamental aspect of its existence
that its mention seems more like stating the obvious than making
an argument for the participation of women in sectarian life in the
time of Jesus. Furthermore, it could be argued that the Therapeutrides
(as the female adherents of the sect were designated) are not a viable
example for the simple reason that they flourished in Egypt and
may, thus, represent what may have been acceptable in Egyptian-
Jewish society but unheard of in Palestine. Thus, it is important to
search for evidence of women's roles in sectarian activity closer to
home.

Of course, the sect closest to the Therapeutai in Palestine are the
Essenes and they clearly shunned female company, being a monastic association of males.[20] However, this is precisely the issue on
which the identification of Essenes with the Dead Sea Sect breaks
down. The texts of the Dead Sea Scrolls clearly speak of families
and even contain laws relevant specifically to women, perhaps suggesting that these were members in their own right and not just
wives of members.[21] But even if we accept the suggestion of some
scholars that the sect was divided into followers who lived all over
the country and the more devout members who resided in Qumran
and its vicinity,[22] it is worthwhile noting that both in the cemeter-
ies of Qumran and in those of neighbouring Dead Sea settlements,
female skeletons were found alongside men's at a ratio of 1:3.[23] Thus,

---

[19] R. Shepard Kraemer, "Monastic Jewish Women in Greco-Roman Egypt: Philo
on the Therapeutrides," *Signs* 14 (1989), pp. 342–70.

[20] Jos., *War* 2:120.

[21] For a detailed discussion of these rulings, see my "The Attraction of Aristocratic
Jewish Women to Pharisaism," *HTR* 88 (1995), pp. 1–33. This issue is discussed
on pp. 28–33. See now also P. R. Davies and J. E. Taylor, "On the Testimony of
Women in 1Qsa," *Dead Sea Discoveries* 3 (1996), pp. 223–35.

[22] On this theory and its shortcomings, see H. Stegemann, "The Qumran Essenes:
Local Members of the Main Jewish Union in Late Second Temple Times," in
J. Trebolle Barrera and L. V. Montaner (eds.), *The Madrid Congress* I (Leiden: Brill,
1992), pp. 126–37.

[23] R. de Vaux, "Fouilles au Khirbet Qumrân: Rapport Préliminaire," *RB* 60
(1953), pp. 83–106. The relevant details are on p. 103; idem, "Fouilles au Khirbet
Qumrân," *RB* 63 (1956), pp. 533–77. The relevant data is found on pp. 567–71;
S. H. Steckoll, "Preliminary Excavation Report in the Qumran Cemetery," *RQ* 6
(1968), pp. 323–36. See relevant details on p. 335; P. Bar-Adon, "Another Settlement
of the Judaean Desert Sect in En el-Ghuweir on the Shores of the Dead Sea,"
BASOR 227 (1977), pp. 12–17. I demonstrate this further in "Bone of My Bone:
The Use of Skeletal Remains for the Study of Gender and Social History in Second

if full membership in the sect entailed a rejection of past life style and a removal to the Dead Sea region, women, like men, took upon themselves these hardships.[24]

However, not just marginal ascetic groups, such as the Therapeutai and the Dead Sea Sect, attracted Jewish women. Elsewhere[25] I have shown that early sectarian Pharisaism of the Second Temple period held a certain appeal to women. I was able to show this with reference to some statements about Pharisee following found in Josephus and in rabbinic literature and with reference to specific women who adhered to this group's outlook, primarily the Jewish Queen Shelamzion, who was in a position to elevate the Pharisees to a position of power. Since Pharisaism was a movement which did not withdraw from society at large, and since what membership in the sect entailed is not entirely clear, we have no way of knowing whether women were actually members of the sect. It is, however, worthwhile noting that our sources are equally unclear as to whether men were members of the Pharisee sect and what that actually meant. For example, Josephus' confession that he himself was an adherent of the Pharisees, is usually considered suspect by many scholars.[26]

All this data together tend to support the view that women could and did make political and religious choices of this sort at the time of Jesus. This does not mean that making such a choice did not entail social censorship and derision. It does not mean that it was easy or commonplace to become a female sectarian. All it suggests is that women who were so inclined could join a sect of their choice, and once they made the step they probably found support groups of other females who had acted likewise and who were now happy

---

Temple Times," in *Integrating Jewish Women into Second Temple History* (Texts and Studies in Ancient Judaism, 76; Tübingen: Mohr Siebeck, 1999), pp. 195–214.

[24] See also L. Cansdale, "Women Members of the *Yahad* according to the Qumran Scrolls," *Proceedings of the Eleventh World Congress of Jewish Studies, Vol. A* (Jerusalem: World Union of Jewish Studies, 1994), pp. 215–22; E. Schuller, "Women in the Dead Sea Scrolls," in M. O. Wise, N. Golb, J. J. Collins, and D. G. Pardee (eds.), *Methods of Investigation of the Dead Sea Scrolls and the Khirbet Qumran Site* (Annals of the New York Academy of Science, 722; New York, 1994), pp. 115–31.

[25] Ilan, "Attraction of Aristocratic Women."

[26] See M. Smith, "Palestinian Judaism in the First Century," in M. Davis (ed.), *Israel: Its Role in Civilization* (New York: Jewish Theological Seminary, 1956), pp. 67–81. The relevant discussion is on pp. 74–8; S. Mason, *Flavius Josephus on the Pharisees* (Leiden: Brill, 1991), pp. 325–41; S. Schwartz, *Josephus and Judaean Politics* (Leiden: Brill, 1990), pp. 209–16.

to render assistance to their new colleagues. The Jesus movement
with its female following was another such support group.

2. *Women's Particular Attraction to the Jesus Movement*

The fact that women could join the Jesus movement says only so
much about the social background of the Jesus movement. It certainly does not explain why they would want to join it. As opposed
to claims put forward by some early, over-simplified Christian feminist studies,[27] it is impossible to claim that the Jesus movement was
particularly feminist, or that it legislated in women's favour. This is
certainly not true. In fact the only legal pronouncement Jesus ever
made on the issue of women, his logion banning divorce (e.g. Mark
10:2–12), could easily be understood as a piece of strong anti-feminist legislation.[28] Thus, we have to dismiss the urge to suppose that
Jesus' message appealed to women because it was particularly relevant to their social oppression. The attraction will have be looked
for elsewhere. The following is an attempt to uncover some of the
movement's appeal to women.

2.1 *Healing*

Jesus' activities are generally characterized by two interrelated features, healing and prophecy. Jesus claimed for himself both, and his
disciples followed him because he healed and because his prophecies about the radiant future of the poor were seductive indeed. How
were these features interpreted by the ruling Jewish oligarchy and
other sectors of the establishment? The answer to this question can
only be superficial, because we know of it from nowhere aside from
the Gospels themselves. From this source it appears that Jesus' healing activities were received with hostility, and Jesus was charged with
using demonic powers in the process (Mark 3:22; Matt. 9:34; 12:24;
Luke 11:15).

This reminds one of similar ambivalent attitudes displayed in near-
contemporary Jewish sources toward the art of healing. The Jews,

---

[27] E.g. L. Swidler, *Biblical Affirmations of Women* (Philadelphia, PA: Westminster,
1979), pp. 173–6; Witherington, *Genesis of Christianity*, pp. 48–51.

[28] See for example, B. Brooten, "Early Christian Women and their Cultural
Context: Issues of Method in Historical Reconstruction," in A. Yarbro Collins (ed.),
Feminist Perspectives on Biblical Scholarship (Chico, CA: Scholars, 1985), pp. 65–91. Her
discussion on this topic is on p. 74.

like their neighbours, viewed with suspicion the healing powers of certain individuals, and often identified them as originating in the domain of evil. This suspicion it probably based on the large number of medical failures which healers experienced during their career. Jesus himself is reputed to have failed in his healing activities when he came to his home town, Nazareth (e.g. Mark 6:5). However, a healer's failures may be foreshadowed by other cases of success, which would explain why people continued to seek his advice and prescriptions.

One piece of data that seems to stand out in our investigation of Graeco-Roman Palestinian Judaism is the large number of women who practised the art of healing. Thus, for example, in a discussion of the permitted means of healing on Sabbath, the Tosefta comments that these should not be done "according to women" alone, but their opinion should be seconded by a male Israelite (*t.Shab.* 15:15). Such a statement naturally suggests that on any other day women were duly consulted in this matter. This fact is exemplified nicely in a story found in the Palestinian Talmud about Rabbi Yohanan and his physician, a certain woman referred to as Bat-Domitianus, who treats his ailment with the application of an ointment. From the story it appears that the recipe for the ointment was a trade secret, known only to the members of a certain guild (*y.Shab.* 14:4, 14d). This guild was obviously open to the participation of women (and may in fact have been exclusively female in composition). Another story in the Palestinian Talmud relates how Rabbi Meir (falsely) complained of a sore eye and asked for a woman to come and heal him. We are further told that the remedy for the sore eye required saliva of the woman healer and thus that she spits into the sick person's eye (*y.Sot.* 1:4, 16d). It may be of interest to remember here that in healing a blind man according to the Gospel of Mark, Jesus also spat in his eye (Mark 8:23), and according to the Gospel of John, Jesus applied to it saliva mixed with dust (John 9:6). Thus, if Jesus was primarily a healer he could have received some formal education in a professional guild of healers, many of which were women.

The association of women with the art of healing obviously had positive aspects. They were the midwives who brought babies into the world. Thus, they were called חיה—life-givers, or חכמה—wise women. On the other hand, when their cures failed, the blame was obviously laid at their doorstep and they were accused of what in modern terminology we would call malpractice, and what in the ancient world would amount to witchcraft accusations. In Jewish tradition all women were, to some degree, suspected of engaging in witchcraft. "Most witchcraft is found in women," says one source (*Mekh. d. R. Shimeon b. Yohai* 22:17). "Most women engage in witchcraft," says another (*y.Sanh.* 7:9, 25d). In the third century B.C.E. Jewish book of 1 Enoch, we are informed that witchcraft came into the world with the fallen angels who seduced the daughters of men (1 Enoch 7:1; cf. 8:3), and that together with other elements of the trade, the fallen angels taught their women allies the medicinal properties of plants and roots, the sources of beneficial medicine as well as malignant poison. Women were, thus, the first healers and the first sorcerers. Healing and sorcery were inseparable. No wonder Jesus the healer was accused by his opponents of being a magician and of using the powers of evil in his cures.

2.2   *Prophecy*

Morton Smith has written an entire book in which he set out to justify the accusations of Jesus' opponents. In his *Jesus the Magician* he defines what magicians were and shows how Jesus' actions could be understood as being of the same fabric.[29] The book is fascinating, and the parallels it presents are undeniable. And yet, Smith assumes that magicians were real people, rather than the brainchildren of their opponents, that there were people who took up sorcery as a profession and that this is what Jesus did.

Jesus, however, would not have viewed himself as a magician or sorcerer but rather as a prophet. He saw himself and his movement as part of an ancient prophetic tradition. His healing activities would have been viewed by him as similar to those of Elijah and Elisha. Elisha had cured a leper (2 Kgs 5:1–19); so did Jesus (e.g. Mark 1:40–45). The two biblical prophets had raised sons from the dead (1 Kgs 17:17–24; 2 Kgs 4:18–37); so did Jesus (Luke 7:11–17). In Luke, the similarity to Elisha is intentional and conscious. Jesus raises the widow's son from the dead in Nain, just across from Shunem, where Elisha had acted in a similar way. In this, as in his healing activi-

---

[29] M. Smith, *Jesus the Magician* (London: Gollanz, 1978). I am much indebted to Smith for the data presented in this paper and for many insights, despite citing him in this note in order to refute him.

ties, Jesus experienced difficulties, as is evident from his statement about himself: "A prophet is not without honour except in his own country and among his own kin and in his own house" (Mark 6:4). Obviously Jesus' opponents claimed he was no prophet and they accused him of practising witchcraft.

Why was Jesus' claim to prophecy disbelieved by many, and why was he accused by his opponents of practising witchcraft? One of the reasons which has been brought up by scholars is the claim that, with the last prophets of the post-exilic period, prophecy in Israel had ceased. Shaye Cohen, in his book *From the Maccabees to the Mishnah*, describes the phenomenon as follows:

> Prophets no longer enjoyed the prestige and authority that had been theirs in pre-exilic times. In second temple Judaism prophets became apocalyptic seers, mystics, healers and holy men. A new type of authority figure emerged to replace the classical prophet: this was the scribe, whose authority derived not from his pedigree and institutional setting (like the priest), not from his charismatic personality and direct contact with God (like the prophet) but from his erudition in the sacred scriptures and traditions.[30]

Certainly very little prophetic literature of later periods has survived and none of it has been canonized. Nevertheless, other scholars have maintained that this is not the result of a historical situation but rather of a later ideology, which suppressed any traces of post-biblical prophecy. Ephraim Elimelech Urbach, for example, maintained that the claim put forward for the end of prophecy with Haggai, Zechariah and Malachi was a Jewish response to the Christian claim of the true prophecy of Jesus.[31] If this were true, then there is no difficulty in Jesus' claim that he, as a Jew, belonged to a long chain of prophets. The reason for the sorcery accusations must lie elsewhere.

In his important book on Old Testament prophecy, Robert Wilson, who studied prophecy in a broad range of societies and from an anthropological perspective, gives another, perhaps more adequate, explanation:

---

[30] S. J. D. Cohen, *From the Maccabees to the Mishnah* (Philadelphia, PA: Westminster, 1987), p. 23.

[31] E. E. Urbach, "When did Prophecy Cease?," *Tarbiz* 17 (1946), pp. 1–11 [Hebrew].

A powerless minority [like the Jesus movement—T.I.], sometimes feels that society is not responsive enough to the group's demands and that the supernatural message of the [prophetic] intermediary [of the group, in this case Jesus—T.I.] is not taken seriously. These feelings usually lead to frustrations and to an escalation of its demands . . . Social tensions between the group and society increase, and . . . society comes to regard the group as a threat to social stability. When the point of toleration is passed, the society will take steps to reduce social tension and restore the social order. Societies have various ways of dealing with the situations of rivalry and social friction, but the one which is most important for our discussion is the witchcraft accusation. Accusations of witchcraft are employed in cases where there are social tensions that cannot be handled by normal, rational or legal means.[32]

Thus, according to Wilson's criteria, society's reaction to uncontrollable prophets is similar to its reaction to inexplicable healing powers; both come from unclean, evil and ungodly sources. Both healers and false prophets are servants of the devil rather than God. This should be considered more in the context of the way a society views other and self than to any "real" historical situations. What is legitimate when performed by the representatives of a society is often viewed by the same as evil when practised by the members of a rival group. Magic, for example, was widely believed in all ancient societies. When the rabbis practised it, it was viewed by rabbinic literature as good, white magic, whose ultimate source is God. But when others, such as peripheral leaders and women, did the same, it was considered bad, black magic, whose ultimate source are the powers of evil, that is, demons, and ultimately the devil himself. The reverse, of course, is just as true. Jesus and his followers viewed his practice of healing as emanating from the true God.

It is no great revelation that in Israel, as in other societies, women had access to prophecy. This could be explained in any number of ways, but from ethnographic observations, Wilson concluded that

intermediaries with peripheral social background can be found in many cultures, but the best examples come from . . . patriarchally oriented religion. In these societies political and religious power is usually concentrated in the hands of the older males, while the younger males and women play little role in government or in the official cult. Yet most of the intermediaries come precisely from these powerless groups.

---

[32] R. R. Wilson, *Prophecy and Society in Ancient Israel* (Philadelphia, PA: Fortress, 1980), pp. 73–4.

Many of the intermediaries are women, who frequently experience peripheral possession and become members of peripheral possession cults which are counterparts of the male-dominated central cults.[33]

Women prophets in biblical Israel conform to a similar pattern. The reason why they eventually received formal prophetic status is because biblical historiography is essentially a product of a peripheral prophetic circle, the Deuteronomic circle, in which women were full-fledged members.[34] Thus, one can find hardly any difference between the Deuteronomic prophecy of Huldah and that of King Josiah (2 Kgs 22:14–20) and that of other male counterparts.[35] Prophetesses, no less than prophets, were subject to false prophecy accusations. Thus, Nehemiah accuses the woman Noadiah as falsely prophesying against him (Neh. 6:14). From the title he gives her, "prophetess," it is clear that society at large viewed this woman as possessing prophetic powers.[36] That he calls her prophecies false is naturally the result of the polemic nature of the Book of Nehemiah and not a reflection of the woman's status. Witchcraft accusations against prophetesses were no less common, even from within competing prophetic circles, and presumably because of their gender. Thus, Ezekiel, when condemning false prophets and accusing them of witchcraft, does not rest content leaving his hearers to deduce that "prophets" is a generic term, but refers also specifically to women who claim to possess prophetic capabilities: "Therefore you shall see no more vanities nor perform witchcraft (קסם תקסמנה לא) for I will deliver the people out of your hands and you shall know that I am the Lord" (Ezek. 13:23).

While Jesus was alive, his dominant presence undoubtedly silenced other prophetic voices in his movement, but after his death an outburst of prophetic uttering could be heard in the emerging Christian movement. Not surprisingly, some of them were women. Thus, the evangelist Philip's four daughters are said to prophesy (Acts 21:9). Some women in the emerging Christian community of Corinth

---

[33] Wilson, *Prophecy*, pp. 46–7.

[34] For this, see Wilson, *Prophecy*, pp. 46–7. For an elementary view of the Deuteronomic school, see R. E. Friedman, *Who Wrote the Bible?* (New York: Summit Books, 1987), pp. 89–135.

[35] On Huldah and the Deuteronomic tradition, see D. L. Christensen, "Huldah and the Men of Anathot: Women in Leadership in the Deuteronomic History," in K. Richards (ed.), *SBL Seminar Papers* (Atlanta, GA: Scholars, 1984), pp. 399–404.

[36] On Noadiah, see T. Eskenazi, "Out from the Shadows: Biblical Women in the Postexilic Era," *JSOT* 54 (1992), pp. 25–34, here p. 41.

claimed similar powers (1 Cor. 11:5). Christians themselves resorted to false prophecy accusations against rival claimants. Thus, the Christian prophetess from Thyatira, whom the author of Revelation calls Jezebel, is accused by him of acquiring her powers from Satan himself (Rev. 2:20).

The stories of women in the Jesus movement, too, seem to suggest that they displayed some prophetic traits. In the Gospel of John, Martha proclaims to Jesus: "You are the Christ, the Son of God" (John 11:27). In the Synoptic Gospels, a similar proclamation is made by Peter (Mark 8:27–30; Matt. 16:13–20; Luke 9;18–20). In the Gospel of Matthew, Jesus answers this proclamation of Peter with the words: "Blessed are you, Simon Bar-Jona, for flesh and blood has not revealed this to you, but my father who is in heaven" (Matt. 16:17). These words imply that the knowledge of the true nature of Jesus requires prophetic vision; a vision which, according to the Gospel of John, Martha also has.

2.3 *Possession*

Another prophetic trait may be found in Mary Magdalene. According to the Gospel of Luke, we are informed that Mary had joined the Jesus movement as a result of his exorcizing seven demons from her (Luke 8:2). Demonic possession is another confusing situation which could be interpreted differently by different groups. In the Hebrew Bible, for example, prophecy seems to seize people as a form of possession. The spirit of God descends upon them, and prophets are made to prophesy against their own will, speaking and acting in a strange way. Of King Saul it is related that "the Spirit of God came upon him also, and as he went he prophesied . . . and he too stripped off his clothes and he too prophesied before Samuel and lay naked all that day and all that night" (1 Sam. 19:23–24). This episode suggests that prophetic behaviour is often associated with possession and lunacy. When Elisha comes to anoint Yehu as king of Israel, the latter's followers inquire of him: "Why did this mad fellow come to you?" (2 Kgs 9:11), but when Yehu tells them of the prophecy, Elisha's words are easily believed.

Jesus, too, is accused by his opponents of being possessed by demons and charged as being a madman, who should be kept under lock and key (Mark 3:21–22). Yet Jesus himself exorcizes demons from others who are possessed. The most famous case recorded in the Gospels is the case of the man from Gerasa (Mark 5:1–20; Matt.

8:28–33; Luke 8:26–39). We are informed that the man was considered by all as mad, that he was chained because he could not be controlled, but most surprising of all, possessed as he was, and just before being released from the demon, he pronounces Jesus to be "Son of the Most High God" (Mark 5:7). Thus, though he may be possessed and a madman, he is certainly no false prophet according to the Gospels. Whatever the source of his possession, it also endows the person possessed with prophetic abilities. Similarly, in Philippi Paul encounters a possessed slave girl, whom he exorcizes, but just before he does so, the girl follows him prophesying correctly: "These men are servants of the Most High God, who proclaim to you the way of salvation" (Acts 16:17).

Thus, the issue of exorcism, possession and prophecy is slightly mixed up in the Hebrew Bible and truly confused in the New Testament. Jesus, who appears to others to be possessed, exorcizes demons who possess others. Among those he exorcizes is Mary Magdalene, his most staunch supporter and clearly the woman who was witness to and told of his resurrection. Yet the people he exorcizes, while seemingly mad and clearly possessed by evil spirits, have the gift of true prophecy. Mary Magdalene may also have had such a gift.

Conclusion

My major argument is, in conclusion, that the powers and authority Jesus claimed for himself derived not from the main bodies of power of his time such as the Temple, the priesthood, even the Torah and its study, but rather from the peripheral, charismatic fringes. Leaders who emerged from these fringes claimed authority through direct contact with supernatural powers rather than through exalted birth or knowledge of Scriptures. With neither as prerequisites, women could and did emerge from these fringes in similar capacities. Jesus is, thus, to be found in typical feminine settings and accused of typical feminine transgressions. His message, even when entirely not feminist in character, would be understood by women, because he spoke in a familiar language and went through familiar motions.

Even Jesus' fate must have seemed familiar. The Bible says explicitly, "You shall not suffer a sorceress to live" (Exod. 22:18), and the

rabbis object asking, "Does this not refer to men as well as women?,"
and then add an explanation: "The Torah has only spoken in the
language of common use, since most witchcraft is found in women"
(*Mekh. d. R. Shimeon b. Yohai* 22:18). Indeed, we hear that Simeon
ben Shatah hanged 80 women in Ashkelon (*m.Sanh.* 6:4). These are
identified by the Palestinian Talmud as witches, and the hanging is
interpreted as crucifixion (*y.Sanh.* 6:9, 23c). Who or what these women
were, is hard to tell,[37] but the event described comes too dangerously close to post-medieval witch-hunting to be dismissed as a-his-
torical. Thus, the high degree of self-identification with the Jesus
movement that women felt and their refusal to part with their dead
leader would seem understandable.

---

[37] Two interpretations, which I reject, were suggested by J. Efron, "The Deed
of Simeon ben Shatah in Ascalon," in A. Kasher, *Jews and Hellenistic Cities in Eretz
Israel* (Tübingen: Mohr Siebeck, 1990), pp. 318–41; M. Hengel, *Rabbinische Legende
und frühpharisäische Geschichte: Schimeon b. Schatach und die achtzig Hexen von Askalon*
(Abhandlungen der Heidelberger Akademie der Wissenschaft, Philosophisch-Historische
Klasse; Heidelberg: Winter, 1984).

GENDER, ETHNICITY, AND LEGAL CONSIDERATIONS IN THE HAEMORRHAGING WOMAN'S STORY MARK 5:25–34

MARIE-ELOISE ROSENBLATT

A woman suffered from an issue of blood for twelve years. When she surreptitiously touched the cloak of Jesus in a crowded street, she was suddenly healed of her illness. Despite her reluctance to come forward, Jesus prompted her to tell her story to all the bystanders (Mark 5:25–34; Matt. 9:18–26; Luke 8:40–56). Like many women in the Gospels, she is provided no name, no regional identity, and no designation of ethnicity. The setting is the northern region of the land of Israel, on the western shore of the sea of Galilee (Mark 5:22).

Transformation of consciousness by readers of the Gospel, mediated by the faith of first century witnesses, will not be generated by noting appreciatively the presence of women as "good examples." This is because unquestioned "malestream" interpretations require readers' obedience to the "master narrative" of "preconstructed kyriarchal discourse of women's marginality and victimization," in the words of Elisabeth Schüssler Fiorenza.[1] Feminist interpreters resist the assumption that Gospel women are all passive followers, silent sufferers, receptive believers, or grateful sinners. While patriarchal social interests are clearly at work in the Gospels to re-inforce the social subordination of women, a counter-force is at work as well. A redemptive and transformative reading requires a willingness to challenge certain versions of "revelation." Feminist exegetes counter-read versions of Gospel interpretation which present silent submission to male authority as the loyalty test of women's faith in Jesus. One interpretive strategy is to suspend the debate about which theological ideas are associated with which texts, and turn instead to the exploration of women's actual experience, as encoded in these first century documents.

---

[1] E. Schüssler Fiorenza, *Jesus. Miriam's Child, Sophia's Prophet: Critical Issues in Feminist Christology* (New York: Continuum, 1994), p. 29.

Luise Schottroff has proposed that the methodology appropriate to this task of transformative reading is socio-historical interpretation. She defines her aim that readers "investigate as concretely as possible the living conditions of classes, races and sexes, and the meaning of faith for the everyday life of the people in the past."[2] Focusing on the social reality of ordinary women challenges the reigning Western model of biblical scholarship which relies on a meta-structure of the history of ideas imposed on biblical texts, an approach which ignores the specific details of the social backdrop of both the first century as well as the particularities of the modern world of the reader.[3]

The present study focuses on questions related to the ethnicity or racial identity of the haemorrhaging woman (Mark 5:25–34). As context for the woman disclosing the intimate details of her medical condition, I also use some legal texts from the Oxyrhynchus Papyri as evidence that women were not silent in public or secretive about their lives when it was a matter of justice. Women in the northwestern part of Egypt (a few days' walk from Galilee) routinely formalized their contracts before magistrates and adjudicated their disputes in court. The stories of their domestic conflicts and economic transactions became part of the public record. Against this social backdrop of women who publicized their private affairs before civic officials, the Gospel account of the haemorrhaging woman making a public record of her story may be less violative of her privacy than women readers assume.

Ethnicity is another element of the social-historical reality behind the healing narratives about women in particular, and about the presentation of women generally in the New Testament writings. The question principal posed for this study concerns the ethnic identity of the haemorrhaging woman. Is she Jewish, or is she gentile, and what effect does that determination have on the interpretation of her healing for a first-century readership?[4]

---

[2] L. Schottroff, "Working for Liberation: A Change of Perspective in New Testament Scholarship," in F. F. Segovia and M. A. Tolbert (eds.), *Reading from This Place, Vol. 2: Social Location and Biblical Interpretation in Global Perspective* (Minneapolis, MN: Fortress, 1995), pp. 183–98, here p. 184.

[3] Schottroff, "Working for Liberation," p. 185.

[4] The question of racial heritage is one significant for the author, who bears a Jewish surname and Jewish heritage through her father, was raised Roman Catholic, and has belonged to a religious community, the Sisters of Mercy, since 1967. Racial

Historical Interpretation: Sources, Community Setting, Literary Form

How do we account for the evolution of this particular story of the woman with the issue of blood from oral tradition into Gospel text? The process shares the uncertainty of the provenance of Mark's Gospel itself. Was the story remembered by Peter in Rome and handed on to his interpreter Mark, who wrote for the Christian community in that city during the persecution by Nero? Do hints about Christian persecution and the theme of Jesus the martyr argue for a Roman origin of Mark's Gospel prior to 70 C.E.? Even though Mark had not personally witnessed this healing, was he specifically conscious of Roman Christians when he cast the woman's recovery into a sequence of healings packed into the practically breathless, non-stop report of Jesus' public ministry? Was this woman's story aimed at having a specific appeal for Roman Christians, particular for Roman women?

Or is another location for Mark's Gospel viable, such as Syria or Palestine, since the warnings to believers can evoke the Jewish Revolt (66–67 C.E.) in the land of Israel itself? The first chapters in Acts of the Apostles, from Pentecost (2:14) to the Council (15:7), link Peter solidly with the origins of the Church in Jerusalem, without reference to Rome. If John Mark, the missionary in Acts of the Apostles (15:37), is the composer of the first Gospel, then a Palestinian or Syrian provenance is credible.[5]

The uncertainty of the origin of Mark's Gospel affects a reading of the haemorrhaging woman's story. Should we imagine that the original hearers of Mark's account of the miraculous healing story lived in Rome, or in Syria-Palestine? Which would be demographically more likely to have a majority of gentile Christian members?

---

heritage and religious affiliation are separable in theory, but in first-century practice, as well as contemporary consciousness, unambiguous lines cannot always be drawn. The manuscript of this article was completed on October 11, 1998, date of the canonization in Rome of Edith Stein, the Jewish philosopher who died at Auschwicz, also known by the name she took after she converted to Catholicism and became a Carmelite nun, Sister Teresia Benedicta a Cruce.

[5] For a brief review of the bases of arguments for Roman, Palestinian, or Syrian provenance for the composition of Mark, see C. Setzer, *Jewish Responses to Early Christians: History and Polemics, 30 to 150 C.E.* (Minneapolis, MN: Fortress, 1994), p. 196, n. 3, 4. See the discussion of a Palestinian or Syrian setting in S. L. Harris, *The New Testament*, 2nd edn (Mountain View, CA; London; Toronto: Mayfield, 1995), pp. 80–2.

If a Palestinian origin of Mark's Gospel is assumed, does this argue for a predominantly Jewish-Christian audience? I lean toward the qualification that it is impossible to determine the ethnic mix or exact proportion of gentile and Jewish Christians for any of the audiences of the evangelists. Demographically, however, given the minority status of Jews throughout the Mediterranean, it is more likely that by the time the Gospels were composed, that of the Christian communities of the second generation, in general these were largely gentile in origin.

In considering the sources for the haemorrhaging woman's story, we distinguish the oral tradition, which was linked to Jesus' ministry in Galilee and based on the testimony of persons who witnessed the healing, perhaps extended family members or neighbours of the haemorrhaging woman. But thirty or forty years after the healing event itself, what community interests and social realities were influencing the way Mark cast the narrative? Was it a community of predominantly Jewish Christians which outnumbered gentile converts? Or was the ethnic balance just the reverse, with Christians of gentile origin outnumbering the first-generation Christians of Jewish heritage? Majority of numbers is not necessarily the equivalent of social power, so we might press further to ask which voices were the most compelling in shaping Mark's response, and these could belong to an influential social minority.

Mark fuses two stories: one, the woman with the issue of blood, and the other, the twelve year old daughter of Jairus. The fusion survives in successive redactions (Matt. 9:18–26; Luke 8:40–56). Should the stories be analysed separately, or are readers to understand them as a single pericope entitled "two women cured" as a weaving so tight it cannot be unravelled, since the texts interpret each other?[6] Doubling or pairing of characters is a compositional convention among biblical writers, and Dominic Crossan notes that Mark relies on such pairing. The hermeneutical fusion is akin to the more elaborate use of doubling by Luke in his account of the vision Saul had of Jesus on the road to Damascus (Acts 9:3–8), paired with the corresponding vision Ananias had of Jesus directing the elder to receive Saul once he arrives in the city (Acts 9:10–16).

---

[6] J. D. Crossan, *The Historical Jesus: The Life of a Mediterranean Jewish Peasant* (New York: HarperCollins, 1991), p. 312.

There is little doubt that the stories of the haemorrhaging woman and of Jairus' daughter are separable as literary units; they were most likely historical distinct events. Nevertheless, Mark and his redactors retain the geographical contiguity and chronological overlap for these encounters of women with the restorative life-force of Jesus. Mark's compositional device of pairing the two women focuses the hearer/reader's attention on the fact that the power of Jesus benefits women. These particular stories summon women in the congregation to identify with them.

Historical Interpretation: Women's Ethnic and Economic Status

On what basis would Christian women feel kinship with the double tragedy of a chronically ill woman and a deceased adolescent girl? And which women in the evangelist's community are we designating? Christian women of Jewish ethnicity? Christian women of gentile origin? The child has a father, Jairus, who is noteworthy enough to be named as one of the rulers or leaders of the synagogue. These details make evident the young daughter's Jewish religion and ethnic heritage. The details also suggest the respected social level of her family, perhaps also its economic status, since a large group of mourners and musicians have gathered for the expected funeral (5:38–39).

By contrast, the haemorrhaging woman's economic status is opaque and must be gleaned first from hints and fragments in Mark, then by considering additions to the Markan version by Luke,[7] while noting the omissions in the Matthean redaction.[8] This woman's story is

---

[7] Luke's redaction specifies the girl as an only child, or, in contrast to "my son, my only child" (Luke 9:38) healed after the transfiguration, Luke says "only daughter" (*thugater monogenes*, Luke 8:42). It modifies the criticism of doctors by reducing the woman's quest to simply the fact that "she could not be healed by any one" (Luke 8:43). It omits the prior knowledge the woman had about Jesus through reports about him, and omits any reference to her inner thoughts, leaving out the Markan interior monologue, "If I touch even his garments I shall be made well" (Mark 5:28). Luke alone singles out Peter as the disciple who says it is impossible to tell who touched him because of the crowd. The blessing of Jesus in Luke repeats Mark's "Daughter, your faith has made you well; go in peace" (Mark 5:34, Luke 8:48), but omits Mark's final clause, a reference to her illness, "and be healed of your disease" (*mastigos*, Mark 5:34).

[8] Matthew is the most highly edited version of the woman's role and of Jesus' posture. Matthew omits Mark's criticism of the medical profession and only says the woman suffered from a haemorrhage for twelve years and comes up behind Jesus. He retains Mark's interior monologue in direct discourse, "If I only touch

unique in Gospel healing stories, in one instance, because of its gynae-cological focus. However, that medical category says little about her individually, except that she is not old, and not so sick that she is an invalid. She must have had enough money at one time to place herself under the care of "many physicians" (*hupo pollon iatron*, 5:26). A further aspect of her tragedy is her economic failure combined with the regression of her health. "She spent all that she had but had grown worse instead of better" (5:26). What about her religion and her ethnic heritage? Are we to assume that both she and the daughter of Jairus share Jewish tradition simply because the women's stories occupy the same compositional space, as though they lived almost next door to each other in Mark's imagination?

Historical Interpretation: Women's Legal Status

Besides the gynaecological focus, another unique aspect of the haemor-rhaging woman's story is the publication of the painful secret of her serious medical condition, and the disclosure of both her treatment history and her financial woes. The seemingly forcible disclosure by Jesus elicits sympathy for the woman's embarrassment. "But the woman, knowing what had been done to her, came in fear and trembling and fell down before him, and told him the whole truth" (5:33).

One fascinating aspect of legal documents of the first century is that we know quite a few details of "the whole truth" of several women. A number of documents from the Oxyrhynchus Papyri record the fact that Mediterranean women's private lives were routinely brought to magistrates, and their stories publicly disclosed in official juridical records. In the context of this discussion of the haemor-rhaging woman, two documents from the period of the composition of the New Testament illustrate disclosure of women's lives analo-gous in intimacy to that of the haemorrhaging woman.

The first is a contract of apprenticeship (66 c.e.) in which a mother, Taseus, hands over (*egdedosthai*)[9] her minor son Heraclas to a weaver,

---

his garment I shall be made well" (Mark 5:28; Matt 9:21). Matthew leaves out the queries of Jesus, and the interchange between Jesus and the woman. Here, she has no story to tell, and only receives healing after Jesus blesses her, "Take heart, daugh-ter; your faith has made you well" (Matt. 9:22). Her healing is thus not a result of her seizing it for herself, but of a magisterial act of Jesus, who grants it to her.

[9] P. Oxy. 2971, line 5. See *The Oxyrhynchus Papyri*, Vol. XLI, ed. with transla-

Seuthes, for a period of two years and six months. Heraclas will serve as apprentice to Seuthes, learning the trade. In return, Heraclos will be maintained by Seuthes, who will also pay any taxes owed on the boy for the apprenticeship period. The boy can choose to live on his own, and maintain himself; if this is the case, Seuthes is to pay him five silver drachmas each month.[10] If Heraclas takes extra time off, besides permitted holidays, he is to make up the time to Seuthes, or pay a penalty of a drachma per day. The penalty to Taseus, if she withdraws her son from the apprenticeship before expiration of the contractual period, is a fine of one hundred silver drachmas to the state. Correspondingly, if Seuthes does not teach the boy the skill of weaving, he must pay a like fine.

The poignancy of Taseus' situation is suggested by a reference to her son, "Heraclas, son of Apollo," but the formalities of the contract are a public statement that her guardian (*kyrios*) is her brother. This implies that her husband is either dead or absent, and possibly also indicates that her father is dead. Since her brother—either older or younger—is serving as her guardian, it makes public her vulnerability and social marginality. There are neither older male relatives from her husband's family nor from her own father's family able or willing to act in this guardianship role. The official documents from the Oxyrhynchus Papyri of the Roman period indicate that women required male guardianship from a relative to initiate legal transactions. The contracting of her minor son into apprenticeship, with the guarantee that Heraclas will be housed and fed, implies that Taseus cannot support her son herself, and that the son must learn a trade immediately if he is to survive. Such a contract expresses a mother's economic desperation.

A second example of disclosure is a declaration of manumission from 86 C.E., in which a woman slave-owner, Aline, daughter of Komon, sets free her slave Euphrosyne.[11] The record states the birth record of Euphrosyne. She is "home-bred from the female slave Demetrous" (*oikogene*) and thus Euphrosyne's paternity is either unknown or unstated.[12] It is possible that Euphrosyne is her half-sister, if it

---

tions and notes by G. M. Browne, R. A. Coles, J. R. Rea, J. C. Shelton, E. G. Turner (Greco-Roman Memoirs, No. 57; London: Egypt Exploration Society, 1972).

[10] P. Oxy. 2971, lines 25–6.
[11] P. Oxy. 2843. *The Oxyrhynchus Papyri*, Vol. XXXVIII.
[12] P. Oxy. 2843, line 14.

was Aline's father who "home-bred" Demetrous; if it was a brother
or male relative who "home-bred" Demetrous, Aline may regard
Euphrosyne as more than a slave. Lack of a paternal name, however, designates Euphrosyne's legal status, social class and economic
powerlessness.

Aline's guardian is her own son "Komon the son of Mnesitheus,
son of Petesouchus," which implies an honourable paternal lineage.
The honour encodes a tragedy. Neither Aline's father nor her husband is able to act as her guardian. A man of the same city, Theon
"son of Dionysius, son of Leon and of Isione" is willing to pay Aline
a large sum of money, the equivalent of eight hundred drachmas of
imperial silver coin, as ransom price for Euphrosyne. Theon's
patronymic and economic resources convey his status as a free man,
who, at 43, is several years older than the 35 year old freed-woman.

Complex motives for the manumission can be suggested. The
widow Aline exercises her power to liberate Euphrosyne who, as
daughter of the slave-woman Demetrous, possibly grew up alongside
her as though she were a sister. On the other hand, there is economic advantage to Aline if she commands a high price for her
slave from Theon, a man who can afford to buy Euphrosyne's freedom. However, the document is not a contract of sale in which
Theon purchases Euphrosyne as a slave, so it is possible he intends
to marry her. The manumission ransom paid to Aline is then analogous to a marriage price which would have been paid by the bridegroom to the father of Euphrosyne had she been a free woman.

The relational details of Aline's family history are recorded in such
a document, as well as the class status of women in relation to each
other. Theon pays the ransom price to Aline as owner (*despoditi*)
because Euphrosyne is her property.[13] The "ransom" re-imburses Aline
for the market value of her slave as it re-defines the slave's new status as freed-woman. The "whole truth" of the manumission necessarily states Euphrosyne's humiliation. She is "home-bred" of a
slave-mother in Aline's household. At the same time, the legal doc-
umentation certifies her new status as liberated woman.

These two examples show that the procedural form of contracts
identified the parties to an agreement by their family history. In
addition, the full text of the manumission indicates that parties could

---

[13] P. Oxy. 2843, line 16.

be identified not only by class, but by physical characteristics, such as age, scars, colour of hair or complexion, and shape of face. Such a legal convention necessarily publicized the details of a family's marital history and their present economic interests.

Summary of Historical Issues

Mark's focus on female characters serves a reciprocal theological effect. As his christology and soteriology are refined by showing Jesus as the healer of women, so is the representation of women legitimated by their healing and their presence made visible and, in the case of the haemorrhaging woman, her autobiography memorialized as proclamation of the power of Jesus as she has experienced it. The inter-relation of gender and ethnicity is crucial. It orients the female reader to identify with the healing and re-construct the story as access to God through her ethnic identity, whether Jewish or gentile.

A feminist focus on the woman's experience affirms Jesus' power as a wonder-worker, though this approach does not analyse the story for theological assertions about christology or soteriology. A discussion of each text's source and redaction history is placed at the service of the socio-historical question concerning her ethnicity.[14] The central refrain of this study is a query about the racial designation of the haemorrhaging woman and what impact the feminist reader's assumptions about her ethnicity have on the story's interpretation, both for the first-century audience and for women today.

When the haemorrhaging woman achieves her healing, she experiences a transformation which is more than physical: she acquires a public voice. The voice is "official" by analogy with the voices of

---

[14] For analysis of historicity, redaction, and theology of each healing story, see R. Latourelle, *The Miracles of Jesus and the Theology of Miracles* (transl.). M. J. O'Connell; New York, Mahwah, N.J.: Paulist, 1988), pp. 128–32 (haemorrhaging woman). For an alternative discussion based on the same method, see J. P. Meier, *A Marginal Jew. Re-thinking the Historical Jesus. Vol. 2: Mentor, Message and Miracles* (Anchor Bible Reference Library; New York: Doubleday, 1994), pp. 708–10 (haemorrhaging woman). For a more diffuse treatment based on arrangement of the healing stories according to synchronic, diachronic, and functionalist divisions for motif, theme, genre and symbol, see G. Theissen, *Miracle Stories of the Early Christian Tradition* (transl. F. McDonagh; Philadelphia, PA: Fortress, 1983. German edition originally published in 1974). For historical context, see W. Cotter, *The Miracles in Greco-Roman Antiquity: A Source Book* (London and New York: Routledge, 1998).

women in the Oxyrhynchus Papyri who enter into contracts or give testimony before a magistrate in seeking redress of injustice they have suffered. She no longer speaks in private to doctors about her illness, but in public to the crowds about her healing. Gender and ethnicity of this proclaimer are categories which excavate the story in two ways. Ethnicity—whatever it is assumed to be—evokes identification with the healed woman, and simultaneously structures the interpretation of what her healing means for her position in her social world. Readers understand the significance of the woman's transformative encounter with Jesus through the lens of their own social situation determined not only by gender but also by their national origin, culture and ethnic heritage.

The Jewish Reading and Its Implications

In recent years, feminist interpreters, as well as New Testament exegetes generally, have shared the assumption that the haemorrhaging woman is Jewish. As an adult woman, she is paired with the young Jewish girl, the daughter of Jairus the synagogue leader, who falls ill. The commentaries seem to assume the woman is Jewish "by association" with Jesus and with the story of Jairus' daughter. Her Jewish ethnicity is also taken for granted because of her association with Jesus, a presupposition re-inforced by a contrast with the decidedly non-Jewish, Syrophoenician mother who begged Jesus to cast a demon out of her daughter (7:24–30). Scholars' identification of her Jewish heritage reflects an effort to take seriously the Jewish milieu and religious tradition of the historical Jesus. Commentaries and annotated Bibles routinely cite intra-textual sources from Hebrew Scripture as explanation of the social and religious status of the haemorrhaging woman, particularly passages from Leviticus, which supposedly provide the legislation and cultural backdrop for understanding the social isolation she felt.

One editor, representative among many examples, defines her illness as inseparably linked with her Jewish ethnicity: "Hemorrhages, an unusual menstrual flow producing a state of ritual impurity that entailed social restriction or exclusion (Lev. 12:1–8; 15:19–30).[15] The

---

[15] See note under Mark 5:25 in *The HarperCollins Study Bible, New Revised Standard Version* (San Francisco and New York: HarperCollins, 1989), p. 1926.

main line of interpretation requires her to be Jewish. Diana Culbertson assumes the woman was "forbidden" to touch the body of Jesus, and so touched his cloak instead.[16] Joanna Dewey assumes the religious homogeneity of this narrative. It is a Jewish crowd, with a shared culture and religious traditions. Jesus compromises his ritual purity by initiating the touch and taking the hand of Jairus' daughter, a child said to be dead. The bleeding woman seizes the moment and breaks out of her conventional submissive role which bound her to directives from a series of physicians. Here, she takes the initiative herself.[17]

In her ground-breaking analysis of Jesus' erotic power and relational vulnerability as a source of healing, Rita Nakashima Brock notes that "she bleeds endlessly and is perpetually polluting." She describes the woman's "courage to violate a patriarchal social taboo. Though an unclean woman, she touches Jesus in public . . . Her courage in violating a taboo has made her whole."[18]

Sharon Ringe notes that, in contrast to the daughter of Jairus, surrounded by a supportive family, the woman with a haemorrhage may or may not have a household, or a husband; the story says nothing about her familial circumstances.[19] Joanna Dewey notes that she has no status, in contrast to the derivative status of the daughter of the synagogue leader. "She is destitute and apparently without male kin to protect her."[20] Hisako Kinukawa asserts: "Jesus' radical actions of acceptance and healing broke through the distinction of pure and impure and declared that all are welcome in God's reign. We can also detect in the Gospel texts that women took initiative to cross over the religious impurity laws and create a stage for Jesus to become truly a boundary breaker."[21]

---

[16] D. Culbertson, *The Poetics of Revelation: Recognition and the Narrative Tradition* (Studies in American Biblical Hermeneutics, 4; Macon, GA: Mercer University Press, 1989), p. 151.

[17] J. Dewey, "The Gospel of Mark," in E. Schüssler Fiorenza (ed.), *Searching the Scriptures, Vol. 2: A Feminist Commentary* (New York: Crossroad, 1994), pp. 470–509, here p. 481.

[18] R. Nakashima Brock, *Journeys by Heart: A Christology of Erotic Power* (New York: Crossroad, 1988), pp. 83–4.

[19] Sh. H. Ringe, *Luke* (Louisville, KY: Westminster John Knox, 1995), p. 120.

[20] J. Dewey, "Mark," pp. 481–2.

[21] H. Kinukawa, "Purity-Impurity," in L. M. Russell and J. S. Clarkson (eds.), *Dictionary of Feminist Theologies* (Louisville, KY: Westminster John Knox, 1996), pp. 232–3.

The assumption of some Christian commentators seems to be that impurity/uncleanness is a moral designation, rather than a ritual category. The woman is "rescued" by Jesus from the restrictions of Judaism which represses women. After touching Jesus, the woman reclaims her health, her purity, her honour, and her ability to move freely in Jewish society which, without the healing of Jesus, would otherwise have left her abandoned.

Cautions Against Anti-Judaic Readings of the Haemorrhaging Woman's Story

The assumption that the woman is Jewish is part of a paradigm in which the Jewishness of Jesus is affirmed. Nevertheless, the affirmation is not benign. To suffer a continual haemorrhage as a Jewish woman, so goes the well-intentioned Christian view, is to suffer rejection, isolation, and social exclusion from other Jews because of a constant state of being unclean. When Jesus exercises his healing power, he resists the categorization of women within the religious culture of traditional Judaism.

According to the predominant interpretation, Jesus, the Jewish male, endures the touch of an unclean woman, rendering him ritually unclean. He is compassionate and tolerant, in contrast to the legalistic restrictions on this abnormally menstruating woman, which prevents her from being available for sexual relations with a man if she is betrothed, or a husband having relations with her. Some exegetes who apply social-science paradigms to the Bible rely on Mary Douglas' model of clean vs. unclean and purity vs. pollution.[22] Despite the appeal of the model as a tool of social analysis, this grid imposes a cognitive tension upon any healing story about women. The grid binds the text, such as the haemorrhaging woman's story, onto a procrustean bed. The purity-impurity code condemns the story to the interpretive fate of requiring a liberating Jesus to stand on the side of "purity," while the unliberating Old Testament legal code of "pollution" stands on the other.

Focus on the woman's Jewish ethnicity by Christian interpreters almost inevitably leads to a caricature of Judaism. It also re-inforces,

---

[22] M. Douglas, *Purity and Danger: An Analysis of the Concepts of Pollution and Taboo* (London: Routledge & Kegan Paul, 1966).

despite all expressions of tolerance and good will, an anti-Jewish reading because it implicates Jesus as healer in a rejectionist stance toward his own tradition.[23]

Christian interpreters may propose that Jesus was a proto-feminist and supportive of women, in contrast to the legalism, purity codes and patriarchalism of Jewish tradition. When the "master discourse" governing homiletics takes a christological focus, it can incorporate an anti-Judaic edge. For instance, so they argue, Jesus proves by his compassionate actions that he transcends biblical prescriptions referring to impurity of menstruants. His compassion transcends purity boundaries imposed by Judaism. Jesus proves he transcends the ethnocentric pre-occupation of his religion with ritual purity.[24]

The accumulation of this brand of homiletics supports a theological conclusion that Christianity is superior to Judaism in the sense of "fulfilment," and mirrors a super-sessionist impulse which is heir to a "history of ideas" approach to biblical interpretation. For the last twenty years, Jewish feminists, such as Judith Plaskow, Susannah Heschel and Amy-Jill Levine, have pointed out the anti-Semitism inherent in such an approach.[25]

It is essential for a socio-historical approach, and for an accurate depiction of the social milieu of the Gospels, that exegetes acknowledge the complex religious pluralism expressed by regional, theological and political interests in what is more accurately termed first

---

[23] For more extensive discussion, see R. A. Guelich, "Anti-Semitism and/or Anti-Judaism in Mark," in C. A. Evans and D. A. Hagner (eds.), *Anti-Semitism and Early Christianity: Issues of Polemic and Faith* (Minneapolis, MN: Fortress, 1993), pp. 80–101.

[24] An earlier draft of this study was presented on March 3, 1998, at a conference "Biblical Scholars' Workshop for Christian Preachers and Teachers: Being Fundamentally True to Jesus—Avoiding Anti-Judaic Preaching," sponsored by The National Conference of Community and Justice, in San Jose, California, U.S.A. I am grateful for responses from conference organizer Ms. Lillian Silberstein and from participants Rabbi Harry Manhoff, Dr. Anthony Petrotta, Dr. Bruce Bramlett, Dr. Andrew Kille, and Dr. Glenn Earley.

[25] J. Plaskow, "Christian Feminism and Anti-Judaism," *Cross Currents* 33 (1978), pp. 306–9; S. Heschel, "Anti-Judaism in Christian Feminist Theology," *Tikkun* 5 (May–June, 1990), pp. 25–8, 95–7. See the response of E. Schüssler Fiorenza to J. Plaskow, "The Power of Naming: Jesus, Woman and Christian Anti-Judaism," in *Jesus. Miriam's Child, Sophia's Prophet* (New York: Continuum, *1994*), pp. 67–96. Also J. Plaskow, "Anti-Judaism in Feminist Christian Interpretation," in E. Schüssler Fiorenza (ed.), *Searching the Scriptures, Vol. 1: A Feminist Introduction* (New York: Crossroad, 1993), pp. 117–29. For an accessible popular treatment of corresponding and contrasting Jewish and Christian views on Scripture, Jesus and God, see W. Harrelson and R. M. Falk, *Jews and Christians: A Troubled Family* (Nashville, TN: Abingdon, 1991).

century "Judaisms." In healing various women, Jesus was not opposed to Judaism or "the law" as though he were no longer a Jew. Rather, the record of the Gospels indicates that he and the communities of the evangelists were involved in vigorous intra-Jewish theological controversies over interpretation and application of prescriptions for religious observance. If readings of the haemorrhaging woman's healing replay the assumption that she is Jewish, then Christian interpreters also need to educate themselves about the meaning of ritual purity as seen both from a Jewish perspective and against the cross-cultural setting of the first century.

Mary Rose D'Angelo provides a philological survey which reviews a good number of unfamiliar Greek and Latin texts referring to menstruation.[26] It was not just a Jewish view that menstruation, ejaculation and sexual intercourse involved pollution and the need for purification, especially in relation to worship. Greek, Roman, and Jewish texts all made references to pollution in association with menstruation. In Greek, as well as Jewish, codes women's menstruation was a source of pollution, for herself and for men who had intercourse with her during her period. Considering the relation of the haemorrhaging woman's story and that of Jairus' daughter, she proposes:

> ...for an ancient audience, there may have been an inherent connection or perhaps symmetry between the two stories in Mark 5:21–43. The two stories belong together because they record healings/wonders that offset two opposing dangers to the female body. The woman with the flow of blood for twelve years suffers a womb that is inappropriately open. The twelve-year-old girl may well represent the young girl who dies because her womb is closed; at twelve, she is just at the age for marriage in Roman law.[27]

D'Angelo proposes that the narrative be re-named "the woman who healed herself." Commentary should emphasize a spirituality of shared power and a christology in which persons experience power by participation with the work of Jesus.

---

[26] M. R. D'Angelo, "Gender and Power in the Gospel of Mark: The Daughter of Jairus and the Woman with the Flow of Blood," in J. C. Cavadini (ed.), *Aspects of the Miraculous in Early Judaism and Christianity* (Notre Dame, IN, and London: University of Notre Dame Press, forthcoming).

[27] D'Angelo, "Gender and Power," p. 11 of the unpublished manuscript. See also "Gender and Power in the Gospel of Mark: The Daughter of Jairus and the Woman with the Flow of Blood (Mark 5:21–43). Paper presented at the Annual Meeting of the American Academy of Religion/Society of Biblical Literature, Orlando, FL, November 24, 1998.

Jewish Perspectives on Niddah

In parsing the prescriptions of Lev. 15:19–33, Rachel Biale distinguishes the state of *niddah* (normal menstrual flow) from *zavah* (abnormal vaginal bleeding) and both of these from bleeding originating in the bladder or vaginal walls, which, like the bleeding from any wound, is not associated with ritual uncleanness.[28] From a medical point of view, uncleanness may not be defining the haemorrhaging woman's status at all. Men, too, had both normal emissions (as in sexual intercourse) and abnormal ones (as from infection or disease), both of which rendered men ritually unclean for either one day (for normal) or for seven days (for abnormal). The ritual prescriptions around uncleanness were originally associated with the Temple cult, to distinguish those who could enter the precincts from those who had to wait. "The state of impurity in and of itself is no transgression, only approaching the Temple in such a state is . . . The state of impurity in general, and the state of the *niddah* in particular, are not associated with sinfulness or condemnation in Lev. 15."[29]

The intimacy of marriage defined periods of separation between spouses based on the woman's menstrual cycle, but the prescriptions regarding men's contact with the woman's bedding and furniture referred to the area bounded by their shared dwelling. According to Rachel Biale,

> . . . the impurity of a *niddah* retained its legal significance for her intimate relationship with her husband, but lost its importance in the arena of the woman's contact with other members of her family and with strangers. However, while the Halakhah requires segregation of the *niddah* only in her own home and mostly "in the bedroom," many communities preserved a significant measure of segregation in public life as well. Customs of segregation and exclusion prevailed particularly in the realm of the synagogue worship, perhaps because the synagogue was perceived as a symbolic substitute for the Temple.[30]

---

[28] R. Biale, *Women and Jewish Law: An Exploration of Women's Issues in Halakhic Sources* (New York: Schocken Books, 1984), especially "Niddah," pp. 147–74. See the generally favourable commentary on R. Biale's presentation, in T. Ilan, *Jewish Women in Greco-Roman Palestine: An Inquiry into Image and Status* (Tübingen: Mohr Siebeck, 1995), pp. 16–17.

[29] Biale, "*Women and Jewish Law*," p. 154. She suggests that association of uncleanness with immorality or sin is made in texts much later than Lev. 15, i.e. Ezek. 36:17, and Ezra 9:10–11, where "impurity" is used analogously to symbolize land and peoples whose social customs would pollute the ethics of the Israelites in exile if they allowed themselves to become culturally assimilated.

[30] Biale, "*Women and Jewish Law*," p. 148.

Implications for Jesus

The historical fact is that Jesus, as a Jewish male, would also have entered and exited regularly from periods of ritual uncleanness, quite apart from the abstentions associated with a marital relationship. According to the catalogue of E. P. Sanders, if Jesus experienced bodily discharges, helped neighbours remove dead animals from their fields, or had physical contact with the dead in the course of comforting grieving relatives and friends, he would have become unclean at various times. Depending on the strictness of interpretation given to his contact with furniture which his mother and female relatives used when they were menstruants, he could contract secondary impurity within his family environs.[31] It is unknown whether he observed a system of guarding his association with Jewish women outside his own home or family. It is not clear whether it would have included, for example, his mother's cousin Elizabeth within Zachary's household, especially in light of the stricter observance by a family with priestly lineage.

The purification normally would involve ritual bathing and waiting for a day to remove his impurity. Did Jesus' contact with women disciples on the road (Luke 8:2–3), or in their house, as with Martha and Mary, or sitting in the same space as Mary (Luke 10:38–42) place him at risk of contracting ritual impurity? In Jesus the Galilean's style of observance, were there any social or religious inconveniences for him, and would those have been greater had he been a Judean Jew? Was there any assumption that Jesus needed or sought purification after his contact with unrelated women outside his immediate family, or with relatives of his disciples, as with Simon Peter's mother-in-law (Mark 1:29–31), or with the Samaritan woman at a place such as a well used by women (John 4:9)?

Left unconsidered is the question of the haemorrhaging woman's spouse and his ethnicity. If she is married to a gentile, his culture mandates no restrictions on when he may or may not expect sexual relations. This raises the matter of the God-fearers. If a gentile man married a Jewish woman, and was sympathetic to Judaism, did this entail observance of Jewish purity codes in relation to his wife?

---

[31] See the discussion of E. P. Sanders, "Biblical Purity Laws," in *Jewish Law from Jesus to the Mishnah: Five Studies* (London: SCM; Philadelphia, PA: Trinity Press International, 1990), pp. 134–51.

Did the conservative faction of Jewish-Christians, associated with James in Jerusalem, advocate observance not only of *kashrut*, but of purity codes within marriage (Gal. 2:12)? After all these queries, depending on the nature of the woman's bleeding, she may not have been ritually unclean at all, for example, if she was bleeding from a wound, and her flow was not a menstrual discharge.

The supposition that Jesus contracted impurity from a bleeding woman's touch depends upon a world view made cohesive by assuming that everyone in the story of the haemorrhaging woman is Jewish—Jesus, the woman, the entire crowd, the disciples, the witnesses—and all observe every aspect of the levitical prescriptions in a homogenous way. I suggest, alternatively, that we have no assurance, and no reason to insist that the woman with the issue of blood was Jewish. The text does not require her to be, but the commentaries, notes in various editions of the Bible, and homiletic tradition do. An assumption about the woman's ethnicity determines the paradigm within which we read the story of her healing.

Alternative: Reading the Haemorrhaging Woman as Gentile

While the Jewish identity of the daughter and her father Jairus is clear, since he is the leader of the synagogue, the haemorrhaging woman's religious ethnic or racial membership is not. The alternative possibility, that she is non-Jewish, could also be true. If she is gentile, the social tragedy the story dramatizes is more generically the woman's childlessness for twelve years and therefore the physiological urgency to stop the bleeding which interrupts conception and pregnancy. The economic disaster is her impoverishment, with nothing to show for her investment and effort. As for marital status, she shares the blurry category that most women in the Gospel narratives occupy, namely that of "the woman who appears without companion or advocate."[32]

If the haemorrhaging woman is gentile, levitical purity laws (Lev. 15:19–30) do not apply to her, though they may to Jesus.

Jewish identity is attributed to the woman by association with the crowd "on the other side," i.e. the western shore of the sea of Galilee,

---

[32] Ringe, *Luke*, p. 123.

where people press around Jesus. But there is no indication that the crowd is ethnically homogenous. Jesus' query, "Who touched my clothes? (5:30) is countered by his Jewish disciples who insist it is impossible to identify not only the gender, age or economic status of the toucher, but his or her ethnicity and religion. Once Jesus calls her out of anonymity, generic determiners of social location, gender, age, economic class, health and marital status identify her. Jesus compels her to speak the truth, and this generates an unaccustomed role: she acts as subject and authors her own story. Once she comes forward, the audience understands that she is of child-bearing age, has a passion to be healed, has the economic means to pursue her passion, and has suffered failure in her effort because she has grown worse, not better. She had spent her money on physicians, probably mostly gentile, who might have followed either the spiritual healing practices of dream consultation according to the Asclepian cult at a wide-ranging circuit of shrine-spas around the Mediterranean, or were physicians in the medical tradition of the cult who prescribed herbal remedies or performed surgery.[33]

Some conclusions which do not depend on her ethnicity, but rather her gender, include the fact that she has not been able to become pregnant, and seems to still be in her child-bearing years, and that she had sufficient wealth to spend it all on physicians. Lacking any more financial resources, "she had become part of the population whose lack of financial resources made them dependent on itinerant healers when the techniques of folk medicine routinely practised in the family were not effective."[34] Is her social marginalization then the result of her gentile ethnicity within a region where Jews are the demographic majority?

When the emphasis shifts from pre-occupation with Jewish law and whether Jesus and the woman observe it, the horizon for the woman's transformation is enlarged. Mitzi Minor draws attention to the detail of the woman's hesitation at self-disclosure, and distinguishes the awe of the woman in Mark from the account in Luke. "In Luke's story the woman trembled and fell before Jesus when she realized she was not hidden (Luke 8:47). Mark's woman, however, knew what

---

[33] See S. Kerrigan, *The Impact of the Asclepius Cult on the Christian Healing Tradition*, (Ph.D. Diss.; Donaldson, IN: Graduate Theological Foundation, 1997).

[34] Ringe, *Luke*, p. 125.

had happened to her body and as a result of that knowledge feared and trembled."[35] Is her ethnicity one reason she is afraid of coming forward to tell her story? If she is Jewish, the fear might be shame at anticipating the revelation that she has broken the social codes of her own culture. If she is gentile, her anonymity in the protective crush of a mostly-Jewish crowd gets short-circuited, exposing her as a non-Jew before a Jewish man and his male disciples. With gentile identity, and suspension of the *niddah* question, the emphasis shifts to her role as a witness who acknowledges the restorative power of Jesus. Her journey to the source of transformation finds an analogue in Matthew's presentation of the gentile wise men who left their territory in search of the promised child (Matt. 2:1–2, 11).

The thought, "If I but touch but his clothes" (Mark 5:28) is linked biblically and thematically with gentiles seeking affiliation with Jews. "Thus says the Lord of hosts: In those days ten men from nations of every language shall take hold of a Jew, grasping his garment and saying, 'Let us go with you, for we have heard that God is with you'" (Zech. 8:23). In an earlier passage, Mark emphasizes the diversity of the population, not its homogeneity, for the crowd pressing Jesus on all sides for healing is ethnically mixed, coming not only from the land of Israel, but Idumea, beyond the Jordan, and the region around Tyre and Sidon (Mark 3:10). Luke evokes the same geographical and ethnic diversity in 6:19 at the Sermon on the Plain, in the crowd seeking healing. In Acts 19:11–12, the crowd in the hall of Tyrannus and the residents of the city of Ephesus include both Jews and gentiles. They bring pieces of cloth to touch Paul, as though he were a holy site or a healing-emanating force whose power can be transferred via the medium of an object which has touched him, a surrogate contact with his body.

Corresponding to the action of Jesus when he touches the sick is the taking hold of Jesus' garments by the sick woman. In his discussion of the ritual of laying on of hands and touching the sick, David Daube distinguishes Jesus' action as healer who takes the hand of Jairus' daughter and lifts her up. He offers another contrast which depends on the initiative of the sick person: a cure can be effected by a person in need who touches the miracle worker or something

---

[35] M. Minor, *The Spirituality of Mark: Responding to God* (Louisville, KY: Westminster John Knox, 1996), p. 47.

belonging to him.[36] The woman with the issue of blood "lays hands" on the clothing of Jesus. Daube does not comment whether it was gentile or Jewish practice for a petitioner to touch the garments of a wonder-worker.

The woman's gentile ethnicity is underlined by Jesus' confirmation of her healing and her new socio-religious status as "daughter" (Mark 5:34). The vocative acknowledges that she is no longer an anonymous stranger, but she has a place of respect in the family, analogous to the daughter of the synagogue official. She is no longer a social or religious outsider. The relationship does not flow from Jesus assuming the role of parent. Being called "daughter" in this context is not merely a pastoral expression of care, or a diminutive which subordinates her to the status of fearful child in relation to Jesus as powerful male healer. Rather, in the social context, she is dignified by an acknowledgment that she is a member of the household of the faith; she has been publicly acknowledged and adopted as "daughter" as a badge of honour.

Her testimony belongs to the family as part of its precious heritage of remembering the healing power of Jesus. As Karen Jo Torjesen notes, "The earliest Christians conceived of themselves explicitly as an alternative family or household. The Gospels portray the bonds among the followers of Jesus as familial, superseding even biological bonds."[37] The vocative here has a distinct application to the woman as gentile-daughter; it also has resonance with the dignifying of a Jewish woman as "daughter of Abraham" (cf. the bent-over woman in Luke 13:16) and with the honoured priestly ancestry of Elizabeth, referred to as "from the daughters of Aaron" (Luke 1:5).

The hermeneutical benefits of her gentile identity may outweigh the interpretive fruit of assuming she is Jewish. If gentile, we focus on her human needs which ally her with all women. She is ill; neither Jewish priests nor Asclepian oracles have provided a cure. It is not necessary to describe the sense of betrayal by a sequence of male practitioners of the medical arts, only that she has gotten worse, not

[36] D. Daube, *The New Testament and Rabbinic Judaism* (London: University of London, School of Oriental and African Studies, 1956; repr. Peabody, MA: Hendrickson, pp. 234–5.

[37] K. J. Torjesen, *When Women Were Priests: Women's Leadership in the Early Church and the Scandal of Their Subordination in the Rise of Christianity* (San Francisco and New York: HarperCollins, 1993), p. 126.

better as a result of their provisional diagnoses, magisterial experiments, fruitless guesses, expensive remedies and false assurances of hope. She is impoverished and whether her debts have run in shekels or drachmas, she is a woman who once had money, but now it is depleted by her illness.

Jews and gentiles in Mark's community can identify with her physical and economic condition, and with that sense of her desperation. Unlike the daughter of Jairus, she has no one to act as her intermediary. Her social plight characterizes all women in the Mediterranean, whether Roman, Egyptian, Greek, Asian, Canaanite or Israelite. She embodies the anguish of women who are nameless, adrift, in a land bereft of men who can rescue her from her namelessness. The haemorrhaging woman took hold of Jesus' garments, re-capitulating the prophet's vision of a society's greatest desperation, symbolized by hordes of unpartnered, widowed and childless women during the exile: "Seven women shall take hold of one man in that day, saying, 'We will eat our own bread and wear our own clothes; just let us be called by your name; take away our disgrace'" (Isa. 4:1). In Jewish imagination, the haemorrhaging woman who takes hold of Jesus is a particularly apt symbol for women who feel abandoned or alone, or whose family bonds have been shattered by war or suppressed political rebellions.

But how necessary is it for the woman's ethnicity to be Jewish for an interpretation of her transformative healing? If we resist supersessionist readings which rely on the departure of Jesus from Jewish religious codes, what meaning do the allusions to social and religious legislation have in relation to this female character in the Gospel? There is both a particular and a universal aspect to the haemorrhaging woman. She can exemplify the multiple identities of many Christian believers in communities whose bloodlines run along parallel strands of Jewish and gentile ancestry.

There are, in other words, a number of advantages to reading her story as the healing of a gentile woman. The account is then more effective as a community-building message which supports affiliative relations between Jewish and gentile Christians. If it is a gentile woman who touches a Jewish man's cloak, she represents gentiles who acknowledge that the power of Jesus is holy and health-restoring even though it belongs to a person culturally despised. As a gentile woman, her action counters the Mediterranean's pervasive social climate of anti-Judaism which was officially challenged only

rarely.[38] The silence of the text on the question of her ethnicity permits the reader to consider her a gentile. Curiously, the writer of
Mark's Gospel suppressed mention of her ethnicity, which by contrast, he underlines in the case of the daughter of Jairus the synagogue leader. The absence of any clear designation of her ethnicity
allows both Jewish and gentile readers of the haemorrhaging woman's
story to "see her" as either gentile or Jewish.

It may have been the oral tradition which fused the two stories,
or it may have happened when the writer of Mark's Gospel joined
them together. One story concerned a Jewish girl, the other, quite
possibly, was about a gentile woman (Mark 5:21–43). To have a
Jewish-gentile union makes sense in light of the ethnic mix of Mark's
community, whether the community was located in Rome or in
Syria. Whether the woman was originally Jewish, we don't know.
What Mark has done is universalize her, but still he depicts her
actions taking place within a Jewish world. Thus, she is accessible
textually and homiletically to both gentile and Jewish women as a
model of persistence and self-determination in relation to Jesus. In
light of these considerations of her ethnicity, the question of her ritual impurity or purity falls out of prominence. However, the ambiguity
of her ethnic heritage also allows for the possibility that her actions
can be interpreted within a specifically Jewish religious culture.

Conclusion

Why mention women's experience as relevant or significant to the
truth about Jesus, if men's testimony suffices to meet the requirement
for legal witness in first century Mediterranean society? Carla Ricci,
speaking of Luke, presents the paradox, "What need would the evangelist have had, what purpose would it have served, to refer constantly to the presence of women? . . . The androcentric wider culture
in which he wrote would have led him to seek and see his protag-
onists and witnesses in the male disciples."[39] Is the healing story
about the haemorrhaging women merely a superfluous, decorative

---

[38] Josephus' *Contra Apionem* is one attempt to counter first century anti-Judaism.
For an overview of his treatment of women, see T. Ilan, *Jewish Women in Greco-
Roman Palestine*, pp. 29–31.
[39] C. Ricci, *Mary Magdalene and Many Others: Women Who Followed Jesus* (transl. Paul
Burns; Minneapolis, MN: Fortress, 1994), p. 61.

addendum to claims about the benevolent power of Jesus which are adequately attested by males? Why include this story about a woman healed of her gynaecological disorder, when there are enough men healed so that the point of Jesus's healing power is evident enough?

The haemorrhaging woman, whose ethnic heritage is masked, represents both the marginality of women because of their racial identity, and the universality of women's experience of discrimination based on gender and ethnicity. A feminist approach acknowledges the "master discourse" and its focus on the power of Jesus. However, the more fruitful exploration is to identify the transformation of the social status of the haemorrhaging woman. Jesus is a Jewish wonder-worker whose healing power is universal. The ethnicity of women in relation to his Jewishness raises important socio-historical considerations. If the haemorrhaging woman is gentile, the application of Jewish purity codes from Leviticus 15 are not as relevant to the understanding of her transformative encounter. Instead, we note her childlessness, her social marginalization, her economic bankruptcy at the hands of physicians and the compelling power of her story told in public.

A case can be made that religious regulations concerning *niddah* did not apply in social relationships outside marriage, or in public forums in general (other than the Temple). By admitting the possibility that the haemorrhaging woman is gentile, the reading drops numerous complications of an interpretation which too easily feeds Christian contempt for Jewish law as allegedly originating the oppression of women. In this paradigm, Jesus is cast as a proto-feminist male, and the "liberator" of women from Jewish law. In the alternative paradigm, with the woman imagined as gentile, Jesus remains liberator, but the liberation becomes less pre-occupied with contextually mis-informed readings of Jewish religious practices. Instead, the story focuses on the restoration of the woman's fecundity, her emergence from female voicelessness and anonymity, and respect for the power of her witness before both the male disciples and the great crowd, a testimony which confirms their faith in Jesus.

Such a pericope might have represented an affirmation of women who served as missionaries and teachers and in other pastoral roles at the time of Mark. Like the haemorrhaing woman, they had personally experienced the healing power of Jesus; they could recount their autobiographical history in a coherent fashion in public; they expressed emotion, acted and spoke in a human and memorable way; their experience was capable of universal application and understanding by a broad number of persons; and they reached the emotions and fostered faith in their hearers. Mark addressed a community accustomed to functioning within a cross-cultural, multi-lingual world. The haemorrhaging woman of unknown ethnicity who announced her recovery in public was a credible witness to the benevolent power of Jesus the Jewish healer.

The ambiguity of the woman's ethnicity allows greater latitude to the community of interpretation. For Mark and Matthew, the story memorializes a transformation from outsider to insider status, modelled by the woman's approach to Jesus in confidence that he can heal.[40] The haemorrhaging woman dramatizes the truth that the compassion of Jesus in this instance transcends ethnic, linguistic, geographical, economic and religious boundaries.

If we focus on ethnicity as an element of the socio-historical reality of women in the first century, the haemorrhaging woman can still represent both Jewish and gentile converts in the church. But features of her racial heritage and ethnicity will also be acknowledged, revealing a richer repertoire of their significance for women. Timeless aspects of her experience become more compelling when we consider her as either aligned with a racially numerous but oppressed class, or belonging to a victimized minority. She represents, for example, the unpartnered, childless woman who lacks a male advocate or spokesperson. As a chronically ill woman she is at the mercy of a male medical profession and at risk from incompetent treatment because the female body is less valued and understood than the male body. As a woman whose economic resources are depleted, she suffers disempowerment in a patriarchal society. Without a protector or patron, and linked with no land, city, family, father, husband, or son, she belongs to all marginalized women whose vulnerability leaves them prey to physical danger, legal discrimination, social disadvantage and commercial opportunism.

The transformation of the haemorrhaging woman finds expression in public testimony in the street, not private confession to family members at home. Like the women in Luke 8:1–3, her personal experience of Jesus' healing makes her a witness for the evangelical

---

[40] C. Osiek and D. L. Balch, *Families in the New Testament World: Households and House Churches* (Louisville, KY: Westminster John Knox, 1997), p. 128.

mission in ways the male disciples cannot provide, since none of them, according to the Gospels, could testify to their own healing from physical ailments because of a word or touch by Jesus.

From a legal standpoint, the witnessing has a dual reference. It can refer to the woman's status as official narrator of the deeds of Jesus. On the other hand, when the haemorrhaging woman disclosed "the whole truth" of her medical and financial history to the crowd, she may have provided the disclosures that a legal document would have required, had she entered into a formal contract for healing with a medical practitioner, or had she sought redress when a doctor failed to cure her. In the context of legal transactions, the haemorrhaging woman's complaint is appropriately documented and memorialized.

By the time the Gospels were written, in the late first century C.E., the demographic balance between Jewish Christians and gentile Christians had shifted; the communities of Mark, Matthew and Luke were predominantly gentile, with Christians of Jewish ancestry in the minority. The ethnic ambiguity in the case of the haemorrhaging woman both represents and resolves tensions between gentile and Jewish Christians. The evangelists attempted to reconcile a larger gentile membership and a smaller Jewish-Christian population. Ethnicity as much as gender drove the "identity politics" of evangelists who strove to affirm Jewish origins as they sustained a climate of welcome for gentiles into the family of faith.

If the haemorrhaging woman was understood as a gentile, she represented the majority of Mark's hearers. Her alliance with a young Jewish girl, Jairus' daughter, represented a sisterhood among women, no matter what their ethnicity. Their stories were intertwined because they represented the hope of a united community. As a gentile woman healed and a Jewish girl awakened, they witnessed to a healing greater than the healing of any physical ailment: the overcoming of ancient hatreds between ethnic groups, and discrimination based on racial heritage.

JESUS THE WINE-DRINKER: A FRIEND OF WOMEN

SÉAN FREYNE

It is noteworthy, though perhaps predictable, that the role of women in the Jesus movement has received relatively little attention in recent writing, despite the remarkable resurgence of historical Jesus studies in the past decade or so. With the notable exception of Elizabeth Schüssler Fiorenza, feminist scholars have concentrated on literary rather than historical investigations in dealing with the androcentrism of the New Testament writings.[1] The omission is all the more regrettable since many of these studies, including my own, have focused on the social world of Jesus, who appears to have ignored or deliberately set aside the stereotypical social role of women in his context. This article is, therefore, an attempt to redress the imbalance in my own explorations of that social world. Taking a cue from one particular hint in the Gospels, namely the charge that Jesus was a wine-drinker, hitherto unexplored to the best of my knowledge, I seek to open up a larger vista on the issue of women members of the original Jesus movement.

Each of the Synoptic Gospels indicates that women formed part of the permanent retinue of Jesus in Galilee, though Luke is the most explicit (Mark 15:40–41; Matt. 27:55–56; Luke 8:1–3; 23:55). While the Fourth Gospel does not focus on a Galilean ministry except in passing, the intimate relationship between Jesus and Mary Magdalene is a feature of the presentation (John 20:1–2, 11–18). Even more interesting than these reports is the saying of Jesus from the triple tradition which profiles his movement as one in which those who do the will of his Father take on a fictive-kin-relationship with him as mothers, brothers, *and sisters* (Mark 3:31–35; Matt 12:46–50; cf. Luke 8:19–21). The addition of sisters, strangely omitted by Luke, is all the more noteworthy in view of the fact that the response of Jesus is prompted by a report that his mother and brothers (but no mention of sisters) are outside seeking him. That women as well as

---

[1] E. Schüssler Fiorenza, *Jesus. Miriam's Child, Sophia's Prophet: Critical Issues in Feminist Christology* (New York: Crossroads, 1995).

men feature in the orbit of Jesus' activity is clear from other instances
in the Gospels: the woman with the issue of blood, the Syrophoenician
woman, the woman who anointed him for burial; the daughter of
Jairus, the Samaritan woman, the poor widow, all come to mind.
Perhaps even more significant, because of its social implications, is
Jesus' own comment on the purpose of his ministry: "Do not think
that I am come to bring peace upon the earth. I am not come to
bring peace but a sword. For I am come to set a man against his
father and daughter against her mother and daughter-in-law against
her mother-in-law" (Matt. 10:34–36; Luke 12:49–53). Affiliation to
the Jesus movement meant, therefore, a radical re-ordering of the
most basic relationships within a kinship society.

How are we to evaluate this evidence historically and culturally?
While redactional and later community concerns have been identified
by various commentators of these episodes and sayings, and allowing for the fact that the androcentrism of the texts silences the presence of women, the evidence available clearly supports the idea that
from the very beginning the Jesus movement included women as
well as men as permanent members. More significant, therefore, is
our evaluation of this evidence in terms of its socio-religious implications. The Jesus movement was undoubtedly disruptive in social
terms because its value system violated prevailing norms with regard
to property and other areas of life, such as use of violence against
one's enemy, the honour/shame codes of Mediterranean society, and
ritual purity concerns as these are known to us from Jewish sources.[2]
But what was the social impact of the inclusion of women as permanent members of an itinerant movement of renewal? This is a
highly significant, if difficult, question to answer, and yet it is one
that the sources raise, especially the Q saying alluded to above: Matt.
10:34–36/Luke 12:49–53. Once we begin to read the Gospel traditions not as generalized statements of universal significance, but as
implying localized settings to which they are specifically directed,
they resonate in an altogether new way.

The attempt to understand Jesus' attitude towards women within
the setting of first-century Galilean society calls for caution, however, in the light of some recent efforts to portray him as a Cynic-
style philosopher in that setting. In order to provide the proper social

---

[2] G. Theissen, "Jesusbewegung als charismatische Werterevolution," *NTS* 35 (1989),
pp. 343–60.

milieu for such a portrayal, some scholars have, in my view, grossly distorted the picture of Galilean society, making it a cross-roads of Graeco-Roman culture, without any distinctions being drawn between urban and rural contexts, not to speak of the demands which Jewish religious life and practice imposed, even for urban dwellers in Galilee.[3] The questions therefore are: What conceivable circumstances might give rise to a movement that was equally attractive to men and women, and how plausibly can such circumstances be postulated for Galilee of the first century?

A Wine-Drinker and the Associations

One avenue of enquiry that has particular resonances for Galilee, as we shall see, is the charge by Jesus' opponents that he was a glutton and a wine-drinker (Matt. 11:19; Luke 7:33). While in the context this might readily be dismissed as a rhetorically motivated label of disparagement,[4] it does bear further investigation because of its realistic local colouring and possible associations with the cult of the wine-god, as we shall argue. At least it raises the question as to how outsiders might have perceived the religious reformer's and his followers' practices in that setting. A Dionysiac background has been discussed in regard to the wine-making miracle of Cana, but it has not won wide acceptance outside the History of Religions School of interpretation.[5] To the best of my knowledge, however, no attempt has been made to discuss the historical Jesus himself against that background, yet the evidence that such a culture obtained in Galilee is more compelling than that which is often suggested in support of the presence of Cynics there.

---

[3] S. Freyne, "Galilean Questions to Crossan's Mediterranean Jesus," in W. Arnal and M. Desjardin (eds.), *Whose Historical Jesus?* (Waterloo, Ont.: Wilfrid Laurier University Press, 1997), pp. 61–91, esp. pp. 68–75.

[4] The term οἰνοπότης is a rare word in secular Greek, a hapax in the NT in the Q passage under discussion and is not found in the LXX. Polybius (*Histories* 20:8,2) describes Antiochus the Great as a "wine-drinker and rejoicing in drunkeness" by way of explaining his infatuation with a young virgin from Chalcis, whom he desired to marry. Dionysiac associations are at best implicit, but not improbable, in view of the Seleucid espousal of the wine-god. At all events the connection between wine-drinking and improper sexual behaviour is clearly intended in the passage from Polybius.

[5] M. Smith, "On the Wine God in Palestine," in *Salo M. Baron Jubilee Volume* (Jerusalem: Israel Academy of the Sciences, 1975), pp. *815–829.

The significance of such an association, were it to be established, would be its potential to explain the attraction of the Jesus movement to women in particular. It is generally accepted that certain mystery cults held a special appeal for women within Graeco-Roman society of the first century. This can be documented for the cults of Isis and Osiris from Egypt, the Magna Mater (Cybele) cult from Phrygia, and the Dionysus cult from Greece. The fact that women were central to the mythological framework of the first two of these cults might explain their particular attraction, but in the case of the Dionysus cult the hero is the god himself, who, having escaped Zeus' thunderbolt, which struck down his mother while he was still in the womb, was eventually raised by the nymph, Nysa, and travelled the earth bringing his gifts to people, especially the gift of wine.[6] According to Euripides' play, the *Bacchae*, the worship of this god consisted in orgiastic celebrations conducted at night by women initiates, who, temporarily abandoning their homes and maternal duties, engaged in dancing and merry-making in a state of frenzy, which had been induced by drinking a mixture of wine, honey and milk, and who were clothed in ritual dress. Instead of feeding their infants, they disgorged their flowing breasts by feeding wild animals, who were subsequently torn apart and the raw flesh was eaten. It is by no means certain that these rites, as described in the play, reflected actual practice in fifth century Athens. Nevertheless, subsequent accounts by writers such as Demosthenes, Diodorus Siculus (c. 40 B.C.E.) and much later, Plutarch and Strabo, as well as epigraphic evidence, would seem to corroborate the general picture. The spread of the worship of Dionysus in Hellenistic and Roman times and the general suspicion towards it from official Roman circles meant a moderation of some of the excesses as described in the *Bacchae*, but also the significant change that men as well as women could become initiates.[7]

At first sight it would appear that there is little resemblance between groups of Dionysiac initiates just described and the Jesus movement, at least as it appears in the Gospels. In particular the induced ecstasy, which seems to have been an essential part of the Bacchic rites, is

---

[6] R. Shepard Kraemer, *Her Share of the Blessings. Women's Religions Among Pagans, Jews, and Christians in the Greco-Roman World* (New York and Oxford: Oxford University Press, 1992).

[7] Kraemer, *Her Share of the Blessings*, pp. 36–45.

entirely absent. It is in the Pauline churches that ecstatic experiences occur within early Christianity. The most significant contrast, perhaps, is the fact that for the Dionysiac initiates the celebrations were a temporary release from their daily chores and responsibilities, whereas in the Jesus movement the call was for total abandonment of home and family on a permanent basis. However, before concluding that this particular analogue has little heuristic value for understanding our topic of Jesus and women, we should examine the likely forms which associations with Dionysus would have taken in differing social situations in Galilee, and whether or not anything might be learned about Jesus' women followers from such an investigation.

Dionysus in a Galilean Jewish Setting

It appears that the wine-god was familiar throughout the Ancient Near Eastern world as a vegetation deity associated with the harvesting of the grape. It was in this guise that Dionysus first appeared in Greece also, long before the more restricted rites of Dionysiac devotees became current.[8] The Syria-Palestine region was also familiar with such a deity, who was connected with fertility in humans and beasts. Wine, the gift of this god, had special importance in cultic settings, where imbibing was thought to lead to a close fellowship with the divine world, a view that is echoed in the Hebrew Scriptures also: "wine that cheers gods and mortals" (Judg. 9:13; Ps. 104:15). In Hebrew lore Noah, the post-deluvian patriarch, was the first to cultivate the vine (Gen. 9:20), and thereafter a plentiful wine-harvest was seen as a gift from God (Gen. 27:28, 37) and associated with messianic blessings to come (Gen. 49:10–12; Joel 2:23–24; cf. Mark 2:22 par). At the same time prophetic critique of wine-drinking is reflected in the example of the Rechabites, who obeyed the command of their ancestor not to drink wine, among other ascetic practices (Jer. 35), as well as in the condemnation of Baal worship, with which it was associated (Hos. 2:10–13). Both these examples have significance for our discussion. The contrast between Jesus and John with regard to wine-drinking echoes the abstinence

---

[8] H. Seesemann, οἶνος, in G. Kittel (ed.), *Theological Dictionary of the New Testament*, X vols. (transl. G. W. Bromiley; Grand Rapids, MI: Eerdmans, 1968), vol. V, pp. 162–6.

of the Rechabites (cf. Luke 1:15), whereas the behaviour of Hosea's wife is described in terms not dissimilar to those of the Bacchae with mention of merry-making, the use of incense and festive clothing at the various festivals of Baal, which, according to the prophet, would lead to the destruction of the vine and revenge of the wild animals as a punishment from Yahweh.

Despite the prophetic critique, the use of wine in a Jewish religious context continued, especially at Passover, and there is some evidence that it also continued to be used in Temple sacrifice (Jos., *Jewish War* 5:565; cf. Exod. 29:28–31). Furthermore, several of the symbols associated with Dionysus were also used in Jewish settings. Thus, the coins of one of the Hasmoneans, Antigonus Mattathias, who opposed Herod the Great in the name of Jewish religious claims, bore the ivy wreath and the grape cluster. Likewise, the coins of both the first and second revolts against Rome bear such emblems as the wine-cup, a pitcher, grape-leaf and grape, iconography that was undoubtedly inspired by the messianic associations of the vine and its fruit in the prophetic texts already referred to. More significant still was the great vine with hanging grape clusters, "a marvel of size and artistry," which, according to Josephus, adorned the entrance to Herod's restored Temple (Jos., *Ant.* 15:395; *Jewish War* 5:224).[9] Tacitus relates that this decoration was understood by some to mean that it was Dionysus who was worshipped in the Jerusalem Temple (*Hist.* 5:5).

Thus, the Jews were certainly no strangers to the joys and mystery of wine, and its religious resonances were shared with the wider Mediterranean and Near Eastern cultures. This was so widespread that it was natural to associate Yahweh and Dionysus, as Tacitus reports. Plutarch also has similar information, intimating that the Jewish feast of Tabernacles was a feast in honour of Dionysus (*Quaestiones Conviviales* 6:1–2). The irony of that particular association is that in all probability the feast of Tabernacles had been an old nature festival associated with the grape harvest, which had later been given a Yahwistic colouring related to the wandering in the wilderness. The fact that it was one of the festivals which the Deuteronomic reform sought to centralize in Jerusalem alone (Deut. 16:13–17) is surely an indication that the older associations continued to function throughout the countryside, as indeed we might expect with a festival

---

[9] Smith, "On the Wine God in Palestine," pp. 820–4.

that had an essentially local significance in a rural rather than an urban setting. Indeed there is evidence from Rome that already in the second century B.C.E. Jews were expelled from the city because they were deemed to worship the god Sabazios, who already in antiquity was identified with Dionysus, due to the similarity of the rites practised in his honour. It has been claimed that it was Roman Jews themselves who made the identification of Yahweh and Sabazios, leading to their expulsion, because of Roman unease with eastern cults in general. Such an identification may have been facilitated by the Hebrew epithet Sabaoth, which had became attached to Yahweh earlier. This would represent an extreme form of the *interpretatio Graeca* of the Jewish God, something that had occurred earlier in the same century in Jerusalem itself, where the introduction of the worship of Ζεὺς ὕψιστος had been inspired by Jews who had opted for an extreme form of Hellenism (1 Macc. 1:11; 2 Macc. 6:4). Yet, among Jews, who had maintained a strong sense of religious identity, various haggadic anecdotes and iconographic representations suggest that even observant circles of a later period were not averse to adapting and adopting Dionysiac motifs that had a very wide currency throughout the eastern Mediterranean from the beginning of the Hellenistic age.[10]

Against this more general background, how can one describe Galilean connections with Dionysus? The Seleucids had been ardent promoters of the god, culminating in the attempt to impose his formal worship, together with that of Zeus, on the Jews in the Hellenistic reform of 167 B.C.E. While the reform failed due to the success of the Maccabean resistance movement, the coins of Scythopolis/Bethshan continued to bear the name Nysa, the nurse who had cared for the infant god according to the myth. This indicates that once the city had been restored after the Roman intervention in Palestinian politics in 67 B.C.E., its earlier connection with the god continued. There is also numismatic as well as literary evidence for the cult of Dionysus in the Phoenician cities of Tyre and Sidon, the former having important commercial links with upper Galilee in particular.[11]

---

[10] M. Hengel, "The Interpretation of the Wine Miracle at Cana: John 2:1–11," in L. D. Hurst and N. T. Wright (eds.), *The Glory of Christ in the New Testament. Studies in Christology in Memory of G. B. Caird* (Oxford: Clarendon, 1987), pp. 83–112, esp. pp. 108–11.

[11] G. Foerster and Y. Tsafrir, "Nysa-Scythopolis—A New Inscription and the Titles of the City on the Coins," *INJ* 9 (1986/7), pp. 53–60.

Thus, the likelihood must be that even rural Galilee was not immune to festivals associated with the gift of wine, under whatever
guise these might have been celebrated.

The discovery in 1988 at Sepphoris in lower Galilee of a beautifully
executed Dionysiac mosaic dating from the third century C.E. raises
the question as to whether or not actual worship of the god may
have taken place there at an earlier date also.[12] This particular mosaic,
adorning the floor of a triclinium in a large villa and consisting of
some seventeen panels with Greek labels on each, deals with a drinking contest between Dionysus and Hercules, who incidentally appeared
on the coins of Tyre, identified with the older Phoenician god Melqart.
It contains various scenes depicting mythological themes from the
god's life, but also more realistic ones in which real life people (men
and women) are portrayed carrying gifts in procession. These panels are surrounded by "an elaborate frame of intertwining acanthus
leaves," forming a number of medallions. The central medallion on
one side contains the bust of a beautiful woman, who has been aptly
described by the archaeologists who discovered the mosaic as "the
Mona Lisa of Galilee." Presumably this exquisitely executed head is
a portrait of the matron of the house, who may well have been a
Dionysiac devotee herself and who arranged for the mosaic to be
placed in this banqueting hall of the villa.

Two possibilities present themselves in terms of Jesus' Galilean
audiences as devotees of the wine-god, according to this evidence,
fragmentary though it may be. Either, they might have been members of the elite urban upper class, pagan or Jewish in name at least,
who engaged in the full-blown worship of Dionysus, or alternatively,
and more likely, they would have been peasants for whom the distinction between Yahweh and the wine-god may have been somewhat blurred, especially at wine-making festivals, provided they were
not in the practice of going to Jerusalem for the feast of Succoth
(cf. John 7:1–9). It is in the larger Herodian centres, such as Sepphoris
and Tiberias, that one might reasonably expect to find Dionysiac
associations, attractive to wealthy women, such as the Sepphoris
matron depicted on the mosaic. The links between Dionysus and
the theatre go back to the very dawn of Greek drama, and there

---

[12] E. Meyer/E. Netzer/C. Meyers, "Artistry in Stone: The Mosaics of Ancient
Sepphoris," *BA* 50 (1987), pp. 223–31; *Sepphoris* (Winona Lake, IN: Eisenbrauns,
1992), esp. pp. 38–59.

had been a theatre in Sepphoris from the first century, possibly even from the time of its re-furbishment by Herod Antipas during the life-time of Jesus. There is no comparable archaeological evidence for first century Tiberias, but we do hear of Antipas' palace there which, because it had animal representations, was destroyed by "the destitute class," aided by some country Galileans, prior to the first revolt (Jos., *Life* 65–6). Given his easy association with people from every background and ethnic origin and those of both genders, there is no reason to rule out *a priori* Jesus' contact with devotees of Dionysus also. Though even then the crucial question would remain: What possible attraction could the Jesus movement as known to us have for such devotees? However, the silence of the Gospels about any visit by him to either of the two Herodian urban centres would seem to make such contact less likely, provided his avoidance was a principled one, as I have argued elsewhere.[13] This, of course, does not exclude affluent women being part of his retinue, as Luke informs us (Luke 8:1–3). However, there is a strong suspicion that Luke is here interested in painting a picture of the new movement's social make-up suitable for his own time.[14] The most that can be stated now is that a charge of being a wine-drinker because some of his followers were or had been members of a Dionysiac circle, is possible, though less probable, given the social location of the Jesus movement within first-century Galilean society, insofar as this can currently be re-constructed.

The alternative suggestion, namely, that many of Jesus' Galilean peasant followers might be identified as dedicated to a particular understanding of Yahweh under the guise of the wine god, also has its difficulties. It raises questions about the nature of Galilean Jewish attachment to the "Yahweh alone" claims emanating from Jerusalem, and how likely the peasants would have been to resist any easy assimilation. In the light of the evidence from pre-revolt Galilee it seems clear that a majority of the country people retained undivided allegiance to the Jerusalem Temple, despite the influences of the urban

---

[13] S. Freyne, "Jesus and the Urban Culture of Galilee," in T. Fornberg and D. Hellholm (eds.), *Texts and Contexts. Texts in their Textual and Situational Contexts. Essays in Honour of Lars Hartman* (Oslo/Copenhagen/Stockholm/Boston: Scandinavian University Press, 1995), pp. 597–622.

[14] M. R. D'Angelo, "Women in Luke-Acts: A Redactional View," *JBL* 109 (1990), pp. 529–36.

centres, both the older ones such a Tyre, Sidon and Scythopolis, or
the newer Herodian foundations of Sepphoris and Tiberias.[15] Yet,
the fact is that wine was one of the principal products of Galilee
according to all the literary sources, and archaeological evidence
indicates wine-making activity at various sites.[16] The plain of Gennosar
has been particularly praised for its lush vegetation, including the
vine, by Josephus (*Jewish War* 3:519), and this territory seems to
have figured prominently in the earliest activities of the Jesus movement also (Matt. 11:19–24). Magdala, the home of Mary, who is
repeatedly named as one of the women in the retinue of Jesus (Mark
15:40–41 par), was not far away along the lakefront also. Even
though the town had received the Greek name Tarichaeae, associated
with the fish-salting industry there, it did not have the same ethos
as Tiberias, as became evident later in the first century when it
differed from the newer, more cosmopolitan centre nearby in adopting a more nationalistic stance towards the revolt. If association with
women such as Mary was the reason for Jesus being described a
"wine-drinker," therefore, it was far more likely to have been in a
Jewish, rather than a pagan, Dionysiac context. Sharing in the rev-
elry on the occasion of the wine-harvest, rather than engaging in
self-induced ecstatic experiences, was the much more probable setting for earning such a designation, therefore.

Re-examining the Charge

The use of the Dionysus analogy to explain the charge that Jesus
was a wine-drinker has not proved particularly illuminating thus far.
The evidence of a suitable background that might make the charge
realistic, rather than a piece of vituperative rhetoric, has at best been
inconclusive, even if Jewish peasant circles might conceivably have
blurred distinctions between certain aspects of their Yahweh worship
and a more generalized version of the wine-god as a vegetation

---

[15] S. Freyne, "Urban-Rural Relations in First Century Galilee: Some Suggestions
from the Literary Sources," in L. Levine (ed.), *The Galilee in Late Antiquity* (New York
and Jerusalem: The Jewish Theological Seminary of America, 1992), pp. 75–94.

[16] S. Krauss, *Talmudische Archaeologie, 3 vols.* (Hildesheim: G. Olms, rpr. 1966),
vol. 2, pp. 227–43; R. Frankel, *The History of the Processing of Wine and Oil in Galilee
in the Period of the Bible, the Mishna and the Talmud* (Hebrew. Unpubl. Diss., Tel Aviv
University, 1984).

deity. A closer examination of the charge in its context may help to decide its implications, if any, for our topic of Jesus and women.

The charge occurs in a Q passage and has been variously analysed in terms of its tradition and redaction. The complete unit consists of three elements: (1) an initial parabolic comparison—the children in the market-place; (2) an application of this to the contrast between Jesus and John, and (3) a concluding proverbial reflection on wisdom's vindication. Recent proposals suggest that these three units reflect three stages of the redaction of Q, relating to the experiences of the so-called Q community as it progressed from witnessing, to rejection by "this generation," to vindication of its claims.[17] While such detailed re-constructions must always remain problematic in view of the putative nature of the source to begin with, they do raise the question as to whether the various elements may have pre-existed, possibly emanating from the historical Jesus, or whether they are purely a later construct of the community faced with rejection by the vast majority of their fellow Jews.

One way out of this impasse which is adequate for our present purposes is to read the whole passage *as presently constructed* as a commentary on the career of Jesus, but for that reason no less important in terms of its historical implications for understanding that ministry in its setting. The opening question, "To what shall we liken this generation," should be read as applying to the whole situation described in the parabolic contrast, namely, the unreasonableness of this generation with regard to God's emissaries. Thus understood, one does not have to find correspondences between individual items in the parable and in the application, a problem that has beset many interpretations. Just as petulant children cannot be easily satisfied, so "this generation" was unhappy with the contrasting styles of John and Jesus. Wisdom's children, by contrast, acknowledge wisdom's gifts and accept them gladly.

When the passage is read in this way there is in fact an *a,b-a',b'* pattern. Jesus' life-style (a') matches the piping and dancing in the

---

[17] J. Kloppenborg, *The Formation of Q. Trajectories in Ancient Wisdom Collections* (Philadelphia, PA: Fortress, 1987), p. 111; D. Smith, "The Historical Jesus at Table," in D. J. Lull (ed.), *SBL Seminar Papers* (Atlanta, GA: Scholars, 1989), pp. 466–86, esp. pp. 477–80; W. J. Cotter, "The Parable of the Children in the Market-Place, Q(Lk) 7:31–35: An Examination of the Parable's Image and Significance," *NT* 29 (1987), pp. 289–304.

marketplace (a), whereas John's ascetic conduct (b') is represented by the wailing and dirging (b). Thus, the activities of merry-making and mourning represent the two extremes of a joyful (messianic) existence and an ascetic (penitential) one. Neither is acceptable to "this generation," that is, those who are not open to the surprise of a totally alternative understanding of God's dealing with Israel, opting instead for the safety of the *status quo*. What is significant about the contrast of the two lifestyles for the purposes of this discussion is the choice of imagery. Piping and dancing are universal human activities of merry-making, but there may well be a definite local colouring also with religious significance. A clay plaque from a bronze-age cultic location at Dan represents a male dancing figure with a lute in his hand, which the archaeologist A. Biran has named "The dancer from Dan."[18] Piping is associated with the god Pan, who from the Hellenistic age was celebrated at the nearby grove of Banias at the foot of Mt Hermon. Coins of Banias represent him playing the pipes, sometimes with a goat beside him, a symbol also associated with Dionysus. Pan was also depicted as the escort of Dionysus, as on an altar with an inscription dedicated to Dionysus, "founder" of the city, from Scythopolis and dating from the year 11/12 C.E.[19]

Thus, there was a very long tradition of both these gods in the neighbourhood of Galilee, and the pagan resonances of piping and dancing would surely not have been lost on Jesus' Galilean opponents. They could, therefore, categorize him as a devotee of these locally venerated deities, presumably because of his general infringement of Jewish identity markers as these were defined by more orthodox circles. His and his followers' joyful attitude, grounded in messianic claims, was capable of being misrepresented and thereby discredited, and there was ready to hand a set of associations which could easily have been evoked to pillory his conduct as betrayal and un-Jewish.

That vilification is the prime intention of the charge may be deduced, not merely from the term "wine-drinker" and its nuance of

---

[18] A. Biran, "The Dancer from Dan, the Empty Tomb and the Altar Room," *IEJ* 36 (1986), pp. 168–87.

[19] V. Tzaferis, "The 'God who is in Dan' and the Cult of Pan at Banias in the Hellenistic and Roman Periods," *EI* 23, *A. Biran Volume* (Jerusalem: The Israel Exploration Society, 1992), pp. 128*–35*; Foerster and Tsafrir, "Nysa-Scythopolis," p. 53, n. 2.

pagan religious worship, but also from the other terms used, "glutton" and "friend of tax-collectors and sinners." The association of these terms evokes the setting of meals, often connected with lewd conduct including women. Thus, according to Kathleen Corley, Matthew's linking of tax-collectors with prostitutes (Matt. 21:31), instead of the usual "tax-collectors and sinners" is a natural one. In Hellenistic literature the term sinner/*hamartolos* referred to various kinds of moral failure, but especially those involving sexual promiscuity. Equally, "tax-collector" may not just have the usual connotations of cheating or collaboration with the enemy, but also with prostitution, being closely related to brothel-keeping in the literature.[20] While all these various associations were no doubt grounded in the everyday social life of the Mediterranean world in which the presence of women at public meals was still regarded as improper, the terms inevitably passed over into use as part of vituperative rhetoric, that highly developed art-form in the ancient, no less than the modern world, in order to discredit one's opponent. In a culture where honour was so highly prized, any such character assassination was intended to shame the opponent publicly, thereby depriving them of their right to status and the influence that went with it.

Our brief examination of the charge that Jesus was a wine-drinker in its original Q setting has, therefore, all the signs of an attempt to discredit him and his movement by religious opponents unhappy with his apparent lack of regard for the mores of Galilean Jewish society. This does not mean that we should discount entirely the particular terms in which this vituperation is couched. Vernon Robbins in particular has drawn our attention to the fact that all rhetorical devices are social codes which can give us insight into the values and ethos of particular societies.[21] Thus, our passage tells us something of how women in public were perceived in that culture, participating fully in the values that were prevalent in Graeco-Roman society generally. Such women were cast in the roles of whore,

---

[20] K. Corley, *Private Women, Public Meals. Social Conflict in the Synoptic Tradition* (Peabody, MA: Hendrickson, 1993), pp. 89–93.

[21] V. Robbins, "Socio-Rhetorical Criticism: Mary, Elizabeth and the Magnificat as a Test Case," in E. Struthers Malbon and E. V. McKnight (eds.), *The New Literary Criticism and the New Testament* (JSNT Supplement Series, 109; Sheffield: Sheffield Academic Press, 1994), pp. 164–209.

temptress, dangerous, and open to foreign and lewd practices under the guise of religion. When such images are compared with those of orthodox Jewish women as described in the, admittedly, later rabbinic writings, the contrast is marked. There, too, women are dangerous, not as objects of sexual temptation but as a potential source of impurity. It is for this reason that they had to be excluded from any direct contact with the sacred. As Jacob Neusner has shown, control of women in terms of board and bed is the generative principle of the Mishnah's division, *Nashim*.[22] Aspects of the social role of women are of no interest to the framers of the Mishnah, other than in removing any grey areas in the law concerning the circumscribing of women and their protection, as potential sources of impurity. While it is not possible to ascribe these detailed rules to first-century Galilee with any great assurance, recent archaeological evidence (e.g. ritual baths, stone jars and absence of pig bones) from Sepphoris, Jotapata and elsewhere suggest that issues of purity were important in some Galilean Jewish circles of the period.[23] The significance of such a public statement of concern for purity in certain households has particular implications for the daughters of the house in terms of their marriage prospects, as Marianne Sawicki notes.[24] It is to such groups, probably of a priestly caste, that we should attribute the efforts to vilify the Jesus movement as being not just unobservant in regard to purity but as being un-Jewish in its basic affiliation.

Taking Vilification Seriously

Those who chose to vilify Jesus and his movement in the terms mentioned in the Q passage we have been discussing, were only too happy to characterize them in terms that were quite familiar to

---

[22] J. Neusner, *Method and Meaning in Ancient Judaism* (Brown Judaica Series, 10; Missoula, MT: Scholars, 1979), pp. 79–100.

[23] D. Adan-Bayewitz and M. Aviam, "Iotapata, Josephus and the Siege of 67: Preliminary Report on the 1992–94 seasons," *Journal of Roman Archaeology* 10 (1997), pp. 131–65, esp. pp. 163–4; E. Netzer and Z. Weiss, *Zippori* (Jerusalem: The Israel Exploration Society, 1994), pp. 20–4.

[24] M. Sawicki, "Spatial Management of Gender and Labor in Greco-Roman Galilee," in D. Edwards and C. T. McCollough (eds.), *Archaeology and the Galilee. Texts and Contexts in the Greco-Roman and Byzantine Periods* (Atlanta, GA: Scholars Press, 1997), pp. 7–28, esp. pp. 15–16, and nn. 29, 67.

Graeco-Roman audiences, and the added suggestion of possible com-
plicity in pagan worship merely strengthened the case for rejection.
By the same token, this observation also supports the claim that
women were members of Jesus' permanent retinue. One cannot agree
with Morton Smith's principle that outsiders invariably give a more
accurate account of things than insiders, yet at the same time their
views, even when hostile, cannot be discounted entirely.[25] Distortion
and misrepresentation of the truth, rather than pure fiction, is the
normal stock-in-trade of vilification. Thus, while we cannot take the
charge against Jesus at face value, we should ask why in fact he is
characterized in this precise way. While Jesus and his followers almost
certainly should not be viewed as forming a Dionysiac group, clearly
there were sufficient similarities at a superficial level to make such
a comparison possible, even plausible for some of the uncommitted
of Galilee. In that event it is worth asking whether the social reasons which made Dionysiac associations attractive to women in the
Mediterranean world might not have applied in the case of the Jesus
movement also.

Ross Kraemer has drawn on the group/grid theories of Mary
Douglas, combined with I. M. Lewis' notion of "oblique aggression
strategy," to explain the attraction of Dionysiac rites for women.[26]
While the group/grid theory with its strong/weak co-relates is by
now familiar in biblical studies, Lewis' idea is based on the observation of Polynesian women who were able "to redress the imbalance
of power between themselves and men without directly challenging
the status quo." Kraemer suggests that, in a similar fashion, through
the rejection of socially ascribed roles of mother and nurse and the
adoption instead of traditional male roles of warrior and hunter,
women Dionysiacs effected a temporary role reversal. The fact that
this was achieved "under inspiration" of the god meant that they
were inculpable, engaging in a form of ritual release at the behest
of the deity. In the classical period and as evidenced in the *Bacchae*,
women displayed strong group relations but weak grid identity.
However, as the character of the Greek city evolved in the Hellenistic
period, the role of women in society also changed. The new cos-
mopolitanism resulted in both weakened group and grid in the form

---

[25] M. Smith, *Jesus the Magician* (New York: Harper & Row, 1978), pp. 1–7.
[26] Kraemer, *Her Share of the Blessings*, pp. 46–9; "Ecstasy and Possession: The
Attraction of Women to the Cult of Dionysus," *HTR* 72 (1979), pp. 56–80.

of traditional roles, but consequently a greater freedom and variety even for women at the lower end of the social spectrum. At the same time this would also explain why men were now becoming members of Dionysiac associations because of their need for strong group connections.

Such models from the social sciences are of necessity highly generalized. Nevertheless, they can function heuristically by suggesting the most appropriate questions to be posed to the data to hand. Greater attention to the changing social context of Galilee in the Herodian period is called for in order to understand not just the fact but the particular shape of the Jesus movement. Elsewhere I have attempted to highlight this situation in terms of the building of two urban centres—Sepphoris and Tiberias—during the life-time of Jesus.[27] Since the pre-industrial city was heavily dependent on its hinterland, the emergence of the two centres inevitably put pressure on the traditional way of life in the village culture of lower Galilee. Land-ownership patterns were affected, and the shift from a subsistence to a market economy changed both the means of production and the market exchange system. An integral part of such changes is the "values revolution" that makes the transition from one system to the other possible. Kinship concerns are replaced by those which have to do with maximizing profits, giving rise to a more stratified society. It was the urban elites and their retainers who stood to benefit most from these changes, while the peasant class came under increasing pressure. The slide from ownership to day labouring to homelessness could be rapid. Brigandage or alternative movements, such as the Jesus movement, became real options for those who found themselves on the margins of the new social reality.

The lives of women were inevitably affected by these changes. Within the structure of a peasant village economy, women's presence and labour are essential to the maintenance of the *status quo*. Many of the tasks necessary for subsistence, for example animal tending, fruit gathering, wine treading, etc., are shared by men and women, in addition to the more traditional female activities such as textile production, baking and child nurturing. The tension between group and grid is minimized when everyday existence dominates the

---

[27] S. Freyne, "Herodian Economics in Galilee. Searching for a Suitable Model," in Ph. F. Esler (ed.), *Modelling Early Christianity. Social-Scientific Studies of the New Testament in its Context* (London and New York: Routledge, 1995), pp. 23–46.

ethos so that the public/private dualism is not as marked as in more advanced economies. It was this way of life that was being eroded by the changes occurring in Galilee. Land was confiscated in order to provide allotments for those who were compelled to inhabit the new foundation, Tiberias. Debt is a constant feature in the tradition of the Synoptic Gospels, and this lead to brigandage. The male population was further depleted by the political disturbances on the death of Herod the Great, especially in the region of Sepphoris, which was sacked by the Roman general Varus in 4 B.C.E. Many women were either prematurely widowed or deprived of the opportunity to marry, such an essential feature of women's status in the ancient world, including the Jewish one. The rigid patriarchal structures which controled marriage were certainly not conducive to women's autonomy, but the alternatives of penury or menial services, including prostitution at the larger centres, were deemed to be shameful.

Thus, class as well as gender were operative factors in women's full participation in the Jesus movement. The involvement of upper-class women in Graeco-Roman religious practices, especially from the early empire, has been well documented.[28] A similar case has recently been argued for upper-class Jewish and non-Jewish women's attraction to Pharisaism, and various reasons, social and psychological, have been suggested for this.[29] In a similar vein, Luke can speak of the women caring for Jesus "from their own resources" (Luke 8:3). As we have seen, this may reflect a later situation in which women of means acted as patronesses of such movements. That there were such women of means, either widowed or divorced, can be documented from the Babatha archive in the province of Arabia, for the early second century. Her *ketubba*, or marriage dowry in the event of divorce or death of her husband, was worth 100 Tyrians, that is 400 denarii, recalling that a silver denarius was the average daily wage.[30] But Babatha was deemed a "noble" (or free) woman. The

---

[28] J. Bremmer, "Why did Early Christianity attract Upper-Class Women?," in A. A. R. Bastiaensen, A. Hilhorst, and C. H. Kneepkens (eds.), *Fructus Centesimus. Melanges offerts a G. J. M. Barrtelink* (Steenbrugis: In Abbatia S. Petri, 1989), pp. 37–47; "Pauper or Patroness. The Widow in the Early Christian Church," in J. Bremmer and L. van den Bosch (eds.), *Between Poverty and Pyre. Moments in the History of Widowhood* (London and New York: Routledge, 1995), pp. 31–57.

[29] T. Ilan, "The Attraction of Aristocratic Women to Pharisaism," *HTR* 88 (1995), pp. 1–34.

[30] Y. Yadin/J. C. Greenfield/A. Yardeni, "Babatha's *Ketubba*," *IEJ* 44 (1994), pp.

situation I am suggesting for the earliest Jesus movement is its attraction for women of a lower social class, those who had been marginalized by the changing circumstances in that world. It was presumably the particular view-point and life-style that would have attracted them to that movement rather than those of the Pharisaic associations, which may have appealed to these village women, since Josephus tells us that the Pharisaic movement was generally attractive to the townspeople.

It would appear, therefore, that we can posit social conditions in Galilee that might have been conducive to women as well as men joining the permanent retinue of Jesus. The social circumstances we are positing are different to those which would have obtained in the case of Dionysiac gatherings with their temporary release from family chores. Rather than providing such a temporary escape, the Jesus movement supplied a real social need by offering an alternative, based on a radically different world-view. Faced with the rapidly changing circumstances of their lives, some women of Galilee found that the Jesus movement was offering a viable and attractive alternative. The apparent lack of concern around purity issues must have been a factor of some importance, but it was not the only reason for the appeal.[31] The message of blessing for the poor and setting captives free undoubtedly resonated with the experiences of repression that such women encountered in their daily lives. The promise of reversal of fortunes that the apocalyptic world-view held out was far more attractive than any alternative. Pilgrimage to Jerusalem offered a thoroughly legitimated escape from familial chores, if such were required. Only the permanent following of Jesus could provide the incentive to remake the world in ways that were different to anything that either Rome of Jerusalem might have to offer.

Conclusion

While the search for an adequate social location for permanent women followers of Jesus on the basis of our initial hunch did not

75–101; M. A. Friedmann, "Babatha's *Ketubba*: Some Preliminary Observations," *IEJ* 46 (1996), pp. 55–76.

[31] R. Horsley, *Galilee, History, Politics, People* (Valley Forge, PA: Trinity Press International, 1995), pp. 197–8.

at first prove particularly fruitful, in the end the implied unfavourable comparison in the description of Jesus as a wine-drinker opened up another avenue of investigation. A social-scientific perspective that is sensitive, not just to gender but also to class, can disclose the hidden lives of women in a particular context, even when hard facts are scarce. Approaches to various aspects of women's life in antiquity that can combine such insights with the evidence provided by the new archaeology will surely help considerably in clarifying what was at stake for women in making choices such as joining the Jesus movement and the kind of vilification that they were likely to encounter even from within their own families. Thus, the very silence of our androcentric sources provides a challenge to the historical imagination to re-image critically the world of women in antiquity in ways that may be suggestive for the present and the future also.

MAGDALENES AND TIBERIENNES: CITY WOMEN IN THE ENTOURAGE OF JESUS

MARIANNE SAWICKI

Curiously paired, the names of Mary and Joanna come down to us in a tradition about wealthy women who financed Jesus' operations, travelled with his road show throughout Galilee, and stuck around for the culminating events of his career in Jerusalem. Apparently the business details of promoting the Gospel were handled behind the scenes by women whom today we would call managers or agents. How appropriate are such modern terms, given what is known historically about first-century Galilee and Judea? This article will argue that the Lake region of Galilee was undergoing development as a tourist attraction by Herod Antipas, in furtherance of his geopolitical agenda. Tiberias was the hub for international industrial expansion in the 20s of the first century; nearby Magdala had to adapt. Changes in the character of shipping on the Lake disrupted old alliances and opened up new opportunities. I suggest that the friendship between Mary and Joanna probably was not the result of their prior separate encounters with Jesus as his clients. Rather, circumstantial evidence suggests that common business interests first brought Mary and Joanna together and then led them to "discover" Jesus and promote him.

The argument on circumstantial evidence will not be conclusive. But neither can it be dismissed out of hand. Geographical and political circumstances obviously cannot determine the course of a relationship between two individuals, Mary and Joanna. Yet, inasmuch as the Gospel was a movement launched in real space and time, the events of its origin undeniably were influenced by geography and politics. Scant information about Mary and Joanna comes down to us, but it is of the sort that permits some startling inferences.

Before considering what it means to place Mary at Magdala and Joanna in Tiberias—capital city of her husband's boss, the tetrarch Herod Antipas—let us begin with a simple question about the whole group of women whom all four Gospels associate with Jesus.[1] Why

---

[1] A large group of women supporters is mentioned parenthetically, almost as an

are they *there*? What are they doing *in the text*? This "why" really
has two levels. First, why was it that *after* Calvary stories about
women supporters were circulating in the Jesus movement? Second,
why was it that *before* Calvary certain women were supporting Jesus?
The first level is the "why" of a historical fact, for there is no doubt
about the existence of the stories after Calvary. Those stories can
be accounted for in various ways: as either straightforward memories, or theological constructions, or a mixture of the two. At this
level, one might ask why only Luke mentions Joanna. A plausible
answer is that Luke was most alert to the international scope of the
tensions among Herodian and Hasmonean/Judean factions, and so
either sought out or invented narrative elements such as the Herodian
lady Joanna and the third phase of Jesus' trial by Antipas.

However, it is the second level of "why" that concerns us here.
Why were women involved with Jesus *before* Calvary? This "why"
has to be investigated without having established beyond any doubt
"the fact that" Jesus' activities were indeed financed and managed
by women in general and by Mary and Joanna in particular. There
is no way to secure that as a fact; we have to accept it as a premise.
But if Luke's premise is true—that is, if there was a Mary from
Magdala and if she associated with the wife of the viceroy of the
tetrarch Antipas, and if together they supported Jesus—then we can
use geographical and archaeological information to fill in some gaps
in the puzzle of the origins of the Jesus movement.

Partners in Management

Generally, the role assigned to the women supporters of Jesus in the
Gospel texts is a function of location. In Galilee, they finance his
operations. In Jerusalem, they witness the climactic events of his
career: the cross, the burial, the emptied tomb, the appearances of
the Risen Lord.

Accordingly, Luke yokes Mary with Joanna in the Galilean role
of financial backer. (In Luke 8:2–3, both have been healed by Jesus

---

afterthought, by Mark and Matthew in the crucifixion accounts. See Mark 15:40–41
and Matt. 27:55–56. In Luke 23:49 the women are unnamed. Luke has first mentioned the women earlier in his narrative and has supplied their motive: they have
been healed by Jesus, Luke 8:1–3. John also places a group of women at the cross,
although he does not report that they supported Jesus' operations, John 19:25.

and both use their resources to provide for Jesus and the Twelve.) Luke also partners Mary with Joanna to witness in Jerusalem: they inform the Eleven about the events of Calvary, the burial, and the significance of the emptied tomb. (While the polite convention of anonymity for the women is honoured in the narrative of Luke 23:49–24:9, v. 10 discloses that the group has included Mary and Joanna all along.) Neither in Galilee nor in Jerusalem does either woman act alone. They are portrayed as partners in the midst of numerous women associates, both named and unnamed, as they perform first their Galilean financial functions and then their Jerusalem witnessing functions.

But Luke has associated each of the women with another group as well. Mary represents the lakeside town of Magdala, also known as Tarichaeae.[2] Joanna is the wife of the chief of staff (ἐπίτροπος) of Herod Antipas, tetrarch of Galilee and Perea. In the early decades of the first century C.E., the Herodians and the Galileans were distinct and opposed factions in a tense and deteriorating political landscape. The Herodian dynasty came to power in 37 B.C.E. with Antipas' father, Herod the Great, who out-maneuvered the Hasmonean leadership of the Jerusalem Temple state, and who made at least ten strategic political marriages for himself. On his way to the top in Judea, Herod the Great had married Mariamme,[3] the daughter of the Hasmonean ruling family.

When they betrothed Mariamme to Herod in 42 B.C.E., the Hasmoneans were in the waning days of a century of administration. Judean independence from the Seleucid Empire had been achieved through the popular revolt led by Judah "the Maccabee" 167–152 B.C.E., with the establishment of an independent Temple-state under Judah's brother Jonathan in 160 B.C.E. and recognition by the Roman Senate about 139 B.C.E. The Maccabees took over the high priesthood as well as civil power. Thereafter the family of the Maccabees, called Hasmoneans, extended Judean control northward into Galilee and the Golan again after many centuries of Galilean independence

---

[2] On Magdala as Tarichaeae (also spelled Taricheae), see J. L. Rousseau and R. Arav, *Jesus and His World: An Archaeological and Cultural Dictionary* (Minneapolis, MN: Fortress, 1995), pp. 189–90.

[3] In Josephus, the name is spelled Μαριάμη or Μαριάμμη, adding an inflectable ending to Μαριαμ, the Septuagint form of this name. In the Middle Ages, the third M was changed to N by manuscript copyists, so the name sometimes is found in today's texts with the spelling *Mariamne*.

from Jerusalem.[4] Thus, by 104 B.C.E., about a century before Antipas and Jesus lived, the Hasmoneans had newly imposed the economic and political hegemony of the southern Temple-state upon the northern territories that previously had followed a decentralized form of Israelite religion.[5]

The Judeans took over Galilee by force and they ran it through a network of fortified administrative centres. That is, they placed garrisons within line-of-sight signalling distance of one another at strategic locations: Sepphoris and Yodfat on opposite hilltops surveilling the Bet Netofa Valley; Gush Halav (Gischala) in the mountainous northwest along the route to the Mediterranean port of Tyre; Gamla in the Golan at the far northeast corner of their territory to monitor travel between Damascus and the Lake region; Qeren-Naftali above the northern Jordan River; Magdala on the shore of the Lake itself, and so forth.[6] Through those towns, the Jerusalem administration projected power northward and extracted tithes southward, gradually effecting the integration of Galilee and the Golan into the Temple-state. Judean officials and their families had to be stationed in the north to carry this out. The indigenous Galilean society in which the expatriate Judeans took up residence already shared their basic religious orientation: to the laws of Moses (though perhaps not in written form), to the prophetic traditions (especially the Elijah stories), to the practices of festivals, sabbath, circumcision, almsgiving, and tithing (involving local cultic personnel), and to Israelite kinship customs (including the reckoning of inheritance and descent). The Galileans probably did *not* share the Judeans' enthusiasm for the

---

[4] The brothers of Judah "the Maccabee," Jonathan and Simon, were the first two rulers in the line of "Hasmoneans." See R. A. Horsley, *Galilee: History, Politics, People* (Valley Forge, PA: Trinity Press International, 1995), pp. 34–61. The term "Hasmonean" came to apply to their administrative officers as well as their kin.

[5] The far-reaching social consequences of the Hasmonean conquest are discussed by R. A. Horsley in two recent works: *Archaeology, History, and Society in Galilee: The Social Context of Jesus and the Rabbis* (Valley Forge, PA: Trinity Press International, 1996); and *Galilee*. Horsley persuasively argues that the demography, the economy, and the culture of Galilee in the era of Jesus were decisively affected by the recently imposed Judean hegemony.

[6] See Horsley, *Galilee*, pp. 132–44. On Qeren-Naftali, see M. Aviam, "A Second-First Century B.C.E. Fortress and Siege Complex in Eastern Upper Galilee," in D. R. Edwards and C. T. McCollough (eds.), *Archaeology and the Galilee: Texts and Contexts in the Graeco-Roman and Byzantine Periods* (Atlanta, GA: Scholars, 1997), pp. 97–105. Judea extended its political hegemony south and east as well.

Davidic capital, Jerusalem, or for the institutions of the Temple and its royal messianic cult.[7]

The Hasmoneans, although generally well loved in Judea, lost their grip on this extended domain through a series of political mishaps in which they were outmanoeuvered. In 42 B.C.E. they attempted an alliance through marriage with the rising strongman Herod, who would become known as "the Great" because of his political and architectural achievements and who was already in favour with the Romans. At the time, the betrothal of Mariamme to Herod looked like a good solution. Herod was not Judean, but Idumean; that is, he was from a people who had been forced to accept circumcision and the Judean laws in his grandfather's generation.[8] The offspring of the union between Herod and Mariamme, then, would be "legitimate" according to the laws of Moses, as interpreted in Jerusalem. The children would be the legacy of both Herod, with his imperial connections, and of the Hasmoneans, with their popular local Judean support.

Mariamme did bear five children; two of her sons grew to manhood. But Herod had ambitions beyond Judea, and in 29 B.C.E. he had Mariamme murdered. He also murdered her young brother Aristobulus, whom he had appointed high priest in 35 B.C.E., as well as his own two sons by Mariamme, in 7 B.C.E. This brought an end to the Hasmonean dynasty as such. Nevertheless, Hasmonean personal names continued to be associated with hopes for Judean independence, and many nationalistic Judeans named their babies John,

---

[7] This summarizes the re-construction offered by Horsley, *Galilee* and *Archaeology*. The Galilean villages probably did not blanket Galilee but existed alongside settlements of other ethnic-cultural heritage, perhaps in an overall sparsely populated interior between the coast and the lakeshore.

[8] In regard to this period, it is anachronistic to ask whether Herod or anyone else was "Jewish." The word Ἰουδαῖος means "Judean" in the ancient texts (Josephus and the Gospels). Outside of Palestine, this term could be applied to anyone from Judea, Samaria, Galilee, Idumea, or even beyond, especially if the person observed the sabbath and the other festivals. Inside Palestine, the term was used more precisely, and regional variances in Israelite religious practices were recognized. (Somewhat analogously, a native of Georgia in the United States might be called a "Yankee" if she travelled to Germany, but never in Atlanta.) In modern English, the term "Jewish" connotes a history of religious development that had not yet happened in the first century B.C.E. Judaism (or Judaisms, plural) was still in its formative period. I do not mean to *define* "Judaism" or "Jewishness." It is surely not my place to do so. But the complexity of the historical phenomena must be acknowledged.

Simon, Judas, Salome, or Mariamme.[9] There were still plenty of Hasmonean nationalists in and around Jerusalem, as well as in the far-
flung administrative towns of Galilee and the Golan. Herod the Great
nominally controlled those towns, with backing from the Roman
empire. But the Herodian administration had to deal continually
with the Hasmonean faction, which included Jerusalem-based elite
priestly families with extensive agricultural holdings, economic power,
and (in Judea) popular support. Unsurprisingly, civil unrest broke
out at the death of Herod the Great in 4 B.C.E., but was suppressed
with help from Roman legions.

Demography and Landscape of Galilee

There were, then, at least three identifiable social factions in the
Galilee of Jesus' childhood: Herodians, transplanted Judeans, and
indigenous Galilean villagers. Since this was the ancient Near East,
individuals did not affiliate with these groups at will; rather, people
were born into them, married into them, or (especially in the case
of the Herodians) entered them in servitude and perhaps rose to
positions of relative power. Who were these people? Let's take a
closer look.

Galileans were the portion of the indigenous population descended
from Iron-Age Israelite stock.[10] They farmed their ancestral plots of
land, herded sheep and goats, produced wine and oil for local consumption, fished in Lake Gennesareth (the "Sea of Galilee"), lived
in villages, practiced trades such as weaving, pottery manufacture,
or masonry, exchanged products with households in other villages

---

[9] See M. H. Williams, "Palestinian Jewish Personal Names in Acts," in R. Bauck-
ham (ed.), *The Book of Acts in its Palestinian Setting* (Grand Rapids, MI: Eerdmans,
1995), pp. 79–113. Williams found that the Hasmoneans' personal names became
suddenly much more common in first-century Palestine, while in the contemporary
Diaspora they became less common. She attributes this to the fact that Diaspora
Jews were used to being ruled by gentiles and did not wish to associate themselves
with the destabilizing independence movement in Judea, where gentile rule was a
novel and unwelcome experience in the first century (pp. 107–9).

[10] That is, they are villagers whose ancestors were overlooked for various reasons when the Assyrians deported most of the Israelite population in the eighth
century B.C.E. Roadside settlements in Galilee by people of different background in
subsequent centuries are likely. There is insufficient evidence to support claims that
Galilee was "empty" or "abandoned" from the seventh through the second centuries B.C.E.

by means of travelling peddlers or hucksters, and maintained their Israelite identity by following Mosaic law concerning festivals, marriage, inheritance, and the distribution of produce to kin, to the poor and to local priests. Speaking an Aramaic dialect, they would have managed community affairs through traditional institutions like a circle of elder men or a network of senior women—each with its proper sphere of competence. Every member of a village could reckon himself or herself kin to every other member, through multiple lines of relation; the customary procedures for re-distribution of commodities were clearly recognized. The difference between the "richest" and the "poorest" member of the village could never be very great.[11] The archaeological signature of indigenous habitation sites has not yet been established.[12] It would have to include traces of the villagers' cuisine, their manufacturing, and domestic architecture adapted to accommodate their complex extended kinship structures. There is no reason to expect that indigenous Galilean villagers built "public" community centres, whether for educational or political or economic or religious uses. Their "synagogues" were not buildings. They had no need of market squares either, for they had no conceptual means of defining anything as "surplus."

Judeans in Galilee of the first century C.E. were the descendants of Hasmonean administrators.[13] They include some members of the priestly and levitical castes. They cluster in the areas around the former Hasmonean outposts, where they still have control over agricultural estates consolidated in the previous century out of small indigenous ancestral holdings. They regard the Galilee as a province in a land whose capital is Jerusalem. Even though political administration of the land was divided among sons of Herod the Great

---

[11] The network of responsibility for kin is perhaps the most distinctive feature of a settled indigenous Israelite population. Kinship determines who is responsible for arranging one's marriage, one's employment, and one's burial. Land and its productivity are allocated by the kinship system. It is this system which is disrupted when an outside population moves in and takes over. There are echoes of an attempt to adapt, after such a disruption, in the Jesus saying that one must now "love the neighbour"—rather than the cousin, that is.

[12] This lack has permitted the hasty conclusion, on the basis of surface pottery finds, that Galilee was "empty" before the Hasmonean influx.

[13] "Galileans" are not "Judeans" ("Jews") in the common parlance of the first century. Horsley points out that Josephus ordinarily uses the terms "Judeans," "Idumeans," and "Galileans" in precise and mutually exclusive senses. See *Galilee*, pp. 44–5.

after 4 B.C.E., so that Jerusalem is no longer in political control of
Galilee, David's city remains the religious capital for the Judeans in
the north. They return there for festivals, and they maintain family
ties with their associates in the south through inter-marriage. In the
late first century B.C.E. and the first decades of the common era, the
descendants of the Hasmoneans are working out a *modus vivendi* with
the new Roman-backed Herodian party. But resentment smolders.
The transplanted Judeans harbour nationalist sentiments, and while
collaborating with the Herodians they find ways to subvert and
impede Herodian projects as well. They seek to undo the annihila-
tion of the Hasmonean dynasty symbolically by naming their daughters after the last Hasmonean princess, whom Herod the Great
murdered. The name "Mary," previously uncommon in Palestine,
suddenly becomes very popular just after the murder of Mariamme
and her sons.[14] This name may serve as an index to families who
support a return to Hasmonean-style Jerusalem-based rule and who
oppose Herod, the emperor's man.[15]

The archaeological signature of Hasmonean habitation would contrast with that of indigenous Galilean villagers in some ways, but
not in others. Their cuisine and their household equipment (pots
and tools) would be quite similar, for they would have been locally
acquired.[16] But there would also be some luxury goods, such as
imported fine ceramics. Their housing and its decoration would be
larger and finer. Unlike Galileans, they might have τρίκλινα, dining
rooms furnished for reclining at formal meals. Traces of Hellenistic
design are to be expected, since Hasmonean material culture in Judea

---

[14] Williams reports that the name *Mariam* apparently was not common among
Palestinian Jews until Herod put his wife to death in 29 B.C.E. "From then on,
there was an explosion in its popularity." See Williams, "Palestinian Jewish Personal
Names," p. 107.

[15] This would mean that the mother of Jesus probably came from a Hasmonean
family or from nationalists who were Hasmonean sympathizers. Nazareth lay close
within the orbit of the Hasmonean administrative outpost at Sepphoris.

[16] This sort of interface in the material culture of domestic spaces has been
reported at New World sites in the period after colonial conquest. Indigenous people serve in the kitchens of the occupying population, where they use the same
pots, tools, fuels, and foodstuffs that they have always used in the area. By contrast,
other rooms of the homes are furnished and used in the manner that the occu-
piers were accustomed to in the region of their origin. See J. Levy and C. Claassen,
"Engendering the Contact Period," in C. Claassen (ed.), *Exploring Gender Through
Archaeology: Selected Papers from the 1991 Boone Conference* (Madison, MI: Prehistory,
1992), pp. 111–26.

was already influenced by Greek Mediterranean motifs in the first century B.C.E. Hasmonean fortifications and housing in Galilee would be found beside or overlaid upon indigenous Galilean villages. The Hasmoneans, with their international connections, might very well have enlarged existing indigenous industrial installations in order to produce goods for export: fishpacking, oil and wine bottling, weaving. They needed warehouses, arsenals, and granaries.[17] They likely improved the roads somewhat as well. It makes sense to look for public buildings—"synagogues"—in Hasmonean sites, because of their administrative character and because the pre-existing local indigenous social institutions of the villages did not belong to the ex-patriate Judeans. With the Judeans also came the first need of organized and dedicated market spaces in the growing towns of Galilee, in order to provide for exchange of goods among people who did not regard each other as kin.

Herodians were the officers of administration in the court of Herod the Great and, after 4 B.C.E., in the court of his son Herod Antipas. They ruled on behalf of the Romans. They built in the Graeco-Roman style: temples, theatres, market fora, colonnaded avenues, baths, hippodromes, harbours, roads, villas, stupendous mountain fortresses, swimming pools in the desert. Their kinship practices were opportunistic. The multiple inter-marriages between pairs whom we would consider uncle and niece, or brother- and sister-in-law, were driven by geopolitical ambitions more often than by lustful whim. The same may be said for their inter-familial murders. They were inventive compromisers. Herod the Great had masons trained from the priestly caste so that he could romanize the Jerusalem Temple without violating religious taboo. Among his other architectural accomplishments was the harbour city of Caesarea on the Mediterranean coast. His son Antipas re-furbished the inland town of Sepphoris as his first capital after 4 B.C.E. About two decades later, Antipas built Tiberias as an entirely new capital city on the shore of Lake Gennesareth. At this period, the non-indigenous non-Judean population of Galilee also was growing, due in part to international commerce and to retirements from the imperial legions.

---

[17] By contrast, presumably Galilean villagers simply stored grain for the year in large jars in each household, to be shared with kin in time of need. They did not stockpile it. Large collection facilities like the vaults in the lower city at Sepphoris are an indication that taxation, foreign trade, or both have been imposed upon the land.

Herodians were thoroughly hated throughout Judea and Galilee as interlopers and as the agents of Roman power. Yet they were a fact of life. You couldn't beat them, but there were various ways of joining them and working out some viable accommodation. Inter-marriage was one way. Although the Hasmonean attempt to forge a high-level alliance through betrothal eventually failed, still it indi-cates that brides like Mariamme functioned as more than passive pawns in the power game. This brings us to a Herodian lady of the first century c.e., Joanna. In Luke's Gospel, she is the link between the Herodians and the Jesus movement.[18]

If Luke is essentially correct about this connection, the reader is confronted with something puzzling. The wily Antipas very much wants to meet Jesus, *but somehow he is prevented from seeing him.* Luke asserts that Herod Antipas is interested in Jesus, whom he regards as an entertainer, and is favourably disposed toward him. Yet, Antipas' curiosity is thwarted, and Jesus is kept out of his clutches all the while that he operates in Galilee. Antipas doesn't get his hands on Jesus until Pilate, the Roman prefect himself, sends the prisoner to the tetrarch for trial in Jerusalem.[19] Antipas earlier had no trouble detaining John the Baptist; but in Luke's account, Jesus seems to have had a powerful and effective protector on the inside of Herod's court.[20] Apparently he needed one, because Luke reports that Jesus'

---

[18] This fact is largely overlooked in recent scholarship, apart from B. Witherington III, "On the Road with Mary Magdalene, Joanna, Susanna, and Other Disciples—Luke 8:1–3," *ZNW* 70 (1979), pp. 243–8. Witherington cites an earlier argument by F. W. Danker to the effect that Joanna may have been a source for Luke's information, and mention of her indicates that "the Gospel has '. . . penetrated Herod's own establishment'." This periphrastic construction seems to be a way of avoiding the obvious inference that Joanna *herself* was the agent through whom the Gospel entered the court of Antipas.

[19] In Luke 9:7–9, Antipas hears about Jesus' activities and his curiosity is piqued. In Luke 13:3 the Pharisees warn Jesus to flee because Antipas wants to kill him, but Jesus sends a taunt back to the tetrarch. In Luke 23:6–12, "Herod was delighted to see Jesus. In fact, he had been eager to see him for quite some time, since he had heard so much about him, and was hoping to see him perform some sign."

[20] The baptizer's name, John, is one of those favoured by Hasmonean national-ist sympathizers. In fact, "John" or Ἰωάννης is the masculinely inflected form of the name "Joanna" or Ἰωάννα. Indeed, Luke provides this John with Jerusalem connections and a priestly lineage on his mother's side as well as his father's (Luke 1:5–25, 57–63). Intra-caste marriage, like that which Luke attributes to John's par-ents Zechariah and Elizabeth, was a means by which the leading priestly families concentrated their power. Although Zechariah is not permanently resident in Jerusalem, neither has he married a woman of mere Israelite or Levite ancestry;

own attitude toward Antipas was rather foolhardy. If Jesus had a protector inside the Herodian inner circle, as Luke implies, most likely she was Joanna.[21]

These three major factions related in complex, conflictive, and collaborative ways in the Galilee of Jesus. The picture was surely much more complicated than can be summarized here. We must conclude, however, that the significant frontiers in that society were not drawn between "Jews versus Romans" or "aristocrats versus peasants" or "village versus city," conceived as simple oppositions. Those clichés are inadequate to the data.

Magdala and Tiberias

The Gospels provide little direct information about Joanna and Mary. But historical and archaeological sources allow us to make some inferences about what it meant to be "the wife of Herod's viceroy." We can also determine with some confidence what it meant to be known as being "from Magdala" in the first century.

Magdala lay on the western shore of Lake Gennesareth, three

---

this detail of Luke's story tends to corroborate the suggestion that Hasmonean sympathies prompted the choice of the name John.

[21] The fact that women were powerful and active in Antipas' court is further attested by the role of Herodias in determining John's fate. It is no less plausible that Joanna protected Jesus, than that Herodias engineered John's arrest and execution (Matt. 14:1–12; Mark 6:14–28; Luke 3:19). To anyone advocating a return to Hasmonean-style national autonomy, Herodias' marital law-breaking portended something much more disastrous than the waywardness of an ordinary woman. Herodias was the granddaughter of Herod, the great polygamist, and Mariamme, which means that her grandmother's grandfather had been the Hasmonean high priest Hyrcanus. But Herodias' own grandfather Herod, who had murdered her father, then chose to become her father-in law as well by betrothing her to another of his sons. (See Josephus, *Ant.* 17:1, 2.) Accordingly, Herodias, descendant of the Hasmonean priestly line through the princess Mariamme, was married into the lineage of the *other* Mariamme: one of the out-caste women who had taken Herodias' grandmother's place as Herod's wife: Mariamme "the second," whose father had been installed in the high priesthood by Herod after he deposed the Hasmonean priestly line. In Herodias' children, then, royal-priestly Hasmonean blood would mix with that of usurpers of the priesthood. (In fact, this was the lineage of the daughter who danced for the party-goers in Matt. 14 and Mark 6, a distasteful detail omitted by Luke.) Herodias later switched husbands—keeping the same father-in-law, interestingly enough. Offspring of this second marriage, to Antipas, would mix Hasmonean blood with that of the Samaritan mother of Antipas. Presumably, this prospect was even more offensive to nationalists who regarded the Hasmonean dynasty as the last hereditarily legitimate rulers of Israel.

miles north of Tiberias (the modern city, continuously inhabited since its foundation by Herod Antipas about 18 c.e.).[22] Josephus calls it "Tarichaeae" after its famous export commodity, salt fish.[23] The material remains of the first-century habitation at Magdala are scant, but they fit the suggested profile for a Hasmonean site. There was a small (18' by 21') colonnaded hall, later converted to a city fountain-house, apparently. Textual references indicate that the city had a shipyard and facilities for processing fish. Josephus, a Judean of priestly caste, found sympathizers here when he was leading a rebel army against the Romans during the First Jewish War (66–73 c.e.). The picture of Magdala that emerges is that of a thriving busy town organized to support its export industry. If Hasmonean encroach-ment in the first century B.C.E. had pushed peasants off their ances-tral farms in the hills and valleys to the west, they could have found new livelihoods in Magdala as shipwrights, net makers, fishers, and fish packers. Not only was the Lake the source of fish, it was also the route for shipping jars of pickled fish across to the ports on the eastern shore that connected with trade routes going north and east to Damascus and on into Babylon. Coincidentally, the region is spec-tacularly beautiful, especially in the springtime.

As noted above, the name Mary was given to girls in the gener-ation ahead of Jesus' as a nationalistic gesture of protest against Herod.[24] Thus, Mary of Magdala may well have been old enough to be Jesus' mother. An older woman would have had greater sta-tus and greater freedom to travel. And this Mary must have trav-

---

[22] Information about Magdala, Tiberias, and the lakeshore comes from personal observation and from the relevant articles in the archaeological dictionary of Rousseau and Arav, *Jesus and His World*, where references to the excavation reports are listed.

[23] Ταριχεῖαι are factories for salting fish, or for pickling, salting, or otherwise preserving any food. The verb ταριχεύω means to pickle or smoke food, or to embalm a human body. Salt would have to be imported in bulk overland to the Lake from the Dead Sea in Judea, and this connection would have been facilitated after the Hasmonean conquest of Galilee. In fact, a Judean family could achieve what we would call a vertical monopoly over the salt, the fish, the processing, and the shipping. A tower in this lakeside town could have been a smokestack or sim-ply a landmark on the shore for the fishing vessels.

[24] The Hebrew name comes from the Torah, and is that of Moses' sister Miriam. In the Septuagint, the name is spelled Μαριαμ (no accent, no inflection). In Latin, the name became Maria; in English, Mary. As Williams points out, the national-istic overtone may not have been consciously embraced. The name may also have been increasingly coopted by the Herodians. One of the later wives of Herod the Great himself was named Mariamme, or perhaps took that name to ennoble her-self and to re-inforce Herod's elevation of her father to the office of high priest, which previously had belonged to the Hasmonean Mariamme's family.

elled, for no one calls you "Magdalene" in Magdala. Significantly, this Mary is not called (in Greek) "Mary of Tarichaeae"—"Pickleworks Mary"—but is identified by the indigenous Aramaic name of the place. Later rabbinic texts refer to the town as *Migdal Nunya*, "tower of fish." So, why is "Mary from Fish-Tower" going abroad in Galilee? Plausibly, she is conducting business related to the export of salt fish. In any event, the association of this Mary with Magdala is circumstantial evidence that she belonged to the Judean-sympathizing, *anti-Herodian* faction in Galilee.

Magdalenes had reason to shun the Herodians in the new resort of Tiberias, planted just an hour's stroll down the beach. Hasmoneans arriving from Judea apparently had established themselves at Magdala about a century earlier and had expanded the village comfortably to suit their administrative and business needs. Assuming a common basic religious heritage and kinship customs between Judeans and Galileans, that transition may be imagined as a relatively smooth one, though there would have been economic conflicts and frictions over land ownership. But the foundation of Tiberias in 18 or 19 C.E. brought more drastic changes to the region's administration and its landscape.

Tiberias was erected from scratch and populated with involuntarily displaced peasants, artisans, traders, foreigners, and whomever else Antipas could grab up. Why did he go to the trouble of building himself a spanking new capital on the shore of the Lake, when he already had adequate facilities in the beautiful inland city of Sepphoris? The answer is to be sought in the geopolitical ambitions of the Herodian dynasty in general and of Antipas in particular. Antipas controlled less territory than his father had. He lacked a Mediterranean port. The Jordan river was the eastern border of his northern territory, Galilee, and it was the western border of his southern territory, Perea. Antipas didn't care about the land as such; he cared about how people crossed it on their way to and from Jerusalem. Jerusalem was a worldwide pilgrimage centre, thanks in part to the magnificent Temple enlarged and renovated by Herod the Great. Travellers disembarking at Herod's new Mediterranean port of Caesarea—that is, those arriving from Alexandria, Rome, and other western imperial cities—were received and entertained in palatial facilities before proceeding on their journeys east overland toward Babylon or south to the Temple city by the coastal route. But Antipas, unlike his father, did not control either Caesarea or Jerusalem. His capital, Sepphoris, apparently could not attract the elite imperial pilgrims approaching the Temple city from the west. And from the east, travellers arriving from Babylon and Damascus were bypassing Antipas as they entered the Decapolis region on the southeast lakeshore, proceeded down the eastern bank of the Jordan, forded at Scythopolis without entering Perea (Antipas' other territory), continued south along the river to Jericho and ascended westward toward Jerusalem.

To divert and capture this traffic, Antipas needed to give elite travellers a reason to sail across the Lake. He chose the site for Tiberias on the southwestern shore opposite the gleaming hilltop city of Hippos/Susita.[25] He built an attractive cliffside palace to entice elite travellers to tarry with him on the way to and from the Temple city. The remains of that palace have not been identified in the archaeological record; however the textual record indicates that it was decorated in the finest imperial style. At Tiberias, Antipas would be the first to greet elite Babylonian tourists on their arrival in Eretz Israel and the last to bid them farewell as they returned home. (Presumably, more modest commercial and civic facilities—synagogues?—would accommodate travellers who were not quite important enough to be Antipas' guests.) Besides the obvious gains in international prestige, this would open up opportunities for business contacts not just for the Herodians, but also for any local agricultural or food-processing interests astute enough to get a piece of the action.[26]

Antipas would need to arrange entertainments for wealthy business travellers and their families. His staff, supervised by Chuza, would take care of this work.[27] Since pilgrimage was a socially accept-

---

[25] The twin names come from the Greek and Hebrew words for horse, respectively. At night the lights of Tiberias would shine out across the black water, like those of Hippos, visible as far as Bethsaida and Capernaum on the northern shore, according to the suggestion of Rousseau and Arav, *Jesus and His World*, pp. 127–8. The voices of party-goers could also be heard across the waters, disrupting the fishing.

[26] Antipas also entertained at the palace of Machaerus in his other territory, Perea. Machaerus was just 30 miles from Jerusalem, and part of the journey was a pleasant cruise across the Dead Sea. Sea travel, even for just a few miles, was not only more pleasant than travel by desert roads; it was also stylishly "Greek" and "Alexandrian." Thus, the cities of Caesarea and Tiberias had the maritime advantage over the sometime capital Sepphoris, with its one puny little municipal swimming pool. Antipas was not the only one who wanted to influence the pilgrims coming and going along the Jordan valley. John the Baptist positioned himself and his challenge to Herodian authority right on the banks of the Jordan, astride the pilgrimage route. This confrontation was the context for Jesus' own baptism.

[27] Chuza's name is known to us only in the transliteration that Luke gives us:

able motive for women to travel along with their husbands, it is likely that Chuza's wife shared responsibility for arranging hospitality for entire families.[28] "Joanna" is a nationalistic Hasmonean name: Ἰωάννα, feminine form of Ἰωάννης or "John." The betrothal of Joanna to Chuza may have been arranged with the same sort of political intentions as the betrothal of the Judean Mariamme to the Idumean Herod one generation earlier. Joanna's marriage may have been intended to forge an alliance between an elite Judean family and one of the first families of neighbouring Idumea or Perea. We then have at least three quite plausible reasons for Joanna to come into contact with Mary Magdalene. (1) Both apparently were born into families with nationalistic Judean sympathies. Perhaps they had even been girlhood friends and their friendship continued during their marriages. (2) Joanna may have assisted Mary to make international business connections through the court at Tiberias. (3) Mary may have assisted Joanna in hosting elite visitors on tours of local sights such as the packing facilities at Magdala, or in pleasure cruises on the Lake. A fourth possible connection is suggested by Luke, who says that both Mary and Joanna were cured of illness by Jesus. There are hot springs at Tiberias. It is not unlikely that the palatial Herodian resort included something like a health spa (as at another Herodian complex, Machaerus in Perea, which Antipas often used). If Tiberias was supposed to be a place of recuperation for weary pilgrims, then a Galilean faith-healer would be an intriguing addition to the list of local attractions. Jesus, Mary, and Joanna may have first come together in such a context. If, as Luke reports, Antipas himself regarded Jesus as an entertainer and a quaint but harmless curiosity, that fact lends substance to this conjecture.

The Lukan Premise: A Double Agent in Herod Antipas' Organization?

If the first contacts among Joanna, Mary, and Jesus occurred in a material context such as I have described, this does not in any way

---

Χουζᾶ. It is probably an Idumean name. Herod the Great was of Idumean heritage, and the region of Perea remained a power base for Antipas. Josephus mentions an Idumean deity named Koze (*Ant.* 15:253). An administrative officer of Herod the Great, Costobar, is said to be from the lineage of the priests of Koze.

[28] This is all the more likely if Joanna had family connections in Judea, site of the Temple and its pilgrimage facilities, but Chuza did not.

rule out a profound transformation of their relationship subsequently. On the contrary, it helps to solve one of the toughest puzzles in early Christian history: how a local Palestinian reform movement, with locally defined issues, began to spread beyond the Jordan and the Mediterranean Sea. The Magdalene and the Herodian lady are the only disciples we know of for whom we can plausibly posit international commercial and political connections. For the international mobilization of the Gospel movement to get going *after Calvary*, as it did, there had to be people close to Jesus who knew something of the world beyond Galilee.[29] Joanna and Mary are the only figures in Jesus' immediate circle who did, according to the circumstantial evidence of their involvement with international trade and their contacts in far-flung Diaspora communities. These likely provided the bridge for the Gospel to travel up to Jerusalem and out to the cities of the eastern and western worlds. No other hypothesis fits the archaeological, geographical, and textual evidence so well.

But that was after Calvary, and I am getting ahead of my story. Let's recall that, as stated above, the Gospel texts distinguish between the Galilean functions of the Jesus women and their Jerusalem functions. In Galilee the women bankrolled and facilitated the road trips of Jesus (Mark 15:40–41; Matt. 27:58; Luke 8:1–3). We have seen how circumstantial evidence allows us to fill in some details about the context in which this occurred—given the involvement of a Mary "from Magdala" and of a Joanna "wife of Herod's viceroy." Our reconstruction suggested that Antipas turned Lake Gennesareth into a tourist attraction. Travellers from Damascus, Babylon, and points east now crossed the Lake to Tiberias, where the cliffside palace of Herod Antipas offered hospitality and a chance to mingle with Antipas' local clientele. The hospitality of the palace, and of auxiliary commercial establishments, would mean party barges, ferry boats, dinner cruises, water sports, and other floating entertainments radiating out from the docks and beaches at Tiberias. This was the first stop in the Promised Land for travellers making their way to Jerusalem for business and/or pilgrimage. The *number* of elite guests for whom these facilities were intended was not large. But the *power* of those

---

[29] *Before Calvary*, the Gospels report, Jesus himself travelled beyond Galilee into the cities of the Decapolis and northward to Tyre and Sidon. While the women financiers are not reported to have gone that far with him, their money probably did, and they may have made arrangements for him with their local contacts.

elite few was considerable. They represented an opportunity for international trading connections that could plug Galilean industries into the Syrian, Babylonian, and other eastern trade networks, and cultivate prestigious international political connections for Antipas.

If the eastern visitors had commercial interests, they would want to meet local managers and tour the industrial facilities along the shore from Tiberias up to Magdala and on toward Capernaum. The Herodian hosts would want to include some local colour in the business itinerary. They also needed to provide diversions for members of travelling families who were not directly involved in business. Jesus the exorcist, healer, and teacher fit the bill. We have no record that he appeared at Antipas' spa or at the palace.[30] But people went out in droves to hear and see Jesus along the shore and in the lakeside hills.[31] Antipas began his makeover of the lake region about the year 18 C.E. The flamboyant Herodian lifestyle provoked vociferous opposition from John and others during the following decade. Jesus bought into that opposition and signalled his agreement by undergoing John's baptism about 28 C.E., shortly before John was arrested and beheaded.[32]

The question is whether Jesus' career began with his baptism and therefore was anti-Herodian from the start. This cannot be pre-supposed. The connection with Joanna suggests that, on the contrary, Jesus may have first functioned as an exorcist under the sponsorship of the Herodians, at least for a time. When he eventually broke with his patron—"that fox," Luke 13:32—Jesus did not sever all his connections with members of the Herodian court. There is an additional consideration that makes this possibility appear more likely. In Jerusalem the Roman prefect Pontius Pilate seems to have recognized Jesus as Herod's kind of guy. By Luke's account (Luke 23:6–17), Pilate sends Jesus to Antipas for a mock trial. Antipas is delighted to see him at last; he expects Jesus to perform tricks. The

---

[30] Jesus seldom made house calls—for example see Mark 5:21–43 and par; Luke 7:1–10. But if he healed Joanna he must have encountered the ailing Herodian lady *somewhere*.

[31] Five thousand are fed in Mark 6:34–44. If the exaggerated story is not pure hype, it may reflect an influx of visitors during tourist/pilgrimage season, when villagers would be prepared to sell food to outsiders (as expected in v. 36).

[32] Tiberias was founded as the capital of Galilee in 18 or 19 C.E. For John's dates, see the extensive discussion in J. P. Meier, *A Marginal Jew: Re-thinking the Historical Jesus. Vol. 2: Mentor, Message, and Miracles* (New York: Doubleday, 1994), especially pp. 1040–1.

entertainer won't entertain, nevertheless Antipas and his soldiers have some fun with Jesus, dress him up in gaudy clothes, and send him back to Pilate. This little exchange occurs in the currency of contempt for indigenous religious idioms, and by Luke's account, sharing it cements a bond of friendship between the Roman bureaucrat and the puppet sovereign.

We cannot here establish the historical reliability of Luke's account of the trial, in all its details.[33] Our discussion goes forward simply on the stipulation that Luke's report is essentially correct: Jesus was taken for a Herodian protégé (or at least a Herodian subject) by the civil authority in Jerusalem. This brings us now to what I have termed the second or Jerusalem functions of the Jesus women. In Gospel hindsight, that is, in Christian religious perspective, the women's role is to *witness* the events of the crucifixion, the burial, and the emptied tomb. But in contemporary secular perspective, it seems that the task confronting Joanna and her associates was to *keep an eye on Jesus* and keep him out of trouble by keeping him away from both Antipas and the Judean religious authorities while in Jerusalem for the festival of Pesach.

Joanna, I have suggested, walked a thin line in Herod's court at Tiberias. Co-operating with local associates like Mary of Magdala, Joanna promoted the teaching and healing career of her protégé Jesus both among Antipas' clients and in villages and towns of Galilee and beyond. Antipas heard rave reviews about Jesus, but Joanna managed to prevent the two from meeting in spite of the tetrarch's curiosity. Perhaps she could have continued indefinitely to juggle Jesus' itinerary against Herod's schedule in Galilee. But Antipas and his court went to Jerusalem for the same festival at which Jesus and his male followers, for whatever reason, chose to stage the political confrontation that quickly brought his career to a close.

The suddenness of Jesus' arrest and execution took his followers by surprise. It happened so fast that they didn't know what hit them; therefore, many commentators assume that the details of Jesus' trial

---

[33] R. E. Brown finds the Herodian trial plausible as an imperial ἀνάκρισις or preliminary investigation. See *The Death of the Messiah: From Gethsemane to the Grave*, 2 vols. (New York: Doubleday, 1994), p. 766. J. D. Crossan disagrees. He argues that the trial narrative was produced by later Christian reflection on Psalm 2 at a time when Herodians remained powerful enemies of the Jesus movement. See *Who Killed Jesus? Exposing the Roots of Anti-Semitism in the Gospel Story of the Death of Jesus* (San Francisco, CA: HarperSanFrancisco, 1995), p. 84.

were unknown to his followers.[34] Some scholars discount the possibility that there was any trial at all, and most agree that the trial "transcripts" in the Gospels are later, theological re-constructions based on various passages of the Hebrew Scripture. But this skeptical view leaves us without a way to account for the fact that the Jesus people knew that Jesus was being crucified *at all*. If Jesus was snatched in the night, and even if Peter skulked along behind the Temple police and eavesdropped on the arraignment before the Sanhedrin, Jesus' friends would not have learned that he was to be marched out to Calvary in the morning. They would assume, rather, that he was kept in custody by the Temple police to hush him up during the festival. The Sanhedrin could not carry out a death penalty. If indeed there were witnesses standing by the cross in the morning, then there had to be someone sympathetic to Jesus on the inside of the Roman-Herodian civil process overnight.

But if there was no such process in Jesus' case, or if it occurred but Jesus' friends had no inside connections, then Jesus' friends would not have learned of his crucifixion at all—before, during, or after the event. The crucifixion of Jesus lasted just a few hours. The chances are slim that one of his companions—out-of-towners staying in unfamiliar accommodations in a city mobbed with visitors like themselves—accidentally happened upon the scene in that small window of opportunity while the execution was occurring. Afterwards the corpse was quickly removed.[35] It stands to reason: as the hours went by, the longer Jesus' companions remained ignorant of his fate, the less likely they were *ever* to learn what happened to him. Yet, they did know afterwards; and, in all four Gospel accounts, they knew

---

[34] Crossan writes: "The hypothesis I am testing is that Jesus' companions knew he had been arrested and executed but knew nothing at all about what, if anything, had intervened. They had no details at all about any judicial process or, indeed, any knowledge about whether any such event took place." See *Who Killed Jesus*, p. 112. Crossan's formulation frames the issues well, but it does not address the major problem of *how* the companions knew of the arrest and execution.

[35] I am assuming that the reports are correct and the crucifixion of Jesus at Passover festival time was cut short. Ordinary Roman practice was to allow crucified bodies to be consumed by animals as carrion. Crossan's suggestion that foraging dog packs regularly patrolled the outskirts of Jerusalem is not compatible with the character of the city as a place offering hospitality to tens of thousands of travellers at regular intervals—not to mention the livestock continually herded into the city for the Temple cult. But Crossan is correct to presume some degree of co-operation in peacetime between the Roman administration and the religious authorities. See *Who Killed Jesus*, p. 117.

soon enough to be present during the crucifixion procedure itself. Specifically, in the Gospel narratives it is Jesus' women associates who show up at the cross in time to watch Jesus die. The plausible explanation for this is that Joanna spread the word to alert her associates after learning of—or perhaps witnessing—Jesus' appearance before Antipas.

In other words, given the evidence that we have, we need to accept the historicity of the Herodian connection if we are to account for the fact that Jesus' companions knew about the crucifixion *at all*, not just while it was happening. The short time and the huge number of visitors in the city made it unlikely that one of the relatively few people who noticed Jesus being crucified, and who also bothered to learn his name, would accidentally have mentioned it afterwards in the hearing of someone who cared. For all Jesus' companions knew, he remained in the custody of the Temple police. Joanna, as a Herodian dignitary, may have been recognizable on sight to soldiers of the Roman death squad; if so, she could safely approach the place of crucifixion. As a mobile and discrete informant she would be an asset to her husband's boss. Antipas had found Jesus innocent and entertaining, according to Luke, and may have been interested in a back-channel report through Joanna about what became of his reluctant wonder-worker. Thus, it appears that Joanna's stakeout at Calvary yielded intelligence that she passed on officially to Antipas and unofficially to the friends of Jesus.

It is quite unlikely (though technically possible) that Jesus' friends received timely word of the crucifixion from the other group that apparently knew about it, the Sanhedrin. In all four Gospels we meet the figure of Joseph of Arimathea, who buries Jesus after asking Pilate to release the body to him while it is still on the cross. Could Joseph have been the insider who leaked word of Jesus' imminent execution? Joseph is presented as an officer of the Sanhedrin, which supposedly prosecuted Jesus before Pilate and before Antipas. Matthew calls Joseph rich; Mark says he was looking for God's reign; Luke insists he was righteous and dissented from the prosecution of Jesus; and John makes him a secret disciple and partners him with Nicodemus. But these appear to be implausible attempts to rehabilitate Joseph in order to account for the disciples' knowledge of the crucifixion; they are not supported by any other evidence of a sympathetic connection between Jesus and the Judean authorities. In fact, the Sanhedrin had every reason to try to keep Jesus' supporters from hearing about the crucifixion during the festival, when there was maximum risk from civil disturbance. It is likely that Joseph of Arimathea, acting for the Sanhedrin, claimed the body in order to complete Jesus' "disappearance," and also to fulfill the provisions of Judean law in capital cases (as later reflected in Mishnah *Sanhedrin* 6:5). An executed prisoner's body was supposed to be kept in the custody of the Sanhedrin, in a special tomb, without the performance of mourning and burial rites, for one year until the flesh separated from the bones.[36] The death sentence was then considered completed, and the bones were released to the family for proper mourning and burial.

The Sanhedrin was supposed to maintain a facility for entombing executed criminals. The court might very well wish to keep the location of the criminals' tomb secret, since families and friends ordinarily might not agree to forego mourning rituals or to let the body rot so shamefully apart from the bodies of kin. Hence the curious detail in the Gospels to the effect that the Jesus-women had to follow Joseph surreptitiously in order to find out where the tomb was and witness the burial (Mark 15:47; Matt. 27:61; Luke 23:55). Had Joseph really been such a friend to the Jesus-people, he himself could have witnessed to the burial and the location of the tomb. In any event, we have now followed the women through the first phases of their Jerusalem witnessing function: explicitly, to see Jesus hung on the cross and to see him buried; and implicitly, to see Jesus fall into the hands of Antipas and be sent back to the Roman prefect for condemnation.

The culmination of the women's witnessing in Jerusalem occurs at the emptied tomb, according to the narratives that come down to us. Having seen Jesus condemned, crucified, and buried, the

---

[36] This was not cruel or unusual punishment according to prevailing customs. In first-century Jerusalem, a two-stage burial was the norm for those who could afford it. The first burial, on the day of death, was really enclosure of the body on a slab in a rock chamber. At the end of a year, the bones were cleaned off and re-buried in a small stone box called an ossuary. (In effect, all tombs were emptied.) There were rituals to be observed by kin at both stages of the process. The difference with penal burial was that the first phase occurred in custody rather than in the family's own tomb. For further discussion of this custom, see M. Sawicki, *Seeing the Lord* (Minneapolis, MN: Fortress, 1994), pp. 237–8, 257, 273. R. E. Brown seems to assert on p. 1206, n. 1, and p. 1243 of *Death of the Messiah* that Joseph was *not* enforcing the provisions of penal burial; but on pp. 1249–50 Brown makes a strong case that Joseph was doing exactly that.

women now see the significance of his death and life. It is they who bring the message of resurrection back to Jesus' male associates.

Through the Eyes of Joanna and Mary

From Calvary to this very day, anyone who sees Jesus as the Risen Lord is looking at him through the eyes of Mary, Joanna, and their women associates. Unlike most disciples, these women knew Jesus in the early days and stuck with him after Calvary. Their relationship *became* faith but may have begun as something else. We cannot look into their hearts, but we have taken a look around their world. Someone saw the possibilities and the needs of that world. Someone after Calvary saw that the words of Jesus deserved repetition not only as a variant of the *halachah* circulating in Galilean and Judean villages, but also as a variant of the Stoic and Cynic χρεῖαι circulating in the Decapolis and other secular cities. Someone facilitated the translations in language and in genre that brought the Gospel out into western imperial society and into the Syrian and Babylonian east.

To understand the Gospel, it is necessary to understand the social mechanisms of its cultural translation and propagation. The distinctive interface of Galilean, Judean, and Herodian factions on the Magdalene-Tiberian lakeshore was the context for a friendship between two women, and through that friendship, was the prelude to the decisive events of Calvary and the emptied tomb.

MARY MAGDALENE AND THE SEVEN DEMONS
IN SOCIAL-SCIENTIFIC PERSPECTIVE

CARMEN BERNABÉ UBIETA

Introduction

Soon afterward he went on through cities and villages, preaching and bringing the good news of the kingdom of God. And the twelve *were* with him, and also some women who had been healed of evil spirits and infirmities (ἀπὸ πνευμάτων πονηρῶν καὶ ἀστςενειῶν): Mary called Magdalene, from whom seven demons had gone (ἀφ᾽ ἧς δαιμόνια ἑπτὰ ἐξεληλύθει), and Joanna, the wife of Chuza, Herod's steward, and Susanna, and many others, who provided for them out of their means (Luke 8:1–3 RSV).

Throughout history, the demons expelled from Mary Magdalene have been a detail in the story that was treated in two ways. On the one hand, no special interpretation of the "demons" was offered because their meaning was taken for granted. On the other hand, when the "demons" were treated explicit, they were generally identified with Satan, or the devil, understood as a "ser personal extrahumano causa decisiva del pecado en el mundo."[1] At the same time, the reference to the demons entailed a moral judgement as well. By means of a literary relation of Luke 8:3 with Luke 7:36–50,[2] the conclusion was often reached that the evil that affected Mary Magdalene was due to prostitution, which is the sin or moral evil "par excellence" attributed to a woman in a patriarchal society.

We might ask, however, whether the usual interpretation is not reductive. By focusing on the presumed moral quality of the afflicted woman, are interpreters not selectively inattentive to political and cultural dimensions that such liberating healing involves? In order to bring into consciousness the hidden dimensions of this passage, we need to know all dimensions of the particular evils that afflicted

---

[1] H. Haag, *El Diablo. Su existencia como problema* (Barcelona: Herder, 1978), p. 30. Literal translation of the quotation: "suprahuman personal being, the decisive cause of sin in the world."

[2] C. Bernabé Ubieta, *María Magdalena. Sus tradiciones en el Cristianismo Primitivo* (Estella: Verbo Divino, 1994), pp. 191–201.

women such as Mary Magdalene. Evils that Luke considers to be possession by evil spirits (especially related to women) play an important role in his Gospel[3] and this implies the author's explicit intention to communicate something significant to his readers.[4]

Not all questions that modern readers ask about the passage are answered by Luke, even if those readers need the answer in order to understand the Gospel's message. It is because of this that appropriate methodological tools are required in order to answer such questions. Among these methods, social-scientific criticism seems quite useful and has been applied in recent years within biblical exegesis. Its value has also been acknowledged by the Biblical Pontifical Committee in its document "Bible Interpretation in the Church" (1993).[5] Theories, models and concepts from the social sciences are introduced into biblical scholarship according to the nature of the phenomenon that is studied in order to obtain a better understanding of it.

The possibility of anachronism and ethnocentrism in applying such social-scientific theories and models is very obvious, but practitioners of social-scientific criticism are far more sensitive to this possibility than are historians whose models of the ancient world remain thoughtless and inexplicit. Furthermore, I believe that the critical and conscious use of those models and theories may help us to achieve a deeper understanding of the facts we study. Social-scientific approaches compare the cultural scenarios of biblical documents with scenarios in other similar cultures; they also apply models and concepts of human knowledge, acting and understanding as applicable in comparatively similar social systems such as those of biblical societies. Such comparative models are good tools to obtain a deeper and more relevant understanding of biblical passages and their messages.

At times, scholars are able to create a frame of reference or model in terms of what the biblical authors themselves attest to, thus allowing us to understand what we find in the Bible in terms of ancient Mediterranean experience (emic perspective: viewpoint, categories of thought, and explanations of the group which is being studied). But

---

[3] The statistic of the term (δαιμόνιον) is as follows: Matt. 11; Luke 22; John 6. Πνεῦμα πονηρόν: Matt. 1; Luke 3; Acts 4.

[4] J. J. Pilch, "Sickness and Healing in Luke-Acts," in J. H. Neyrey (ed.), *The Social World of Luke-Acts. Models for Interpretation* (Peabody, MA: Hendrickson, 1991), pp. 196–7.

[5] Cittá del Vaticano: Libreria Editrice Vaticana, 1993.

more often than not, however, we will apply theories about biblical roles, values and behaviours in terms of our contemporary categories (etic perspective: viewpoint, categories of thought and explanations of the external investigator).[6] I find both perspectives legitimate and necessary, and mutually clarifying.

In this essay about spirit possession, I think it is insufficient to know the cultural frame of reference in which the ancients categorized and studied possessed people in their own cultural categories (although I do a little of this as well). They thought that some strange and powerful forces, personified and called "demons," could take possession of human beings. Such demons then controlled the possessed person's existence and withdrew that existence from the individual's control. Demons would cause evil and destroy the most typically human features in those they possessed. We, however, no longer explain events in terms of personal causality ("every significant event has a personal cause"). Hence, instead of personifying interpersonal and intra-personal phenomena, as the ancients did, we look for immediate and adequate causes of the phenomena. We will label those demons rather differently and seek to know more about the reason why they appeared to certain people, how they increasingly influenced them, and how people were healed. We want to understand what those afflicted people experienced and what they tried to convey as they described their experiences, but in categories meaningful to us.

Consequently, to understand spirit possession in New Testament documents, I find it necessary to employ theoretical perspectives derived from social anthropology and cross-cultural social psychology. There is a set of dimensions that need to be clarified if we wish to grasp, fully and with relevance, what Mary Magdalene's encounter with Jesus meant. For sure, it was a healing encounter which completely changed her life for the better. Hence, for example, we ought to enquire into the social function of possession and exorcisms, the inter-relation between certain kinds of social situations and the types of persons undergoing spirit possession, the roles that gender, kinship structures and socio-cultural norms played both in the aetiology of spirit possession and its healing.

---

[6] J. H. Elliott, *What is Social-Scientific Criticism?* (Minneapolis, MN: Fortress, 1993), pp. 38–9.

I. *Demons and Possession*

1. *Demons and Spirits in the Ancient Mind*

In the Hellenistic period, the term "demon" (δαιμόνιον) came to designate a whole set of personified forces which surrounded human beings, and influenced and controlled their existence, for good or for evil. The neuter form δαιμόνιον (pl. δαιμόνια) was preferred to δαίμων (pl. δαίμονες) because the latter had come to designate a class of semi-divine beings, closely related to the spirits of the dead. In the New Testament, the only two types of demons mentioned somewhat frequently are those who are prone to evil, malignant spirits that damage people's belongings and personality, causing infirmities and disgraceful behaviour, to the point of controlling the actions of the afflicted person. The ideology behind such demon perceptions is rooted in the most primitive of animistic beliefs.

Both in the Synoptics and in Acts, as well as in early Rabbinical documents (b.Pes. 112b, Strack-Billerbeck IV, 514; b.A.Z. 12b, Strack-Billerbeck IV, 532), demons were believed to be capable of damaging persons and property. But although they were perceived as the cause of certain infirmities and afflictions, they were not considered to be intermediate beings (between God and humankind), as they were outside Israel. Similarly, they were not related to the ancestors' spirits, as they were in the Greek world. In the New Testament period such demons were likewise called spirits (πνευμάτα), either good (πονηρός) or impure (ἀκάθαρτος).[7]

It happened that certain people acted in distinctive ways, but the causes of their behaviour could not be traced back to other human beings or the usual experiences of human life, so the inexplicable activity was attributed to personal causes affecting such extraordinary persons and which were called demons. Consequently, these people were thought to be possessed by demons. Those so affected showed external behavioural signs that were judged to be deviant from cultural norms, hence derived from deviant relationships. Whether those "abnormal" actions or attributes were positive or negative, whether they came from God or from the demons, that the community had to find out. In negative cases, consequently, to free a

---

[7] Cf. W. Foerster, "Δαίμων," in *Grande Lessico Nuovo Testamento* II (Brescia: Paideia, 1966), pp. 741–90.

person from a demonic possession involved not only exorcizing the demon, but re-instating that particular person into a meaningful place in society as well.[8] It also involved political overtones, since in order to restore the disturbed correct social order, power was required.[9]

While I do not think it is useful to delve into demonology here, I would like to note that any translation of δαιμόνια in Luke 8:2–3 as "devil" or any synonym for that term would be simply wrong. Further, to relate the activities of demons or spirits to that of "Satan" (or its Greek equivalent διάβολος, "devil") would be totally anachronistic. Generally, the demonic activity is non-moral, affecting the material side of human existence, not the moral side.[10]

2. *Model for a Fuller Understanding of the Phenomenon of Demonic Possession*

There is a wide range of "disciplines" that, from different perspectives, shed light on the subject of demon possession, which they consider to be a problem of relationships between a person and society, including those social groups and persons with which human beings have relational ties. Social anthropology, cross-cultural psychology, sociology, medicine, and psychiatry all provide a range of models and concepts which allow a complex and nuanced approach to a complex problem, its causes, extent, meanings, and solutions.

2.1 *Possession and Trances. Definitions*

From the anthropological point of view, demonic possession is defined as a cultural explanation for certain infirmities, and one of the mystical interpretations of trance.

Trance, in a medical sense, is an altered state of consciousness, belonging to atypical dissociative disorders of the DSM-III.[11] It is produced or induced by different causes, and without physical injury. It is characterized by the alteration in the integrating functions of consciousness (identity, memory, perception), and is translated into dissociative phenomena (visual or aural hallucinations, amnesia, somnambulism, dissociated identities or multiple personalities,

---

[8] B. J. Malina and R. L. Rohrbaugh, *Social-Science Commentary on the Synoptic Gospels* (Minneapolis, MN: Fortress, 1992), p. 312.

[9] J. J. Pilch, "Power," in J. J. Pilch and B. J. Malina (eds.), *Biblical Social Values and their Meaning. A Handbook* (Peabody, MA: Hendrickson, 1993), p. 141.

[10] Cf. H. Haag, *El Diablo*, p. 119.

[11] DSM-III (Diagnostic and Statistical Manual of Mental Disorders. American Academy of Psychiatry, 1987).

self-mutilations, convulsions, etc.). Sometimes, conversion reactions (such as deafness, muteness, paralysis, etc.) arise as well.

Some cultures (and also modern psychiatry) offer non-mystical explanations for trance states.[12] But there are cultures which offer mystical explanations: the subject loses his/her soul, or he/she suffers a demonic possession. It is obvious that for the latter explanation to emerge, a group must previously believe in spirits and demons.[13] "Demonic possession" also can be diagnosed in afflicted people who do not have the more serious "hysteroid" symptoms that are found in trance (cf. supra).

2.2 *Possession as Indirect Protest and Rebellion Strategy (I. M. Lewis)*

After developing a comparative perspective on the phenomenon of possession among very diverse peoples, in his study of ecstatic religion I. M. Lewis divides demonic possession into two main types: *legitimating* and *peripheral*. The difference between these types lies in the subjects who suffer from them, the kinds of spirits that are thought to be involved in them, as well as their function in the social group.

Legitimating possession is produced by the ancestral spirits, or by the spirit of the main divinity. These are the spirits that support the moral code of the group, and they can be found in the main form of worship in a society. Such spirits legitimatize the power, status, and authority of those who experience spirit possession: usually the male elite.

Peripheral possession, however, is much more relevant for the Gospel tradition. Peripheral possession is produced by peripheral spirits—spirits or demons deriving from neighbouring peoples or from the enemies, which are non-moral, because they do not relate to, affect or directly question established morality. More significantly, they affect people who are subjugated, or who are, for different reasons, marginal figures in their own society. For example, women are a target for peripheral possession, no matter what their social situation, since gender is a determining factor because it denies them full participation in public life. And males, too, experience peripheral

---

[12] F. W. Putnam, *Diagnosis and Treatment of Multiple Personality Disorder* (New York and London: Gilford, 1989); C. A. Ross, *Dissociative Identity Disorder. Diagnosis, Clinical Features, and Treatment of Multiple Personality* (New York: John Wiley & Son, rev. ed., 1997).

[13] I. Lewis, *Ecstatic Religions. A Study of Shamanism and Spirit Possession* (London and New York: Routledge, 1989), pp. 32–59.

possession in situations where they are subject to strong dominating powers, or to policies of clear inequality and subjugation.[14]

However, the findings of social anthropologists and cross-cultural social psychologists agree that this type of possession mostly affects women. And among women thus afflicted, researchers have discovered common social problems with very similar features and an underlying common factor: the distortion of family relations with males. This distortion of family relationships has consequences bearing upon the place, function and esteem of women within the family and society. Women experiencing peripheral possession live under family and social pressure, always related to the cultural norms and social roles that are attributed to them as women.

According to the study of C. Kessler,[15] which is supported by many others, the kind of women who are afflicted with possession usually belong to three groups: young wives who were married against their will; old wives who are alienated from their spouses, or who experience strong tensions in their polygamous marriages; and barren, divorced/repudiated or widowed women who have to bear significant family burdens.[16] Thus, in all these women who suffer afflictions diagnosed as possession there is an evident, underlying strong tension between, on the one hand, what these women have been socialized to believe are their goals in life, along with the acknowledgement and self-esteem attached to the various stages of realizing these goals and, on the other hand, the real and actual possibilities open to them in their everyday experience, alongside the

---

[14] Cultures where peripheral possession takes place are characterized by a structure in which women (to whom equality is denied) hold peripheral positions, while males are in power positions. Supporting this deduction (achieved by a number of comparative studies), we have the cases of those cultures where women share positions of responsibility with men and where, consequently, the phenomenon of possession does not appear. R. Shepard Kraemer, in the study *Her Share of the Blessings. Women's Religions among Pagans, Jews, and Christians in the Greco-Roman World* (New York and Oxford: Oxford University Press, 1992, p. 48), describes the relationship between the greater possibility of public performance for the women in the Hellenistic period, and the decrease in ecstatic worship, such as Bacchanals, among women (at least, in the most severe expressions).

[15] Cf. C. S. Kessler, "Conflict and Sovereignity in Kelantanase Malay Spirit Séances," in V. Crapanzano and V. Garrinson (eds.), *Case Studies in Spirit Possession* (New York: Wiley & Son, 1977), p. 316, quoted in I. Lewis, *Ecstatic Religions*, p. 76.

[16] Widowed, barren, or divorced women are precisely the most likely to suffer from hysteria, according to the doctors of ancient times, such as Hippocrates or Galen. Cf. D. Gourevitch, *Le mal d'être femme. La femme et la médecine dans la Rome antique* (Paris: Societé d'édition "Les belles lettres," 1984, pp. 117–19).

sense of alienation in case they are not successful. Because of social expectations, there is a very strong tension between the desire to attain certain goals and available, actual possibilities. Studies point to a connection between stress, illness, possession, and sexual values.

I. M. Lewis believes that we are obviously faced with "a widespread spiritual interpretation of female problems common to many cultures, whose diagnosis and treatment gives women the opportunity to gain ends (material and non-material) which they cannot secure more directly."[17] This author refers to Victorian women as an example of this phenomenon. In fact, the symptoms for some possession are very similar to those of classical hysteria. These so-called hysterical symptoms, regarded as an indicator of a typically female problem in which sexual attitudes play a crucial role, had already been observed by the physicians and writers of ancient times.[18]

Possession serves as a mitigating factor for those tensions mentioned previously. However, it is only a relief, not a solution to the causes behind the tensions. When the peripheral spirits who possess these women are duly diagnosed, the possessed women are free from all responsibility for whatever they may say, demand, or do. The demands that the spirits make on them are accepted and granted within socially determined limits in order for afflicted women to achieve their healing.[19] I. M. Lewis refers to this as "an oblique protest strategy" because such possession does not directly call into question the structure, or the role and distribution of power. Males thus allow for such an "oblique protest" as long as the essential aspects of the social structure are not questioned, and women thereby obtain temporary relief from situations full of tension or from oppressive burdens.

Afflictions interpreted as possession may recur cyclically. When they do return, it becomes possible for those afflicted to become part of a group, made up of women (sometimes including some men),

---

[17] Lewis, *Ecstatic Religions*, p. 77.

[18] Gourevitch, *Le mal d'être femme*, pp. 113–28; M. MacDonald, *Early Christian Women and Pagan Opinion. The Power of the Hysterical Women* (Cambridge: Cambridge University Press, 1996), pp. 1–3, 102–9.

[19] Anthropological studies of peoples from all continents and from pre-industrial cultures, in which the phenomenon of possession is found, have shown that the peripheral spirits demand from the husbands, brothers, or fathers of the possessed women what these women feel they are lacking. By means of this possession, which is always considered authentic, those afflicted (in this case, women) are granted attention. Sometimes this is a way to rebel against and punish (either economically or simply by bothering them) those who are responsible for the oppressive, exploitative, or alienating situations.

similarly affected by possession. The person who leads the group (generally a woman, although a man can also do it), is somebody who has suffered possession, but has learned how to handle the symptoms. Such group leaders are able to introduce spirits into their body at will. Leaders teach how to share their lives with the spirits, giving free reign to them in the cyclical celebrations that these people come to share.

Obviously, such celebration rituals are not very well accepted by local authorities and the representatives of official worship. And this holds all the more true for people who have learned how to handle the spirits, who lead these groups and who help the possessed persons accommodate their afflictions. Thus, these latter are in danger of being accused of witchcraft, that is, of controlling the spirits and directing them against the elite who represent the established order. In other words, the social establishment eventually comes to see a danger in those women (or men) who have suffered spirit possession and subsequently have learned how to handle their spirits and to freely repeat possession episodes. During those episodes, the possessed can behave without moral restraint and express opinions which are theologically or politically critical or heterodox. The establishment attempts to control such deviants by means of witchcraft accusations.

There is a clear relationship between the pattern of the social system and the appearance of possession afflictions in which gender is a determining risk factor. In what follows, this relationship will be considered from the perspective of some other models and supportive findings derived from social anthropology (M. Douglas), and cross-cultural psychiatry (E. Dio-Bleichmar).

2.3   The Body as a Microcosm of the Social Body (Mary Douglas)

In her work Natural Symbols,[20] Mary Douglas describes and analyses the relationship between the social and personal dimensions of the self. She also describes the way in which social pressure affects people and shapes their self-awareness. Her descriptions are based on a model which classifies society in terms of two variables: the way individuals regulate their personal existence (grid) and the pressure that the group exerts on the individual (group). The manner in which

---

[20] M. Douglas, *Natural Symbols. Explorations in Cosmology* (London and New York: Routledge, 1996).

these two variables intermingle, in different degrees and combinations, configure different types of society, which hold different attitudes towards the physical body.[21] With this model, Mary Douglas could demonstrate how the social body and the categories which make up its world-view determine the way in which the individual physical body is perceived and experienced.

Working on the anthropologist Marcel Mauss' idea of the human body as an image of society, Douglas developed her theory about the physical body as a microcosm of the social body, that is, the correspondence between body control and social control, while the former is a reflection of the latter. The more structured, formalist, rigid, and hierarchical a society is, the greater will be the control over the human body and the more its member will neglect the body, both in daily life and ritual. The less tolerant of foreigners a society is, the greater the control of its members relative to bodily limits and body orifices (mouth-food, sexual organs—sexual relations . . .); the more structured, hierarchical and controlling a society is, the less accepting of dissociative phenomena will its members be (that is, of trances and spirit possession, as a community indicator and source of power). As Douglas says in her own words: "I here argue that a social structure of the situation which requires a high degree of conscious control will find its style at a high level of formality, stern application of purity rules, denigration of organic process and wariness towards experiences in which control of consciousness is lost."[22]

The fact that a certain society holds a negative opinion of trances or possession, however, does not mean that such altered states of consciousness do not exist. Douglas likewise agrees that the loss of consciousness may be a consequence of alienation. In other words, neglect of the body as a form of social expression is not due to any lack of strongly articulated social structure, but rather due to the experience of oppression in the social system, structured rather rigidly to the benefit of a male elite. This elite keeps other members of society away from the benefits of society. In turn, those excluded express their protest by disregarding social boundaries, abandoning bodily control, and thus rebelling against social control. Douglas notes that "this is how the fringes of society express their marginal-

---

[21] Douglas, *Natural Symbols*, pp. 54–68 (diagram p. 60).
[22] Douglas, *Natural Symbols*, pp. 80–6 (quotation p. 86)

ity."[23] Insofar as the physical body is a system, it readily functions as a natural symbol of the prevailing social system.

2.4 *Hysteria as an Unconscious Protest against Gender Roles and Social Images (E. Dio-Bleichmar)*

Anthropological studies often witness a relationship between spirit possession and so-called hysterical symptoms attributed particularly to women. It is, therefore, of interest here to analyse this feature of spirit possession and discover its meaning and connections. As previously noted, physicians and writers in antiquity already spoke about hysteria as a female sickness (hysteria comes from ὑστέρα, "uterus"). Celsus accused Mary Magdalene of being πάροιστρος (Origen, *Contra Celsum*, 2:55; 2:59), a term that the Greek-English Lexicon[24] translates as "frenzied," or "frantic." The Greek term has the connotation of a person who moves frantically and compulsively, desperately and beside him/herself. It was later translated as "hysteric," because that was the adjective used for this sort of women. The designation derives from the false idea that the behaviour in question was due to the factor that the uterus had moved out of place because of the lack of sexual relations and the desire for them.

Ancient physicians understood hysteria as an illness of the whole woman, notably in her relations with males. But they could not understand that in this illness the women might in fact show their own problems and those of their own society.[25] Gourevitch says:

> Peut-être parce que les médecins, presque tous des hommes, n'ont pas pu mettre en question leurs propres rapports avec les femmes, et par conséquent leur place causale dans ces manifestations pathologiques. Car la femme n'est pas hysterique parce qu'elle a un uterus, mais parce qu'il lui manque un homme, ou parce qu'elle n'a pas celui qu'il lui faut.[26]

What the "hysterical" woman was thought to be lacking, such as pleasure or protagonism, comprised everything that was socially more valuable, but which was prohibited to her because she was a woman.

"Hysteria," therefore, indicates a relationship between the sexual ideology of a society and the symptoms of some women, very often

---

[23] Douglas, *Natural Symbols*, pp. 85–9 (quotation p. 89).
[24] Liddell/Scott, *Greek-English Lexicon* (Oxford: Clarendon, 1968, 9th reimp. edn)
[25] Gourevitch, *Le mal d'être femme*, pp. 113–27; MacDonald, *Pagan Opinion*, p. 3, n. 7.
[26] Gourevitch, *Le mal d'être femme*, p. 128.

interpreted as spirit possession, who are affected by that ideology, understood as norms socially imposed in order to govern women's everyday life and behaviour.

In her work *El feminismo espontáneo de la histeria*, E. Dio-Bleichmar has studied the phenomenon of hysteria in depth. Her conclusion is that hysteria is closely related to the cultural norms of the society that define and constitute what a woman should be. For this author, hysteria is an unconscious expression of protest against the conflicting dimension of culturally defined femininity. Hysterical women find themselves trapped between the social definition and their innermost desires. The outcome is a narcissistic or self-assessment conflict, since we are dealing with a negative cultural evaluation of the female gender (or an evaluation which in practice is experienced as secondary or subordinated to the male gender). The hysterical woman tries to raise that evaluation to a neutral level, or to invert it, using the body and sexuality as a symbolic and expressive system. But this latter proves to be a strategy that turns against her, because it locks her up in the socio-cultural stereotypes that caused her protest in the first place.[27]

Hysteria is a response that has several clinical manifestations with a common factor, that is, the degree of acceptance or refusal of the social gender roles.[28] It is a response which is reflected in the individual's body and personality, since self-esteem includes the representation of the anatomical body. Both affect each other, and that is the origin of hysteria's dissociative and conversion symptoms.[29] For E. Dio-Bleichmar, hysterical symptoms are always the proof of social inability that entails a message:

> Existe un feminismo espontáneo en la histeria que consiste en la protesta desesperada, aberrante, actuada, que no llega a articularse en palabras,

---

[27] E. Dio-Bleichmar, *El feminismo espontáneo de la histeria. Estudios de los trastornos narcisistas de la feminidad* (Madrid: Siglo XXI, 1985), p. XXIII.

[28] Dio-Bleichmar talks in depth about three different types of hysteria: the childish-dependent symptoms, the hysterical personality, and the phallic-narcissistic or aggressive type. Each type has different features, but all types represent a rejection of the definition of and the roles attributed to women.

[29] The conversion symptoms (for example, deafness, paralysis, muteness, etc.) can be considered such only when they do not have a physical basis, and they are in symbolic relation with the conflicting person's story, since, "el síntoma somático es la expresión simbólica, debidamente disfrazada por los mecanismos de condensación y desplazamiento de las ideas, deseo y temores reprimidos" ("the somatic symptom is the symbolic expression, concealed adequately by the mechanisms of condensation and by displacement of the ideas, and by the repressed desire and fears").

una reivindicación de una feminidad que no quiere ser reducida a sex-ualidad, de un narcisismo que clama por poder privilegiar la mente, la acción en la realidad, la moral, los principios y no quedar atrapada sólo en la belleza del cuerpo.[30]

In short, hysteria would then be the symptom of the conflicts aris-ing from being a woman in a particular society. That is why the symptom has changed in its manifestations throughout the ages, depending upon the socially shared models of and guidelines for what a woman should be. Fainting, convulsions, spirit possession and the like, are not usual any longer in contemporary Western society, but according to E. Dio-Bleichmar, the aggressive (phallic-narcissistic) response is becoming more and more significant. Thus, hysteria would not be so much a protest against the sexual difference but rather a protest against social inequalities and injustice between the sexes.

II. *Application of the Models to Luke 8:1–3*

1. *The Text in its Narrative Context*

The passage is located in the larger section that renders Jesus' min-istry in Galilee (4:14–9:50). Formally, these verses serve as a sum-mary which closes the small Lukan insertion (6:20–8:3), and hinges together two sections of the long section which narrates Jesus' min-istry in Galilee (4:14–9:50).

On the one hand, these summarizing verses close the previous section where Jesus has performed several miracles (healings, exor-cisms, etc.) which revealed him as the prophet-saviour who brings the good news of God's kingdom (such as he had announced in the synagogue at Nazareth in 4:14). Only the "children of Wisdom" (7:35), the poor and alienated, such as the woman who anointed Jesus' feet and who is known as a sinner (7:36–50), have been able to see these signs. Only those people who have received the word and liberating action of Jesus as the true good news, have been able to understand the meaning, perhaps because they were suffering from

---

[30] Dio-Bleichmar, *El feminismo*, p. 181. The literal translation of the quotation would be: "There is a spontaneous feminism about hysteria, which consists of the desperate, aberrant, acted protest that does not get articulated in words, the exigency of a femininity which does not want to be reduced to sexuality, of a narcissism which demands to be able to give privilege to the mind, to action in reality, to morality, to the principles, and not to remain trapped only in the beauty of the body."

unjust and oppressive situations. On the other hand, this summary gives way to a new, more didactic section (8:4–22), where Jesus speaks of the necessary attitude towards life in order to receive the word. Disciples are those who know how to receive the word. And this reception transforms their existence, even in the most basic institution in which a person lives and which is the basis of society: the family (vv. 19–21). The word of Jesus affects and transforms lives and relations in society's basic institutions, such as family, and, as a consequence, society at large. This fact seems to be of special interest for Luke, since in these verses he alters Mark's order (Mark 3:31–35) and places them after the parable of the sower, thus shedding some light on the relation between God's word and the followers of Jesus.

This passage is found in the minor insertion consisting of Luke's own material where narratives about women seem to be abundant. Some scholars, such as H. Schürmann,[31] have even suggested a specific female tradition (a tradition where the main characters were women, and perhaps even transmitted by women). Proving this is virtually impossible, but it is true that within the material that Luke introduces in his two insertions, the stories about women are frequent (7:11–17; 7:36–50; 8:1–3; 10:38–42; 13:10–17).

2. *The Twelve and Many Women Accompanied Him*

In these verses, Jesus is depicted as being on the road. He has not yet started going up to Jerusalem (cf. 9:51), and is travelling through towns and villages. He is accompanied by two groups who are present because of his previous activity: the Twelve and some women healed of difficult infirmities. Actually, both groups are a living sign of his mission, as introduced in 4:14, that is, to preach and to announce the arrival of God's kingdom as the good news for the poor.

The Twelve are the symbol for Israel's re-unification that is announced for the end of time when God will realize his salvation. The women from whom the evil spirits and infirmities have been expelled are the living proof of the beginning of that liberation which is announced to the oppressed for the last time as the good news. Thus, Luke describes a symbolic gesture and a present reality, a demonstrable testimony of the real nature of what Jesus preaches

---

[31] H. Schürman, *Das Lukasevangelium* (HThK III/1; Freiburg: Herder, 1969), pp. 445ff. This author thinks we are before a group of narratives about women (7:11–17; 7:36–50; 8:1–3).

and of the arrival of the final time. All of them (the Twelve and the women) have listened to the word and received it, a word which is a summary of all the liberating activity which precedes it. In the women's case, their gender strengthens this liberating symbolism which, in turn, makes them particularly visible, both in their previous and present situations.

Luke mentions a group of women who, after experiencing salvation in their lives, followed Jesus. Luke identifies three of this group by name. This is probably due to their importance. When referring to the first one, named Mary, Luke points out how spectacular her healing was. The second and third women appear only in Luke's list. Joanna is defined as Chuza's wife, thereby indicating her relationship to the Herodian court, while Susanna's name appears only here.

The women are described as travelling in Jesus' company. This is notable, since first-century Eastern Mediterranean society divided space by gender, ascribing the public realm to men and the private to women. This division was accompanied by the corresponding judgements as to the lack of honour (called shame in the case of women) of those who did not follow such rules,[32] and did not stay within the gender boundaries. Thus, it is surprising, although Luke does not present it this way, to find these women "on the road," travelling through towns and villages. This same fact places them in an ambiguous situation. What might other women have thought who observed them travelling along, while they themselves could feel constrained in their daily lives? And what would men think of them?

3. *Women Healed from Evil Spirits and Infirmities*

Even if these women did not preach the good news with words, they made their new existence evident to everybody just by their presence in Jesus' company. Thus, their way of life was already a joyful announcement of the historic beginning of the eschatological salvation, although only for those who experienced the heavy burdens that the society (or the powerful men who governed it) in which they lived imposed on them. For other people, these travelling women would remain considered as sick or possessed by evil spirits, since their behaviour did not follow the social norms. Only strange and

---

[32] For an introduction to the cultural reference frameworks of that society, cf. B. Malina, *The New Testament World. Insights from Cultural Anthropology* (Louisville, KY: Westminster John Knox, rev. edn, 1993).

evil spirits, so they would argue, would cause these women to question the established order, its norms and boundaries.

The women who accompanied Jesus together with the Twelve had
experienced in their lives the truth and reality of what Jesus proclaimed. They surely encountered the closeness and justice of God
since they had been healed from evil spirits and infirmities, both of
which were so closely linked that Luke combines them in 13:11–17,
an episode only found in Luke. It relates to the healing of a bent-
over woman and views it as a release from Satan's clutches. By the
Hellenistic period, Israel saw Satan as God's enemy; the name now
personified the forces that oppose God's saving power. In this episode
here, Jesus' healing quite clearly entails an exorcism, interpreted as
an act of liberation. The very affliction (the woman walks with a
stoop) seems to symbolize the oppressive weight that this woman has
carried for so many years. Jesus heals her, and introduces her into
the community of Abraham's children, which is where her unprecedented title, "Abraham's daughter," comes from. On the other hand,
we might consider her healing as being due to the fact that she felt
part of that privileged community. This aspect, and the fact that her
healing takes place on a sabbath and in a synagogue highlight the
incident as a sign of the eschatological liberation that Jesus had
announced in 4:16–22.[33]

In Luke, sickness not only indicates an organic dysfunction, but
is also something more comprehensive, pointing to a breakdown in
the meaning of life as a whole, a breach in the activities and relations that make life full and meaningful. Consequently, sickness affects
not only the individual, but also those to whom the individual is
related in one way or another, mainly kin group members and neighbours, because individuals are related to a range of persons within
their group.[34]

The women mentioned in 8:1–3 are labelled as healed, hence
freed by Jesus. They belong to the ranks of women in Luke's Gospel
who underwent healing experiences: Peter's mother-in-law (4:38–39),
the widow of Nain (7:1–11), the haemorrhaging woman (8:43–48),
Jairus' daughter (8:40–56), and the above mentioned woman who

---

[33] This is also T. Karlsen Seim's opinion in *The Double Message. Patterns of Gender
in Luke-Acts* (Studies of the New Testament and its World; Edinburgh: T&T Clark,
1994), pp. 42–3.
[34] Pilch, "Sickness and Healing," pp. 190–2.

was bent-over due to Satan's action (13:10–17). They all experienced their healing by Jesus as the renewal of their lives.

Luke indicates that the women who went with Jesus had been healed from evil spirits, sometimes also called unclean spirits (8:29; 9:42), which indicates that the afflicted women had some symptoms and behaviour that were considered inappropiate for women and deviant from the accepted norms of society: they were "impure" or "unclean." In other words, their spirit possession was an affliction that signified a challenge to the established social order. As we have previously noted when referring to social anthropology, such a challenge would have been more or less conscious for those afflicted. Therefore, when Jesus healed these women by driving the evil spirits from them and admitted them to his entourage, he was likewise saying something about the boundaries and the definitions of his society and the criteria that governed it. Here, the criteria have to do specifically with gender norms. Jesus exercises power and re-defines social guidelines and values according to new criteria.

4. *Mary, Called Magdalene, out of Whom Went Seven Demons*

Among the women whom Jesus had healed, Luke presents an especially serious case. It is the case of a woman simply called "Mary," without the addition of any male's name. However, her name is followed by the designation of the place from which she probably came, Magdala, which was an important town north of Tiberias on the western shore of the Sea of Galilee.

The *seven* demons that Jesus had expelled from Mary Magdalene can be interpreted as referring to a medical case that had been treated previously, but unsuccessfully. The number of demons points to a case in which, after an initial, apparent improvement in the patient, the symptoms would have returned and become more virulent. This is stated in 11:24–26, where we are told that possession by seven demons is an extremely serious case, the result of a partial but ultimately unsuccessful healing. The demon which initially caused the affliction found no rest, that is, the causes that had produced the affliction had not disappeared. While these causes may have been hidden, they certainly had not been eradicated. So the woman's life continued to be governed by strange forces that worked contrary to the will of God insofar as those forces were uncontrolled and destructive to life.

This interpretation is confirmed by present-day anthropology and cross-cultural medicine. If the causes that produce the altered states of consciousness, with or without dissociated personality disorders (interpreted as possession), are not resolved, the symptoms occur repeatedly each time with greater intensity. Psychiatrists stress that the process following therapy carried out in order to integrate the desintegrated personality (or lay exorcism) is essential. The sick person must find in his/her environment the conditions and support that will enable him/her to live as an integrated personality. The previously afflicted person must come to face everything that was dissociated or repressed (anxieties, desires, feelings, traumas, etc.), recognize it, make it his/her own, and change it. Otherwise, dissociation as a defense mechanism may return, in an even more serious form.[35]

From all said above we can conclude that Mary Magdalene had suffered a serious relapse of an old sickness, and that she probably showed the symptoms of an altered state of consciousness, with dissociative personality features (possibly also affecting her identity). The mention of a multiplicity of demons points to this.

We know that such possession is a bodily reflection of some inner conflict between the person's desires and feelings on the one hand and prevailing social norms and values on the other. In the case of women, this internalized conflict generally relates to social values and norms concerning gender roles and gender identity. In other words, this has to do with the norms that define what a woman is supposed to be. The number of demons, along with the fact that demons are referred to with that particular term (δαιμόνια) probably indicate that the special seriousness of the case was further demonstrated by some spectacular, involuntary symptoms such as self-injury, flight, abandoning of responsibilities, amnesia, convulsions, sexual alterations, paralysis, muteness, sudden personality changes (multiple egos or a dissociated personality), and a range of abnormal behaviour (opinions, actions, gestures, attacks, etc.). In short, the symptoms would cover a whole set of acts which were an outward proof of an unconscious protest against the situation that the woman found herself in, calling (indirectly) for more attention and consideration.

The way Mary is introduced in the passage indicates that it was not known by the Christian community whether she was related to

---

[35] Putnam, *Diagnosis*, pp. 316–21.

any male. At the time this seems to indicate an abnormal situation in that cultural context. The reason for this could well be that she was a young widow, or her husband had divorced her, sending her back to her father's house for some reason or other, burdening her with the stigma and consequences typical of a society where women are considered only in the role of wives and mothers.

The symptoms of possession in such a society seem to indicate a feeling of inadequacy, and at the same time a mute and ineffective protest. On the one hand, Mary Magdalene could have felt that she herself was responsible for her situation, including the consequences that her abnormal situation would have for the honour of her family. On the other hand, she might have nurtured a feeling of protest against this situation, which she re-directed against herself but which nevertheless had an impact on her family and in-group in a derivative way. The greater the feeling of rebellion against social norms and against the situation that one suffers from, the greater the repression and introjection will be. The latter prevent subjugated and afflicted persons from experiencing those impulses, feelings and thoughts that are forbidden by the social norms that people adopt in the process of socialization.

Jesus healed this woman[36] by driving from her the seven demons that made her unclean and deviant and set her outside the social fabric of her community. In healing her, Jesus likewise re-instated her into her kinship and larger community group. As we noted, perhaps others had attempted such healing and social restoration previously, but their attempts proved unsuccessful. Futhermore, Jesus' healing further affirmed that the woman was quite correct in her protest against society and her desire for redress (this protest and

---

[36] We can ask whether the healing that Jesus performs is carried out by means of the word, which Mary Magdalene hears and takes in, and revealed throughout Luke's Gospel to be efficient and healing, or by means of an exorcism. In fact, there seems to be no apparent contradiction between the two of them, since the word is also essential in exorcisms. It is the word that "talks to" the demon, and asks about its identity, that is, the word that asks about the reasons for the situation, the word that questions, that helps to face the hidden aspects, and that puts forward a new perspective, convinces about the existence of another reality, creates another reality, and other possibilities of existence. The therapy for the integration of those altered states of dissociated conscience has a lot to do with the word, since it involves asking the different egos about their story, and making them aware of each other, helping them see other solutions, and unite in a single personality, thereby integrating all the different, painful and conflicting facets, which hitherto were so repressed that they acted on their own.

desire were expressed by means of the unconscious and fruitless cry
of her affliction). Thanks to Jesus, she now had the experience of
being one of Abraham's daughters, just like the woman who was
bent-over (13:10–17), and feeling self-esteem, and self-respect. The
designation "daughter of Abraham" was not customary, hence it
should not be taken for granted either. A woman could not be circumcised, and thus her belonging to the covenant was doubtful or
secondary. The bent-over woman was healed by her full re-intro-
duction into the group in which she was marginalized because of
her gender and, consequently, she could walk upright again. In Mary
Magdalene's case, her healing is confirmed and made effective in
her following Jesus and becoming a disciple. By being introduced
into Jesus' group, where followers lived according to a more kin-
ship-oriented and egalitarian *ethos*,[37] which meant that God's kingdom
that Jesus preached actually became a reality, she was truly healed.

Jesus' exorcisms involved a critique of existing social norms and
values, and also had social consequences because, by means of such
actions, Jesus re-defined the boundaries of society (purity norms),
and the criteria upon which the latter were based. J. Pilch says:
"Jesus' exorcisms can be correctly understood as political actions performed for the purpose of restoring correct order to society."[38] That
may have been the reason why Jesus was accused of witchcraft, that
is, of acting in the power of the Prince of Demons (Beelzebub), hence
of being opposed to God (cf. 11:14–22). In fact, underlying this dis-
pute, we find the question of Jesus' authority. What sort of authority had Jesus assumed in order to change the social order, making
pure what was established as impure, changing criteria and priori-
ties? Is such behaviour sanctioned by God or contrary to God (like
God's adversary, Satan)?

Given the fact that spirit possession was closely connected to the
injustice of social order, the healing of people from this affliction

---

[37] Jesus, through his words and actions, questioned the concept of honour which
existed in that society, and claimed it for the tasks and values attributed to women.
He did so when he used images of women or of their tasks to talk about God and
the kingdom (15:8), or when he adopted roles that were characteristically female
(he welcomed the children, fed the poor, showed tenderness, cried in public, etc.,
(15; 18:15–16; 19:41)), or when he suggested that these attitudes are essential for
discipleship. He also questioned and re-defined the roles of women as only mothers where the interests of the patriarchal family confined them (8:19–21; 11:27–28).
Thereby, the relationship between male and female, and the family's consideration,
are also questioned and re-defined, according to the values of the kingdom.
[38] Pilch and Malina, *Biblical Social Values*, p. 141.

can be interpreted as liberation associated with the final period that Jesus proclaimed once his activity got under way. T. Karlsen Seim says:

> The women are helped by Jesus to achieve a vital transformation in their lives—and by crossing the boundaries created by concepts of impurity and by social marginalisation, the women are rehabilitated as Abraham's daughters with a right to share in the community of the People of God and salvation.[39]

Jesus not only suppresses the demons that possessed Mary Magdalene and other women. He also listened to their mute cries of helplessness which showed up in their bodies and "spoke for in itself." Jesus healed Mary Magdalene completely of her infirmities by assuring her of the legitimacy of her protest and demands. Her life assumed a new meaning, her person a new value. Her life was no longer governed by strange dehumanizing forces that were contrary to God's will. Her body was no longer a burden, nor a barrier. God had begun to act, changing the boundaries that shaped society, and the criteria that were used to establish them. Jesus' healing activity and the reception of his word made Mary Magdalene feel that whatever was inadequate was not in her, in her aspirations and rebellions, but in the political and religious norms that determined life and interpersonal relations.

(Translated by Lucía F. Llorente)

---

[39] Seim, *The Double Message*, p. 48.

"YOUR FAITH HAS MADE YOU WELL."
JESUS, WOMEN, AND HEALING IN THE GOSPEL OF MATTHEW

ELAINE M. WAINWRIGHT

Women have always been healers. They were the unlicensed doctors and anatomists of western history. They were abortionists, nurses and counsellors. They were pharmacists, cultivating healing herbs and exchanging the secrets of their uses. They were mid-wives, travelling from home to home and village to village. For centuries women were doctors without degrees, barred from books and lectures, learning from each other, and passing on experience from neighbor to neighbor and mother to daughter. They were called "wise women" by the people, witches or charlatans by the authorities. Medicine is part of our heritage as women, our history, our birthright.[1]

Ehrenreich and English, who make this broad claim in *Witches, Midwives and Nurses: A History of Women Healers*, undertake a study which participates generally in the contemporary movement to reclaim women's history but is focused particularly on the Middle Ages and the rise of the medical profession. Their work exposes the need to test their claim in other historical eras. For the historian of first-century emerging Christianity this means examining women's participation in healing in the Graeco-Roman world generally and in early Christianity in particular, a task all the more urgent since there is no record of women as healers in the Christian Scriptures. Rather, healing is portrayed as a key characteristic of the ministry of Jesus and significant male apostles. The symbolic world of healing in early Christianity is, therefore, significantly gendered.

Was this emerging Christian movement unwitting participant in the silencing or the obscuring, even the displacing, of women's art and task of healing and of women's history as healers? This paper seeks to explore this question in the context of a re-viewing of the transformative encounters between Jesus and women healed in the Matthean Gospel (the particular focus being Matt. 8:14–15 and

---

[1] B. Ehrenreich and D. English, *Witches, Midwives and Nurses: A History of Women Healers* (London: Writers and Readers Publishing Cooperative, 1973), p. 19.

9:18–26).[2] It will be necessary to develop a methodology suitable to the task of examining the variety of data which can yield a scenario of women as healers and as healed in the Graeco-Roman world. The encounters between Jesus and three women within the Matthean healing narratives (Matthew 8–9) will be studied using the same framework of analysis. Conclusions will then be drawn as to the possible rhetorical effects of the symbolic world created by the Matthean narration of Jesus, women, and healing—whether it was transformative and for whom.

Healing as Constructed and Constructive: A Hermeneutical Model

The emergence of the social sciences has had an effect on a number of disciplines, historical and biblical scholarship being no exceptions. Medical anthropology in particular is currently providing analytic frameworks in biblical studies which will be drawn upon in this essay.[3] I will extend these to an analysis of women's participation in the world of healing within the Graeco-Roman era.[4] This will enable me to bring the two worlds of the biblical text and women's healing in the world of antiquity, analysed social-scientifically, into dialogue and to work toward a further interpretation of the Matthean healing narratives chosen.[5]

When healing is understood not just in terms of healer, recipient of healing, description of an illness or type of cure, but as an entire

---

[2] I have chosen not to include Matt. 15:21–28, which is significant within the Matthean narrative and its construction of healing, simply to allow for more depth of analysis within the confines of this paper.

[3] See in particular the extensive work of J. J. Pilch of which the following are but representative: "Understanding Biblical Healing: Selecting the Appropriate Model," *BTB* 18 (1988), pp. 60–6; idem, "The Health Care System in Matthew: A Social Science Analysis," *BTB* 16 (1986), pp. 102–6; and idem, "Reading Matthew Anthropologically: Healing in Cultural Perspective," *Listening* 24 (1989), pp. 278–89; and also E. van Eck and A. G. Van Aarde, "Sickness and Healing in Mark: A Social Scientific Interpretation," *Neotestamentica* 27 (1993), pp. 27–54.

[4] In my research to date I am aware of only one study which makes use of the hermeneutic model of medical anthropology in a study of women's healing in the Graeco-Roman world of antiquity, namely N. Demand, *Birth, Death, and Motherhood in Classical Greece* (Baltimore ML: Johns Hopkins University Press, 1994).

[5] C. J. Hemer, "Medicine in the New Testament World," in B. Palmer (ed.), *Medicine and the Bible* (Exeter: Paternoster, 1986), pp. 43–83, says of such a dialogue that "[t]here is . . . a special value in the attempt to set the text representatively in its fullest possible contemporary and cultural context. This can help to bring its reality alive" (p. 83).

socio-cultural system which is both semantic and symbolic, the hermeneutical or interpretive model of medical anthropology provides a very useful framework of analysis.[6] This is particularly so for the cross-cultural study entailed in this essay which traverses not only diverse cultures within the Mediterranean world of antiquity but also first and twenty/twenty-first century cultures. Its focus is the human experience of healing and the meaning given to this experience which allows for the multivalence of both intra-cultural and cross-cultural realities. Within such a model both the sources and their interpretations are considered as "text" and as such they construct the meaning of healing and of the healer within the socio-cultural healing system.[7] Braidotti extends this consideration by noting that "[t]he text must . . . be understood as a term in a process, this is to say a chain-reaction which encompasses a web of power-relations" and that "[w]hat is at stake in the textual practice, therefore, is less the activity of interpretation than of decoding the network of connections and effects that link the text to an entire socio-symbolic system."[8] The sources or texts for consideration in this study are various, including:

1. literary sources such as the Hippocratic Corpus, Soranus' *Gynecology*, and other texts which generally present a male cultural perspective on medicine and medical practitioners;

2. inscriptional references to women healers as well as female recipients of healing, especially from divine healers; and

3. folk traditions reflected in the literary works, including the Gospel accounts of Jesus' healing of women.

This hermeneutical approach to healing is particularly appropriate in a study whose focus is the genderization of healing, given the recognition amongst feminist scholars that gender, like healing, is not a cultural "given" but is being constructed in the process of human

---

[6] A. Kleinman, *Patients and Healers in the Context of Culture: An Exploration of the Borderland between Anthropology, Medicine and Psychiatry* (Comparative Studies of Health Systems and Medical Care; Berkeley, CA:, University of California Press, 1980), notes that "[t]he overwhelming distortion in medical anthropology, resulting from several decades of research, has been one in which healers were studied in isolation as the central component of medicine in society" (p. 205).

[7] See H. King, "The Daughter of Leonides: Reading the Hippocratic Corpus," in A. Cameron (ed.), *History as Text: The Writing of Ancient History* (London: Duckworth, 1989), pp. 11–32, p. 13.

[8] R. Braidotti, "What's Wrong with Gender?," in F. van Dijk-Hemmes and A. Brenner (eds.), *Reflections on Theology and Gender* (Kampen: Kok Pharos, 1994), pp. 49–67, p. 58.

meaning-making.[9] Narratives of healing, whether on stone, parch-
ment or alive in the oral tradition of folklore, participate in this construction of gender as well as its representation, maintenance or
disruption.[10] The historian retrieving women's healing within antiquity faces a problem similar to that faced by other historians of
women's perspectives, activities and relationships. When most of the
informants are men, it is exceedingly difficult to uncover women's
voices and hence women's perspectives, just as women's activities
and relationships are often obscured or confined within a different
world view, namely that of the male. It will be necessary to read
for the subsumed or resistant voice within the fissures of texts while
at the same time recognizing that even women's perspectives may
be bounded by the dominant culture.[11] Achterberg notes in this
regard that since "[t]he experience of women healers, like the experience of women in general, is a shadow throughout the record of
the world," then this experience "must be sought at the interface of
many disciplines: history, anthropology, botany, archaeology, and
the behavioral sciences."[12] A cross-disciplinary approach which recognizes the multivalence of the health care system is, therefore, essential to uncover the women of the healing arts of early Christianity.

In antiquity, since healing was, in many instances, associated with
religion and since the healing narratives of the Matthean Gospel are
contextualized in a religious text, the hermeneutic model proves
appropriate for analysis of the religious meaning making system and
its participation in the construction of healing within socio-cultural
systems.[13] The critical analysis which this method allows will, therefore,

---

[9] M. W. Conkey and J. M. Gero, "Tensions, Pluralities, and Engendering
Archaeology: An Introduction to Women and Prehistory," in J. M. Gero and M. W.
Conkey (eds.), *Engendering Archaeology: Women and Prehistory* (Oxford: Basil Blackwell,
1991), pp. 3–30, pp. 8–11; and Braidotti, "What's Wrong with Gender?," pp. 49–67.

[10] B. J. Brooten, *Love between Women: Early Christian Responses to Female Homoeroticism*
(The Chicago Series on Sexuality, History, and Society; Chicago: University of
Chicago Press, 1996), demonstrates this in relation to early Christianity when she
claims that "[a]ncient medical writers represent and helped to create the culture in
which early Christianity originated, which means that they are significant for Christian
history not only because of their later influence, but also because they helped to
shape the frameworks of thinking to which early Christians responded" (p. 145).

[11] H. King, "Bound to Bleed: Artemis and Greek Women," in A. Cameron and
A. Kuhrt (eds.), *Images of Women in Antiquity* (London: Croom Helm, 1983), pp.
109–127, p. 109.

[12] J. Achterberg, *Woman as Healer* (Boston, MA: Ahambhala, 1990), p. 2.

[13] Hemer, "Medicine," p. 43. Pilch ("Understanding Biblical Healing") notes
that the "biomedical model . . . is incapable of appreciating ethnic or religious
differences in interpreting human misfortune" (p. 60).

bring into dialogue, throughout the remainder of this essay, the categories not only of gender but also of class and ethnicity, and constructions of healing within the context of social and cultural institutions including religion. This will be directed to our inquiry as to whether the focusing of the healing power in Jesus and significant male apostles in early Christian narratives displaced women's healing powers and gendered healing as male within the Christian sociocultural system.[14]

Women in the Health Care System of Greece and Rome

In order to understand the broader cultural context of women within the health care system in the Mediterranean world of the first century C.E., the historian must not only examine a wider historical period but also the various sectors of the health care system, and it is the medical anthropological model which allows for this more holistic view of those sectors. Kleinman highlights three of them: the popular, the professional, and the folk.[15] He notes, however, that the lines are blurred between them and an exploration of women healers indicates that female gender can function to further blur such neat distinctions, as we will see below. Examination of the available data has led me to collapse the folk and popular distinction. Under the umbrella of folk medicine, I will give particular attention to women as healers in its secular stream and women as patients in its magico-religious stream, the particular sources for the second stream being the inscriptions and dedications from the Asklepieia. Within the professional sector, I shall place the representation of women in the Hippocratic Corpus and Soranus. A final comment will be made on the lack of specific data from Israel during this Graeco-Roman period in relation to women as healers and women healed.

---

[14] E. Schüssler Fiorenza, "Miracles, Mission and Apologetics: An Introduction," in idem (ed.), *Aspects of Religious Propaganda in Judaism and Early Christianity* (Notre Dame, IN: University of Notre Dame Press 1976), who notes that "any adequate discussion of the early Christian movement must consider both the relationship of the early Christian movement to the Jewish propagandistic movement, on the one hand, and the impact of the Greco-Roman religious and cultural movement on both movements, on the other hand" (p. 4).

[15] Kleinman, *Patients and Healers*, pp. 50–60. Demand emphasizes in *Birth, Death, and Motherhood*, that "folk" is not a pejorative but a descriptive term within the medical anthropological model (cf. p. xix).

Secular Folk Medicine

Kleinman says of the folk sector, which he calls "non-professional, non-bureaucratic, specialist," that it "shades into the other two sectors of the local health care system. Folk medicine is a mixture of many different components; some are closely related to the professional sector, but most are related to the popular sector."[16] In seeking to re-construct such a sector of a number of systems over four or more centuries and to situate women within that, account must be taken of the paucity and scattered nature of the data, the chronological and cultural boundaries which are transgressed, and the hints of only a blurred image which may, therefore, emerge. To begin this construction, I turn first to the brief passing comment made by Plato in the *Republic* 454d2: "we meant, for example, that a man and a woman who have a physician's mind have the same nature."[17] This text is located in a developing argument toward claims as to who is best suited to be educated for the administration of the affairs of the state, and it seems to suggest by its use of the male and female terminology for physician or doctor [ἰατρικόν and ἰατρικήν] that the imaginative possibility of women healers was not unknown in fourth-century Athens.[18]

This symbolic world of healing and its genderization can be further constructed by literary and inscriptional data from the late fourth century. Agnodike, of whom account is given in Hyginus' *Fabula* (274:10–13), is situated in ancient times when "there were no midwives (*obstetrices*); women and slaves were forbidden by the Athenians to learn medicine."[19] In order to study medicine, Agnodike cuts off her hair, dresses as a man and becomes a student of Herophilus. By revealing her sexuality to female patients she is able to give assistance to them when they are "crying out in labour." Her growing popularity brings upon her the ire of male doctors and she is brought

[16] Kleinman, *Patients and Healers*, p. 59.
[17] This translation is taken from Plato, *Republica*, transl. by P. Shorey (London: Heinemann, 1943). See also the discussion of the manuscript tradition as well as possible interpretations given by S. B. Pomeroy, "Plato and the Female Physician (*Republic* 454d2)," *American Journal of Philology* 99 (1978), pp. 496–500.
[18] G. E. R. Lloyd, *Science, Folklore and Ideology: Studies in the Life Sciences in Ancient Greece* (Cambridge: Cambridge University Press, 1983), rightly says of this text that "[t]here is ... no firm indication in this passage either that this happened *regularly* or that it *never* happened" (p. 70, n. 47).
[19] I am using the translation in H. King, "Agnodike and the Profession of Medicine," *Proceedings of the Cambridge Philological Society NS* 32 (1986), pp. 53–77.

230 ELAINE M. WAINWRIGHT

to trial at the Areopagus where once again she reveals her "true sex." Innocent of the charge of seducing female patients, she faces the further charge of having broken the law and studied medicine as a woman. It is only the agitation of the "wives of the leading men" which saves her.

King studies this text in much more detail than is possible here, raising the question of the historical or mythic/symbolic nature of the account and concluding that it functions symbolically in "defence of women's medicine and women's roles" in the social order.[20] Viewed from the point of view of medical anthropology and the symbolic universe being created, one notes that the account genders the tension between the folk and professional sectors of ancient medicine and as such contributes to the construction of both gender and health in that world: socially and systemically, female gender prevents women from becoming professional healers; linked to the privatization of female health, this can be fatal for women; and yet women can, in fact, carry out the healing role with significant success; and the legalization of social roles can, indeed, be changed.[21]

While maintaining the construction of gender and health, the account of Agnodike may also have functioned constructively to authorize what may have been a significant body of female *obstetrices*, midwives and physicians giving assistance to other women in the secular stream of the folk sector of the health care system. In such a context, the late fourth-century stele praising Phanostrate as μαῖα καὶ ἰατρός may likewise point to the possibility of significant numbers of women working as midwives and physicians ("Phanostrate, a midwife and physician, lies here. She caused pain to none, and all lamented her death").[22] This may have functioned to blur the distinction between a naturalised and visible world of male professional healers and an invisible world of women who may not only have attended childbirth but also treated other diseases of women. King recognizes how uncertain factual claims made from this evidence can

---

[20] King, "Agnodike," p. 68.
[21] Once again Lloyd (*Science, Folklore, and Ideology*) reminds readers that this account may not be descriptive or mimetic since there is no other evidence of women being forbidden to study medicine or of the law being changed. This does not, however, detract from its contribution to the construction of a symbolic universe (p. 70, n. 47).
[22] Pleket 1.G, quoted in M. R. Lefkowitz and M. B. Fant, *Women's Life in Greece and Rome: A Source Book in Translation* (Baltimore, ML: Johns Hopkins University Press, 2nd edn, 1992), pp. 266–7, § 376.

be, but she also warns against seeing Phanostrate and Agnodike as the few exceptional women who differed from that whole body of women considered marginal rather than integral to the health care system.[23] In light of the above, women healers and women healed need to be re-inscribed at the centre of the health care system rather than on its margins.

Before closing this examination of the almost invisible world of women's folk healing in Greece and early Imperial Rome, attention should be drawn to the inscriptions which commemorate female physicians—Antiochis, Primilla, Terentia Prima, Julia Pye, Minucia Asste, Venuleia Sosis and Melitine—most from first-century Rome.[24] To these can be added epitaphs of midwives.[25] Although small in number, they point toward a more significant incorporation of women into the professional sector of the health care system together with public recognition of this shift in the secular arena.

Magico-Religious Folk Medicine

From his anthropological study of the sacred folk healer-client relationship, Kleinman makes the claim that "[m]ost clients in folk practice are females."[26] It is of interest in this study, therefore, to examine the data presented by Aleshire in her analysis of the dedicatory inscriptions from the Athenian Asklepieion.[27] She notes that they register what she calls "a high proportion of women dedicants"—for all the inventories, 51.39 per cent women to 45.82 per cent men.[28] Since most of these inscriptions simply record the gift and the name of the giver, there is little else which can be drawn from this material for the purpose of this study apart from the high proportion of women who come for healing to the Asklepieia.

The stelai from the Epidaurian Asklepieion differ from the dedicatory inventories of Athens in that they contain tales or accounts of healing.[29] From Stelai A and B, the two of the four stelai of

---

[23] King, "Agnodike," p. 60.

[24] See Lefkowitz and Fant, *Women's Lives*, pp. 264–5, § 369–72, for a readily accessible compilation of this data.

[25] Lefkowitz and Fant, *Women's Lives*, p. 267, § 377.

[26] Kleinman, *Patients and Healers*, p. 206.

[27] S. B. Aleshire, *The Athenian Asklepieion: The People, their Dedications, and the Inventories* (Amsterdam: Gieben, 1989).

[28] Aleshire, *The Athenian Asklepieion*, p. 45.

[29] These are available in L. R. LiDonnici, *The Epidaurian Miracle Inscriptions: Text, Translation and Commentary* (Texts and Translations, 36; Graeco-Roman Religion

Iamata inscriptions which escaped severe damage, we can determine that Stele A contains three out of twenty accounts of women healed (15 per cent); and Stele B contains seven of twenty-three (32.8 per cent). LiDonnici discusses the tradition history of the tales whose earliest sources may lie in votives, some without names and then with the name of the one healed. The Athenian inventories represent an intermediate stage before the redactional stages of the explanatory tales by the priests of the temples, a process in which the biblical scholar recognizes similarities with the tradition history of the Gospels even before LiDonnici draws attention to this.[30] One aspect of the process that is readily visible in a gender analysis is the drop in the percentage of women between the Athenian inventories and the Epidaurian tales. Similar percentages occur within the Matthean Gospel with healing narratives of women accounting for three out of nine (33.3 per cent) in the miracle collection of Matthew 8–9 and four out of eleven (27.5 per cent) in the entire Gospel. One questions whether women's greater exclusion from literary resources and the control of the narratives in their final composition phase predominantly by men account for the smaller percentage in literary tales of women healed. The votive offerings may reflect more realistically women's actual participation. It should also be noted that in this process women's perspectives, which may have been more visible on their dedicatory votives, become obscured within the confines of male storytelling.

From the Epidaurian Iamata inscriptions, one glimpses the semantic and interpretive nature of healing within the health care system. As LiDonnici notes, the inscriptions "recount personal afflictions, but ones that reflect and support public ideology."[31] It is significant in this regard that of the fifteen inscriptions that name women specifically, seven are concerned with women becoming pregnant, four of which conclude with her bearing a son (A1, B11, B14, B22) and only one a daughter (A2). The remainder of the healings of women are likewise concerned with curing women's illnesses so that the women are re-established within the socio-cultural system which the temple and

---

Series, 11; Atlanta, GA: Scholars, 1995), who notes in relation to the different types of text that "Epidauros is best known for narrative inscriptions, represented by the Iamata; Corinth lacks inscriptions but is rich in terra-cotta body-part votives, while Athens and Piraeus have many stone votive reliefs, without any text" (p. 42).

[30] LiDonnici, *The Epidaurian Miracle Inscriptions*, pp. 50–82.

[31] LiDonnici, *The Epidaurian Miracle Inscriptions*, p. 1.

its healings support. Both healing and gender are being constructed and the dominant social ideology in which both reside is being maintained.

Some characteristics of the interpersonal interaction between the supplicant and Asklepios are significant in terms of the symbolic universe being created by the inscriptions within the world of health care generally.[32] The relationship between supplicant and healer is negotiated in a number of instances by way of a vision (A2, A4, B3) or dream (A4, B1, B11, B14, B19). In only three of the fifteen accounts of women's healing are any human intermediaries mentioned, the "sons of the god" (B3–Asklepios being absent from Epidauros at the time), and a handsome man/young boy (B5 and B11). A snake is associated with the healing in B19, B22, and C2. In each of these instances, however, it is clear that it is Asklepios who is the source of healing, in particular in B3 where the god must complete the healing which the "sons of the god" were unable to do.[33]

The repeated meaning given to the healing of a number of the women in these accounts is that they have been "made well," the adjective ὑγιής being used repeatedly (A1, A4, B1, B5, B21). Order is established also in the lives of women and therefore in the universe through the benevolent care of Asklepios. Within this system, however, the power of healing is confined to the male god and his intermediaries who are likewise male, which renders women healers invisible in the folk magico-religious sector and genders divine healing power as male. This is reflected also in the gradual diminishment of the power of the daughters of Asklepios, Hygeia and Panacae, female divine healers, and their disappearance from the pottery, statuary and frescoes. By the beginning of the Roman period, therefore, divine healing in the cultural system of the Graeco-Roman world was symbolized male. Women's participation in this divine healing was transformative in that their lives were restored at least physically, but it was within the confines of a very ordered world.

---

[32] In drawing on this category of "interpersonal interaction" I am reliant on the criteria for analysis of cross-cultural healing systems developed by Kleinman, *Patients and Healing* (cf. pp. 207–8), which I have already used minimally in examining the account of Agnodike and which I will continue to use throughout the remainder of my analysis.

[33] One is reminded here of Jesus healing the epileptic boy whom the disciples were unable to cure (Matt. 17:14–18).

Professional Sector

A study of the "professional" sector of the health care system of Greece and Rome finds its earliest sources in the Hippocratic Corpus, an extensive body of medical literature attributed to the mid-fifth century B.C.E. physician Hippocrates, but believed to be drawn from a number of sources and compiled over decades into the fourth century B.C.E.[34] It seems that these treatises functioned in the training of health care professionals and their focus was on diseases and their cures. As a result, they contributed significantly to the construction of health within antiquity as well as to the construction of the human body. Lloyd notes in this regard that "little attention is paid to differences between men and women until we reach the section devoted to women's complaints."[35] The Hippocratic patient is constructed, therefore, as male, women are considered as "other" on the grounds of genitalia since their particular diseases are largely gynaecological, as a brief glance at the treatises on women reveal. I do not wish to focus in this paper on that construction of the female body,[36] nor on women as patients in the Hippocratic Corpus which would be unique studies in their own right.[37] Rather, I will simply give brief attention to women as healers.

Women are referred to as healers within the Hippocratic Corpus almost in passing. In *Fleshes* 19, there is reference to ἀκεστρίδες or female healers who attend births, and in *Diseases of Women* 1:68 it is the ἰητρεύουσα or the "female who is doctoring,"[38] who is instructed

---

[34] For insights into this history and its significance for women and healing, see King, "Daughter of Leonides," pp. 16–20; and A. E. Hanson, "Continuity and Change: Three Case Studies in Hippocratic Gynecological Therapy and Theory," in S. B. Pomeroy (ed.), *Women's History and Ancient History* (Chapel Hill, N.C.: University of North Carolina Press, 1991), pp. 73–9.

[35] Lloyd, *Science, Folklore and Ideology*, p. 65.

[36] For this, see L. Dean-Jones, "The Cultural Construct of the Female Body in Classical Greek Science," in Pomeroy (ed.), *Women's History*, pp. 111–37; and A. Rousselle, *Porneia: On Desire and the Body in Antiquity* (transl. F. Pheasant; Cambridge: Blackwell, 1988), pp. 24–46.

[37] See in particular, H. King, "Self-help, Self-knowledge: In Search of the Patient in Hippocratic Gynaecology," in R. Hawley and B. Levick (eds.), *Women in Antiquity: New Assessments* (London and New York: Routledge, 1995), pp. 135–48; and the extensive treatment in Lloyd, *Science, Folklore and Ideology* (pp. 58–111), who notes, that "[i]n not one of the seven books of the *Epidemics* taken as a whole are female patients in the majority," corroborating what has already been noted in relation to male-produced literary material on women's healing (p. 67).

[38] Demand, *Birth, Death, and Motherhood*, p. 66. For the text of the gynaecological treatises, see E. Littré, *Oeuvres complètes d'Hippocrate*, 10 vols. (Paris, 1839–1861, repr. Amsterdam: Hakkert, 1961).

on the removal of a dead foetus. There are other passages which give instructions to a woman presumed present at the consultation to carry out examinations of female patients.[39] Indeed, Rouselle points to an extensive study which reveals evidence of only two vaginal examinations carried out by male doctors. This is not to say that the doctors, constructed male within the Hippocratic Corpus, did not perform such examinations but the text points to women undertaking self-examinations themselves or other women performing this task.

This raises the vexed question as to the sources for the gynaeco-logical treatises. Rouselle suggests that the above data point to women's knowledge located in the popular/familial or folk sector of the health care system as the source of the developing body of professional knowledge of women's illnesses and healing.[40] King warns against too simplistic an assumption of women's remedies and knowledge being appropriated by men, examining the interplay of power within the Hippocratic system and what she calls "strategies women used within the system."[41] Demand suggests that the Hippocratic treatises *Diseases of Women* 1 and 2 were addressed to midwives or female healers who were significant participants in the professional sector.[42] Drawing this into the medical anthropological model she concludes:

> As a member of the folk sector, the traditional midwife controlled a well-developed body of information and had skills that were recog-nized and valued, especially in the community of women. My claim that some midwives rose in status and became professional through their association with Hippocratic doctors is made in the context of Kleinman's model: I am arguing that these women probably moved up in status in the male patriarchal society by associating themselves with the sector that was recognized as the most prestigious by that society, which for that reason we identify as professional in Kleinman's terms. This by no means implies that as traditional midwives operat-ing in the folk sector they had lacked knowledge or skills; on the contrary, it was their knowledge that became gynecology when male doctors took it over and incorporated it into the form of the Hippocratic treatise.[43]

Demand's conclusions raise the question of the intersection between women, healing and literacy. It is Soranus, a late first century C.E.

[39] Lloyd, *Science, Folklore and Ideology*, pp. 70–3.
[40] Rouselle, *Porneia*, pp. 24–5.
[41] King, "Self-help, Self-knowledge," p. 136.
[42] Demand, *Birth, Death, and Motherhood*, p. 66.
[43] Demand, *Birth, Death, and Motherhood*, p. xix.

physician, who provides a possible answer. In his *Gynecology*, he gives instructions that those women who become midwives should indeed be literate "in order to be able to comprehend the art through theory too."[44] Women were to be instructed in medical knowledge since they were significant assistants to the male medical professionals. As with other data, it is difficult to deduce the extent of women's participation as healers within the developing professional sector of ancient Greece and Rome. It is clear, however, that from behind the written text there emerges an image of a significant body of well-trained female medical professionals whose knowledge and skill was central to the entire health care system especially as it related to women.

Women and Healing in Israel in the Graeco-Roman Era

In the light of this data, scattered though it might be, one is struck by the paucity of material on which to draw any conclusions in relation to women's participation in the health care system in Israel in the same chronological period. It is generally agreed that healing was depicted as the exclusive work of Israel's God or what Seybold and Mueller call "Yahweh's healing monopoly."[45] By the Hellenistic period, the Testament of Job 38 and Sirach 38:1–15 recognize physicians and their healing power but within the symbolic universe of healing as the prerogative of Israel's God who is predominantly gendered male without any accompanying female divine healers as was Asklepios. There is no indication of the gender of the physicians in either of these texts.

Israel's foundational story, the Exodus, does, however, provide just a brief glimpse of another element in the system, namely the midwife (Exod. 1:8–21), suggesting that midwives may have been as natural in Israel's health care system as was divine healing power, though rarely mentioned in the biblical texts whose authors are male and whose concerns were not women's care of women. Tal Ilan includes the profession of midwife among the occupations available to the women of Palestine in the Graeco-Roman period, noting that this profession must have been limited to women since only feminine

---

[44] Soranus, *Gynecology*, § 3 in *Soranus' Gynecology* (transl. O. Temkin; Baltimore, ML: Johns Hopkins University Press, 1956).

[45] K. Seybold and U. B. Mueller, *Sickness and Healing* (transl. D. W. Stott; Biblical Encounters Series; Nashville, TN: Abingdon, 1981), p. 105.

forms of related words are used in rabbinic literature.[46] She conjectures from this that women may have supplemented the knowledge gained in midwifery to enable them to work as physicians also. Data in this regard is so scarce though that one is left with the image of women's healing in Graeco-Roman Palestine functioning almost invisibly in the socio-cultural construction of healing and especially within its semantic and symbolic universes.[47] It is this world that is the backdrop to the concluding section of this study which examines Jesus, women and healing in the Gospel of Matthew.

Jesus the Healer and Women the Healed (Matt. 8:14–15; 9:18–26)

Consideration of women as recipients of healing as recounted in the Gospel of Matthew traverses two worlds. The healing narratives originated in oral storytelling contexts within early first-century Galilee. They were developed within the broader provenance of Matthean traditioning across the arc of cities linking upper Galilee with Antioch later in the century.[48] Since the focus here is more specifically on the rhetorical or symbolic function of the narratives attention will be directed to the later Matthean context and the world constructed by that Gospel's accounts of women's healing.

For this analysis, I will use more explicitly the five categories of Kleinman's cross-cultural criteria—institutional setting; characteristics of the interpersonal interaction; idiom of communication; clinical reality; and therapeutic stages and mechanisms[49]—allowing them to overlap somewhat as the analysis unfolds. In this paper, I can only apply these to the three healing narratives chosen. It will not be possible to compare these accounts with the others in Matthew 8–9 nor with the healing narratives beyond these chapters, especially Matt. 15:21–28. Such comparisons would, however, certainly enrich this study.

The *settings* for the healings of Peter's mother-in-law, the ruler's daughter, and the woman with the haemorrhage are all non-institutional. Two take place in a house: the first in the house of Peter

---

[46] T. Ilan, *Jewish Women in Greco-Roman Palestine* (Peabody, MA: Hendrickson, 1995), p. 189.

[47] Attention has already been drawn to the fact that there is no explicit reference to women as midwives or physicians or exercising any of the healing arts in the corpus of the Christian Scriptures.

[48] I have argued for this provenance of the Gospel narrative in *Shall We Look for Another? A Feminist Reading of the Matthean Jesus* (Maryknoll, N.Y: Orbis Books, 1998).

[49] Kleinman, *Patients and Healers*, pp. 207–8.

(8:14),[50] and the second in the ruler's house (9:23). The haemorrhaging woman is healed along the way to the ruler's house (9:19).
The events are episodic in nature and are performed for individuals. In two of the accounts, however, those located within a house,
the women are embedded within a familial context. One is named
mother-in-law of the owner of the house, Peter, who is a key character in the Matthean narrative. The other is the daughter of the
ruler who is active in seeking the healing. The haemorrhaging woman
stands alone and initiates her own healing. Except for this small
fissure in the text, the narratives construct women as passive and in
need of male healing power, as in the dominant narrative of the
Hippocratic treatises as well as in the Epidaurian inscriptions. The
symbolic universe of women healers is all but obscured in this narrative. Only the initiative of the haemorrhaging woman and her
undertaking of an action which she believed would bring her healing constructs woman in an active mode in the healing process. Like
the Epidaurian texts, these Gospel narratives participate in and hence
maintain the ideology of healing and its genderization current in first-
century c.e. Palestine and in Jewish communities beyond its borders.

In none of the Matthean accounts, or elsewhere in the Gospel, is
Jesus named a physician and hence belonging to the professional
sector of the health care system.[51] He would likely have been located
by the majority of the Matthean readers/hearers within the world
of the holy ones of charismatic Judaism—those who drew their healing power from God.[52] This would place Jesus within the folk sector, as Pilch also suggests,[53] and he goes on to define the folk healer
as "real and effective but ... not accepted by everyone as legitimate."[54] The type of healing being predicated of Jesus in this early
stage of analysis, locates him firmly within Israel's health care system as mediator of divine healing.

The quality of the relationship between healer and healed within

---

[50] For a much more extensive analysis of the possible symbolism of this location,
see E. M. Wainwright, *Toward a Feminist Critical Reading of the Gospel according to
Matthew* (BZNW, 60; Berlin: de Gruyter, 1991), pp. 184–5.

[51] The only time the word ἰατρός is used in the Gospel is in the parabolic saying of Jesus in Matt. 9:12—"Those who are well have no need of a physician, but
those who are sick."

[52] G. Vermes, *Jesus the Jew: A Historian's Reading of the Gospels* (London: Collins,
1973), pp. 65–80.

[53] Pilch, "The Health Care System in Matthew," p. 105.

[54] Pilch, "The Health Care System in Matthew," p. 105.

the context of *the interpersonal interaction* being developed by these
Matthean healing accounts is a much less formal one than in the
Asklepian healings while at the same time constructing a world of
divine compassion similar to the world they construct. The person
in need of healing does not have to make a pilgrimage to a distant
shrine but rather the healing power of Jesus is integrated into the
normal activities of both the healer and the healed. Jesus enters
Peter's house for a purpose that is unstated in the narrative, healing Peter's mother-in-law when he sees her lying sick with a fever
(8:14). It is while he is in a discussion with his disciples that the
ruler approaches him to bring his daughter back to life (9:18), and
on the way to the ruler's house a woman along that way touches
his garment for healing (9:20). The use of the verb of movement
ἔρχομαι (ἐλθὼν in 8:14 and 9:18; and προσελθοῦσα in 9:20) conveys
this sense of the integration of Jesus' healing into ordinary everyday
activities.

In each of these accounts the *idiom of communication* of healing within
the context of the relationship is by way of touch. Jesus touches the
hand of Peter's mother-in-law (8:15), the woman with the haemorrhage touches Jesus' garment [9:20], and Jesus takes the young
woman's hand (9:25). This constructs the healing conveyed by Jesus
in each of these accounts within a much more intimate encounter
than that of sleep, dream or vision, as in the Asklepian temple.

The attitudes of the participants in the healing interaction are
significant toward the development of the semantic and symbolic
world of healing. There is an apparent silence in this regard in the
account of Jesus' healing of Peter's mother-in-law. We learn nothing of her attitude to Jesus as healer prior to her healing. The immediate reaction of Jesus upon seeing her lying sick with a fever may
have been understood to imply his desire that healing and wholeness be extended to those whose world was shattered, broken or
controlled by forces that debilitated or destroyed body or spirit.[55]

On the other hand, the listener to the narratives encounters the
attitude of the haemorrhaging woman. She expresses to herself the
profound conviction that if she but touch the hem of the garment

---

[55] See Wainwright, *Feminist Critical Reading* (pp. 180–2), for a more lengthy discussion of the significance of the verb 'to see' in this verse for the construction and
reception of this story as not only an account of healing but also a narrative of
call or vocation.

of the charismatic holy one, she would be made well. Her use of the verb σῴζω constructs the semantic world of healing in terms of freedom from disease but also situates that healing within a broader religious framework, given that the verb carries with it connotations of divine salvation or preservation from eternal death.[56] Within the Matthean narrative, it is in fact the verb used to designate Jesus' future role at the time of his conception—he will save his people from their sins (1:21). It is the cry for help on the lips of the disciples during the storm on the lake (8:25) expressing a profound desire for transformative or restorative intervention similar to that of the haemorrhaging woman. At a number of other points in the narrative it carries stronger connotations of final transformation or restoration (10:22; 16:25; 19:25; 24:13, 22). Only as an ironic challenge to Jesus as healer by divine power but dying on the cross, does the meaning revert to that of the more immediate—save yourself (27:40, 42, 49).

Jesus' desire to restore life and wholeness is further emphasized by his immediate response to the ruler's request to come and heal his daughter who, in the words of the narrative, "has just died" (9:18). In the language of the father's request—"Come and lay your hand on her, and she will live"—the semantic world of healing is extended to include the restoration of life which was symbolically included in the verb σῴζω in the enclosed narrative (9:20–22). Within the Matthean narrative the verb ζάω of 9:18 is predominantly used as descriptive of God, who is called the "Living God" or "God of the Living" (16:16; 22:32) and therefore intimately associates restoration to life with divine power. Thus, this brief analysis of the attitudes of both healer and healed within the healing encounter has enabled us to uncover elements of the belief system among first-century Jewish Christians who constructed healing as a transformative and restorative encounter with divine power, mediated through the one commissioned with this healing or restoration. These narratives of women's healings in their turn functioned rhetorically to shape belief in Jesus as the one so commissioned as well as belief in divine power for healing accessible in the ordinariness of everyday life and in the intimacy of human touch.

---

[56] W. Bauer, W. F. Arndt and F. W. Gingrich, *A Greek-English Lexicon of the New Testament and Other Early Christian Literature* (Chicago, IL: University of Chicago Press, 2nd edn, 1979, p. 798), for these possibilities within the semantic range of the verb.

Turning to the *clinical reality*, it appears from the above analysis that the efficacy of these healing encounters between Jesus and the three women is derived from their sacred quality. Kleinman, while recognizing the therapeutic strengths of this aspect of the system of healing, also acknowledges that therein lies one of its limitations in that the very sacred nature of the encounter "limits the extent to which it can be 'rationalised' as part of a secular organization of health care."[57] In terms of this study, this may be one of the characteristics of the system which has virtually displaced women healers from the symbolic universe of early Christianity in the Graeco-Roman world, especially in light of the fact that in the Matthean narrative, immediately following the construction of this sacred aspect of healing in Matthew 8–9, twelve male disciples are singled out to be commissioned to heal as Jesus healed (10:8), thus sharing Jesus' sacred power. However, there is no explicit account of women who share that same power.

Attention to the language which describes both the clinical reality as well as the *therapeutic stages and mechanisms* reveals layers of the semantic and symbolic world of healing within the Matthean narrative. In each case, the problem is named in terms of a very concrete disease: one woman is "lying sick with a fever" (βεβλημένην καὶ πυρέσσουσαν); another has "suffered from a haemorrhage for twelve years (αἱμορροοῦσα δώδεκα ἔτη); and the young girl has "just died" (ἄρτι ἐτελεύτησεν). Those descriptions would have evoked varieties of intertextual meanings within the Matthean Jewish Christian audience in the Roman world. For some fever may have been commonly associated with malaria,[58] while the professional sector had constructed it multivalently, requiring a variety of cures.[59] It was a disease, often serious to fatal, which needed to be cured. Given the construction of women as suffering predominantly from gynaecologically related diseases within the professional sector and perhaps too in the folk sector, the general reference to a woman suffering with a haemorrhage for twelve years may have evoked the construction of female haemorrhage as uterine.[60] The Levitical laws within Judaism and their interpretation during the first century may have likewise

---

[57] Kleinman, *Patients and Healers*, p. 241.
[58] Hemer, "Medicine," p. 70.
[59] See *Affections* 1:10–15 by way of example in *Hippocrates*, vol. 5 (transl. P. Potter; Cambridge, MA: Harvard University Press, 1988), pp. 19–27.
[60] See Soranus, *Gynecology*, 3:10.

contributed to such an understanding.[61] Within the Hippocratic Corpus, a significant section deals with haemorrhages but it seems that generally when the sick one is not specifically gendered, they can refer to nasal haemorrhages.[62] Whatever its origin, the length of the woman's suffering would have rendered her physically vulnerable. That a young girl had just died and healing was requested for her by her father, would have recalled for the hearers the social, familial and personal precariousness of the time of transition from young girl to nubile maiden.[63] From this it is clear that one layer within the health care system of early Christianity is that of actual diseases or even physical death as needing therapeutic attention. As such these conditions are given a culturally legitimated name or label according to Kleinman within the health care system.[64]

We saw above that in each of the three accounts under consideration, the cultural label was manipulated by Jesus as healer by way of the instrument of touch. As a result, a new label was sanctioned. It is these which are of interest in terms of both the semantic and symbolic nature of healing and gender, especially its Christian construction. The woman of Matt. 9:20–22 can no longer be described in terms of her illness but she has been made well or saved (ἐσώθη), participating, therefore, in the fullness of what that word entails within the symbolic universe of the Matthean narrative as described above. Both Peter's mother-in-law and the young girl are labelled anew as having been lifted or raised up (ἠγέρθη). While this new description of the two women can be understood simply on a clinical level, it must be remembered that it also evokes the new interpretive lens through which the emerging Christian community understood the most destructive of forces, namely death (see in particular 28:6 in relation to Jesus). Peter's mother-in-law is not only raised but she also ministers to Jesus (διηκόνει αὐτῷ). Pilch understands this as restoration to a "desirable state of being," but he considers that for women

---

[61] For a detailed study of this, see S. J. D. Cohen, "Menstruants and the Sacred in Judaism and Christianity," in Pomeroy (ed.), *Women's History*, pp. 273–99.

[62] Hippocrates, *Prorrhetic* 1:132–150. See also A.-J. Levine, "Discharging Responsibility: Matthean Jesus, Biblical Law, and Hemorrhaging Woman," in D. R. Bauer and M. A. Powell (eds.), *Treasures New and Old: Contributions to Matthean Studies* (Atlanta, GA: Scholars, 1996), pp. 379–97, who warns against too ready an assumption that the haemorrhage is uterine.

[63] A. Clark Wire, "Ancient Miracle Stories and Women's Social World," *Forum* 2.4 (1986), pp. 77–8; and Demand, *Birth, Death, and Motherhood*, p. 11.

[64] Kleinman, *Patients and Healers*, p. 243.

in Mediterranean culture the state more proper to women, rather than men, is that of "doing" rather than "being" and the sphere for that is the home.[65] Examination of the semantic value of διακονέω within the narrative world of the Matthean text and the call or vocation element in the story type[66] leads to a recognition that the healing accounts function not only to construct healing as transformative of somatic aspects of women's lives but also of their socio-cultural and religious lives as well. Each woman is named as participant in the transformative universe associated with Jesus—that of service (20:28), of saving (1:21) and of being raised to new life (28:6).

Conclusion

It is clear that at least the three healing narratives of women examined in this paper can function rhetorically and symbolically as transformative. Transformation takes place in the ordinariness of everyday activities and by way of human touch. Women's bodies are the site of the most significant transformative powers associated with Jesus—service, saving and resurrection.[67] Certainly, they are not the healers in these transformative encounters but the healed. Women's bodies, however, configure the divine healing power, mediated through Jesus. There is a reciprocity within these narratives, especially as analysed by way of the medical-anthropological model, which suggests that the healer and the healed cannot be isolated from one another nor constructed hierarchically within the symbolic universe of early Christianity. Within the entire socio-cultural and religious system, Jesus cannot be isolated even as mediator of divine healing from those healed. Women healed carry in their restored bodies the signification of those aspects of transformation that Jesus himself both represents and enacts.

As their stories are appropriated beyond the constructions of healing and gender of the Graeco-Roman world, the transformative healing of Jesus may be configured more explicitly by the bodies of women: their bleeding, their dying and their rising, contributing to

---

[65] Pilch, "Reading Matthew Anthropologically," p. 286.

[66] Wainwright, *Feminist Critical Reading*, pp. 85–6, 186–7.

[67] As well as drawing this conclusion from the study undertaken herein, I have also been informed in this insight by Levine, "Discharging Responsibility," pp. 396–7.

a more multivalent metaphoric construction of Jesus among contemporary communities of believers. Women too can be configured
anew as initiators of the transformative powers inscribed on the bodies of their foresisters as well as recipients of divinely mediated healing. This is to read the Gospel narrative symbolically and rhetorically
for today's world. Women as active participants in their own healing, in the healing of human relationships and human brokenness,
and in the healing of the universe may be transformed by their faith
to be healers as well as healed in the interplay of movement toward
transformation.

PORTRAYALS OF WOMEN IN 1 AND 2 MACCABEES

GERBERN S. OEGEMA

1. *Introduction*[1]

In 1 Maccabees, which is a history of the Maccabean revolt and was written under the reign of John Hyrcan or Alexander Jannaeus (134–104–76 B.C.E.), women are usually portrayed as being dependent on men. On the one hand, they are presented as victims of the Syrian occupation (1 Macc. 1:26–27, 32) and are killed because they have their children circumcised (1 Macc. 1:60). On the other hand, they are important only if a man wants to marry them in order to enter a priestly family (1 Macc. 16:11). Another example of the neglect of female characters in the book is the figure of Matathias, the leader of the revolt against Syria, to whose five sons the author constantly refers, but whose wife or possible daughters are never mentioned (1 Macc. 2:1–5; cf. 8:10). According to the ideology reflected by the "war epic" of 1 Maccabees this lack of interest may point to the fact that women played a subordinate role in the Hasmonean kingdom.

In contrast, in 2 Maccabees, which originated under the reign of Salome Alexandra (76–67 B.C.E.) or somewhat later, women are highly glorified. Not only the "Song of Praise" for the mother and her seven sons, who had died the death of martyrdom shortly before the Maccabean uprising (2 Macc. 7:1–42), but also other parts of the book stress the important role of women. Women can be economically independent and emancipated. For instance, they control their own possessions (2 Macc. 3:10). In the case of their martyrdom

[1] This paper was written in the context of the project "Jewish Writings of the Hellenistic-Roman Period" (Introduction, Bibliography and Index), supported by the *Deutsche Forschungsgemeinschaft* and directed by Prof. Dr. H. Lichtenberger, Tübingen (cf. *ZNW* 87 (1996), pp. 294–5). I wish to thank my colleagues for providing me with the preliminary results of their research necessary for writing this article: Prof. Dr. F.-W. Horn, Dr. H. Löhr, H. Omerzu, and C. Büllesbach (Mainz and Duisburg) and Prof. Dr. H. Lichtenberger, Dr. U. Mittmann-Richert, A. Lehnardt, M.A., D. Rieß, and J. Dochhorn (Tübingen). For improving my English as well as for many useful suggestions concerning gender studies I thank D. Dimitrova (Heidelberg).

for the Jewish religion we are dealing with an important aspect of the history and possible origin of Jewish and Christian martyrology in New Testament times.

Both this aspect as well as the theological and ideological background of the portrayals of women in 1 and 2 Maccabees will be discussed in this article. Furthermore, it should especially be noted that both books belong to the very few historiographies which may have been read by educated Jewish (and later on possibly also Christian) men and women at the time of Jesus of Nazareth. 1 and 2 Maccabees may, therefore, not only reflect the ideas of their authors in the second and first centuries B.C.E., but also, in the history of their reception, those of the readers in the first century C.E., especially of those members of the upper class in Jerusalem, who were able to read Greek and felt connected with the Hasmonean ideology.

1.1 *The Literary Character of 1 and 2 Maccabees*

The fact that 1 and 2 Maccabees were written several generations after the Maccabean uprising in 164 B.C.E. points to two important characteristics as regards both historiographic writings.[2] Firstly, their authors must have made use of older literary sources unknown to us, as they are well informed about the history of the Jewish people and know of many details concerning the conflict with the Syrian rulers at the beginning of the second century B.C.E. Secondly, they not only had the opportunity but also a reason to portray history and especially the events connected with the Maccabees in an apologetic way, as they were writing during and in favour of the Hasmonean rule in the late second and early first century B.C.E. The Hasmoneans were the successors of Matathias and his five sons, of which Judas "Maccabaios" was the most prominent one.

---

[2] Introductions to 1 and 2 Maccabees are found in H. W. Attridge, "Jewish Historiography," in R. A. Kraft and G. W. E. Nickelsburg (eds.), *Early Judaism and Its Modern Interpreters* (Atlanta, GA: Scholars, 1986), pp. 311–43 (history and state of research), and H. W. Attridge, "Historiography," in M. E. Stone, et al. (eds.), *Jewish Writings of the Second Temple Period* (CRINT, II.2; Assen: Van Gorcum and Philadelphia, PA: Fortress, 1984), pp. 157–84; E. Schürer, *The History of the Jewish People in the Age of Jesus Christ (175 B.C.–A.D. 135). A New English Version. Revised and edited by* G. Vermes, F. Millar and M. Goodman, Vol. I–III.2 (Edinburgh: T&T Clark, 1986), Vol. III.1, pp. 180–5, as well as in A. Lehnardt and H. Lichtenberger (eds.), *Bibliographie zu den jüdischen Schriften aus hellenistisch-römischer Zeit* (JSHRZ, VI.2; Gütersloh: Gütersloher Verlag Gerd Mohn, 1998), and H. Lichtenberger, U. Mittmann-Richert and G. S. Oegema (eds.), *Einleitung zu den jüdischen Schriften aus hellenistisch-römischer Zeit* (JSHRZ, VI.1; Gütersloh: Gütersloher Verlag Gerd Mohn, forthcoming).

In the centre of 1 Maccabees, an apologetic history of those events from 333 to 135 B.C.E. leading to the Maccabean revolt, stands the priestly familiy of Matathias and his sons, their resistance against the Syrian occupation and the latter's effort to abolish the Mosaic religion. The sixteen chapters of the book, written in Greek, like 2 Maccabees (as well as 3 and 4 Maccabees later on), contain several references to older literary sources as well as many documents (letters, decrees and treaties), and were most probably written in Jerusalem. The author represents the standpoint of orthodox Judaism by stressing both the legal hegenomy of the Hasmonean priest-kings as well as Jewish patriotism and national independency. Behind both stands the unshakable trust in God's protection of his people and the centrality of Jerusalem. The credibility of the narrative is guaranteed by its many details and by a style similar to that adopted in the Hebrew Bible, to whose Greek version, the Septuagint, it has been added quite early. The book was known to Flavius Josephus as well as to some of the authors of the New Testament and to some of the Pseudepigrapha. Through the Latin translation of the Vulgate this highly important work on the history of the Jewish people in Hellenistic times became known to the Christian world, in the Protestant tradition as one of the Apocrypha.

Of central importance for the portrayal of history in 2 Maccabees is God's miraculous acting in history, which stands in contrast to 1 Maccabees, where the military skills and political wisdom of the Maccabean princes are highlighted. The author of 2 Maccabees, who presents himself as the *Epitomator* of a five-volume history on Judas written by Jason of Cyrene, clearly belongs to the epoch of Hellenistic Judaism. Although he probably lived in Alexandria, the connection with the Palestinian homeland was still of central importance to him. The fact that the author made use of an older, though lost work, not only indicates that in the case of 2 Maccabees we are dealing with a description, but also with an interpretation of those events resulting in the Maccabean revolt. Despite the importance of the literary sources and their redaction by the author of 2 Maccabees we can only take the book in its present state as the basis of our investigations.[3]

---

[3] Concerning the sources, see also the letters in 2 Macc. 1:1–9, 1:10–2:18 and 9:19–27, as well as the documents mentioned in 2 Macc. 11:17–21, 23–26, 27–33 and 6:34–38.

1.2   *The Historical Situation Described in 1 and 2 Maccabees*

If we want to describe the historical situation of Palestine from
Alexander the Great to the Hasmonean priest-kings, we can consider not only the information and chronology provided by the authors
of 1 and 2 Maccabees but also their account of this history. As
regards the latter, we may be able to discern between facts and
views, a distinction which is of great methodological importance for
our subject, the portrayal of women, although any historian knows
that precisely this distinction is the most difficult of all undertakings.[4]

---

[4] On the role and portrayal of women in the literature of the Hellenistic-Roman
period see (in alphabetical order): L. J. Archer, *Her Price is Beyond Rubies. The Jewish
Woman in Graeco-Roman Palestine* (JSOT Supplement Series, 60; Sheffield: Sheffield
Academic Press, 1990); M. M. Brayer, *The Jewish Woman in Rabbinic Literature. A
Psychological Perspective*, Vols. *1–2* (Hoboken: KTAV Publishing House, 1986); B. J.
Brooten, *Women Leaders in the Ancient Synagogue. Inscriptional Evidence and Background Issues*
(Brown Judaic Studies, 36; Chico, CA: Scholars, 1982); C. A. Brown, *No Longer Be
Silent. First Century Jewish Portraits of Biblical Women* (Louisville, KY: Westminster John
Knox, 1992); H. M. Cotton, "The Archive of Salome Komaise Daughter of Levi.
Another Archive from the 'Cave of Letters'," *ZPE* 105 (1995), pp. 171–208; L. A.
Hoffman, *Covenant of Blood. Circumcision and Gender in Rabbinic Judaism* (Chicago, IL,
and London: University of Chicago Press, 1996); T. Ilan, *Jewish Women in Greco-
Roman Palestine. An Inquiry into Image and Status* (TSAJ, 44; Tübingen: Mohr Siebeck,
1995); T. Ilan, "Premarital Cohabitation in Ancient Judaea. The Evidence of the
Babatha Archive and the Mishnah," in *HTR* 86 (1993), pp. 247–64; T. Ilan,
"Women's Studies and Jewish Studies—When and Where Do They Meet," in *JSQ*
3 (1996), pp. 162–73; R. Shepard Kraemer, *Her Share of the Blessings. Women's Religions
Among Pagans, Jews, and Christians in the Greco-Roman World* (New York and Oxford:
Oxford University Press, 1992); M. Küchler, *Schweigen, Schmuck und Schleier. Drei
neutestamentliche Vorschriften zur Verdrängung der Frauen auf dem Hintergrund einer frauen-
feindlichen Exegese des Alten Testaments im antiken Judentum* (NTOA, 1; Freiburg: Universitätsverlag, and Göttingen: Vandenhoeck & Ruprecht, 1986); G. Mayer, *Die
jüdische Frau in der hellenistisch-römischen Antike* (Stuttgart, et al.: W. Kohlhammer, 1987);
R. Radford Ruether, *Religion and Sexism. Images of Women in the Jewish and Christian
Traditions* (New York: Simon and Schuster, 1974); *Sara en Maria. Vrouwen in synagoge
en kerk* (OJEC, 5; Kampen: Kok, 1987); E. M. Schuller, "Women in the Dead Sea
Scrolls," in M. O. Wise, et al. (eds.), *Methods of Investigation of the Dead Sea Scrolls and
the Khirbet Qumran Site. Present Realities and Future Perspectives* (New York: The New
York Academy of Science, 1993), pp. 115–31; D. I. Sly, *Philo's Perception of Women*
(Brown Judaic Studies, 209; Atlanta, GA: Scholars, 1990); A. Standhartinger, *Das
Frauenbild im Judentum der hellenistischen Zeit. Ein Beitrag anhand von Joseph und Aseneth*
(AGJU, 26; Leiden et al.: Brill, 1995); L. Swidler, *Women in Judaism. The Status of
Women in Formative Judaism* (Metuchen, N.J.: The Scarecrow, 1976); J. R. Wegner,
Chattel or Person? The Status of Women in the Mishnah (New York and Oxford: Oxford
University Press, 1988); P. W. van der Horst, "Portraits of Biblical Women in
Pseudo-Philo's *Liber Antiquitatum Biblicarum*," in idem (ed.), *Essays on the Jewish World
of Early Christianity* (NTOA, 14; Freiburg: Universitätsverlag, and Göttingen: Vandenhoeck & Ruprecht, 1990), pp. 111–22; P. W. van der Horst, "Conflicting Images
of Women in Ancient Judaism," in idem (ed.), *Hellenism—Judaism—Christianity. Essays
on their Interaction* (CBET, 12; Kampen: Kok Pharos, 1994), pp. 73–95.

We will, nevertheless, try to give an overview of the historical events which form the basic contents of both books and which events are necessary for their understanding. In the analysis of those passages dealing with the role of women during the Maccabean period we will focus on the portrayal of women in both books and on the ideology on which these portrayals are based.

The first two chapters of 1 Maccabees describe the historical situation on the eve of the Maccabean uprising and the beginning of the Hasmonean hegenomy. In 1 Macc. 1:1–10 the author looks back on Alexander the Great and the four diadochs who ruled over Greece, Egypt, Syria and Babylonia. Palestine was mainly governed by Egypt (the Ptolemeans) in the third century B.C.E. and by Syria (the Seleucides) at the beginning of the second century B.C.E. In 1 Macc. 1:11–64 the oppression of the Jewish religion by Antiochus IV Epiphanes is described and followed by a narrative in 1 Macc. 2:1–70 on the uprising of Matathias and his five sons. 1 Macc. 3:1–9:22 highlights the military successes of Judas "the Maccabee," one of the five sons of Matathias, and the freedom of religion secured by him. In 1 Macc. 9:23–12:53 it is described how the Hasmoneans are politically accepted by the Seleucides, due to Judas' brother Jonathan, who thereupon is appointed high priest. Under the reign of Simon, Judas' other brother, Judaea becomes independent, and Simon himself unites all political and religious power in one person (1 Macc. 13:1–16:10). His son John Hyrcan takes over power after the death of his father (1 Macc. 16:11–24).

After two introductory chapters, 2 Macc. 3–7 treats the time before the Maccabean uprising in great detail and focuses on the inner-Jewish conflicts concerning the highpriesthood and the martyrdom of the faithful, whereas 2 Macc. 8–15 presents the events described in 1 Macc. 1:11–7:50 in a different order. Due to its character 2 Maccabees is less historical than 1 Maccabees, if one is only interested in the *bruta facta*, but it nevertheless gives us important insights into the way the Maccabean revolt, the events leading to it and the situation resulting from it were perceived in those days. For instance, the author of 2 Maccabees blames inner-Jewish conflicts (mainly Jason's and Menelaos' striving for the highpriesthood and the Hellenization of Judaea) for the abolishment of the Jewish religion by Antiochius IV.

From what was said above, it follows that the Seleucide oppression of the Jewish religion and the succeeding Maccabean uprising in the year 164 B.C.E. resulted in an independent Jewish state. Whereas its political independence lasted until Pompeius' conquest of Jerusalem in 63 B.C.E., its religious independence ended only—after a period of Roman supremacy—at the end of the First Jewish War (66–73 C.E.). As Jesus of Nazareth was born and early Christianity originated in a time of lasting religious independence of the Jewish people, it is of great importance to stress the theological relevance of 1 and 2 Maccabees and their reception history in the first century C.E. An investigation into the portrayal of women, its role in Palestine from the second century B.C.E. to the first century C.E. and its ideological background should, therefore, also take this reception-historical point of view into consideration.

2. *Portrayals of Women in 1 Maccabees*

After having described the ideological background of the account of history in 1 and 2 Maccabees, we now come to speak of the portrayal of women within the context of both writings. Already at the beginning of our investigation we can make the observation that there are only very few verses that relate to women (1 Macc. 1:26–27, 32, 60; 2:1–5; 8:10; 16:11 and 2 Macc. 3:10; 6:10). However, there is the important passage 2 Macc. 7:1–42. All relevant texts will be presented in a translation followed by a short commentary on the basis of which we will draw our conclusions.[5]

1 Macc. 1:26–27, 32

> 26   And the leaders and the elders groaned,
> the virgins and the young men languished,
> and the beauty of the women faded away.
> 27   Every bridegroom took up his lament,
> and she who sat in the bridal camber mourned.

---

[5] If not indicated otherwise, the translations are my own. Editions and translations of and commentaries on 1 and 2 Maccabees: W. Kappler (ed.), *Maccabaeorum Liber I, Septuaginta Vetus Testamentum Graecum, Auctoritate Societatis Litterarum Gottingensis*, Vols. 9.1 and 9.2 (Göttingen: Vandenhoeck & Ruprecht, 2nd edn, 1967); A. Rahlfs (ed.), *Septuaginta. Id est Vetus Testamentum graece iuxta LXX interpretes* (Stuttgart: Deutsche Bibelgesellschaft, 2nd edn 1979), pp. 1039–99; J. R. Bartlett, *The First and Second Books of the Maccabees* (CNEB; Cambridge: Cambridge University Press, 1973); J. A. Goldstein, *I–II Maccabees* (AncB, 41–41A; Garden City and New York: Doubleday, 1976–1984); W. Dommershausen, *1. Makkabäer – 2. Makkabäer* (NEB, 12; Würzburg: Echter, 1985).

[. . .]
32 And they took captive the women and the children,
and they took possession of the cattle.

1 Macc. 1:26–27, 32 is part of the two introductory chapters: ch. 1
describes the oppression of Antiochus IV, and ch. 2 describes the uprising of the Maccabees. Vv. 26–27 and v. 32, as part of the smaller
text unit 1 Macc. 1:20–40, in which the plundering of the Temple
and the occupation of Jerusalem by the Syrian army are described,
have, therefore, a mainly narrative purpose. The terrible fate that
has come over Israel is emphasized by using literary technique. The
verbs "groaning," "languishing," and "fading away" express the passive aspect of lamentation and mourning, whereas the verbs "taking
up a lament" and "mourning" have a more active connotation. We
know this technique from many prophetic texts in the Hebrew Bible
(but also from the Greek tragedies), in which the respective authors
lament over a great loss.[6]

Consequently, the women mentioned in these verses are portrayed
mainly by referring to their weakness or dependence, expressed by
such attributes as virginity, young age, beauty, and waiting for a
wedding which will not take place. They are mentioned together
with other weak and independent beings like young men (boys at
the age of 13 and older), children and cattle. Once they were living under the protection of the leaders and elders of Israel, but now
they are held in captivity. However, although the captivity of women
and children is mentioned in the same sentence as the taking possession of the cattle, we cannot state explicitly that women and children are considered to range on the same level as cattle, because a
certain order is implied (women, children, cattle). Nevertheless, they
do have something in common, that is, their dependence on those
men who are in power.

---

[6] Cf. Lam. 1:4, 18, 19; 2:10, 20; 4:10; Lam. LXX 5:13; Ezek. 24:18; Dan. 6:25;
Nah. 3:13; Ps. 109:24; Ps. LXX 108:24. On the use of the Hebrew Bible (style
and motives) in the poetic sections of 1 Maccabees, see G. O. Neuhaus, *Studien zu
den poetischen Stücken im 1. Makkabäerbuch* (fzb, 12; Würzburg: Echter, 1974). See also,
F.-M. Abel and J. Starcky, *Les Livres des Maccabées* (SB (J); Paris: Gabalda, 1961),
pp. 12–13, and R. H. Charles, *The Apocrypha and Pseudepigrapha of the Old Testament
in English*, Vols. *1–2* (Oxford: Clarendon, 1913), here *Vol. 1*, pp. 69–70. Though the
images are clearly taken from the Hebrew Bible, we may also point to several texts
from later times applying the same literary technique and offering a similar portrayal of women (cf. Mark 13:14–19 par, and m.Sota 9:14).

1 Macc. 1:60–61

> 60   And the women who had circumcised their children
> they put to death according to the decree;
> 61   and they hanged the infants round their necks,
> and their inmates and those who had circumcised them
> (they put to death).

We are dealing here with a description of the cruelty of the Syrian occupation (the women are killed and the infants are hanged around their necks). But a new aspect is added here which is important for an understanding of the chapters following chs. 1–2: the women are punished for circumcising their children, i.e. for obeying the Mosaic law (cf. Exod. 4:25; 2 Macc. 6:10, and Jos., *Ant.* 12:5 for women circumcising their children), and the infants are killed for being circumcised, i.e. for being Jewish. In other words, it is the Torah of the God of Israel that should be abolished, and the women and children, despite their piety, become the victims of the anti-Jewish orders of the Syrians (a clear example of pagan anti-Semitism in pre-Christian times; see also Matt. 2:16).[7] Nevertheless, the reaction of the people and especially of Matathias nevertheless leads to resistance against the Syrian occupation (1 Macc. 1:62), and he starts to organize the uprising (1 Macc. 2:15–48).

1 Macc. 2:1–5

> 1   In those days Matathias rose up,
> (who was) the son of John, (the grandson) of Simeon,
> a priest of the sons of Joarib from Jerusalem,
> and he dwelt at Modiin.
> 2   And he had five sons: John surnamed Gaddi
> 3   Simon, who was called Thassi,
> 4   Judas, who was called Makkabaios,
> 5   Eleazar, who was called Avaran,
> (and) Jonathan, who was called Apphus.

In 1 Macc. 2:1–5 it once again becomes clear that it is not the purpose of the author of 1 Maccabees to discuss either the role of women or their fate. On the contrary, he uses the topic of women's weakness to stress certain aspects of the military and political relationships between the Maccabees/Hasmoneans and the Syrian and

---

[7] On anti-Semitism in antiquity, see P. Schäfer, *Judeophobia. Attitudes toward the Jews in the Ancient World* (Cambridge, MA: Harvard University Press, 1997), with bibliography.

Roman powers. 1 Macc. 2:1–5 is part of the first chapters, which introduce the main actors of the "war epic" of 1 Maccabees: Matathias and his five sons, of whom Judas the Maccabee leads the revolt and Simon and Jonathan become the first Hasmonean priest-kings after the death of Judas.[8] The hereditary lineage is solely based on sons (although, according to the Halakha, Jewishness depends only on one's mother), moreover on a priestly descent. In other words, the pespective of 1 Maccabees is exclusively male.[9]

1 Macc. 8:10

> [. . .] and how they [= the Romans]
> had made many wounded among them [= the Greeks]
> and had taken captive their wives and children.

The observation made already in 1 Macc. 2:1–5 is confirmed in this verse which is part of 1 Macc. 3:1–9:22 and highlights the military success of Judas the Maccabee. Contrary to 1 Macc. 1:26–27, 32, 60, the taking of women and children into captivity is not understood as a vice or crime here, but as the expression of power and strength. In the first example the Syrians are portrayed in a negative way by pointing to the fact that they are the ones who have taken the women and children of Israel into captivity and have killed them; in the second example the Romans are praised because they have taken into captivity the women and children of Greece (which probably took place during the war of the Romans against the Aecheans in 146 B.C.E.).

In the former case, according to the perspective of the narrator, the Syrians had to be portrayed negatively, because they were the enemies of the Jews; in the latter case, from the same point of view, the Romans had to be portrayed positively, because they were going to become the future allies of the Jews. We may, therefore, conclude that, according to the political theory of the author of 1 Maccabees, women and children were to be subjected to the more important goals of a nation, namely its military and political independence.

---

[8] On the names and identities of the five sons, see Abel and Starcky, *Livres*, pp. 30–2.

[9] The name Matathias means "gift of God;" on Joarib, see 1 Chron. 24:7 and Neh. 12:4. The grandfather of Matathias, Simon, was a son of Hasmon, from whom the name Hasmonean(s) is derived; cf. Jos., *Ant.* 12:265, and *War.* 1:36. On the other names in 1 Macc. 2:1–5, see K.-D. Schunck, *1. Makkabäerbuch* (JSHRZ I.4; Gütersloh: Gütersloher Verlag Gerd Mohn, 1980), pp. 303–4.

In the case of the Jewish nation one small but important difference
deserves attention: although, in general, women and children may
be subjected to military and political activities, in the case of Israel
women are also and foremost subjected to their Jewish identity.
Although the Syrians took into captivity women and children, like
any other nation had done before them, they took them into captivity not only because they were women, but because they were
Jewish, whereas the Romans (e.g. in the example mentioned above)
took into captivity only Greek women, that is, only non-Jewish women,
and therefore they were worthy to be praised because they made
an exception for the Jewish women.

According to these observations, Jewish women are considered to
be first of all Jewish and only secondarily female: only for this reason they are killed by the Syrians and spared by the Romans.
According to the author of 1 Maccabees, a Jewish woman has to
be praised, and actually is praised for, having circumcised her children, because circumcision is the most important marker of Jewish
identity.

1 Macc. 16:11–12

> 11   And Ptolemaios, the son of Abubus,
> had been appointed captain of the plain of Jericho,
> 12   and he had much silver and gold,
> for he was the son-in-law of the high priest.

1 Macc. 16:11 is part of the concluding vv. 11–24 of ch. 16, in
which it is rendered how John Hyrcan takes over power after the
death of his father Simon. 1 Macc. 16:11–12 exemplifies the supremacy
of maleness, military strength, and political and economical power,
which are all inherent in the ideology of 1 Maccabees. As it is mentioned in 1 Macc. 16:12 that Ptolemaios is the son-in-law of a high
priest and captain of the plain of Jericho (see Josh. 10; Luke 10:30,
and Jos., *War* 4:467 as well as *Ant.* 13:228), we implicitly know
of the existence of his wife and that she is the daughter of a high
priest, who has paid a lot of silver and gold for her marriage.
However, neither her identity nor her name are mentioned, nor the
fact that she is the one who owns (or owned, in case the husband
has taken over her property) the silver and gold. Her identity is of
no importance, from a male point of view, for emphasizing the meaning of Ptolemaios (cf. 1 Macc. 10:51).

However, the real reason for mentioning Ptolemaios is not to point out his importance, but to introduce and present him as the murderer of Simon. After he has killed Simon following a treachery plan, his son John Hyrcan kills him and his men and in turn becomes the next Hasmonean high priest. The focus on the latter was the main goal of the narrative of 1 Maccabees.

3. *Portrayals of Women in 2 Maccabees*

2 Macc. 3:10

> And the high priest pointed out that the deposits
> belonged to the widows and orphans [. . .].

2 Macc. 3:10 is part of 2 Macc. 3–7, which treats in great detail the period before the Maccabean uprising. These chapters focus on the inner-Jewish conflicts, which the author of 2 Maccabees considers to be the cause of the Syrian occupation of Jerusalem and the desecration of the Temple. Ch. 3 describes how a certain Simon from the tribe of Benjamin plans to organize the robbery of the Temple treasure by informing the Syrians about its enormous richness (2 Macc. 3:1–6). Thereupon the Syrian ruler sends a certain Heliodorus to take possession of the Jewish treasure (2 Macc. 3:7–21). However, miraculously the crime does not take place (2 Macc. 22–40).

From Simon's point of view, and even more so from the point of view of the Syrians, the treasure in the Temple of Jerusalem is just silver and gold, which thus kindles their greediness. For the author of 2 Maccabees, however, the true meaning of the silver and gold is that of being the deposit of and pension for the widows and orphans, according to the the Law of Mose (cf. Deut. 14:25, 29; 27:19; Job 24:3; Isa. 1:23; Ezek. 22:7).

As in 1 Maccabees, also in 2 Maccabees women and children are portrayed as weak and in need of protection, but this time not in order to portray them as the victims of adversary powers. They are weak according to creation, and it is within God's order that they are taken care of. The Mosaic Law prescribes that, when they have lost either their husband or their father, other members of the Jewish community should care for them.

In 2 Maccabees, the care for women and children forms one of the central pillars of Jewish social security in the Palestine of those days. Also in the Jewish communities of the Diaspora, where the author probably lived, such a social system was in practice. Furthermore,

the author juxtaposes a non-Jewish way of life, which is characterized by greediness, to a Jewish way of life, which is focused on loving one's neighbour. Therefore, the message of 2 Macc. 3:10 may
not only be addressed to a Jewish audience, but also to non-Jewish
readers, as in the case of Philo of Alexandria.

2 Macc. 6:10

> Two women, for example, were brought up
> for having had circumcised their children;
> and with the infants hanging on their breasts
> they were led about in public (paraded round the city)
> and then hanged upside down (flung from the walls).

Contrary to the description of the same event in 1 Macc. 1:60, in
2 Macc. 6:10 the women and their children are less anonymous. This
is due to the fact that this passage does not deal with a number of
unknown women, but with two exemplary women. Although their
names are not mentioned, they are depicted in a detailed, vivid and
passionate way, as if their identities were known to the author and
his readers. The great concern of the author of 2 Maccabees for
women and their fate can, therefore, be contrasted to the attitude
of the author of 1 Maccabees, who portrays women rather as anonymous objects.

2 Macc. 7:1–2, 20–23, 25–29, 41

> 1   It also happened that seven brothers together with their mother
> were arrested and shamefully lashed with whips and scourges,
> by the king's orders, in order to force them
> to taste the abominable pork.
> 2   But one of them spoke up for the others and said,
> Why question us? What would you learn from us?
> We are prepared to die sooner than transgress the laws of our fathers.
> [. . .]
> 20   The mother, however, was a perfect wonder;
> she deserves to be held in glorious memory,
> for, thanks to her hope in God,
> she bravely bore the sight of seven sons dying in a single day.
> 21   Full of noble spirit and nerving her weak woman's heart
> with the courage of a man, she exhorted each of them
> in the language of their fathers, saying,
> 22   How you were ever conceived in my womb,
> I cannot tell!
> 23   It was the Creator of the world who fashioned men
> and devised the generating of all things,

and he it is who in mercy will restore to you the breath of life
even as you now count ourselves naught for his laws' sake
[. . .]
25   As the young man paid no attention to him,
he summoned his mother and exhorted her
to counsel the lad so save himself.
26   So, after he had exhorted her at length,
she agreed to persuade her son.
27   She leaned over to him and,
befooling the cruel tyrant,
spoke thus in her father's tongue:
My son, have pity on me.
Nine months I carried you in my womb,
three years I sucked you;
I reared you and brought you up to this age of life.
28   Child, I beseech you, lift your eyes to heaven and earth,
look at all that is therein,
and know that God did make them out of the things that existed.
So is the race of men created.
29   Fear not this butcher,
but show yourself worthy of your brothers,
and accept your death,
that by God's mercy I may receive you again
together with your brothers.
[. . .]
41   Finally after her sons the mother also perished.

2 Macc. 7 consists of 42 verses, in which three elements predomi-
nate: firstly, the dialogue between the Syrian king Antiochus and
each one of the seven brothers and their mother (2 Macc. 7:2,
7b(9–19), 24–26, 39–42); secondly, the speeches of several of them
(2 Macc. 7:5b–6, 30–38), especially of the mother (2 Macc. 7:20–23,
27–29); and thirdly, the description of the cruel way in which they
all are killed (2 Macc. 7:1, 3–5a, 7a, 8b, 9–19). The reason for the
conflict is the Syrian king's attempt to force the seven brothers and
their mother to eat pork and thereby abandon the Mosaic Law. The
contents of the speeches is the assurance that, no matter how cruel
death may be, they should never give up believing in their God and
living according to his laws.

Therefore, the main topic of 2 Macc. 7 is sacrifice, neither for
men in general nor for the Syrian religion, but for God. The purpose of the narrative is to demonstrate the exemplary role that the
seven brothers, and even more so their mother, had in times of persecution. According to the author, this exemplary role is also valid

for later times similarily endangered by the possible loss of the belief in the God of Israel.

Furthermore, the narrative stresses the importance of raising up one's children to live according to the Mosaic religion. The didactic and ethical character of the passage may either point to the Pharisees in Palestine or to certain (sapiential?) circles of Jews in the diaspora as its "Sitz im Leben."

In her speech to the Syrian king the mother, who has to witness the cruel deaths of her sons and is killed herself in the end, glorifies the greatness of God, the real king of the universe (2 Macc. 7:22–23). In 2 Macc. 7:20–21 she herself is praised as a "perfect wonder" and a "believer in God," for being full of noble spirit and nerving her weak woman's heart, for having "the courage of a man" and for deserving to be held in glorious memory.

In her second speech, in which the Syrian king argues that she should persuade her son to eat pork (2 Macc. 7:25–26), she does the exact opposite. She fools the cruel king by speaking in Hebrew (her "father's tongue"), so that he cannot understand her. Again she praises God, the creator of all things that exist. So there is no need to fear "this butcher," because after they all have died they will meet again at the time of the resurrection (2 Macc. 7:27–29).

Contrary to 1 Maccabees, in 2 Macc. 7 women are not portrayed as weak and as dependent on men, but as brave—despite the greatest cruelties inflicted on them by men—and as independent of men. The mother of the seven sons is even more estimated by the author of 2 Maccabees (and his readers), because, unlike the seven brothers, she loses not only her own life but also "the flesh of her flesh," because the seven men have come from her womb. This high esteem is based on her willingness to sacrifice everything dear to her for the one and only God, the creator of the world and the king of the universe, because it is he who has given her and her people the Law of Moses, which the Syrian tyrant wants her to abandon.

From a present-day point of view, one may question this type of woman, but the portrayal of women in 2 Maccabees leaves no doubt about the ideal behind it: The mother (together with her seven sons and, therefore, *pars pro toto* humanity in general) is sacrificing her life to God and not to men or to the values of a patriarchal society constructed by men. She sacrifices her life for her personal belief in God. Therefore, her independence is highlighted, and she is presented as a believing, thinking, feeling and acting human being (see 2 Macc. 7:20–21).

Understood this way, the woman and the other martyrs of the Maccabean revolt not only became perfect models for the first Christian martyrs who suffered a similar fate in the first centuries C.E., but later on became even saints in the Catholic Church. However, they have not become perfect models and saints because they were women, but because they were righteous believers in the one true God.

4. *The Reception of 1 and 2 Maccabees in New Testament Times*

If we investigate into the reception in New Testament times of the female characters as portrayed by the authors of 1 and 2 Maccabees, there are only a few texts which may provide some information. These are Heb. 11:35–36 and some passages in the works of Josephus and in the Pseudepigrapha. In other words, neither the authors of the Gospels nor the Apostle Paul may have been acquainted with the women in these historiographic works. This observation in turn may point to the fact that Jesus and his disciples (including Paul) did not belong or have access to those circles in which the women of the Maccabean-Hasmonean period played an important role, namely the priestly dominated upper class in Jerusalem on the one hand, and learned men like the historian Josephus on the other hand. However, this argument from silence becomes invalid, if research of the social structure of the first Christian communities and, for instance, of the use of Hasmonean names by early Christians would prove the opposite.

Heb. 11:35–36

> 35 Women received their dead raised to life again:
> and others were tortured, not accepting deliverance;
> that they might obtain a better resurrection.
> 36 And others had trial of cruel mockings and scourgings,
> yea, moreover of bonds and imprisonment.

The Epistle to the Hebrews was written by an unknown author, probably in Rome between 80 and 90 C.E. Hebr. 11:1–40 stresses the exemplary role of the believers in Israel's past and is obviously directed to the Christian addressees so that they may follow these models. The author lists among the believers of the past Abraham, Isaac, Jacob, Joseph, Moses, Rahab, Gideon, the prophets, and probably also the martyrs known from 2 Maccabees. For him, not only the Bible itself (e.g. the Septuagint, from where he may have known 1 and 2 Maccabees as well as such parallel texts as Sir. 44–49), but also Israel's history "proves" that God, and only he, is worthy to be believed in.

As the author was familiar with the Greek Bible (including 1 and 2 Maccabees), shows affinities with Jesus Sirach and Philo (cf. *Abr.* §§ 268–70 and *Her.* §§ 90–95) and may have lived in Rome, one could postulate the existence of a connection between the cultural centres of Alexandria and Rome, for which Jerusalem was not necessarily the intermediator.

Josephus

Ant. 12:256

> Indeed, they were whipped, their bodies were mutilated,
> and while still alive and breathing, they were crucified,
> while their wives and the sons whom they had circumcised
> despite of the king's wishes were strangled,
> the children being made to hang from the necks of their crucified parents.

Ant. 13:228

> Now he ruled over the Jews for eight years in all,
> and died while at a banquet,
> as a result of the plot formed against him by his son-in-law Ptolemy,
> who then seized and imprisoned his wife and two sons,
> [. . .][10]

In both texts Josephus, who lived at the end of the first century C.E. in Rome, writing his *Jewish Antiquities* and *Jewish War*, takes over material from 1 Macc. 1:60 and 16:11–12 without changing or adding anything, as far as the portrayal of women is concerned. Only the way women were put to death is described in greater detail. In *Ant.* 12:256 he adds that they were first whipped and then crucified or strangled, thus adapting the description of the punishment to the Roman mode of sentencing someone to death. In *Ant.* 13:228 he provides details about the political background of Ptolemy (Ptolemaios) and his remaining in power, and he explicitly adds the imprisoning

---

[10] Translation according to, *Josephus With An English Translation, by R. Marcus, in Nine Volumes* (London: William Heinemann and Cambridge: Harvard University Press, 3rd edn, 1961), Vol. VII, pp. 31–2, 343.

of his wife and two sons (this information is lacking in 1 Macc. 16:11–12).

The point of view in Josephus' portrayal of women, as far as the two parallel narratives in 1 and 2 Maccabees are concerned,[11] is totally dominated by his perspective of a historian, who, after having been defeated as a former leader of the revolt against Rome (66–73 C.E.), worked for the Flavian house (until about 100 C.E.). In writing "a history of the Jewish people" he tried to find a compromise between the needs of his Roman audience and his own belief in the important role the Jewish people played among the nations. This audience-oriented approach may explain why he adds physical, military and political details in his description of the deaths of the women in the two relevant texts. However, in the overall context of the terrible fate of the Jewish nation the fate of individual women is of less importance, or expressed in the message of 2 Maccabees: being Jewish is more relevant than being female.

Pseudepigrapha

Apart from the earlier, or approximately contemporary, descriptions of the Syrian occupation and the Maccabean uprising in the apocalyptic writings of Dan. 7–12 and 1 Enoch 85–90,[12] 4 Macc. 5–18 treats the martyrdom, as we know it from 2 Macc. 7, in great detail. In this case the author of 4 Maccabees may also have had access to sources other than 1 and 2 Maccabees.

4 Macc. 14:11–18:23 deals in great length with the fate of the mother, after describing the fate of the seven sons in the preceding chapters. Apart from the fact that we do not know when exactly the period between Pompey and Hadrian (63 B.C.E. to 120 C.E.) 4 Maccabees was written, the extensive treatment of martyrdom is by all means noteworthy. It may be explained within the historical context of the two Jewish Wars against Rome (66–73 and 132–135 C.E.) as well as the Diaspora revolt in 115–117 C.E. Moreover, the narrative

---

[11] On the portrayal of women by Josephus, see the dissertation of C. Gerber, *Ein Bild des Judentums für Nichtjuden von Flavius Josephus. Untersuchungen zu seiner Schrift Contra Apionem* (AGJU, 41; Leiden, et al.: Brill, 1997).

[12] On the relationship between, for instance, 2 Macc. 6–7 and Dan. 3 and 6, see J. C. H. Lebram, "Jüdische Martyrologie und Weisheitsüberlieferung," in J. W. van Henten, et al. (eds.), *Die Entstehung der jüdischen Martyrologie* (SPB, 38; Leiden, et al.: Brill, 1989), pp. 88–126, here pp. 91–3. See the contributions in, van Henten, et al. (eds.), *Entstehung.*

may form a bridge between Jewish and Christian martyrology.[13] However, we are only interested in the portrayal of the mother in 4 Macc. 14:11–18:23 and will limit ourselves to the concluding section 4 Macc. 17:11–16.

4 Macc. 17:11–16

> 11   Truly divine was the contest in which they were engaged.
> 12   On that day virtue was the umpire
> and the test to which they were put
> a test of endurance.
> 13   The prize for victory was incorruption in long-lasting life.
> The first to enter the contest was Eleazar,
> but the mother of the seven sons competed also,
> and the brothers as well took part.
> 14   The tyrant was the adversary
> and the world and the life of men were the spectators.
> 15   Piety won the victory
> and crowned her own contestants.
> 16   Who did not marvel at the champions of the divine Law;
> who were not amazed?[14]

In the apologetically oriented philosophical tractate of 4 Maccabees the martyrdom of the mother and her seven sons, as we know it from 2 Macc. 7, is changed in two ways. First, it is portrayed as the philosophical "contest" between the Jewish and the non-Jewish people dealing with the question, whether there is a greater "virtue" than "piety" at all, "virtue" being a term from Greek philosophy and "piety" being the highest goal of the Jewish Law. Second, the role of Eleazar is emphasized and the role of the mother is diminished. Already in 4 Macc. 1:1 the author describes the subject of his tractate: "Highly philosophical is the subject I propose to discuss, namely, whether devout reason is absolute master of the passions [. . .]". After presenting many examples of the victory of reason over passion, he gives us a hint as to how he thinks about women in 4 Macc. 14:11–14:

---

[13] Translation according to H. Anderson, "4 Maccabees (First Century A.D.). A New Translation and Introduction," in J. H. Charlesworth (ed.), *The Old Testament Pseudepigrapha, Vols. 1–2* (Garden City and New York: Doubleday, 1983–1985), Vol. 2, pp. 531–64.

[14] On this, see also J. W. van Henten, "Das jüdische Selbstverständnis in den ältesten Martyrien," in idem, et al. (eds.), *Entstehung*, pp. 127–61, here pp. 143–5; idem, *The Maccabean Martyrs as Saviours of the Jewish People* (JSJ Supplement Series, 57; Leiden, et al.: Brill, 1997), and B. Dehandschutter, "Martyrium und Agon. Über die Wurzeln der Vorstellung von ΑΓΩΝ im Vierten Makkabäerbuch," in van Henten, et al. (eds.), *Entstehung*, pp. 215–9.

11   Do not count it amazing that in those men reason triumphed over tortures,
when even a woman's mind scorned still more manifold torments;
12   for the mother of the seven youths endured the agonies inflicted on every one of her children.
13   Consider how tangled is the web of a mother's love for her children so that her whole feeling is the profoundest inward affection for them.
14   Even animals not possessed of reason have an affection and love for their young similar to that of human beings.

Despite the impression this quotation may have on us (the love of the mother for her children is compared to the love of animals for their young), one's gender is shown as being subject to reason. Unlike the animals, which would have fought for their youngs, and thus passion would have triumphed over reason, the mother did *not* stand the tortures because of her *affection* for her seven sons. She triumphed out of *reason*, understood as piety. In other words, she was able to endure the tortures only because she believed in God. As in the case of 2 Maccabees and Josephus, gender is subject to Jewishness.

5. *Concluding Remarks*

As both the author of the Epistle to the Hebrews and Josephus lived and wrote in Rome at the end of the first century C.E., 1 and 2 Maccabees must either have been kept in their libraries or they must at least have had access to them somehow. The earliest evidence for the reception of both historiographic works is, therefore, to be found in Rome around the year 90 C.E. Before 70 C.E. both books have certainly been kept in the libraries of Alexandria, as they belong to the Septuagint, and also in the archives of the Hasmonean and Roman rulers in Jerusalem. From there they may have been brought to Rome after the destruction of Jerusalem.

Evidence of knowledge of 1 and 2 Maccabees in Galilee and Syria is not available. In Asia Minor and Greece both books may have been known, as they belonged to the Septuagint. We may, therefore, conclude that the followers of Jesus and the earliest Christians, as far as they spoke Aramaic or Syriac, did not have much knowledge of the contents of 1 and 2 Maccabees, whereas the Greek speaking churches founded and visited by Paul may have had some knowledge, as the Septuagint was their Bible. Evidence from the social sciences and, for example, from the use of Hasmonean names in the New Testament may either be able to verify or to falsify these *argumentia e silentio*. For the time being, all we can say is that the earliest Aramaic or Syriac speaking Christians may have had little or no knowlegde of the female characters in 1 and 2 Maccabees, whereas the Greek speaking churches with contacts to Rome must have had some knowledge.

PART THREE

ACTUALIZATIONS

BORDER-CROSSING AND ITS REDEMPTIVE POWER IN JOHN 7:53–8:11: A CULTURAL READING OF JESUS AND *THE ACCUSED*

LETICIA A. GUARDIOLA-SÁENZ

1. *Introduction*

"Cultural texts do not simply reflect history, they make history and are part of its processes and practices."[1] The Bible, like any other cultural text, can be studied not only as an archaeological piece that *reflects history* and ideological traces of its time, but also as a text that *makes history* and does an ideological work.

The influence of the Bible in the formation of Western thought epitomizes the potential that cultural texts have to make histories and conceive ideologies. This influence, however, is not unilateral. The Bible has certainly influenced deeply the history and ideology of the Western world, but equally important has been the influence of the Western world in the history and ideology of biblical interpretation. So closely intertwined are the Bible and the Western thought that it is difficult to conceive one without the other. Because of this "dangerous liaison" the Bible cannot be read innocently, as a distant text that narrates experiences of a people from the past, as a story detached from our realities. To understand its active role as a text that has made and makes history and ideology in our culture, the biblical text needs to be studied in both its socio-historical conditions of production and its socio-historical conditions of consumption.[2]

---

[1] J. Storey, *Cultural Studies and the Study of Popular Culture: Theories and Methods* (Athens, GA: University of Georgia Press, 1996), p. 3.

[2] The hybrid reading approach I am proposing in this article has its basis in cultural studies, a critical perspective highly informed by Marxism with a particular interest in the patterns of cultural consumption (See Storey, *Cultural Studies*, pp. 3–7). Within this particular approach, the act of reading is performed dialogically. The reader engages the text in conversation, acknowledging and scrutinizing both the socio-historical context in which the text was written (produced), and the socio-historical conditions in which the text is read (consumed) and interpreted. From this perspective, the history of scholarship of the biblical text can be examined as the history of consumption (readership) of the text at different points in times, under different cultural circumstances, performed by readers from different social locations with particular perspectives and ideologies.

A text is never read in a vacuum. Every time that a reader encounters a text, a cultural process is set in motion. The act of reading or "consuming" texts is a cultural practice that exposes the relations of power and politics involved in all cultural transactions aiming at producing meaning. Readers are not disinterested; every reader has a particular agenda which evidences her/his political engagement in society and influences the ways in which texts are read, interpreted, transmitted and used to *make history* and *ideology*.

In some instances, however, there are readers who believe they are immune to our human "subjectivity" and to the influence of cultural processes. The wide use of the historical-critical method— praised for its objectivity and universality—as the main reading approach to the Bible among Western male scholars proves the point. They have monopolized and manipulated academia in the last decades with the myth of the text-as-window to the past. Blinded, perhaps, by the symbiotic existence of the Bible and their Western thought they seem to overlook the cultural fibres of their readings. Consciously or unconsciously, they hide their agendas under their supposed objective view which can retrieve the "original" and "proper" meaning of the text.

Postmodernity, however, has launched into academia, together with new readers and readings, different approaches that reflect the changes of a world that, after all, has always been inhabited by many worlds. The collapse of the latest empires brought to trial the subtle readings that nourished the expansionist spirit of the Christian world. Readings that once were regarded as universal and objective, *reflecting the history* of the text, were later proven to be socially constructed.

In the end, the West has been found guilty of reading the biblical text subjectively, *making history* according to its imperialistic and patriarchal agendas. Today, the exposé of Western subjectivity vindicates the marginalized voices previously dismissed as subjective, non-scholarly readings.

Gradually, the presence of minority voices from the Two-Thirds World doing biblical criticism in the U.S. arena has been increasing. But there are still very few methodological approaches that engage the presence of non-Western subjects and their cultural contexts as seriously as one time the supposedly objective readers were taken. Therefore, the aim of this article is twofold: first, to present a cultural, regional reading of John 7:53–8:11 from the hybrid experience of a bi-cultural Mexican-American subject from the border-lands, living in the diaspora; and second, to begin theorizing and systematizing the elements of a reading strategy aimed at empowering minority readers as agents of historical change in the ongoing process of de-colonization and liberation of the Two-Thirds World.

This cultural, regional reading of Jesus and *the Accused* in John 7:53–8:11 represents only an alternative reading, which is by no means objective or universal. Rather, it is an interested reading, performed by a subjective reader from the borderlands.

This article is developed in five steps. First, I briefly review the old and new critical paradigms at work in biblical criticism as theoretical framework. Second, I map my hybrid, border identity under Cultural Studies and Border Theory as the basis for my reading strategy. Third, I survey some of the cultural conditions that launched the production of John 7:53–8:11. Fourth, I critically read and acknowledge some of the existing interpretations of the text, entering into conversation and reading with other readers as a way of finding my own voice.[3] And finally, I present a reading of Jesus and *the Accused* from my border perspective, concluding with some remarks on the political ramifications of border-crossing practices.

2. *Mapping Biblical Criticism: Old and New Territories*

Four main critical paradigms have dominated biblical scholarship in the past 25 years: historical criticism, literary criticism, social-scientific criticism, and cultural studies.[4] The emergence of these four paradigms can be broadly explained as a direct result of historical and social changes. Particularly, the key catalysts that have prompted the shift in paradigms have been the roles that culture and experience have played in the reading strategies.[5] As readers have gradually came to recognize the inevitable influence of culture and experience in their readings, they have equally came to admit the non-universal

---

[3] Regarding the importance of acknowledging and affirming the legitimacy of other readings, see D. Patte, *Ethics of Biblical Interpretation: A Reevaluation* (Louisville, KY: Westminster John Knox, 1995), pp. 113–29.

[4] See F. F. Segovia, "'And They Began to Speak in Other Tongues': Competing Modes of Discourse in Contemporary Biblical Criticism," in F. F. Segovia and M. A. Tolbert (eds.), *Reading from This Place. Volume 1: Social Location and Biblical Interpretation in the United States* (Minneapolis, MN: Fortress, 1995), pp. 1–32.

[5] Segovia, "They Began to Speak," pp. 1–32.

view of their perceptions. As a consequence of this process of sub-jectivization—humanization of the readers—the focus of their ap-proaches has evolved. They have moved from the illusory objectivity inherited from the Enlightenment to the chaotic subjectivity of the *flesh-and-blood-readers* of postmodernity.

First, influenced by the positivism of the 19th century, historical criticism focuses mainly on the historical context of author and text. The reader, as objective observer, is capable of retrieving the text's original meaning in an almost scientific way. Later on, with the influence of the scientific empiricism and its emphasis on semiotics, literary criticism centres on the text. The text, as a literary universe, is isolated from its context of production and studied as a coherent unity, a meaningful whole that responds to an internal structure. In this paradigm the reader is still objective, however, under particular lenses like feminist readings, she/he starts questioning her/his social location. Thirdly, under social-scientific criticism, influenced by a post-modern and fragmented post-colonial thinking, the focus starts consistently moving toward the reader. Now the reader is seen as a subject informed of her/his ability to construct meaning(s) from the text.

It is under this latest focus on the reader that the fourth para-digm of cultural studies emerges, pushing the presence of the *flesh-and-blood reader* into biblical studies. Cultural studies integrates within biblical criticism "the questions and concerns of the other paradigms on a different key, a hermeneutical key, with the situated and inter-ested reader and interpreter always at its core."[6]

The evolution of the reader has been gradually changing accord-ing to the level of acknowledgement that each paradigm has given to the cultural context and experiences of the reader. Acknowledgement and evolution have come, as mentioned before, through the irruption of marginalized and minority voices in academia. By acknowledging the borders of social location, the *flesh-and-blood reader* has expanded the political horizons of her/his reading, and in so doing has exposed the hidden agendas of the presumed apolitical-disengaged readers.

Regarding its political agenda, cultural studies is informed by Marxism in two aspects: first, the cognizance of the socio-historical

---

[6] F. F. Segovia, "Cultural Studies and Contemporary Biblical Criticism: Ideological Criticism as Mode of Discourse," in F. F. Segovia and M. A. Tolbert (eds.), *Reading from This Place. Volume 2: Social Location and Biblical Interpretation in Global Perspective* (Minneapolis, MN: Fortress, 1995), pp. 1–17, here p. 8.

conditions in which cultural texts, practices, and events are produced (generated) and consumed (engaged) to understand their meaning; and second, the awareness that capitalistic societies are divided unequally, thus culture is a site of ideological struggle.[7]

In cultural studies, culture is defined as the texts and practices of everyday life. Since different meanings can be ascribed to the same text or practice, minority groups always resist dominant groups and their imposition of meanings. Culture is the terrain where meaning is incorporated or resisted, where hegemony can be won or lost.[8]

The reason for the use of this approach is twofold: first, as reader I can use my cultural identity both as hermeneutical lens and as a reading strategy; second, I can read texts from the perspective of the political dimension of everyday life. Under cultural studies, the reader participates openly in constructing meaning, because "a text does not carry its own meaning or politics already inside itself. [T]exts do not define ahead of time how they are to be used."[9]

By working under this umbrella paradigm of cultural studies the text is then the site where the socio-historical conditions of consumption (in which I read) and my social location as reader merge with the text to produce what I call a hybrid text, a *crossroads-text*. This *crossroads-text* has no fixed meaning, but multiple meanings produced via the constant readers' readings.

Besides, cultural studies fosters the perspectives and realities of diverse groups, like border theory, which emerged from Chicano studies.[10] Border theory "as analytic tool or as a privileged site for progressive political work,"[11] addresses and analyses the experiences of life in the borderlands. Although border theory has grown out of the studies of "the hybrid culture from the Tex-Mex region," as

---

[7] See Storey, *Cultural Studies*, p. 3.

[8] Storey, *Cultural Studies*, pp. 1–4.

[9] Storey, *Cultural Studies*, pp. 6–7.

[10] According to D. E. Johnson and S. Michaelsen, "Border Secrets: An Introduction," in D. E. Johnson and S. Michaelsen (eds.), *Border Theory: The Limits of Cultural Politics* (Minneapolis, MN: University of Minnesota Press, 1997), pp. 1–39; ". . . the U.S.—Mexico border [is] the birthplace, really, of border studies, and its methods of analysis" (p. 1). They also say that "while it is true that other critical discourses both implicitly and explicitly have recourse to borders—geopolitical and metaphorical—it is equally true that Chicano studies, more than any other, has refocused critical attention on the concept of the border. Chicano studies—more than ethnic studies or post-colonial studies or U.S.—Mexico border studies—has made the idea of the border available, indeed necessary, to the larger discourses of American literary studies, U.S. history, and cultural studies in general" (p. 22).

[11] D. E. Johnson and S. Michaelsen, "Border Secrets," p. 3.

Russ Castronovo asserts, "other contact zones, such as those between race and gender, or between women's writing and patriarchal canons, raise the contention that culture itself can be mapped only by changing margins of identity and fluctuating fringes of power."[12]

Surrounded by cultural differences, we operate within all sorts of borders, literal and figurative.[13] Our identity is shaped not only by the limits of the borders we inhabit but also by the political ramifications of respecting or crossing those borders. In speaking of the functions of a border, Alejandro Morales says,

> A border maps limits; it keeps people in and out of an area; it marks the ending of a safe zone and the beginning of an unsafe zone. To confront a border and, more so, to cross a border presumes great risk. In general, people fear and are afraid to cross borders. People will not leave their safe zone, will not venture into what they consider an unsafe zone.[14]

For Gloria Anzaldúa "the borderlands are the privileged locus of hope for a better world."[15] In a similar way Russ Castronovo celebrates the potential of the contact zone, but he advises us not to forget "the trappings of power that patrol the boundaries of any area of culture."[16] The borders, as permeable boundaries, prove advantageous not only for border-crossers, but for the hegemonic ideologies that structure social realities.[17]

Whether we celebrate the subversiveness of border-crossers, or lament the repressiveness of border patrols, it is important when reading cultural maps to "pay attention to the borders, for it is in these uncertain regions where the landscape of politics is most susceptible to sudden change and reversal."[18] And to better understand borders, it is vital to pay attention to border identities and the hybrid

---

[12] R. Castronovo, "Compromised Narratives along the Border: The Mason-Dixon Line, Resistance, and Hegemony," in D. E. Johnson and S. Michaelsen (eds.), *Border Theory*, pp. 195–220, here p. 9.

[13] See R. Rosaldo, *Culture and Truth: The Remaking of Social Analysis* (Boston, MA: Beacon, 1993), p. 217.

[14] A. Morales, "Dynamic identities in heterotopia," in J. A. Gurpegui (ed.), *Alejandro Morales: Fiction Past, Present, Future Perfect* (Tempe: Bilingual Review, 1996), pp. 14–27, here p. 23.

[15] Michaelsen, "Border Secrets," p. 3.

[16] Castronovo, "Compromised Narratives," p. 203.

[17] S. Hall, "Gramsci's Relevance for the Study of Race and Ethnicity," *Communication Inquiry* 10 (1986), pp. 5–27, here p. 22.

[18] Castronovo, "Compromised Narratives," p. 217.

realities that emerge from the borderlands. The following is a description of some of my hybrid identity parameters for reading texts.

3. *Border/Hybrid Identity and Reading Strategy*

Every reader makes sense of a text in the ways in which it seems to fit her/his needs. And each reader uses the interpretive resources that better help her/him to make sense of her/his world.[19] As a woman from a border zone, I have chosen to read John 7:53–8:11 as a case of border-crossing, bringing into dialogue some aspects of the story that resemble the hybrid reality of the borderlands, with its political ramifications, in the midst of an era of trans-national and multi-cultural realities.

With culture and experience as key factors for a *flesh-and-blood reader's* reading strategy, I proceed to explore my own story to ground my hybrid reading strategy.

As a Mexican woman, born and bred in the bi-cultural, neo-colonialist context of the Rio Grande Valley borderlands, living now as a resident alien in the U.S., I read *the Accused's* story as the encounter of two *border-crossers* who defy the politico-religious, moral and cultural borders of their time.

As a child, living ten blocks from the International Bridge of Reynosa, a border zone between Mexico and the U.S., I grew up well informed of the historical struggle hidden (symbolically) behind that bridge. That bridge represented the negative result of the rupture we suffered as a nation at the hands of our imperialist neighbour, but paradoxically it was also the source of a new connection—a hybrid culture coming out of the encounter of two worlds, one struggling for survival under economic oppression, and the other thrashing about in the waters of interventionism.

Ever since the loss of our territory, feelings of depravity and displacement have haunted our people. However, those Mexicans who ceaselessly cross the U.S. border and succeed in obtaining a better life for themselves and their families represent the silent gradual victories of recovering the seized territory. Regardless of all the laws and patrols enforced to stop the immigration, the influx of border-crossers searching for a better way of life never stops.

---

[19] Storey, *Cultural Studies*, pp. 6–7.

The stubbornness of crossing the border in spite of all the failed attempts, and the ability to camouflage intentions and desires tricking the system—like a chameleon—have become traits of the hybrid identity of this community that feels at home in this ambiguous and divided life. Life in the borderlands is in constant change, from certainty to insecurity, from open lives to hidden identities. Smuggling is the ethos of survival. It is not just the material smuggling of goods that is at stake, but the smuggling of lives of the risk-takers who dangerously cross the borderlands because "to survive the Borderlands you must live *sin fronteras*, be a crossroads."[20]

Now, the old bridge of my childhood, the site of struggle, rupture and hybridity, depicts not just the broader picture of the divided identity of the Mexican-American population of the borderlands, but it is also a place for dialogue and construction from which I can assemble[21] my hybrid identity, denounce oppression, fight for justice, and call for liberation.

Through my hybrid/border subjectivity, assembled in the political grounds of neo-colonialism, I read and appropriate the texts that surround me as hybrid-texts, with a hybridity described by Homi Bhabha "as the sign of the ambivalent and shifting forces of colonial power which cannot be registered at a purely mimetic level within colonial discourse but exceed it, resisting containment and closure."[22] Likewise, I read the shifting forces of patriarchal power inscribed in John 7:53–8:11 as resisting containment and closure. The revolt of *the Accused* against patriarchy, evident in the interstices of the Johannine discourse of law and authority, proves the hybrid/political value of this text for liberation.

Besides using my hybridity as reading strategy and as strategy for survival, I also take it as a model for political change, as Homi Bhabha's hybrid moment, where "the transformational value of change

---

[20] G. Anzaldúa, *Borderlands/La Frontera* (San Francisco, CA: Aunt Lute, 1987), p. 195.

[21] *Assembling* is a very well known word in the borderlands. One of the main sources of economic survival in the borderlands in Mexico are the Maquiladoras. In the Maquiladoras, people assemble goods which they probably will never use or which are too expensive. Maquiladoras are alienating places, not just because of the fragmented work people do, but also the fragmented lives they live, where members of a family work at different shifts and have no chance to see each other. Maquiladoras have become a world inside the borderlands' world. People struggle daily to assemble their lives while assembling goods.

[22] S. Sim (ed.), *The A–Z Guide to Modern Literary and Cultural Theorists* (London: Prentice Hall, 1995), p. 52.

lies in the re-articulation, or translation, of elements that are neither the One nor the Other but something else besides, which contests the terms and territories of both."[23]

From my experience as hybrid/border woman I present two basic assumptions for this proposed reading strategy from the borderlands: First, the recognition of the reader's hybridity as a way of avoiding the illusion of universal and objective readings; and also as a way of identifying the contesting extremes of her/his different reading axes. Second, the acknowledgement of the text as a hybrid product with different sides and positions in itself inscribed at the moment of its production, as well as a site where multiple meanings converge and are produced in the context where the text is read/consumed.

I shall proceed now to explore the socio-cultural conditions of production of John 7:53–8:11 within the Johannine community.

4. *Community and Text at the Crossroads: Context of Production*

The Bible, through the centuries, has become a hybrid, crossroads-text. It is not a hermetic, self-contained narrative, but a *text* that has been read, translated, represented, interpreted and transmitted in so many ways that it is common to see it in movies/TV, to hear it in songs, to admire it in sculptures and paintings, and to perceive it in a wide variety of other means that sometimes it is overlooked. The biblical text certainly belongs to the culture that produced it, but now belongs to us and all the cultures that have consumed it before us, and have re-produced and re-enacted it in various ways. However, to say that the text belongs to the present, or that it is *sin fronteras* and hybrid, does not mean it is ahistorical. On the contrary, it is precisely the historical re-enactment of the text throughout the centuries that has emphasized its historical nature and its influence in the process of making history.

The (hi)story of the text shapes the way I read my own story, and my story shapes the way I read the (hi)story of the text. So, to appreciate the strategical value of the hybrid nature of this pericope, and of the hybridity of the Gospel of John as a whole, it is necessary to highlight the socio-historical situation of the community that produced such a text.

---

[23] H. K. Bhabha, *The Location of Culture* (London and New York: Routledge, 1995), p. 28.

According to Raymond Brown, as quoted by Craig Koester, the Gospel of John emerged from and reflects the struggles of a mixed (hybrid) community of Jews, Gentiles and Samaritans who were striving to accommodate to their different theological positions.[24] The Johannine community, constructed here as a marginal group that was expelled from the synagogue, had to deal with issues such as "the relationship to Judaism, with questions of self-identity, and with Christian life in a situation of minority status and some oppression."[25] These sociological presuppositions used to describe the community that produced (wrote) the Gospel of John as an attempt to make sense of its surroundings, illumines my proposed reading strategy to re-read the text from my hybrid community. It also helps to explain the migratory nature of *the Accused's* story.

Although the historicity of the incident has been widely accepted as part of the Jesus tradition by most scholars, its textual location is still debatable. What is important from my perspective of border theory in this case is that the story has crossed canonical borders and seized a place in the text for more than sixteen centuries. As Gail O'Day has precisely said: "John 7:53–8:11 is a story without a time or place, a story to be read on its own terms without sustained reference to its larger literary context."[26] In a sense, John 7:53–8:11 has become a hybrid story in the midst of a Gospel that has been adopting it and rejecting it through the readings of millions of consumers (readers) who have debated the issue. This is a *crossroads-text* that depicts the existence and survival strategies of two border-crossers living at the crossroads.

Due to the mobile nature of this pericope in the written sources, the opinions about the spacial location of the text are divided. Frederick Schilling considers the story as an *intrusion* into the original text, since the earliest manuscripts do not include it.[27] Herman

---

[24] C. R. Koester, "R. E. Brown and J. L. Martyn: Johannine Studies in Retrospect," *BTB* 21 (1991), pp. 51–55, here p. 53.

[25] R. Kysar, "The Gospel of John," in D. N. Freedman (ed.-in-chief), *The Anchor Bible Dictionary. Volume 3* (New York: Doubleday, 1992), pp. 912–31, here p. 918. The three most common causes used to explain the expulsion from the synagogue are: "the introduction of another group of Christians into the community [...], the enforcement of a formal benediction against the heretics [...], the destruction of the Temple in 70 C.E." (p. 918).

[26] G. R. O'Day, "John," in C. A. Newsom and Sh. H. Ringe (eds.), *The Women's Bible Commentary* (Louisville, KY: Westminster John Knox, 1992), pp. 293–304, here p. 297.

[27] F. A. Schilling, "The Story of Jesus and the Adulteress," *ATR* 37 (1955), pp. 91–106, here pp. 92–3.

Ridderbos says the story is "a clear *interruption* and it differs sharply in language and style from John."[28]

Harold Riesenfeld explains that the reason for the late inclusion of the pericope in the Gospel of John was the strict penitential discipline at work in the early church. The tolerant forgiveness Jesus extends to *the Accused* was against the teachings of the church. Later, when penitential practice became more liberal, the story received acceptance in the text.[29] This incident shows how the weight of popular readership/consumption, and not the text itself, is what determines its textual borders. The hybridity of this text is evident: the borders of the text were subjected to the interests and values of the culture that consumed (read) the text.

For Rudolf Schnackenburg the text is not from "the original fabric of John's gospel."[30] A similar position is taken by Leon Morris[31] and Daniel Wallace.[32] For Fausto Salvoni[33] the pericope's style is Lukan, and it is, as for Eugene Nida and Barclay Newman, who also favour the Lukan origin, an interruption of the sequence of John 7:52 and 8:12.[34]

Among the scholars in favour of the present location and its Johannine origins are Allison Trites[35] and Alan Johnson, who says that "the traditional and popular internal linguistic criticism of this disputed passage is not as strong as it has usually been represented."[36] Using linguistic theories, John Paul Heil attests that the narrative sequence in this "masterfully dramatic story adeptly contributes to rather than disrupts the narrative flow in John 7–8."[37]

---

[28] H. Ridderbos, *The Gospel of John. A Theological Commentary* (Grand Rapids, MI: Eerdmans, 1997), pp. 285–6.

[29] See R. E. Brown, *The Gospel According to John (i–xii)* (The Anchor Bible, 29; New York: Doubleday, 1966), p. 335; Ridderbos, *The Gospel of John*, p. 286.

[30] R. Schnackenburg, *The Gospel According to St. John. Volume 2* (New York: Seabury, 1980), p. 162.

[31] L. Morris, *The Gospel According to John* (Grand Rapids, MI: Eerdmans, 1995), p. 779.

[32] D. B. Wallace, "Reconsidering 'The Story of Jesus and the Adulteress Reconsidered'," *NTS* 39 (1993), pp. 290–296, here p. 296.

[33] See F. Salvoni, "Textual Authority for John 7:53–8:11," *Restoration Quarterly* 4: (1960), pp. 11–15.

[34] B. Newman and E. Nida, *A Translator's Handbook on the Gospel of John* (New York: United Bible Societies, 1980), p. 257.

[35] A. A. Trites, "The woman taken in adultery," *Bibliotheca Sacra* 131 (1974), pp. 137–46, here p. 146.

[36] A. F. Johnson, "A Stylistic Trait of the Fourth Gospel in the Pericope Adulterae?," *BETS* 9 (1966), pp. 91–96, here p. 96.

[37] J. P. Heil, A Rejoinder to "Reconsidering 'The Story of Jesus and the Adulteress Reconsidered'," *Église et Théologie* 25 (1994), pp. 361–6, here p. 366.

Whether the scholars consider this pericope Johannine or non-Johannine, it is a fact that the text has assured its place in the canon by popular demand, and the choice is now ours, either to read or to reject it. Either way, our decision to accept the conditions of production of the text enacts already a cultural reading. Explicitly or implicitly, our rejection or acceptance of the text shows the imprint of our cultural values, political agendas, and in sum, maps the borders of our subjectivities in the context of our cultural conditions of consumption (readership).

5. *Reading the Story of the Accused with Others*

Historically, the biblical text has proven to be powerful. The Bible has gone beyond its temporal and spatial boundaries not just for good but also for evil, including massive destruction. Because of some evil interpretations of the biblical text, many people have been erased from the face of the earth and others subjugated and oppressed for not conforming to hegemonic, often biblically grounded, ideologies.[38] Evidently, there is more power in the way in which biblical texts are consumed by readers than we would like to acknowledge. The Bible, read by a variety of readers, has certainly been proven to be not only redemptive but also destructive, and all the possibilities in between.

Although the interpretations of the story of the *accused* woman might seem harmless and have not caused physical extermination of people, the fact is that they have been equally destructive by reinforcing the patriarchal morality of double standard that oppressed women. Analysing some interpretations of John 7:53–8:11 done during the last 40 years, I would say that Johannine scholarship has explained the story of the *accused* woman using mainly two scenarios or hypothetical plots. It has not been until the last decade that a third and a fourth scenario or hypothesis have joined the academic dialogue. The first interpretive scenario focuses on God's grace and

---

[38] Five centuries ago, faithful to the endeavour of Christianizing the New World (cf. Matt. 28:18–20), the Spaniards massacred hundreds of indigenous people in Latin America. Last century, the U.S. with the myth of the *Manifest Destiny* based on the ideology of God's chosen people, seized half of the Mexican territory as their "promised land." The expansionist dreams ended up in massacres. In both cases the Bible was the excuse to mask political ambitions, justifying appropriation of lands and subjugation of peoples.

Jesus' example of forgiveness. The woman in the story is used to show the divine mercy; she is a passive recipient of God's love. The second scenario is more interactive. God and Jesus call sinners to forgiveness, but it is still God or Jesus who has the central voice in the story. These two first scenarios assume that the woman is guilty of adultery. However, in the third scenario, the image of the merciful God disappears. The focus is on the characters, the woman and the Pharisees, and the equal treatment they received from Jesus. The guilt of the woman is not the point of entry to the text, in fact, men are also confronted with their sins. Jesus is seen as sharing the experience of being on trial together with the *accused* woman. In the fourth scenario, the focus is on the structural sin, that is, the patriarchal system. Jesus confronts the religiosity of a patriarchal system that has restrained women and men from having a more fulfilling way of life. The following review of scholars' interpretive scenarios shows their conclusive ideas on the main teaching of the story, and emphasizes their approaches to the woman.

In the first scenario, focused on God's mercy, Frederick Schilling states that the purpose of the story is to "illustrate the principle of forgiveness, the unearned grace of God."[39] Frederick Schilling focuses on forgiveness, a word never mentioned in the story, and ignores the patriarchal oppression inflicted on the woman, who is taken as an object to set Jesus on trial. Likewise, for Beverley Coleman the story is about "our Lord's divine authority as Law-giver, the giver of the love which can save every repentant sinner and give eternal life."[40] She ignores the woman's dehumanization by the Pharisees. The focus is on the act of repentance, which is not even clear in the story.[41]

For Bart Ehrman "the story has to do with Jesus' teaching of love and mercy even to the most grievous of offenders. Judgment belongs to God alone, who forgives sinners and urges them to sin no more."[42] The woman is the "offender," "urged to sin no more." The accusers need no forgiveness, they leave free of guilt.

---

[39] Schilling, "The Story of Jesus," p. 96.
[40] B. W. Coleman, "The Woman Taken in Adultery [John 7:53–8:11]," *Theology* 73 (1970) pp. 409–10, here p. 410.
[41] See also in the first scenario: Brown, *The Gospel According to John*, pp. 336–7; B. Lindars, *The Gospel of John* (New Century Bible; Grand Rapids, MI: Eerdmans, 1972), pp. 310–12.
[42] B. D. Ehrman, "Jesus and the Adulteress," *NTS* 34 (1988), pp. 24–44, here p. 38.

In the second scenario, Rudolf Schnackenburg argues that the theme of the story is not the condemnation of sin but the calling of sinners: "Jesus accepts sinners in God's name; his will is not to judge but to save."[43] Rudolf Schnackenburg excludes the male characters as sinners from the scene.

For Leon Morris, "the guilty woman had as yet given no sign of repentance or of faith[,] what Jesus does is to show mercy and to call her to righteousness."[44] He emphasizes the urgency to call the woman to make a "clean break with sin," but there is no such call to the accusers, who enforce the law that gives them the freedom to commit adultery blamelessly.

The shift to the third scenario comes with Patricia Castro. Reading from a feminist perspective, she observes that the presence of the adulterer is neither important nor needed; Jesus, as a man, has symbolically taken his place. The accusers "not only want the death of the woman, but also the death of the man-Jesus."[45] The woman and Jesus are considered as equals, two law-breakers, two border-crossers who are judged equally.

Robert Maccini focuses on the woman and addresses gaps in the story that need to be questioned when he states, "the narrator takes for granted that the woman is guilty of adultery and does not discuss background details or address tangential issues."[46] The woman, who comes into the scene as the pawn of the accusers, leaves as a free person. She was silent in the story, and she had not even a chance to defend herself, but "no one has condemned her . . . [and] her simple statement to that effect is her only testimony, and her testimony is true."[47]

Gail O'Day, in her commentary on John,[48] says that the story's structure shows how Jesus' attention is equally divided between the woman and the accusers. Both are treated as social subjects and human beings at equal levels. Jesus speaks to both about their sins.

---

[43] Schnackenburg, *The Gospel According to St. John*, p. 168.

[44] Morris, *The Gospel According to John*, p. 786.

[45] P. Castro, "La mujer en la pastoral de Jesús y de los fariseos," in I. Foulkes (ed.), *Teología desde la Mujer en Centroamérica* (San José: Seminario Bíblico Latinoamericano, 1989), pp. 105–19, here p. 113.

[46] R. G. Maccini, *Her Testimony is True. Women as Witnesses According to John* (JSNT Supplement Series, 125; Sheffield: JSOT, 1996), p. 235.

[47] Maccini, *Her Testimony is True*, p. 235.

[48] See O'Day, "John," in *The Women's Bible Commentary*, p. 297.

Both receive the invitation to live life anew. When the male accusers dehumanize the woman, Jesus humanizes her by talking to her as equal to the men. Under Jesus' care, women and men are invited to live life anew, to become part of a new system where both are humanized by Jesus.

Two years later, in her commentary "The Gospel of John," Gail O'Day inaugurates the fourth scenario. She strongly emphasizes that the story is not about the accusers' sin or self-righteousness, nor about the woman's sexual sin, but is about the structural sin, the accusers' religious authority that Jesus challenges: "Jesus places his authority to forgive and to offer freedom over against the religious establishment's determination of the categories of life and death."[49] Jesus attacks what needs to be changed, the system, so that men and women can live new lives, a new vision, in a new hybrid age.

By and large, the interpretations that have prevailed in academia and in non-academic forums are those performed by male readers of the two first scenarios. These readers have taken the woman as sinner and have believed the testimony of the patriarchal accusers, overlooking the fact that the Pharisees are breaking the law by not bringing the adulterer to the trial. They have no regrets in using the woman, whether guilty or innocent, as a bait.

More work is needed to be done in the third and fourth scenarios to bring about political change or re-articulation and transformation of the present, and with it, the fracture of the patriarchal system. Working within the fourth scenario, the proposed hybrid reading seeks to highlight the redemptive power involved in the act of crossing oppressive and tyrannical boundaries. In doing so, new ways of re-defining the borders of marginalized identities will emerge, contouring new territories that invite social transformation and political change.

6. *Crossing Borders with Jesus and the Accused: Reading for Liberation*

The first step towards a liberating reading of this story is to approach the pericope with a new title. Whenever a new edition, revision, or translation of the Bible is prepared, the cultural context, language,

---

[49] G. R. O'Day, "The Gospel of John. Introduction, Commentary and Reflections," in *The New Interpreter's Bible. Volume 9* (Nashville, TN: Abingdon, 1994), pp. 496–865, here p. 630.

values and preferences of the scholars working on the project per-
meate in the translation of the text and in the titles assigned to the
pericopes. The suggestive and categorical titles given to the pericope
of John 7:53–8:11 in most of the translations and studies of this text
have explicitly proved the readers' biased common and undisputed
conclusions about the guilt of the woman. In order to treat her fairly,
with the benefit of the doubt, I address her as *the Accused*, not the
adulteress.[50]

As a way of mapping my reading strategy, I have identified four
general contact zones in the story to analyse the text from my border perspective: spacial borders, gender/moral codes, political/reli-
gious factions, and communication codes. Regarding space, there are
two contact zones in the story: one is between public (Mount of
Olives—8:1) and private (people's homes—7:53) space, the other is
between sacred (Temple—8:2) and profane (other than Temple)
space. These spacial contact zones are closely related to the second,
the contact zone of gender, which defines the cultural roles for women
and men. Women and men had different spacial privileges, and
different moral codes. The third contact zone is the one between
politico-religious factions: Moses' Law vs. Roman ruling, the Pharisees
and scribes vs. Jesus and *the Accused*. The fourth contact zone is established by the communication codes between groups and their verbal and non-verbal discourses.

Beginning with John 7:53–8:1, the first contact zone is one of space
between private and public space: "Each of them went home, while
Jesus went to the Mount of Olives" (7:53; 8:1). Although there is no
explicit reference to the time when the people and Jesus withdrew
from the scene, it can be inferred that it was at the end of the day,
since 8:2 refers to the next morning. So, while the multitude from
7:40–44 (and/or the group from 7:45–52)[51] seems to conclude the
day in the private spaces of their homes, Jesus spends the night in
an open public space, on a hill at the margins of Jerusalem. Jesus,

---

[50] As far as I know, the only biblical scholar who also mentions something about
the bias displayed in the titles given to the pericope, is Gail O'Day. See G. R.
O'Day "John 7:53–8:11: a study in misreading," *JBL* 111 (1992), pp. 631–40.

[51] When the narratives in 7:45–52 and 7:40–44 are read as separated, but simultaneous, stories, 7:53 becomes the perfect link between 7:44 and 8:1. The narrative is ended with the typical Johannine way of concluding conflict scenes (cf. 6:15:
"he withdrew again . . .;" 8:59: "Jesus hid himself and went out . . .;" and 10:39:
"he escaped . . ."). Reading 7:44 as the conclusion of a conflict scene brings a
smoother continuity between 7:44 and 7:53, than the one between 7:44 and 8:12.

as an alien, non-resident individual of the city, wanders outside the walls of Jerusalem.

Excluded from the private spaces of the people's homes, voluntarily or involuntarily, Jesus takes over some of the public spaces, like the Mount of Olives, and transforms them into his private space/home. He knows well enough how to use the public spaces for his benefit so that, whenever he needs to hide from the mob (6:15), he almost becomes invisible to the point of even crossing among them without being harmed (8:59; 10:39). According to Renato Rosaldo, "Immigrants and socially mobile individuals appeared culturally invisible because they [are] no longer what they once were and not yet what they could become."[52] This is shown in Jesus' life in John chapters 1 through to 11. Culturally, as a heavenly immigrant (6:38), Jesus becomes invisible for those who seek to arrest him (7:30). He is no longer what he was with God, and he is not yet what he could become but later on. Through the signs he performs and because the people begin to believe in him (2:23), the authorities will realize that Jesus is a menace to their culture, the powerful leader that could fracture their authority (11:45–53). His presence and identity, although still hybrid, will no longer be invisible to the law-enforcers and the culture's border-keepers. Jesus' hybrid identity helps him to survive while crossing borders and moving frontiers in his subversive acts of creating spaces for transformation. In the end, when his hour comes, he will pay a high price for his behaviour as a border-crosser.

The next day Jesus comes back to the Temple (8:2), the sacred place he adopts as his teaching space. In the Gospel of John, where the community is depicted as a marginal group, Jesus has no synagogue in which to teach. The fact that the synagogues, the common forums of Jesus' teaching in the Synoptics, are replaced by the Temple in the Gospel of John reveals the tension of a community expelled from that sacred space of the synagogue. This event shaped and moved the Johannine community to construct a Jesus who inhabits not just the margins of the city, but who teaches at the borders of the sacred places of the Temple and the synagogue, and in fact advocates for an in-between and different worship space (4:21). Living in the fringes of their religious community, the Johannine community re-creates its story in search of its new identity as border people.

---

[52] Rosaldo, *Culture*, p. 209.

Their struggles and conflicts are personified in the Johannine Jesus, who creates alternative spaces out of the traditional sites. Jesus, the border-crosser who has come from above, becomes the model for survival in the hostile world which the Johannine community inhabits.

Suddenly, the alternative space Jesus opened for all who came to receive his teachings is invaded (8:3). Those who dare to cross the oppressive boundaries of the system and liberate others by teaching them how to cross those borders, live in constant risk. The scribes and the Pharisees irrupt into the scene and break Jesus' teaching discourse by imposing their own discourse (8:3–5). Several borders are at stake in this scene and care is needed to ensure their place and the system's order. Scott Michaelsen says that "the 'border' is always and only secured by a border patrol."[53] If imposed borders were meant to benefit all the subjects in contact zones equally, there would be no need to secure them, everybody would respect them. The Pharisees, "ever-watchful and suspicious adversaries of Jesus,"[54] know they need to rise as the *border patrol*, ready to secure the benefits of their gender, religious group, and authority. They need to watch over the borders of gender/moral codes established by patriarchy and supported by their interpretations of Moses' Law; they have to defend their teaching authority (12:42), which is being threatened by the marginal presence of Jesus' new teachings; and they must secure their political power (endorsed by the chief priests' allegiance with the Roman empire)[55] which is being menaced by Jesus' subversive power.

The Pharisees and scribes bring along with them a woman whom they say has been caught in adultery, and therefore deserves punishment. They have come to defend the territory that patriarchy has granted them, and do not hesitate to cross personal borders and invade the private space of the woman's house to bring her to trial. Several pieces are missing in the puzzle: Who found the woman and where? Where is the adulterer? Where is the husband? These are some of the timeless questions scholars have been debating without definite answers, since there are several lose strings in the scene for speculation.[56]

---

[53] Michaelsen, "Border Secrets," p. 1.
[54] A. J. Saldarini, "Pharisees," in D. N. Freedman (editor-in-chief), *The Anchor Bible Dictionary. Volume 5* (New York: Doubleday, 1992), pp. 289–303, here p. 297.
[55] Saldarini, "Pharisees," p. 296.
[56] For legal details on the arrest and historical considerations on adultery in first-

Scholars have found several reasons to prove that the woman was married, and therefore deserved to be punished.[57] Married or not, the fact is that she is there by herself, the adulterer has run away from the consequences of his actions (cf. Deut. 22:22–24); and there is no husband fighting to get her back, and maybe, as Duncan Derrett says, he was the one who arranged the situation to intentionally catch her and benefit somehow from it.[58]

After arresting the woman, the scribes and the Pharisees come to trap Jesus and defend the borders of their religious authority to rule and teach according to Moses' Law. They call him "Teacher," preparing him to be interrogated and make him prove himself as such. Then the *border patrol* informs Jesus of the arrested woman being accused of crossing the borders of her marriage and defying the power of patriarchy to control her body and will. The interrogation begins: What do you say? What should we do with such a woman? You know that Moses' Law command us to stone "such women." By using the woman as a pawn, they want to trick Jesus and make him confess that he, like her, is also a border-crosser, so that they can accuse him. Likewise, the U.S. immigration patrol uses illegal border-crossers (particularly from Latin America) to catch others in similar situations in order to deport them to their place of origin, once they have confessed where they came from. The Pharisees have cornered Jesus and they are asking him to confess his *place of origin*, just like the border patrol ask the border-crossers. In order to *deport him to where he belongs*, they need to know where is he coming from, and whose side is he going to take. They want to know where he belongs to. They need to know whether he is one of them or whether he is against them.

Jesus and the woman are on trial for trespassing boundaries. The Pharisees are expectant, waiting for Jesus' response which will decide his as well as her destiny. Many possible responses can be concluded from that question. Which one do they expect to hear? Evidently, they are looking for one particular, "they said this to test him" (8:6). They could be testing his subversiveness, his knowledge of the law, or his ability to teach. Allison Trites says that the Pharisees see him

century Christianity, see J. D. M. Derrett, "Law in the New Testament: The Story of the Woman Taken in Adultery," *NTS* 10 (1963–64), pp. 1–26.

[57] See Schnackenburg, *The Gospel According to St. John*, p. 164; Morris, *The Gospel According to John*, p. 782, n. 15; Nida and Newman, *Translator's Handbook*, p. 259.

[58] See J. D. M. Derrett, "Law in the New Testament," p. 4.

as a lawbreaker,[59] that is why they go to him with a question regarding the law. They want to test him and *catch him in the very act of breaking/crossing the law.*

According to the historical construction of the story's context, the Sanhedrin no longer had the power of execution under the Roman empire. The trap becomes evident: no matter what Jesus says, he will be wrong. He is between two dangerous borders, the religious border of the Mosaic Law, which he will violate if he is in favour of the woman, and the political border of the Roman empire, which he will violate if he orders them to stone her.[60]

Jesus makes silence. His discourse, which is a subversive, liberating message, has been invaded by the Pharisees' discourse of punishment, violence, and death. He opens a space of silence between his discourse and theirs when he writes in the dust.[61] It is a space of transformation, a hybrid moment in which they are invited to re-define their own borders, and let the others define their own borders too. In the meantime, the woman is still standing there in the midst of the crowd, as a wall, demarcating the borders between Jesus and the Pharisees.

Facing such a wall and listening to the intensity of Jesus' silence the men are confronted with the validity of their male system. They, like the men in most Mediterranean cultures at the time, are the ones "responsible for the shame of their women which is associated with sexual purity and their own honor derives in large measure from the way they discharge their responsibility."[62] However, in this scene there is only an abandoned woman, who is considered by the patriarchal system as someone "not self-contained, with personal boundaries diffuse and permeable,"[63] who stands by herself with no

---

[59] Trites, "The woman taken in adultery," p. 146.

[60] See Brown, *The Gospel According to John*, p. 337. See Derrett, "Law in the New Testament," p. 11. It was not until the third century that adultery became a capital offense for the Romans.

[61] Several versions have circulated about Jesus' writing in the dust, but none of them offers convincing evidence of what Jesus wrote. See Schnackenburg, *The Gospel According to St. John*, pp. 165–6; Derrett, "Law in the New Testament," p. 19. I agree with the basic idea that "if what Jesus wrote on the ground had been of importance as far as the account itself is concerned, doubtless the author would have included it" (Nida and Newman, *Translator's Handbook*, p. 260).

[62] D. D. Gilmore, "Introduction: The Shame of Dishonor," in D. D. Gilmore (ed.), *Honor and Shame and the Unity of the Mediterranean* (Washington, DC: American Anthropological Association, 1987), pp. 2–21, here p. 4.

[63] C. Delany, "Seeds of Honor, Fields of Shame," in Gilmore (ed.), *Honor and Shame*, pp. 35–48, here p. 41.

responsible husband fighting for his honour. She is accused of bringing shame to the male system by not living within the established
boundaries. Women were not considered as autonomous beings, self-
defined or self-bordered. Therefore, borderless as they were, they
had no way to negotiate their existence as equal human beings.
Paradoxically, this borderless woman, incapable of mapping out her
own identity because her body/territory has been occupied by patriarchy, becomes the metaphorical border between the Pharisees and
Jesus. The Pharisees compel Jesus to continue overriding the woman's
borders, those they have erased by dehumanizing her and treating
her as an object "to achieve narcissistic gratifications and dominance
over other men."[64] They want him to trespass this woman, to ignore
her voice, and deny her the chance of breaking out from the oppressive system. If Jesus condemns her, his decision will help the Pharisees
to keep their privileges, and therefore they will control him and
confine him to their borders.

The Pharisees insist on breaking his silence, ignoring the first
moment of transformation Jesus is giving them (8:7). Jesus responds
to their shock: "Let anyone among you who is without sin be the
first to throw a stone at her."[65] There is silence again (8:8), the second hybrid moment. The silence between discourses is a possible
interstice to subvert their oppressive system, for them to reflect, transform and break the patriarchal ideology behind their actions.

Unlike those who were afraid to oppose the empire at the expense
of their little power, Jesus, having nothing to lose, declares subver-
sively against the imperial control telling them, *go ahead, stone the
woman, do it.* Even though he lives under the Roman jurisdiction he
dictates his sentence under the Jewish Law. This assertion sounds as
if Jesus, by responding positively to the Pharisees' demand, was being
insensitive to the woman, and in complete agreement with the Law.
However, from the border, his response indicates that he does not
subscribe to the Roman empire. The empire does not define the
limits of who he is; he decides on his borders and constructs his

---

[64] Gilmore, "Introduction," p. 4.
[65] According to Nida and Newman, Jesus was referring to Deut. 17:6–7, "a person could not be given the death penalty apart from the testimony of two or three
witnesses. They were to throw the first stones at the condemned person" (p. 261).
But Jesus offers a different interpretation of the law, challenging the system by ironically stating that only a witness who himself is sinless may be the first to throw
the stone, implying the need of a new way of life.

identity. And by the same token, he reveals that neither is he sub-scribing to Moses' Law. Jesus offers them a new alternative, a mid-dle ground between their discourses. If they want to follow the Law, they can do it; but they need to fulfill the whole Law first and obey every single detail in order to be fair. Jesus pushes them to realize that their system is collapsing: first, because they themselves are not respecting the borders they seek to secure; and second, because their interpretations of the Law are co-opting the Other's possibility of defining her borders and mapping her own identity. Any system that takes away the individuals' privilege of defining their own borders and identities is an oppressive system.

The teaching space that Jesus opens (8:9) and the hybrid moment provided by his spoken and silent discourses overcome the Pharisees' intrusion, suppressing their discourse of violence and death. Unable to relinquish their privileges, but aware of their fault in nullifying the borders of the Others, the women, the scribes and Pharisees get out of the hybrid territory Jesus opened for transformation. Like the adulterer who fled from the consequences of his action, one by one they disappear silently, running away from their false discourse of righteousness.

Ironically, the leaders who expelled the Johannine community from the sacred space of the synagogue, are expelled by their guilt from the sacred border/space. The space is empty, and only Jesus and the woman remain in that new space, a site for the new community that is "neither the One, nor the Other, but something else be-sides which contests the territories of both."[66] It is one of the sites where the hybrid community of Jesus begins to emerge. By defining the borders of the identity of those who are willing to live at the crossroads, Jesus begins to map the borders of his new hybrid com-munity. The two border-crossers are left alone, face to face. In a moment in which she also could have run away like the Pharisees did, *the Accused* decides to stay; perhaps she is innocent and has noth-ing to fear, or maybe she, like Jesus, is tired of the system and wants to change it.

Jesus speaks to *the Accused* (8:10). The woman, who was invaded in her space, accused, silenced, and publicly exposed by the Pharisees and their oppressive system, is now privately addressed by Jesus. She is asked to speak for herself. Freed from her accusers and their crim-

---

[66] Sim, *A–Z Guide*, p. 50.

inal charges, she is now invited to the sacred space Jesus offers to those who, oppressed by the structures, are looking for liberating alternatives. The Pharisees and their male system were not treating women as separate entities, as subjects with their own borders who deserve to be respected equally. In addressing *the Accused* as equal to the Pharisees, Jesus gives her the opportunity to express herself and her identity, to build her own borders, and to re-claim the territory of her body for herself.

"Has no one condemned you?," Jesus asks the woman. And for the first time in the story the woman is enabled to express herself, "No one, sir" (8:11). She is *accused*, but not condemned. Jesus releases her from that predicament when he respectfully acknowledges her presence and invites her to speak for herself. Through the dialogue, "the potential of borders in opening new forms of human understanding"[67] becomes real for the woman. Only with self-determined borders respectful dialogue can take place and fair demarcation of identities can come true.

The inhabitants of contact zones are at risk of extinction when their particular cultures exist in isolation. It is only through interdependent relationships that such contact zones can save their particular elements and, therefore, the identity and borders of their inhabitants. For borderland subjects, "salvation involves increasing attention to border crossing: a kind of coming to consciousness of proliferating psychological crossing."[68] This is part of the salvation that Jesus is granting to the woman, the Pharisees, and the rest of the crowd; the realization that contact zones such as gender can only be constructive through interdependency. Crossing systemic borders in order to allow the Other to *assemble* her identity's borders is the only way in which salvation and liberation can come for all the inhabitants of the borderlands. The scribes and Pharisees do not want to see the redemptive power of border-crossing which Jesus demonstrates as a possibility for a new way of life. They are certainly crossing the system's borders, but for their own benefit. When Jesus challenges them to subvert the system that oppresses them through their isolation, they refuse to do so and, therefore, miss the salvation and the opportunity to live in balanced interdependence with the Other.

---

[67] Rosaldo, *Culture*, p. 216.
[68] Michaelsen, "Border Secrets," p. 11.

The Accused is now a free woman. Jesus tells her, "Neither do I condemn you. Go your way, and from now on do not sin again" (8:11). The accusers, who came with a self-righteousness attitude, end up being accused by their own consciousness and silence and are still bounded to their systemic/institutional sins. They refuse to give up their oppressive borders and miss their chance for transformation. The woman, on the other hand, is freed from the sins of the system, and is told not to return to it, not to sin again by entering into relationships that are dictated by an oppressive and dehumanizing system. She is now a free human being, redeemed and called by Jesus to become a border-crosser, in search of new and better ways of life. *The Accused*, like all the other "border crossers [who] create new myths ... provide[s] radical alternatives to the existing social structures."[69] By redeeming the border-crosser, Jesus the border-crosser becomes not just the new myth for radical alternatives, but also the new ethos for survival for those who strive for a better world.

7. *Final Remarks*

In his broader context, the Johannine Jesus seems to live between borders, in a hybrid space which is an experience similar to that of Hispanics/Latin Americans in the post-colonial and neo-colonial era. Jesus, the *border-crosser*, the traveller between cities and villages, between heaven and earth, between suffering and bliss, comes to redeem the *border-crosser* who refuses to conform to the limits and borders of a society that has ignored her voice, her body, and the borders of her identity as the Other.

The hybrid moment of transformation perceived in the story of *the Accused* is an affirmative statement of the redemptive power involved in the border-crossing behaviour. The borders traced in the story become the sites of transformation for the future that emerges in the in-between of the present needs. By confronting the Pharisees and addressing the *accused* woman, Jesus reconciles a past of oppressive traditions and a silent present of subversiveness into an "in-between space that innovates and interrupts the performance of the

---

[69] A. L. Keating, "Myth Smashers, Myth Makers: (Re)Visionary Techniques in the Works of Paula Gunn Allen, Gloria Anzaldúa, and Audre Lorde," *Critical Essays: Gay and Lesbian Writers of Color* 26 (1993), pp. 73–95.

present."[70] The new identity of the *accused* woman announces the interstitial creativity of the future: freed from the oppressive borders of the system, she is sent as a border-crosser, a model for building the future of the hybrid Johannine community and a model for a better life.

On his part, Jesus, the hybrid being *par excellence* in John's Gospel, contests all contact zones. He removes the structures that have been adopted by those in power and acts in ways that respond to a reality different from the one in which he is located. He is a model for transformation for those readers who, like him, live in the interstices, the in-between, and who look for a political change to alter reality. Reading and inhabiting the interstices that the Johannine Jesus reveals in the text opens the opportunity to trigger a hybrid moment for a political change. It is an invitation to re-articulate or translate the elements of the contact zones which are neither the One nor the Other, but *something else besides*, as Homi Bhabha explains, giving way to the transformational value of change.[71]

The relationship of Jesus and *the Accused* opens some redemptive possibilities for all border-crossers who are looking for another way of being, out of the traditional and oppressive boundaries of the present society.

As a Mexican-American I read the story of *the Accused* as a hybrid subject, living an experience of conflicting border zones like the experience of John's community. In their need of affirmation in a transitional process, the Johannine community constructs a narrative that can help them accept their new identity. The excluded community that once belonged to the official religious institution is now being confronted with the system. They have to decide to go in silence and do nothing to change the system, or be free from condemnation, and be aware of the oppressive borders that need to be transgressed in order to create alternative spaces for liberation.

---

[70] Bhabha, *Location*, p. 7.
[71] See Sim, *A–Z Guide*, p. 50.

THE MIRACLE STORY OF THE
BENT-OVER WOMAN (LUKE 13:10–17).
AN INTERACTION-CENTRED INTERPRETATION

HISAKO KINUKAWA

Text: Luke 13:10–17

> 10 Now he was teaching in one of the synagogues on the sabbath.
> 11 And just then there appeared a woman with a spirit that had crippled her for eighteen years. She was bent over and was quite unable to stand up straight.
> 12 When Jesus saw her, he called her over and said, "Woman, you are set free from your ailment."
> 13 When he laid his hands on her, immediately she stood up straight and began praising God.
> 14 But the leader of the synagogue, indignant because Jesus had cured on the sabbath, kept saying to the crowd, "There are six days on which work ought to be done; come on those days and be cured, and not on the sabbath day."
> 15 But the Lord answered to him and said, "You hypocrites! Does not each of you on the sabbath untie his ox or his donkey from the manger, and lead it away to give it water?
> 16 And ought not this woman, a daughter of Abraham whom Satan bound for eighteen long years, be set free from this bondage on the sabbath day?"
> 17 When he said this, all his opponents were put to shame; and the entire crowd was rejoicing at all the wonderful things that he was doing. (NRSV)

1. *Introduction*

In her excellent article, "The Structure of the Gospel Miracle Stories and their Tellers," Antoinette Clark Wire[1] proposes to use the interactions between and among the characters as the interpretive key when she deals with the Gospel miracle stories. According to her, "all gospel miracle stories fall into one of four categories

---

[1] A. Clark Wire, "The Structure of the Gospel Miracle Stories and their Tellers," in R. W. Funk (ed.), *Early Christian Miracle Stories* (*Semeia*, 11; Atlanta, GA: Scholars, 1978), pp. 83–113.

according to their organizing interaction: the exorcism, the exposé, the provision and the demand."[2]

The story of the bent-over woman, which I would like to analyse in this paper, is classified as an exposé of moral and social restrictions, though Wire does not deal with this particular story in detail in her article. There are two characteristics of the exposé stories as described by Wire. First, "the exposé features a struggle between Jesus and religious authorities concerning what is permitted in individual conduct."[3] And second, "the interaction results in an exposé of standard procedures and exalted egos and a fissure in an otherwise closed legal system. The miracle re-enforces this fissure."[4]

I understand her contention to mean that a miracle may occasion an interaction between Jesus and religious authorities, which results in exposing a fissure and engendering a struggle between both parties. I would like to follow her analysis and apply the interpretive key she proposes to the story of the bent-over woman. Then, I would like to go further by interpreting the interactions not only between the two parties represented by Jesus and the synagogue leader in this particular story but also among the characters that appear in it, that is, Jesus, the leader of the synagogue, the bent-over woman, and the crowd. Throughout the process, I would like to tear off layers of transformation added to a probably oral tradition, with various intentions at work on different occasions, so that we may work our way as closely as possible to the original incident: an encounter between the woman and Jesus.

Needless to say that I would like to read the story from my own social location and would like to discern what the story might imply for our contemporary churches in Japan. I have studied the story with several groups of women whose perspectives have produced insightful interpretations of the encounter between the woman and Jesus. I cannot forget what a woman, who is an Ainu, an indigenous and ethnic minority in our country, said from her marginalized experiences. She and her people have been socially alienated throughout history, pushed back into a corner of the northern part of Japan. She said the double bending of the woman symbolizes the inexpressible pain of her people who have been denigrated by the

---

[2] Wire, "Structure," p. 83.
[3] Wire, "Structure," p. 83.
[4] Wire, "Structure," p. 83.

power of our country. When I had a discussion on the story with a woman from El Salvador, she discerned the bending as symbolic oppression that has repeatedly been inflicted on them by colonizers. Every time she and her people tried to straighten up their bent backs, they were bent with even heavier pressure. I was touched hearing the Ainu woman say that the woman's straightened back reminded her of the time of transformation of her inner self and when she could meet other people on an equal basis for the first time.

2. *The Story of the Bent-over Woman*

From the beginning of the story we are cautioned that both the occasion and the place of this event may cause trouble: the event occurred on a sabbath, which is the important day for Judaism, and it took place in a synagogue, which is the sacred place. These two elements, however, signify that Jesus, a Jew, started his mission among his compatriots, and that his movement was formulated within the framework of Judaism. It seems less clear which part of a synagogue women could enter or sit in, in Jesus' time. Women might not have been marginalized in their place of worship. And if that was true, such circumstances might have motivated the bent-over woman to come into the synagogue.

Luke's Redactional Intention in the Story

Luke is the only one among the four evangelists that recorded this story. It seems true that the story of this woman has hardly been referred to and the woman has almost been forgotten throughout the history of the church. Since Luke is the only one that was concerned about the story, the attention of interpreters has concentrated on exploring Luke's intention in adopting the story. Therefore, when the story is taken up by them, more words are spent clarifying Luke's editorial scheme by using the methods of historical criticism.

Form criticism classifies the story as structured upon an apophthegmatic saying. A miracle story about a sabbath healing was connected with it and the former might have influenced the style of the latter. An apophthegm is found in Jesus' response to the synagogue leader, "Hypocrites, each of you on the sabbath does not liberate his ox or ass from the manger and give drink by leading away?"

(v. 15).[5] The final point in the account on the miracle was made clear by the phrase, "all the ones opposing him were put to shame" (v. 17a).[6] Thus, the fissure between the two parties, namely between Jesus and his opponents, has been publicly exposed.

Redaction criticism affirms that Luke added the sentence at the end, "all the crowd rejoiced over all the glorious things happening through him" (v. 17b). According to Bultmann, some suspect that the phrase "a daughter of Abraham" might also be Luke's invention. This is probable because nowhere else in the New Testament can the phrase be found.[7] The story is set as the last occasion for Jesus to teach in a synagogue and as the second of the three healing stories on a sabbath (6:6–11; 14:1–6).

From a socio-literary critical point of view, it is held that Luke, as a non-Jewish Christian, living in the early age of the Christian church formation, was in conflict both with the Roman society, to which he needed to adjust his church, and with Judaism, which he wanted his church to outgrow. Thus, his concern resulted in changing the miracle story into a debate on the sabbath.[8]

Tradition criticism notices that an oral tradition or a text which was transmitted as a miracle story was made use of by Luke for his own intention.[9]

The Three Contrasts in the Story Devised by Luke

It may be helpful to determine Luke's intention in recording this story in his Gospel through the contrasts we can locate in the text.

---

[5] Literary translation of v. 15; I will pursue the same policy throughout this paper when necessary.

[6] R. Bultmann, *History of the Synoptic Tradition* (transl. J. March; Peabody, MA: Hendrickson, 1963), pp. 12–13.

[7] Bultmann, *History*, p. 63.

[8] E. Schüssler Fiorenza, *But She Said* (Boston, MA: Beacon, 1992), pp. 208–9. She continues as follows: "Although she has become occasion and object of male debate, she no longer inhabits a subject-position in the text. The Lukan text transformed the whole story from a woman-focused to a male-centered sacred text by merging a Sabbath controversy with the healing story. . . . Thus, in the controversy story the woman has become invisible again. . . . By turning the miracle story into a controversy dialogue, Luke or one of his predecessors has transformed the healing story into a debate with the leadership of the synagogue which reflects the tensions between the early Christian community and its Jewish mother-community in the last quarter of the first century."

[9] S. Arai, *Sin-yaku Seisho no Josei-kan* [Women in the New Testament] (Tokyo: Iwanami, 1988), pp. 169–71.

First, the contrast between the attitudes of liberating one's ox or ass from the manger on a sabbath and at the same time rejecting the healing of the sick. This shows the contradiction found in the behaviours of the religious authorities as represented by the synagogue leader. Second, the contrast between Jesus and the people, when Jesus declares the woman as a daughter of Abraham and thus shows that she is to be treated as a member of their community. Third, the contrast between the philosophies of life shown in the inclusive attitude of Jesus and in the exclusiveness seen in the hypocritical mind of the synagogue leader.

By way of summary, the contrasts are set in such a way that the command of loving one's neighbour is valid even on a sabbath and thus is more important than piety pursued by the religious authorities.[10]

What Is Our Main Concern?

It seems clear that Luke tried to overcome the conflict which had developed between the church he was related to and its mother-community of Judaism. But if our concern is also closely focused on this, we may find ourselves ignoring the encounter that occurred between the woman and Jesus. As a result, we have to admit that the woman and her experience were used by Luke as well as by readers for other purposes. In fact, she is not just a scapegoat, but is the subject of the miracle story. We need to read the story carefully so that we do not lose our vision to see the interactional relationship between the two, which I would like to name "life communion."

For us, the most important aspect seems to be the liberation experience of the woman. What the event looked like in its primary stage will be our focus in the exploration that follows, and thus we hope we will be able to see her as a main character of the story.

"And, Behold, a Woman . . ."
After a general statement on the setting of the story, the next sentence begins with important words which call our attention to the woman: "And, behold, a woman," according to the Greek words in

---

[10] In this analysis I conferred as representing a traditional interpretative standing, K. H. Rengstorf, *Luka ni yoru Hukuin-sho* [Das Evangelium nach Lukas] (transl. H. Izumi and H. Shibuya; Tokyo: NTD Publishing Committee, 1968), pp. 361–2.

that order. Thus, our interest is focused on the woman. And further: "She, having a spirit of infirmity for eighteen years, was bent double and not able to raise herself up entirely" (v. 11). The stirring word "behold" placed in front of "woman" explains that she is one of the "others" whose existence has been ignored. Even though she is there, nobody notices her. Nobody dares to see her. Nobody cares about her even if they do see her. She is left in complete indifference. She is there in silence. She is virtually anonymous.

She obviously has never tried to touch Jesus' clothes from behind, like the woman with haemorrhage (8:42b–48). She does not have any vicarious man who is qualified to ask for Jesus' help, like Jairus did for his sick daughter (8:40–42a, 49–56). There is also no indication that she is trying to attract Jesus' attention. At the same time, she does not seem to be completely avoiding Jesus noticing her. She seems to be there, but in complete silence. My question is whether we should interpret her silence as characteristic of women's traditional receptive attitudes toward men, as Turid Karlsen Seim does in her reading of Luke's stories.[11] Though she uses gender difference as an analytical constant, she focuses her reading on understanding the Lukan construction.[12] Her reading is somehow in line with the popular reading I have already pointed out. She characterizes the role of the women in the Lukan miracle stories as "remarkably respectful to common convention regarding women's behavior."[13] I am interested to find out whether Seim's generalization of the characteristic of women also fits in the case of the bent-over woman.

The Bent-over Woman: Marginalized Yet Not Broken
Luke describes her illness in detail. She has been bent double for a long time. In Japanese, the Chinese character used for the lower back, or waist or hip, signifies the linchpin of the whole body. This implies that if one's linchpin is broken, one cannot support one's body. We can imagine that this woman has suffered various types of pains caused by being bent double: shortness of breath, limited

---

[11] T. Karlsen Seim, "The Gospel of Luke," in E. Schüssler Fiorenza (ed.), *Searching the Scriptures. Vol. 2: A Feminist Commentary* (New York: Crossroad, 1994), pp. 728–62, here p. 738.
[12] Seim, "Luke," p. 729. She states: "This approach may, of course, be seen as lacking a certain feminist suspicion, but the rationale behind it is the wish and the need to see the full construction before deconstruction and reconstruction can take place."
[13] Seim, "Luke," p. 738.

eye sight, constricted mobility, malnutrition, etc. Her suffering is even
more serious because it is not only physical, but she is defined as
"having a spirit of infirmity" (v. 11), and later we are told that it is
Satan that bound her (v. 16).

The root of the Hebrew word "Satan" means "one who opposes,
obstructs, or acts as adversary." Its Greek term, διάβολος, translated as "devil," literally means "one who throws something across
one's path."[14] Elaine Pagels, who investigated the social history of
Satan in her groundbreaking book, shows the evolution of Satan
from its origins in the Hebrew Scripture to the New Testament as
that from merely being obstructive to being the bitter enemy of God
and humanity. Generally speaking, the four evangelists identify those
who refused to worship Jesus as the Messiah as being under Satan's
control. In Luke, Pagels says, "Spiritual warfare between God and
Satan—which is reflected in conflict between Jesus and his followers and the Jewish leaders—intensifies throughout the gospel."[15] In
other words, "Luke wants to show that those who reject Jesus accom-
plish Satan's work on earth."[16] In Luke, those who reject Jesus are
described as the scribes, the Pharisees, and others plotting to kill him.

In Luke's Gospel, only five times do we find the word "Satan"
(10:18; 11:18; 13:16; 22:3, 31), the Greek word, διάβολος, only
twice (4:3; 8:12). When he uses the word "demon" in connection with
the two words above, it is connected with unclean spirit (4:33). The
spirit of infirmity is also connected with evil spirit.

When Luke puts the phrase, "Satan bound her," on Jesus' lips as
a response to the synagogue leader whom we expect Luke to define
as a part of Satan, he means that she is under Satan's control and,
therefore, deprived of God's protection. Thus, she does not belong
to the true Israel. It is contradictory for the people in the synagogue·
to reject the woman, who is a daughter of Abraham and is, therefore, to be saved from the control of Satan. Following Pagels' social
analysis, we might say that Jesus identifies the religious authorities
with Satan, and accuses them of not wanting her to be liberated.
In other words, he points out that she has been excluded from the
faith community by their satanic definition of piety. More exactly,

---

[14] I took this definition from E. Pagels, *The Origin of Satan* (New York: Random
House, 1995), p. 39.
[15] Pagels, *Origin*, p. 91.
[16] Pagels, *Origin*, p. 98.

or based on oral tradition, we might say that he is accusing the faith community of considering her to be bound by Satan and therefore ignoring her, even though she is one of them.

In sum, we understand her social alienation as being under Satan's control and her physical alienation as pollution. Thus, she might be defined as impure and untouchable by her religious authorities and alienated from her society. Besides her physical suffering, she is excluded from the circle of the pure, and is marginalized both socially and religiously.

She was looked down upon as a social burden. Actually, she could barely see her surroundings because of her bending double position. What makes her so remarkable is that none of her difficulties prevented her from being there. It is worth noting that she did not give up looking up and remained there in complete silence. This woman appeared and did not raise her voice until, as we read afterwards in the narrator's comment, she "began praising God" after experiencing the miraculous interaction with Jesus.

I would like to interpret this as her positive outlook toward life. She came out by breaking boundaries which hindered her full participation in her society. She never raised her voice, but she pursued a way to life by daring to cross several boundaries set before her.

3. Who Are the Bent-over Women in Our Contemporary Situation?

Sometimes mouths are forced to be kept shut. That happens either as a result of the threatening pressure exercised by those in power or by the ethical mores imprinted on individuals. The bent-over woman remains in complete silence for both reasons. I see the same kind of silence enforced upon the so-called "comfort women" who were forced to become sexual slaves by the Japanese Imperial Army during the Asia-Pacific War (1931–45). There was almost a 50–year period of complete silence around this issue. Both the victimized and the victimizers kept silent. And even after the victimized dared to start talking about their horrifying and humiliating experiences, encouraged by the women who believed it necessary to help them retrieve their human dignity, there has been silence on the part of the victimizers. It is true that even those who were not directly involved with the war or the issue were hesitant to speak up because of the delicate nature of the issue.

It is not only indifference but also ignorance that has produced such silence among the people of the victimizer, Japan, my mother country, because the issue was never taught at school, while it was always taught in detail in the victimized countries in Asia. It is also true we did not want to open our eyes and see the reality thrust in front of us. We have simply ignored the issue, even though we noticed that the women were there just like the bent-over woman in the synagogue, who the people ignored.

If the silence among us is justified with some incomprehensible reason, the agonizing courage of the victimized to speak up is going to be ignored and forgotten again in the darkness of history. Silence means assisting in preserving the social and political structure of our country that has left compensation for the war crime unsettled.

Pagels says: "I invite you to consider Satan as a reflection of how we perceive ourselves and those we call 'others.' Satan has, after all, made a kind of profession out of being the 'other;' and so Satan defines negatively what we think of as human."[17] I fully understand her claim based upon my own experience of being involved with the "comfort women" issue since 1987. It was in 1992 when I first heard the living voices of the victimized women. I was astounded by their bearing witness to what kind of sexual assaults they had to endure while still teenagers. I, as a mother of two daughters, almost lost consciousness when I heard about how they were taken to the front camps of the army and "raped" by ten to twenty Japanese soldiers every day.

One of the victimized said that numerous women whom she met at the camps committed suicide at the end of the war. They were tormented by feelings of guilt that they had somehow defiled their bodies and brought shame to their own parents, families, home towns and mother countries. Most of the survivors did not go back to their home towns, but cut themselves off from the society that defined them as polluted and shameful. As a result, they had to remain in complete silence if they wanted to live. Most of those who married have not been happily married. One witness said she has never experienced the joy of being a woman. Memories of the rapes tormented her all through her life even though she never mentioned her previous history to her husband. These women have suffered from men-

---

[17] Pagels, *Origin*, p. xviii.

tal as well as physical traumas. And voicing their experiences implies re-living the whole rape experience once again.

In most Asian countries where young women were drafted for military sexual slavery, the patriarchal mind-set of the societies considered it shameful to get one's body defiled in such a way. The mind-set was re-inforced by religions such as Confucianism and Buddhism. Thus, the "comfort women" have become socially alienated and religiously defined as polluted.

Violence Against Women is a Human Rights Issue

As I listened to the voices of the survivors, I realized that the issue was not only addressing the guilt of war and invasion pursued by my country, but pointing out that this was an issue of violence against women, of the destruction of women's bodies, which quite often resulted in mental disorders. I see the same structure here as we have already seen in the story of the bent-over woman. That is, the victimized women were forced to remain in complete silence, but they did not stop trying to make their own way in life. After 50 years of silence, they were given attention by women who were aware of the issue and felt they had to deal with it so that the survivors might overcome their "otherness" and retrieve their human rights.

If we women in Japan did not listen to the voices, which were very small in the beginning, we could be said to be taking sides with Satan. Therefore, the initial word in the Lukan story, "behold," plays a very important role. What is challenged here are the eyes so that we see what needs to be seen, but which has been ignored so far. As has been said, it is true that we only see what we have been prepared to see. Therefore, the issue of the "comfort women" requires that we confess where we stand and whom we advocate.

Keeping this contemporary issue in mind, I would like to go back to the story of the bent-over woman.

4. Where Do We Locate Our Concern in the Story of the Bent-over Woman?

Interaction Between Jesus and the Woman

As the story goes, Jesus shocks the people. As soon as he sees the woman, he calls her. Did he call her over to a place where she was not supposed to be, or did he dare to go into the place where the

woman was and he was not expected to go? In either case the abnor-
mality of the situation is obvious. Then, "a thundering sentence of
liberation"¹⁸ was declared to her: "Woman, you have been liberated
from your infirmity" (v. 12). The verb used here, ἀπολύω—literally meaning "to liberate"—is the key word for the whole story. The
word is quite different from the word θεραπεύω, which means "to
cure or heal." Jesus never uses θεραπεύω, while the synagogue
leader never uses ἀπολύω. The word ἀπολύω with its variants is
used three times, and only by Jesus (vv. 12, 15, 16). The first use
is constructed in the present perfect tense, emphasizing the fact that
she has already been liberated from her infirmity and that her liberated condition is lasting. From Jesus' words to her, we understand
that what she sought was the liberation from alienation and the contempt she had suffered from in society. This liberation was naturally
accompanied by a cure from her illness. It is very interesting to note
that Jesus' declarative words preceded any concrete action, which
usually makes the incident a miracle.

Compassion with Her Suffering: Jesus' Advocacy Stance

Jesus saw her and acted right away. He did not pose any questions
about whether she had sinned to deserve such punishment, as people in her surrounding might have asked, or if she had a husband
to act as a vicar for her. Jesus' actions must have appeared most
unusual. He went ahead and touched her with both his hands. In
order to lay his hands on her, he must have bent down to her level.
Through this action, he showed his empathy and compassion—which
literally means "to have the bowels ache"—with her as well as accepting the consequences of being disgraced by her impurity.
    Thus, he himself broke down the boundary of pollution. I would
like to stress here that Jesus was standing face to face with the woman
and restored her life to its wholeness. There was life communion
between the two. She was liberated from her physical, religious and
social bondage at the same time. Therefore, she immediately stood
up straight, and began to praise and kept praising God. Her long
silence was broken and she burst into glorifying God. The significance
of glorifying God as one of the important elements that characterize the sabbath will be explored in the next section.

---

¹⁸ R. Conrad Wahlberg, *Jesus and the Freed Woman* (New York: Paulist, 1978),
p. 20.

We cannot say that the "comfort women" have been liberated to the extent that the bent-over woman was liberated. Though the Japanese government finally admitted it as a historical fact that the sexual enslavement was systematically executed by the government, and even though it was publicly recognized in August 1993 that the Japanese military forced numerous young women to serve as military slaves on battle fields, the government has rejected compensating individual women who have raised their voices and have witnessed that they were made "comfort women." For them, this means that the Japanese government has not formally apologized for what it did to them in the past.

Legalism of the Synagogue Leader

Looking at the entire process of the personal interaction between Jesus and the woman, the synagogue leader reacts in three ways. First, he is indignant because Jesus "healed" the woman. He uses θεραπεύω and thereby shows his inability to understand that Jesus has liberated her from her religious and social fetters. Second, he speaks only to the crowd and not to Jesus or the woman. Third, he believes that work ought to be done only on the six days of the week and not on the sabbath.

It should be noticed that he uses the verb θεραπεύω, which means "to cure diseases," twice (v. 14), instead of ἀπολύω. For him, Jesus' liberating action is merely equivalent to the physical treatment given by a physician. What makes him furious is Jesus' therapeutic work, which is prohibited on the sabbath, according to the law.

We may define sabbath in its simplest sense in two ways. It connotates being free from work, which premises that on the other six days one can work. The second meaning refers to receiving God's blessings, which premises that one is liberated from pain, both physical and spiritual. Only after liberation is one enabled to glorify God. However, the synagogue leader concentrates all his attention on the law and the detailed regulations based upon it. He sticks to the definitions and descriptions of the law and ignores the value of a person's life, which should be underlined by the law. He has no ability to discern Jesus' act as liberating and as making the woman whole by retrieving her human dignity. Nor can he understand Jesus' actions, which have transformed the woman and, through that transformation, have made her whole and thus were most appropriate to have taken place on a sabbath.

So the synagogue leader keeps admonishing Jesus in front of the crowd. From the beginning he ignores the woman as "other" and unworthy of being addressed. He also avoids talking to Jesus face to face. Maybe he feels threatened by Jesus' miraculous act and tries to avoid attacking him directly in front of the crowd, who must be astounded. His strategy is very devious because his attack seems to be directed toward the woman, when he says, "Six days are there on which it is necessary to work. Therefore, coming on those days, be you healed and never on the day of the sabbath" (v. 14). To him, healing is a category of work; he speaks from the standpoint of those who work, not from that of those who suffer or are alienated. His statement is made to guarantee the honour and respect of men who do proper work.

What an intrusive woman this woman is to expect a man to work for her, so he might have speculated. Her disease is not terribly serious or urgent since she has been in that condition for eighteen years. Doesn't she know the law? She is wrong. She is to be blamed for drawing Jesus' attention to her by appearing there on a sabbath.

But the truth is that she is made the scapegoat in order to allow the synagogue leader direct his real attack at Jesus. His strategy is very suspect because his anger is ultimately directed at Jesus. The woman offered him a convenient chance to attack Jesus. To keep the sabbath is the only concern of the synagogue leader. He believes this is the only way he can keep his religious institution in order.

In a hierarchical society such as the one in Palestine of Jesus' time, it is safest to blame the powerless, such as women who have no men to protect them and whose social status is very low. Attacking Jesus, however, might be dangerous because there could be many among the crowd that would stand by him.

Most of the women who were forced to become "comfort women" were between 16 and 18 years old. They were too young to even know what they would be doing. Most of them were just shocked when their bodies were abused by so many men. They were too powerless to defend themselves against the force of the soldiers. In addition, they had grown up in cultures where the raped were made feel guilty because they were considered unguarded and seductive. This is true in most Asian countries where Confucian teachings have functioned as norms of daily life. Thus, they were made doubly silent. It was like they were caught by Satan and brought under his control. Who should liberate them from such a cursed life? They were left alone, unnoticed and untouched by anybody for the next 50 years.

When courageous women began to search for the hidden "comfort women" and struggle for retrieving their human rights, the Japanese government and the governments of the related countries started official negotiations and settled the issue diplomatically, with mainly political concerns in mind. All discussions and negotiations were carried out without hearings that included the victimized women. They were ignored and dealt with as though they were merely a diplomatic affair that should be settled according to various national benefits. Just like the bent-over woman, these women were overlooked as "others."

The Interaction Between Jesus and the Synagogue Leader

As Jesus faces the synagogue leader and the crowd, he asks a question, as he often does: "Each one of you on the Sabbath does not liberate his ox or ass from the manger and give drink by leading it away?" (v. 15). Here we notice his second use of the key verb ἀπολύω. He refers to a traditional convention which has been commonly practised on the sabbath. This is not a special rule set aside as an exception. Everybody knows and actually practises what Jesus is talking about. This is a very good educational strategy often used by Jesus in his response; it cannot raise protest. He meets his adversaries on their ground and begins his discourse from a stance well accepted by them. Thus, he poses an ironical question so that the synagogue leader cannot help but answer positively.[19]

Through an analogy, Jesus refers to the woman using the key verb ἀπολύω for the third time: "And she, a daughter of Abraham, whom Satan bound, behold, for ten and eight years, ought not to be liberated from this bond on the day of sabbath?" (v. 16). Again, he is facing the woman and is standing by her side. It is now obvious that being liberated from bondage and regain wholeness of life is of utmost importance for him. It is typical of Jesus to advocate an isolated suffering person and liberate her/him from her/his suffering. His action is almost always motivated by his will to retrieve one forgotten "other" person from the control of Satan. In Jesus' question, the woman becomes the subject of the sentence.

---

[19] Cf. Bultmann (*History*, p. 41) notes: "The reply to the attack follows more or less a set form, with special preference for the counter-question or the metaphor, or even both together."

The women who were forced to become "comfort women" have kept themselves hidden and in silence, yet have survived for 50 years with their buried torments. The very fact that they survived should have been a challenge for us to realize what we should have seen. But we, Japanese, did not have eyes to see it. It was the women of the victimized countries that raised our consciousness and involved us in the struggle for recovering the wholeness of those surviving women. Unless they had dared to keep on living, the issue would have been lost in the darkness of history.

It is to be regretted that the human rights of these women have still not been regained even though tremendous efforts have been made by women and men of the victimized countries and of our country. We are blocked by the strong measures exercised by the Japanese government. Often we have been thrown down to the ground and made feel as if we ourselves were the bent-over women, sick, socially alienated and ignored. As we can see, the movement has made some progress, and through our struggle with the victimized women and in solidarity with women and men around the world, we are also encouraged by the daring courage shown by the bent-over woman.

Interactions in Pluri-form

Though Jesus was not officially dealing with the law issue raised by the synagogue leader, he eventually addressed the issue. He did not ignore or reject the sabbath law. Rather, he fulfilled the basic premises of the sabbath by (1) making it possible for the woman to work on the other six days, and (2) by liberating her from her pain so that she could glorify God, which she did as soon as she was liberated from her bondage. It is well known that in Israel the sabbath has its origin in remembering the liberation from bondage in Egypt.

Therefore, we are reminded that the exposé in the narrative was only made possible by this woman who dared to place herself in the synagogue on the sabbath. She initiated Jesus' liberating action in the form of a miracle, which re-enforced the split between Jesus and the religious authorities of the time.

Needless to say, it is her distorted life that motivated Jesus to perform a miracle. I am afraid that if we concentrate only on the relationship between Jesus and the religious authorities, we end up reading the narrative in such a way that Jesus as a miracle worker domi-

nates the whole story. Yet, the interactions are found in pluri-form
and the role the woman plays in this story is so decisive. I would
like to read the whole story as an event initiated by the woman's
daring appearance, which resulted in an interaction between the
woman and Jesus. Then, pluri-form interactions between Jesus, the
synagogue leader and the crowd followed.

"Abraham's Daughter . . ."

Jesus calls this woman "Abraham's daughter." In fact, there is no
other instance in the entire New Testament where women are named
daughters of Abraham. Furthermore, there is only one instance when
"son of Abraham" is used (19:9), and that is when Zacchaeus, a
chief tax collector and socially alienated, is brought back into the
faith community which has set up a boundary of impurity and thereby
excluded him. The term "child/ren of Abraham," which may include
both women and men as a generic expression, is used more often
(Matt. 3:9; Luke 3:8; John 8:39, etc.).

Thus, when Jesus dared to call her "Abraham's daughter," he suggests an extraordinary way of connecting Abraham with, first, a
woman, and second, one bound by Satan. The legitimate Israel, the
children of God, excluded those who were defined as impure due
to their threatening collective purity. Jesus reversed this traditional
idea and invited the excluded ones into the centre of the circle.

This story is particularly noteworthy because the incident happens in a place where no-one would ever expect that she, a stigmatized woman, might be considered as progeny of Abraham in
such a patrilineal society, where women's lives are defined as men's
property. It is distinctive to hear Jesus declare that she has been
a daughter of Abraham from the beginning, not that she has become one. As Seim says, "The woman is Abraham's daughter; she
does not become one. It is one of the premises of the healing, not a
consequence of it, but it is not a statement about great piety on
the woman's part." She continues, "The surprising element is not primarily the fact that a Jewish woman is called Abraham's daughter,
but rather that the woman about whom this is said is not a paragon
of virtue and piety." . . . "Abraham plays no role as model or typolo-
gical prototype."[20] I fully agree with her on this point. Jesus' challenge

---

[20] Seim, "Luke," pp. 730, 736–7.

to the synagogue leader is expressed in the question why not make her appropriate to the sabbath on which she also deserves to praise God (v. 16).

If the border which excludes those defined as "others" is broken down, the faith community will naturally become open to all those who would like to join it. Therefore, even though Jesus' declaring her as a daughter of Abraham may be considered his or Luke's limitation of being unable to go beyond the ethnic border of Israel,[21] it is not impossible to interpret Jesus' behaviour as breaking down the border, which certainly results in excluding the people outside the community. How can he or Luke be universalists if they cannot overcome the infra-structural strife?

When our struggle lasts long and does not show us any light ahead, divisions and contentions occur concerning the strategies we should use. When (in July 1995) the Japanese government pushed its policy of compensating the "comfort women" by the so-called "Asia Peace and Friendship Fund for Women," which should mainly consist of money collected from citizens, the grass-roots groups that had worked together until then were in danger being of divided.

Despite the danger, there have been various non-governmental grass-roots activist groups engaged in activities against the Fund. Women's groups continued having campaigns such as the rally with Asian activists, the "Public Hearing in the Court Held for the Rights of Asian Women" in March 1994, and the "First East Asian Women's Forum" in October 1994, all of which worked as preliminary meetings for the "Beijing Women's Forum" in August 1995, and they did not break apart.[22]

5. *Interaction Between the Text and Us as Its Readers*

Concluding her paper, Wire returns to "the question of why the gospel miracles as whole stories were told."[23] From the structure of a miracle story, she projects "the interaction between teller and hearer in which the story might function."[24] Theissen supports her position

[21] Seim, "Luke," p. 737.
[22] Very helpful in understanding the internationally offered support for our campaign is the article by E. Totsuka, "Actions of the UN on Military Sexual Slavery by Japan," *In God's Image* 15 (1996), pp. 69–73.
[23] Wire, "Structure," p. 110.
[24] Wire, "Structure," p. 110.

by his statement that, "All miracle stories seek to provoke a response to the miracle-worker: it is with this purpose that they address listeners and readers. Their missionary function arises out of their structures."[25] Wire continues, "The stories are structured around an extraordinary rift in a given, closed system. This shows that the teller of the story affirms both a realistic, even tragic, view of the human condition and a transforming event that changes the human condition."[26] From this statement, I am sure she would urge us, from her feminist perspective, to pay more attention to the primary interaction between the woman and Jesus. As readers of the scriptural texts, her statement also implies that she expects a similar interaction between the texts and us as contemporary readers.

A Case of the Patriarchal Translation of the Text

First, I would like to deal with an issue that appears in the translation from the original Greek text into the Japanese language. The patriarchal mentality that tends to ignore women as "other" and as worthless is reflected in the words chosen for various Japanese translations. As a result, the interaction between Jesus as a miracle-worker and the synagogue leader is over-stressed and becomes the centre of attention, so that the real and serious rift which the text is about is in danger of being obscured.

We can see this in several instances, even in the newest Japanese translation done by the cooperative work for more than ten years of Protestant and Catholic churches in Japan and finally published in 1993. The Japanese text reads, "The sickness is cured," instead of, "You have been liberated from your infirmity." First, the key verb ἀπολύω is mistranslated. The woman is not considered as the subject of the event, but the attention is focused instead on Jesus' miraculous act.

Second, in Greek, the synagogue leader uses the word θεραπεύω, "to cure," and its translation clearly shows that he did not take Jesus' action as the liberation from the social and religious bondage. The Japanese translation is not only vague about this point but hides the decisive event by mistranslating the verb ἀπολύω as "to cure."

---

[25] G. Theissen, *The Miracle Stories of the Early Christian Tradition* (Philadelphia, PA: Fortress, 1983), p. 167.
[26] Wire, "Structure," p. 110.

The third problem arises from how to deal with the text: "Each
of you even on the Sabbath sets free his ox or his donkey from the
manger . . .?" The translation adds the emphatic word "even" and
thus turns the praxis into an exception, while Jesus referred to it
only as a common convention normally practised on the sabbath. If
it were an exception of the law, the healing of the woman would
be one more example, though the degree of exceptionality may be
relatively strengthened exactly because she is not an animal but a
human being.

The same idea is found in a more emphatic way when the word
is repeated for the woman. The translation reads, "Even if it is the
sabbath . . .," and thereby emphasizes the exceptionality of the miracle. Jesus' primary intention was simply to make her appropriate
to the true meaning of the sabbath and, therefore, his action serves
its true purpose. From the original text, we can never take that he
has broken the law of the sabbath or applied an exceptional measure to her. Furthermore, the translation fails to recognize the woman
as a subject. It translates, "We should liberate this woman from this
bondage," instead of, "This woman should be liberated from bondage."

Thus, the interaction between the woman and Jesus is intentionally made ambiguous, and, as a result, Jesus' liberating message is
weakened. On the other hand, his characterization as a miracle-
worker is over-emphasized. We need to practise a "hermeneutics of
suspicion" even when we deal with translations. I am afraid they
may give the wrong idea of the meaning of the original texts.
Patriarchally biased messages must not overshadow the radically
liberative voice of the texts, which seems hard to discern unless we
carefully read between the lines.

I must point out that it is not a simple linguistic adjustment that
the newest Japanese translation changes the subject from the woman
to Jesus. The patriarchal mind-set and Jesus-centred theology have
been operating in such a translation. In addition, "behold," one of
the key words of this story, is lacking in the translation. We are thus
made to overlook the challenge by Luke, or the previous story-tellers,
that calls for our careful attention to what needs to be looked at.

6. Conclusion: What is an Example of a Contemporary Miracle that We Can Experience?

Finally, we must ask what kind of miracle we could expect. Another question this story imposes on us may be what it means for us to celebrate the sabbath. The woman, when she was straightened, "kept glorifying God." What was she doing to glorify God? The people joined in after the debate on the sabbath.[27] That was the moment her silence was broken. What did she voice? She voiced her gratitude at re-gaining her wholeness and dignity as a human being. Her gratitude might have been expressed concretely by becoming a follower of Jesus. She might have been found among "some women who had been cured of evil spirits and infirmities: Mary, called Magdalene, from whom seven demons had gone out, and Joanna, the wife of Herod's steward Chuza, and Susanna, and many others, who provided for them out of their resources" (8:2–3).

It is very helpful when thinking over these questions to read Theissen, who tries to distinguish between apophthegms and miracle stories. According to him, "in the synoptic apophthegms one group affirms its own convictions and behaviour by differentiating itself from other surrounding groups. The Gospel apophthegms define social identity. In this they are clearly different from miracle stories because the fears, values, and hopes expressed in the latter transcend the boundaries of any particular group—everyone can identify with them."[28] And he summarizes as follows: "we could say that apophthegms tend to have a socially demarcating function, while miracle stories tend toward social transcendence."[29]

Both Wire and Theissen mostly agree in their classifications of miracle stories of the kind: the ones classified as exposé by Wire[30]

---

[27] Theissen, *Miracle Stories*, pp. 166–7: "The model for this Lucan treatment of the acclamation conclusion is cultic thanksgiving, which was performed by an individual before the community, which then joins in. . . . This treatment ties the acclamation, which is part of the oral framework where it is self-explanatory, more firmly into the development of the narrative, and at the same time makes its original position clear. The people's praise refers not only directly to the miracle, but also to the individual's praise, to his account of the miracle healing."

[28] G. Theissen, *The Gospel in Context: Social and Political History in the Synoptic Tradition* (Minneapolis, MN: Fortress, 1991), p. 116.

[29] Theissen, *Gospel*, p. 116.

[30] Cf. Wire ("Structure," p. 92), who classes the following stories as exposé miracle stories: Mark 3:1–6; Luke 13:10–17; 14:1–6; Matt. 12:22–30/Luke 11:14–23; Matt. 9:32–34; Matt. 17:24–27; Mark 2:1–12.

and the miracle stories described as having apophthegmatic character by Theissen.[31] While Theissen makes a distinction between miracles and apophthegms, he does not inquire into what kind of social transcendence miracles bring about and what the implications are for us.[32] Wire seems to go a step further to connect the distinctions made by Theissen or to make the social transcendence clearer in her statement that through "juxtaposition of an accepted oppressive context and an extraordinary breaking out of it," miracle stories show "a marvelous break-through in the struggle against oppressive restrictions on human life."[33]

Certainly, the true meaning of the text is lost when we ignore the significance of the wholeness and value of any human life. Jesus exemplified this by facing what is artificially defined as pollution or labelled as "other" by society, through becoming involved with such situations and by undermining the hypocrisy that justifies the artificial boundary between the pure and the impure for the sake of keeping the integrity of the collective pure. Through miracles he challenges that the human right to live be provided to those who are outcast, allowing these people to be themselves.

We call it a miracle when something unbelievable happens. What is unbelievable in our circumstances? How are we being challenged? In our society there are many who are born with different types of disability. In some cases disability occurs during the course of life. The progress of medicine has made it possible to deal with more cases of physical and mental disabilities. Maybe not yet completely, but to some degree many are helped to stay alive. But the problem of discrimination caused by artificially created boundaries will never be completely solved, no matter what progress medicine makes. This point has been made clear by the miracle story we have dealt with here.

The real issue is whether we can accept the challenge this story offers to us, the readers, that is, the challenge that the real problem lies in the hypocritical mentality on the side of the able. In other words, the challenge is whether we can realize that such a society

---

[31] Cf. Theissen (*Gospel*, p. 116), who refers to the stories in Mark 2:1–12; 3:1–6; Luke 13:10–17, and 14:2–6.
[32] Cf. Theissen, *Miracle Stories*, p. 114: "In some rule miracles, the argument follows the miracle. In Luke 13:10–17 it is integrated into the miracle story, and the concluding acclamation formally rounds off the miracle and the debate."
[33] Wire, "Structure," p. 109.

in which those who are denigrated for whatever reason, who are defined as "others," who are excluded from society and stigmatized as polluted, re-gain their wholeness as human beings. The challenge is whether those who are disabled are accepted as they are and are able to live without pain. If we can create such a community among us, it should really be called a miracle. And we are called upon to trigger just such a miracle as the bent-over woman did. This is a big task for us, yet we are invited to join in. This is what the miracle that happened to the bent-over woman tells us. This is how we, the disabled and the able, may bring about a miracle among us. The process of getting involved with this challenging project will be the way to glorify God, if we would also like to follow the lead of the bent-over woman.

The synagogue leader symbolizes those who are only too eager to pursue their own righteousness and benefits at the expense of others. Thus, they may accept pollution, environmental disruption, militarization of the land, and so on, if it is to their own advantage to do so.

The woman symbolizes all those who are bent and choked by human selfishness. We women, who are oppressed in this patriarchal society, are empowered by the daring way shown by the bent-over woman, who opened up a way to re-gain her wholeness and Jesus' liberative and affirmative response toward her. We will never give up until we can praise God as she did.

At the same time we are challenged to liberate the bent from their bondage. The last but not least important question is whether we have the keen understanding or sensitivity to recognize whom we are marginalizing. As Wire says: "The probability is that they share the harsh experience which the teller assumes as the given condition of the story but have not heard or are not convinced of a transformation of the condition."[34]

We are asked to continue striving for transformations that may bring all of us peace and justice even though we often experience failure and are overcome by feelings of helplessness. We need to believe in ourselves so that we can engender miracles among us. And we are offered the best possible model in the way the bent-over woman pursued the issue and in the way Jesus dealt with it.

I would like to end this paper by noting how much we, Japanese

---

[34] Wire, "Structure," p. 110.

women and men in grass-roots movements, have been empowered
by the global attention paid to the "comfort women" issue through
various means, such as the report issued by the UN "Working Group
on Contemporary Forms of Slavery" (1994), the preliminary report
submitted by the special rapporteur on violence against women,
Radhika Coomaraswamy, to the "Commission on Human Rights
(1995), and the working paper on systematic rape and sexual slavery by an expert of the sub-commission as special rapporteur on
wartime slavery, Linda Chabez (1995). Behind this world-wide attention, I believe, lies the contemporary serious concern that the same
kind of violence continues to be acted out against women and children in different parts of the world. Linda Chabez, special rapporteur on wartime slavery, submitted her report on "Violence Against
Women in the War and Disputes" to the UN "Commission of Human
Rights" in spring 1998. So that she might reflect in her report on
what Asian women have been struggling with, we grass-roots women
in Japan held an international conference on "War and Violence
Against Women" in November 1997. Women from twenty different
countries gathered together and had hot discussions on the issue. As
long as life is rejected for whatever reason, we cannot experience
the sabbath in its real meaning.

DIVINING TEXTS FOR INTERNATIONAL RELATIONS:
MATT. 15:21–28

MUSA W. DUBE SHOMANAH

Introduction

In 1994, when I was visiting Batswana women leaders of African Independent Churches (henceforth AICs) to ask for their biblical interpretations I encountered an interesting Setswana biblical reading.[1] Whenever I entered an AICs church compound and asked to see the leader (usually a faith healer) it was often assumed that I had come to consult the healer. Thus, when I was brought before some of them, they would hand the Bible to me, ask me to hold it in my hands, to open it, and to hand back to them whatever page I had opened.[2] Had I complied, they would have divined the circumstances surrounding all the relationships of my life through interpreting the passages of whatever page I had happened to open. The diagnosis would have shown which of my relationships were in good shape and which ones were wanting, hence causing illness. Lastly, they would have recommended a treatment or a solution through interpreting the passages. Unfortunately, I was visiting AICs women church leaders with my own chosen passages from the New Testament, asking them to interpret those to me.[3] This forced me to decline their offers lest my own research got compromised.

Nevertheless, this encounter made it apparent to me that the Bible has become one of the divining sets or "bones" (the latter is a popular generic term which I shall adopt in this paper) to Batswana people. This form of indigenized reading strategy was undoubtedly a challenge to me as a Western trained biblical scholar. Following in the steps of AICs' indigenization, this paper shall begin by expounding

---

[1] While Botswana is the country, Batswana refers to the people of Botswana and Motswana to one person. Setswana refers to the language and culture of Batswana.

[2] F. Staugard, *Traditional Healers: Traditional Medicine in Botswana* (Gaborone: Ipelegeng Publishers, 1985), p. 74, discusses this method briefly.

[3] M. W. Dube, "Readings of *Semoya*: Batswana Women's Interpretations of Matt. 15:21–28," in G. West and M. W. Dube (eds.), *"Reading With": An Exploration of the Interface between Critical and Ordinary Readings of the Bible. African Overtures* (Semeia, 73; Atlanta, GA: Scholars, 1996), pp. 111–29.

on divination as an ethical method of reading biblical texts. This exposition is also a presentation of the "other" text of my life, that is, the Setswana oral culture of Southern Africans, which is being read in its own right.[4] To emphasize that I am reading from two different books—the Bible and Setswana cultures—I shall use the term "bones-texts." In the second part of the paper, I shall argue that the category of international relationships (henceforth IRs) is central to all nations and should be considered in the process of reading bones-texts. The latter indicates that I am not simply stuck to the "ancient traditions," but I am more concerned with the current affairs of the world. Lastly, I shall divine Matt. 15:21–28 for IRs.

Divining as an Ethical Method of Reading

In many Southern African ethnic groups, divining sets are a collection of animal bones (especially joints), carved wood (on one side), bean-seeds, coins, sea shells, polished stones, mirrors, crocodile-skins, drums, and even plastic pieces.[5] Manufacturers of divining sets, especially the carved ones, are lay people. Each healer buys or collects his/her own set, but these are regarded as "blind" or "mute" until the healer ceremoniously dedicates them to the Divine Powers for the special purpose of divining. Depending on different healers, a divining set can contain one to thirty bones.[6] Similarly, certain types of healers keep bones made of one type of material, while others mix the materials. Some people divine without using any objects, that is, through dreams, visions and the Spirit. My interest in this paper will be with one particular form of divination: that of casting a divining set of bones and reading them.

Regardless of their number and materials, all divining sets function like social books or authoritative books of life. Divining bones are thrown, and the way in which they settle down in relation to

---

[4] I am grateful to Leslie Nthoi, Seratwa Ntloedibe, Peter Mwikisa, and Ingrid Rosa Kitzberger, who read this paper and significantly contributed to its thought.

[5] See M. Gelfand, *Medicine and Magic of Mashona* (Capetown: Juta and Company, 1956), pp. 122–53, for a detailed discussion of Zimbabwean bones; J. Hall, *Sangoma: Odyssey into the Script World of Africa* (New York: Putman Book, 1994), p. 4, for a description of Swaziland bones, and Staugard, *Traditional Healers*, pp. 75–6, for the context of Botswana.

[6] See Gelfand, *Medicine and Magic*, pp. 124–53. Hall, *Odyssey*, p. 70, and Staugard, *Traditional Healers*, pp. 75–9, for the variation of the divining sets.

one another is read to diagnose the circumstances surrounding the relationships of a person and for the appropriate remedy, where problems are identified.[7] Such a reading is possible because key experiences and relationships of human beings in a society are represented in the set. The carvings on the bones are also symbolic. For example, the set will contain bones and patterns symbolizing Divine Powers (Ancestors or the sacred community of the Living Dead), evil powers (witches), foreign spirits (good or bad), elderly man and elderly woman, young man and young woman, homestead, family, parents, death, birth, etc. The process of divining itself involves several stages, which I shall now outline briefly.

A reading of bones is initiated by a consulting reader (henceforth CR/s) who, upon observing some ill-health in her/his life, will seek to understand the nature of his/her affliction, its causes and how it can be healed. A CR can visit alone for a private problem. In cases where the problem is huge or visible to all and affecting those who are close to him/her, relatives and close friends can accompany the CR to read bones. Traditionally, diviner-healers insisted that a CR should be accompanied by relatives. Sometimes concerned relatives can go to consult on behalf of an absent or very ill relative. Ill-health must be understood here in a wider sense, that is, inclusive of physical affliction but not limited to it. Health is understood "as a state of total physical, mental and social well-being" that includes all other aspects of an individual's life.[8] Accordingly, causes of afflictions are not only attributed to natural factors and bad food but are largely attributed to unhealthy social relationships.

Upon arrival of a CR, the healer begins with a prayer (a chant or a ritual) to the Divine Powers, asking them to open the circumstances surrounding the relationships and life situations of the CR. Sometimes, the CR is asked to utter a short prayer in which s/he requests a revelation of his/her circumstances. Second, the healer assigns one bone from the set to the CR. This is picked up from the bones symbolizing a man, woman, young man or young woman, depending on the gender and age of the CR. Third, the diviner-healer would hand the bones to the CR, ask him/her to hold them in his/her hands, breathe on them, shake them and do the first

---

[7] See Staugard, *Traditional Healers*, pp. 118–24; Gelfand, *Medicine and Logic*, pp. 131–53, and Hall, *Odyssey*, pp. 144–63, who present detailed discussion of reading sessions.
[8] Staugard, *Traditional Healers*, p. 5.

throw. In this first step, the CR puts her/his breath on the bones, thus writing his/her story on the pages of the bones. The healer would then study how they fell. Each fall can be read from multiple angles for many different meanings. What is studied is how the bones relate to each other, or the story they write or tell about the social experiences and relationships of the CR. The reader notes those relationships that are healthy and those that are troubled. If, for example, the bone that represents the CR is far away from the bone representing the Divine Powers, that may indicate the anger of an Ancestor. The visiting reader is possibly estranged from the Divine Powers, a situation that causes his/her ill-health and must be rectified. The reading may indicate a number of other problematic relationships.

A diagnosis, however, is not based on the first reading. In fact, for many diviner-healers, the first throw only serves as part of a prayer that seeks the approval of Divine Powers on whether divination is permitted. (Divination can indeed be disapproved where the CR is an outstanding culprit or pursued by extremely ferocious spirits that can attack any healer who attempts to confront them). The healer then takes the bones him/herself and throws them. The bones can only be thrown and read for a maximum of three times to confirm the story of their first fall. Between these throws, the diviner-healer converses with the Divine Powers and the consulting visitors. As s/he shakes the bones in his/her hands, s/he tells the bones the purpose of the divination, utters a praise poem and implores them to speak and tell the story of the CR. The bones are addressed directly as the mouthpiece of the Divine Powers. Once the bones are down, the diviner-healer reads them aloud to the CR and the accompanying readers, constantly asking him/her to confirm or disagree with the story that the bones have just written about her/his life. The CR has the right to reject a reading as incorrect and unrepresentative of her/his life situation and relationships. In such a case, the healer-reader will throw and read again. If the CR is largely dissatisfied with the whole reading, s/he is free to consult another, and possibly a better, healer. Similarly, the healer is free to declare an incapacity to diagnose some cases. In such a case, s/he would advise the CRs to find another healer. But if, for example, the first reading of an estranged Ancestor re-appears in the subsequent throws, then it will be identified as the main problem, or one of the main problems, causing the CR's ill-health.

The second stage of reading bones involves establishing the cause of the troubled relationship/s. In this stage, too, the healer can throw and read up to three times, each time informing the CR of what the bones say and asking the latter to either approve or disapprove of the reading. Based on the re-occurrence of a pattern or of patterns in the bones and the CR's input, a conclusion on the cause is identified. But most of the time, the anger of an Ancestor points to the CR as the one who caused their displeasure. This could easily happen, for example, when someone neglects his/her parents, relatives, or the Ancestors themselves.

The third stage of divining seeks to establish the correct remedy or treatment. The healer throws not more than three times and studies the bones. Although the healer is the dominant reader in this stage, s/he converses with the Divine Powers, asking them about the appropriate medicine. S/he then discusses the readings with the CR and the accompanying relatives. The appropriate medicine and procedure are recommended to the CR. Or the CR and her/his accompanying relatives are given instructions and are responsible for applying the medicine. In both cases, the healer, the CR, and the relatives work very closely over time until the problem is solved.

For Batswana and other Southern Africans, reading of bones was, and still is, tantamount to reading an authoritative book of social life. Bones are not fixed or closed canons. Rather, each CR writes and reads her/his own story with the diviner-healer. Yet, as my introductory story and the observation of other writers indicate, the Bible has become one more divining set among Batswana. It is one more authoritative book of social life. It is read to diagnose the problems of CRs, the causes of their problems, and to seek the appropriate treatment that heals their troubled relationships and restores them back to society as whole, responsible and fulfilled members. Here I must applaud the AICs readers for their insightful efforts to indigenize biblical reading in a fashion that I could not have imagined as a Western trained scholar.

Learning from this ancient art, what method and ethics of reading can be drawn by today's Batswana, Southern Africans, and all other interested readers of the Bible? How can biblical readers become diviners of bones-texts? I would list the following aspects for those who wish to read as diviners or within the framework of reading as a diviner:

1. Bones-texts encapsulate key social relations of various types and kinds. They also address key experiences of human beings.

2. Reading is not a luxury. CRs go to read bones-texts because

they are either observing some ill-health in their world or they want to make sure their well-being is not threatened by encroaching danger or their own negligence. Above all, reading is a search for healing.

3. Reading must determine whether bones-texts reveal problematic or good relationships, and determine the cause of trouble and the appropriate solution.

4. Reading is a process that involves a study of recurring relationships and life-experiences written by the bones-texts and the interpretation of their meaning.

5. Reading is a joint effort between the Divine Powers, the Living Dead, the diviner-healer, the CR and the accompanying relatives, if present. The specialists and the CRs both share responsibility for their readings. The CR, though unspecialized in reading the bones-texts, is nonetheless an indispensable partner since s/he initiates the reading through seeking the consultation; s/he dialogues (confirming or disagreeing) with the healer-reader's interpretations.

6. Reading bones-texts is fundamentally about reading an individual's relationships and experiences within the society; healing physical afflictions is also about creating and maintaining healthy relationships and experiences of various types in society.

7. Reading bones-texts entails a communal responsibility on the part of the concerned to effect a remedy. Healing involves active participation of the CR, the accompanying relatives, the Divine powers and the healer-reader.

8. Reading bones-texts involves the willingness to be self-critical on the part of the CR and the challenge to accept that one can be responsible for one's own ill-health by having failed to create and maintain affirmative relationships.

9. Bones-texts, Divine Powers, CRs and healer-readers write the story of each CR during the consultation. Each reading session is also a moment of writing the life-story of the CR.

10. Fundamental to the divination framework of thinking is that all people are inter-connected and must stay inter-connected. Health means healthy connections. Ill-health means disconnection or unhealthy connections. Therefore, we are responsible for our own health and the health of those around us, depending on how we relate with them.

These points, I believe, capture some of the major assumptions of divination as an ethical method of reading. They also expound some important aspects of the oral culture of Southern Africa and how it functions as a social book of life.

In Botswana, and in other areas, the Bible has become one more set of social experiences and relationships. Like a set of bones that are read to diagnose the circumstances surrounding each individual's relationships and to seek solutions, the Bible is now read to diagnose the social relationships and experiences of CRs. It is now read to offer solutions to troubled relationships and to encourage the creation and maintenance of life-affirming relations in society. Reading bones-texts is, therefore, about the right to live a whole life, to have healthy and affirmative relationships in society, as well as about the challenge to create and to maintain healthy relationships. Undoubtedly, reading bones-texts is an art that seeks to produce knowledge and that requires a substantial understanding of social relations.

On these grounds, Southern African academic readers, and others, who know or wish to know this ancient art of reading, will not only need to re-capture it for their biblical interpretations, but also to follow the route that has already been championed by AICs readers. That is, biblical reading also needs to be divination for us. It needs to be an act of involving Divine Powers, CRs, specialized healers and accompanying relatives to identify unhealthy social relationships and their sources, and to create ethical, life-affirming and healthy relationships with one another in our world. With this discussion of divination as an ethical method of reading in mind, I will now highlight that we need to pay attention to the IRs in our reading of bones-texts, since IRs are vital to our well-being.

International Relations

The interaction of different nations is widely attested to in many ancient texts such as *The Odyssey* and the Bible. People of different nations have always interacted with each other, both in friendly and unfriendly terms. Biblical literature, for example, attests to the interaction of the Hebrew nation with the Egyptians, Ethiopians, Canaanites, and many other nations. Further, the whole, biblical literature is often framed by the interaction of the Hebrew nation with various empires—Babylonian, Persian, Assyrian, Greek, and Roman imperial powers. Thus, biblical literature is often classified under such categories as First Temple, Second Temple, or pre-exilic and post-exilic periods. Each of these categories commemorates some major impact of foreign empires on the Hebrew nation. Interaction with imperial powers implies a relationship of domination and subordination, no matter how friendly it may seem. The New Testament texts originated in an imperial context, where not only the Hebrew nation but many others were under the domination of the Roman Empire.

International interaction is not only an ancient phenomenon, but has also become a relationship that touches all nations very closely in our contemporary world. The interaction of nations is still characterized by friendly and unfriendly relationships, by relationships of domination and subordination. Through economic and political interests and through advanced media facilities, IRs have become central to all nations in today's world. They shape most of our experiences in our daily lives as individuals and as corporate communities. What we eat, wear, read, the cars we drive, the languages we speak, the radios we play, the computers we use, and the balls that our kids play with, come from many different parts of the world. Yet, how much a reader will pay attention to IRs will largely depend on whether s/he is on the dominating or dominated end. Whether one seeks to read bones-texts for IRs will depend on whether these relationships hurt them or not, for it is pain or affliction that usually leads CRs and their relatives to seek a reading for the purpose of healing.

As a black Motswana woman of Southern Africa, and a Two-Thirds World citizen, I am consciously aware of the centrality of the IRs in my life and my region. Not only did Southern Africans and Africa as a whole get colonized, not only did they fight for their independence and acquire it at high prices; they also moved into neo-colonization and straight into the tremors of the impending globalization of the world economy. IRs have affected us closely, continuously and painfully. We have experienced IRs from the side of those who are dominated. The impact of IRs in my world is, therefore, something that cannot be ignored, overlooked or postponed. I am forced to think about them daily. I think of their nature, their positive and negative impact, and how they could be re-constituted for the good of all nations.

Therefore, I read bones-texts with an acute interest in IRs. I want to find out how they are portrayed in bones-texts, whether they are healthy or problematic. If they are problematic, I want to know what is identified as the cause of their troubles, and what treatment or solutions are presented to create and maintain healthy IRs. Further, I am willing to join hands with Divine Powers, healer-readers, CRs and their concerned communities[9] who are searching for healing and who are willing to create healthy and liberating IRs. Similarly, in my reading of bones-texts, I am keenly interested in identifying affirmative IRs. That is, to ask what makes them healthy and affirmative and how they can inform contemporary IRs. As a consulting diviner-reader, I am, therefore, searching and reading for the healing of nations in bones-texts.[10] This brings me to the divination of Matt. 15:21–28 for IRs.

Divining Matt. 15:21–28 for IRs

The story of Matt. 15:21–28 is a good passage for divining in general and for IRs in particular. It is a story with a search for healing and international contact. It also portrays relationships between Canaanites and Israelites, males and females, daughters and mothers, dogs and children, masters and servants, students and teachers, evil and good spirits. In short, it encodes diverse human relationships. Although I must emphasize that divination is a holistic reading that checks the health of all relationships in the process of reading, I shall focus mainly on the search for healing and international contact.

To begin with the search for healing, there is a health problem in the story. The consulting woman identifies its cause for us: evil spirits have taken possession of her daughter (v. 22). She is, therefore, an affected or concerned relative. She hears of a famous healer and embarks on a journey on behalf of her seriously ill daughter. She is in search of her daughter's healing. Upon arrival, she presents a request to Jesus. This healer, however, is not just a human being, a "Son of David" and an Israelite (vv. 22, 24). Jesus is also a Divine Power. He is "Lord" (vv. 22, 25, 27). This woman notably utters three requests before her daughter's healing is granted to her (vv. 22, 25, 27). The woman's repeated appeals to Jesus before the final result resembles the appeals of a diviner-healer, when negotiating

---

[9] See M. W. Dube, *Towards a Post-colonial Feminist Interpretation of the Bible* (Ann Arbor, MI: UMI Company, 1996), where I engaged feminist readers (whom I regard as ethical readers) and challenged them to shoulder international concerns in their readings.

[10] In fact, divination is also done on a community level, for example, when there is a severe drought that affects the whole community.

with the Divine Powers. A divining healer usually appeals to the
Divine Powers for assistance on behalf of a CR. Jesus, however, is
already such a power.[11] The woman, therefore, appeals directly to
the Divine Power, and yet it takes her three requests until Jesus
grants her daughter's healing.

Turning to the international contact, the story takes place on the
boundaries.[12] Jesus travels to the foreign area, and the woman comes
to meet him. The woman is a Canaanite, and Jesus is an Israelite.
The Hebrew Bible characterizes the Israelites as those possessing a
divine mandate to annihilate the Canaanites and their culture (Exod.
23:1–18). As Robert Allen Warrior describes it, "the narrative tells
us that Canaanites have status only as the people Yahweh removes
from the land to bring the chosen people in."[13] In short, Canaanites
and Israelites belong to two different nations that have had centuries
of close contact and unhealthy IRs. It was not a mutual relationship but one of domination and suppression. Theirs was a relationship that made the invaded Canaanites possessed and sick, and hence
the woman's appeal to Jesus for healing.[14]

As a Southern African citizen of Botswana, whose experience of
IRs is from the side of the dominated, I closely notice the proceedings of this meeting. I identify with the Canaanite woman. She
travels to ask for help that she desperately needs. She comes to ask
for help from a member of a people that has oppressed and exploited
her people. This reminds me of the many journeys undertaken by
our African presidents, ministers and other representatives to foreign
countries to ask for aid and investors from our former colonizers. I
also notice how this woman is forced to beg to the point where she

---

[11] Sometimes Jesus seemed to appeal to the Higher Powers for healing a patient,
like in Mark 7:33–34.

[12] For Two-Thirds World women readers of Matt. 15:21–28 who have paid
attention to IRs, see Kwok Pui-lan, "Woman, Dogs, and Crumbs. Constructing a
Postcolonial Discourse," in idem, *Discovering the Bible in the Non-Biblical World* (New
York: Orbis Books, 1995), pp. 71–83; L. Guardiola-Saénz, "Borderless Women and
Borderless Texts: A Cultural Reading of Matthew 15:21–28," in K. Doob Sakenfeld,
Sh. H. Ringe, and Ph. A. Bird (eds.), *Reading the Bible as Women. Perspectives from
Africa, Asia, and Latin America* (*Semeia*, 78; Atlanta, GA: Scholars, 1997), pp. 69–91.

[13] R. A. Warrior, "A Native American Perspective: Canaanites, Cowboys, and
Indians," in R. S. Sugirtharajah (ed.), *Voices From the Margin: Interpreting the Bible in
the Third World* (New York: Orbis Books, 1991), pp. 287–95, p. 291.

[14] For spirit possession and its link to political oppression, see R. Horsley, *Sociology
and the Jesus Movement* (New York: Crossroad, 1989), pp. 83–96. See also M. Taussig,
Shamanism, Colonialism and the Wild Man: A Study in Terror and Healing (Chicago, IL:
Chicago University Press, 1987), pp. 3–127.

completely loses her dignity. First, she addresses her request to Jesus who ignores her (v. 21). Second, the desperate woman then follows from behind shouting for help (v. 23). The disciples, who are obviously irritated or embarrassed by a Canaanite woman who is shouting behind them, ask Jesus to dismiss her and not help her (v. 23). In response, Jesus explains his silence, stating that he has been sent solely to the nation of Israel (v. 24, see also Matt. 10:5–16). It is at this point that she manages to take her third step. She pushes her way through the group of disciples and falls down on her knees before Jesus, stating, "Lord, help me" (v. 25). But not even her emphatic language moves Jesus to help her. Instead, Jesus, as an Israelite, asserts the superiority of his people over the Canaanites, saying, "It is not fair to take the children's bread and throw it to the dogs" (v. 26). This answer asserts the validity of their ancient and problematic IRs. Jesus is speaking from his own context, asserting that only Israelite children are children; only Israelite children deserve food; only Israelite children can sit at the dinner table. The Canaanite children, on the other hand, are dogs; they do not deserve any food, or, as Warrior expresses it, "Canaanites have status only as the people Yahweh removes from the land to bring the chosen people in."[15]

Nonetheless, the suffering of the Canaanite daughter (who, as some readers have observed, symbolizes the future of Canaan) and its impact on her relatives is greater than the refusal of Jesus. The woman does not allow their unsound IRs to get in the way of healing. She needs the healing of her daughter, and she is determined to attain it. This brings us to the fourth stage of her request. The woman assures Jesus that she is not seeking to dispossess the children of Israel for the sake of the children of Canaan. Rather, she seeks to assert the rights of all, that is, "even the dogs eat!" Their need for food is self-evident by the very fact that they pick up and "eat the crumbs that fall from the master's table" (v. 27).[16]

In her assertion, the woman underlines not only the rights of all children to food, but also the inseparability of Canaanites and Israelites. Regardless of whether we label them "children and dogs" or "masters and dogs," they eat together, in the same room, from the same table, and they eat the same bread. Therefore, their needs are the

---

[15] Warrior, "Canaanites, Cowboys and Indians," p. 291.
[16] For this reading, see Dube, "Readings of *Semoya*," pp. 118–19.

same. The woman's response acknowledges the racial difference between Canaanites and Israelites, but underlines their common need for food and their inter-connectedness. That is, while their IRs have reduced the Canaanites' differences to deficiencies, she is re-asserting the rights of those who have been labelled as dogs and their inter-connection with those who have designated themselves as children and masters.

I must admit, however, that my first reading-divination of this story as a black African Motswana woman and a Two-Thirds World citizen is particularly difficult. I see myself in the Canaanite woman's position and I identify Jesus with the powerful donor countries, who have indeed exploited our countries, but whose help is something we beg for. When I hear the dog statement thrown into the face of the Canaanite woman, I remember insulting statements which hold that giving aid to Africa is like throwing money into a bottomless pit. However, those of us who are on the dominated end of the IRs have to put aside our pride and focus on getting the healing of nations that we all need. The act of putting pride aside should not be confused with accepting the current IRs. Rather, it is an act of questioning the existing IRs and of showing their injustice, as well as an act of seeking healing. It is imperative to seek healing, against all odds, primarily because the unhealthy IRs authorize the exploitation of some nations by others. The exploitation of the dispossessed leads to extreme poverty that manifests itself in real physical symptoms of illness. It manifests itself in demons taking possession of people so that relationships, even amongst themselves, become impossible. In short, all kinds of diseases that invade the poor in their lands cannot be healed by simply attending to their physical symptoms. Rather, they also require examining all their key relationships, identifying the normal and the problematic ones, the causes of the latter, and taking the responsibility to create liberating and healthy relationships. It is those who are in pain, the dominated, who, unfortunately, must seek to understand and rectify the anomalies in their inter-connections. Accordingly, the Canaanite woman as a member of the dominated swallows all her pride as she searches for healing.

Furthermore, I find the findings/framework of my first divination of the story quite disturbing, for it does not seem to assert once and for all the birthright of all children to food and health. Rather, the framework seems to work within the paradigm of unequal nations, of domination and suppression, of dogs and children, indeed, of beggars and charitable organizations. As a consulting diviner-reader, one who is searching for her own healing and the healing of nations, I find myself, like the Canaanite woman, refusing to accept that our IRs must be that of dogs and children. This leads me to a second throw: a second reading of the bones-texts, a re-reading for liberating IRs.

It is in the subsequent throws and re-readings that I am able to make sense of the difficulties in my first reading. That is, I begin to understand that the story, first of all, seeks to acknowledge that there are many such unhealthy IRs in the world. Here, I also note that the bones-texts do reveal that the dialogue between the oppressor and the oppressed nations is a difficult dialogue to a point where it is sometimes "a dialogue of the deaf."[17] The subsequent re-reading of bones-texts in search for an appropriate solution indicates that the powerful and the powerless, the oppressor and the oppressed, must undertake the difficult task of working together to effect healing: to create healthy IRs in our world. The final and positive answer of Jesus strongly suggests to me that all unsound IRs must be put aside, by both the oppressed and the oppressor nations, in pursuit of life affirming and healthy relationships.

From this perspective, healing is indeed granted by Jesus, but the road to this healing is characterized by combined efforts of Jesus and the woman. Both Jesus and the woman embarked on journeys to the place of healing. We often tend to emphasize, as I did, the journey of the Canaanite woman. But Jesus also embarked on a journey to Tyre and Sidon. In fact, the text does not tell us why Jesus left his home and travelled to this region, but as soon as he has met and dialogued with the Canaanite woman he returned. This mysterious journey and the encounter with the Canaanite woman indicate that Jesus and his disciples also needed something: they needed their own healing as children of Israel. They needed to be liberated from perceiving the Canaanites as faithless dogs. They needed to repent and begin to realize that Canaanites are just like any children who deserve food from the table. Therefore, on their arrival, Jesus and the disciples indeed embody and express the perspective of Israel towards Canaan. By so doing, they, like the Canaanite woman who comes shouting for the healing of her daughter, have also journeyed in search for the healing of the children of Israel.

---

[17] A. Mazrui, *Cultural Forces in World Politics* (London: James Curry, 1990), p. 116.

This is evident in the conversation of Jesus with the Canaanite woman and the disciples' request for her dismissal. In other words, the story re-activates the IRs of Canaan and Israel as they were in their traditions, precisely to suggest a way out.

The woman led the way by presenting her request and negotiating with Jesus for the healing of her daughter. Jesus allowed himself, not without difficulty, to be persuaded that a Canaanite daughter who is possessed by evil spirits is estranged from healthy relationships. The daughter has an unhealthy relationship with evil spirits. Therefore, she needs to be restored to healthy relationships with all the members of her family and society. But Jesus also realized that the Israelite children, who call Canaanites "dogs" and who would not share their bread, were estranged from their neighbours. He realized that the Canaanite and Israelite children had an unhealthy relationship and that they needed to be restored to each other. Thus, he declared, "Woman, great is your faith! Let it be done for you as you wish." "And her daughter was healed instantly" (v. 28). It was this combined effort, of an Israelite and a Canaanite, of the oppressor and the oppressed, who met each other at the meeting place—the boundary—that brought a healing of their IRs.

In conclusion, three points are notable. First, while the woman requests health, Jesus refers to it as bread. Health is equated to food that sustains life. Second, before the physical symptoms of the daughter are attended to, the social relations of Canaanites and Israelites are addressed. Health is thus portrayed as healthy relationships with those we interact with. Healthy relationships are vividly portrayed as food that sustains all people. Third, on conferring healing on the daughter, Jesus acknowledges the faith of the woman as a major factor in the process. Jesus is a human healer and a Divine Power, but without the initiative and faith of the CR, without her willingness to dialogue with Jesus, healing would have failed. In short, health for all, healing for all, food for all, or liberating IRs for all will only be realized through combined efforts and the solidarity of different reading communities. It will begin when all the consulting diviner-readers begin to acknowledge that a problem exists in our IRs; when they are willing to read-divine for the healing of all relationships, including the international ones.

LILIES OF THE FIELD AND WANDERING JEWS: BIBLICAL SCHOLARSHIP, WOMEN'S ROLES, AND SOCIAL LOCATION

AMY-JILL LEVINE

The "lilies" of the title refer to the thousand flowers of feminist inter-pretations of Scripture; the "Jews" are those who wander through these writings: both as literary figures (e.g., Pharisees) and as inter-ested readers (e.g., myself). Among the lilies, liberationist and fem-inist[1] perspectives offer a bouquet of hermeneutical strategies: the hermeneutics of suspicion, historical interpretation and re-construc-tion, ethical and theological evaluation, creative imagination and ritualization,[2] indeterminacy,[3] re-vision,[4] wisdom,[5] etc. We feminist readers come from diverse locations, have diverse interests and approaches, take different stances in relation to the Bible, and do not always or even often agree. Whether arguing for biblical rejec-tion or recuperation, whether taking an historical, sociological, or literary-critical approach, we share two common roots: we advocate a liberationist perspective that aspires to be "inclusive, ecumenical, and

---

[1] E. Schüssler Fiorenza, "Transforming the Legacy of *The Woman's Bible*," in idem (ed.), *Searching the Scriptures, Vol. 1: A Feminist Introduction* (New York: Crossroad, 1993), pp. 1–24, see pp. 16–19. For problems with and re-definitions of the term, see e.g., T. Okure, "Feminist Intepretations in Africa," in Schüssler Fiorenza (ed.), *Searching the Scriptures, Vol. 1*, pp. 76–85; Kwok Pui-lan, "The Future of Feminist Theology: An Asian Perspective," in U. King (ed.), *Feminist Theology from the Third World. A Reader* (London: SPCK; Maryknoll, N.Y.: Orbis Books, 1994), pp. 63–76, p. 65; the following in O. Ortega (ed.), *Women's Visions: Theological Reflection, Celebration, Action* (Geneva: WCC, 1995): E. Amoah, "Theology from the Perspective of African Women," pp. 1–7, p. 7; I. Graesslé, "Reflections on European Feminist Theology," pp. 52–60, p. 58; E. Tamez, "Latin American Feminist Hermeneutics: A Retrospective," pp. 77–89, p. 83; and the excellent theoretical comments of M. Kanyoro, "Cultural Hermeneutics: An African Contribution," pp. 18–28, pp. 24–6.

[2] E. Schüssler Fiorenza, "Feminist Hermeneutics," in D. N. Freedman, et al. (eds.), *Anchor Bible Dictionary, Vol. 2* (New York: Doubleday, 1992), pp. 783–91.

[3] A. Suskin Ostriker, *Feminist Revision and the Bible* (Cambridge: Blackwell, 1993), p. 86.

[4] Schüssler Fiorenza, "Transforming the Legacy," p. 11.

[5] R. Nakashima Brock, "Dusting the Bible on the Floor: A Hermeneutics of Wisdom," in Schüssler Fiorenza (ed.), *Searching the Scriptures, Vol. 1*, pp. 64–75, on the importance of the past, the rejection of innocence, and the retention of multi-ple perspectives.

multicultural,"[6] and we recognize the political character of our interpretations regarding not only women, but "class, race, ethnicity, and
other structures of oppression."[7]

We also look at ourselves. Our social location and experiences,
we acknowledge, affect the method we employ, the questions we ask,
and the answers we derive. In good post-modern fashion we realize
that our conclusions are necessarily both incomplete and biased; we
also note, however, that "incomplete and biased" does not mean
wrong. To the contrary, our awareness of the limited and temporary nature of our conclusions demands self-correction; our dialogues
with others, especially but not only other feminists, provide us both
support and the occasional pitch fork. In digging through garden-
variety biblical scholarship, we have found much to uproot in the
plots of objectivist historical critics and androcentric theologians. We
have also had to lay the ax to a few of our own earlier efforts.

First, those of us writing from (relatively) privileged, North Atlantic
positions realized that just as objectivist scholarship did not speak
for all, so we as individual feminist critics could not speak for all
women. Social-location based readings and advocacy positions (Wom-
anist, Latina, Asian, Lesbian, etc.) serve to critique the tendency
of some of us feminist readers to universalize our own experiences,
desiderata, or nature. Thus, we draw from our own experience rather
than adopt a guise of objective neutrality, and we recognize the con-
tingent nature of both the experience and the reading it inspires.

Second, against a certain kind of pest that had bored deep into
the roots of the home-grown interpretations of Christian feminists,
those outside the Christian community provided a much needed
organic pesticide. In 1980, Judith Plaskow descried the frequent anti-
Judaism in Christian-feminist biblical interpretation: in order to make

---

[6] Schüssler Fiorenza, "Transforming the Legacy," p. 9, on the "ethos" of "feminist critical interpretation."

[7] See E. Schüssler Fiorenza, "Rethinking *The Woman's Bible*," in *Searching the
Scriptures, Vol. 1*, pp. ix–xiii, p. x. The absence of "sexual orientation" from this list—
and its general omission from the first volume of *Searching the Scriptures* (but see
Schüssler Fiorenza's comment on p. 3, and the observation on "heterosexism" by
A. M. Cheek, "Shifting the Paradigm: Feminist Bible Study," pp. 338–50, p. 338)
as well as from most "feminist" biblical studies books and anthologies—may indicate the theological agendas of the contributors and/or religious publication houses:
unlike the rest of the Western academy, biblical studies has not demonstrated substantial interest in sexual orientation. Perhaps with the recent publication of B. J.
Brooten's *Love Between Women: Early Christian Responses to Female Homoeroticism* (Chicago
and London: University of Chicago Press, 1996), matters will change.

Jesus look pro-active for women, Christian feminists frequently (necessarily?) portrayed a first-century Jewish context that epitomized misogyny.[8] Today, the majority of (Western) feminist academic readings of biblical materials are explicitly cognizant of this problem.[9]

The social and political problems with which we wrestle remain land for reclamation. Nevertheless, we found ourselves comfortable under own vines and fig trees. Recognized by the Society of Biblical Literature, represented by increasingly numerous publications, taking its place on the biblical studies landscape, feminist interpretation appeared to be in full bloom.

The garden looks nice from the distance, but closer inspection reveals growths of anti-Judaism and the decay of projection. Worse, the rot appears with increasing frequency in precisely those writings stemming from the globalization of the discourse. Not only was anti-Judaism the weed of 1970s and early 1980s Christian feminism, it is now choking 1990s feminist-liberationist works. The examples I unearth all blossomed in the last decade, were all planted by women (although women hardly have a monopoly on anti-Jewish readings), and all appear in volumes that explicitly and self-consciously read for liberation.

The Weeds

The weeds come in several varieties. Most common are single sentences purporting to summarize the situation of all Jewish women in the Second Temple period. Occasionally seen are Marcionite perspectives, in which the "God of Judaism" is distinguished from that

---

[8] J. Plaskow, "Blaming the Jews for the Birth of Patriarchy," *Lilith* 7 (1980), pp. 11–12, 14–17; and "Anti-Judaism in Feminist Christian Interpretation," in Schüssler Fiorenza (ed.), *Searching the Scriptures, Vol. 1*, pp. 117–29 (which, alas, references no Jewish women scholars of Christian origins). See, for a similar argument, S. Heschel, "Anti-Judaism in Christian Feminist Theology," *Tikkun* 5.3 (1990), pp. 25–8, 95–7.

[9] See, e.g., Kwok Pui-lan, "Racism and Ethnocentrism in Feminist Biblical Interpretation," in Schüssler Fiorenza (ed.), *Searching the Scriptures, Vol. 1*, pp. 101–16, pp. 106–7, and several other essays in the two *Searching the Scriptures* volumes. For critiques even of Elizabeth Cady Stanton's anti-Judaism, see C. De Swarte Gifford, "Politicizing the Sacred Texts: Elizabeth Cady Stanton and *The Woman's Bible*," in Schüssler Fiorenza (ed.), *Searching the Scriptures, Vol. 1*, pp. 52–63, p. 60; Plaskow, "Anti-Judaism," pp. 117, 122 (with citations); E. Schüssler Fiorenza, "Transgressing Canonical Boundaries," in idem (ed.), *Searching the Scriptures, Vol. 2: A Feminist Commentary* (New York: Crossroad, 1994), pp. 1–14, pp. 2–3.

of Christianity (an offshoot of the "Old Testament God of Vengeance vs. New Testament God of Compassion" model), and very popular are assertions which make Jesus the only Jewish man in antiquity to have cared about, been nice to, or even spoken with women. No plot is complete without a reference to the "Jewish patriarchal system," although very rare are comments on the similarly patriarchal pagan cultures of antiquity. Studies of the Gospels typically remark on "Jewish purity legislation" as necessarily bad for women, and comments by Paul that sound misogynistic are typically laid at the feet of his "Pharisaic" or "Rabbinic" background. Levitical Laws are assumed to be oppressively implemented in the Second Temple period; Rabbinic innovation and regional adaptation are noted only to show how "the Jews" increased the weight of the "yoke of the Law," which is then described as too heavy to bear.

In contrast to the negative view of Judaism is an entirely positive, and typically docetic, Christology. If Jewish women followed Jesus, so the thesis goes, there must have been something wrong with their own system. If Jesus speaks with a woman, touches a woman, or allows a woman to touch him, he is the only Jewish man in antiquity to do so. Little thought is given to the idea that women followed Jesus not because of a problem with the types of Judaism available in Judea and the Galilee, but for one of many other reasons (e.g., his healings, interpretation of Torah, personal welcoming, charisma). Less thought is given, especially outside of Western readings, to the idea that Jesus' own mission is embedded within formative Judaism, rather than external to it.

For example, one of the presenters at the 1994 Bossey seminar "Women in Dialogue: Wholeness of Vision towards the 21st Century," organized by the World Council of Churches and others in celebration of the "Ecumenical Decade—Churches in Solidarity with Women (1988–1998)," summarizes: "Two thousand years ago Jesus Christ gave women their rightful place despite the heavy yoke of the Jewish culture weighing on them. For women in general and Jewish women in particular the coming of Jesus meant a revolution."[10] How

---

[10] M. Fassinou, "Challenges for Feminist Theology in Francophone Africa," in Ortega (ed.), *Women's Visions*, pp. 8–17, p. 9. No sources are cited in support of this claim. For a similar comment, see I. Gebara, "The Face of Transcendence as a Challenge to the Reading of the Bible in Latin America," in Schüssler Fiorenza (ed.), *Searching the Scriptures, Vol. 1*, pp. 172–86, p. 174. While Gebara correctly prob-

revolutionary was he? "Christ was the only rabbi who did not discriminate against the women of his time."[11] And he was needed, given "the dehumanizing situation in which the women of the time were enslaved,"[12] since "women had no standing in Jewish society."[13]

The following citations echo this reified, rapid view of "Jewish culture:"

– "In Jesus' time, women were not allowed to read scriptures, not allowed to say prayer . . . not allowed to take any form of leadership, not allowed to talk to men in public, not allowed to divorce. . . ."[14]

– "In religion, woman was excluded from all the ministries of worship . . .;" "By Jesus' day, women's freedom had been restricted in various ways, for to the traditional limitations in post-exilic Judaism was added a tendency to separate woman from social life outside the home in order to 'protect her morals.'"[15]

– "The honor of the male is thus based on the sexual purity of the woman related to him (mother, wife, daughters, sisters), not on

---

lematizes the gender-determined presentation of Jesus as a man with authority, she stereotypes the context in which that authority is located: "If Jesus in his time genuinely acted differently with respect to women. . . ."

[11] G. Eneme, "Living Stones," in J. S. Pobee and B. von Wartenberg-Potter (eds.), *New Eyes for Reading: Biblical and Theological Reflections by Women from the Third World* (Geneva: WCC, 1986), pp. 28–32, p. 30. Her example of "nondiscrimination" is that Jesus "allowed Susanna, Joanna and others to minister to him." Yong Ting Jin similarly states that "Women were the most oppressed and powerless of all, but Jesus associated with them and restored the dignity due them. . . . Unlike the rabbinic tradition, Jesus taught women openly." See her "New Ways of Being Church: A Protestant Perspective," in V. Fabella and M. A. Oduyoye (eds.), *With Passion and Compassion. Third World Women Doing Theology* (Maryknoll, N.Y.: Orbis Books, 1988), pp. 101–7, p. 103.

[12] H. Kinukawa, "On John 7:53–8:11: A Well-Cherished but Much-Clouded Story," in F. F. Segovia and M. A. Tolbert (eds.), *Reading from This Place, Vol. 2: Social Location and Biblical Interpretation in Global Perspective* (Minneapolis, MN: Fortress, 1995), pp. 82–96, p. 85.

[13] Comment from R. Rebera (ed.), *We Cannot Dream Alone* (Geneva: WCC, 1990), pp. 72–6, from the "Programme on Women and Rural Development of the World Council of Churches," cited in King, (ed.), *Feminist Theology*, p. 201.

[14] A. Maente Machema, "Jumping Culture's Fences," in M. A. Oduyoye and M. Kanyoro (eds.), *Talitha, qumi! Proceedings of the Convocation of African Women Theologians* (Ibadan: Daystar, 1990), pp. 131–5, p. 133. See the similar comments in T. Cavalcanti, "Jesus, the Penitent Woman, and the Pharisee," *Journal of Hispanic-Latino Theology* 2.1 (1994), pp. 28–40, p. 29. I thank Teresa Hornsby for this reference. For an alternative, see below, n. 15.

[15] A. de Rocchietti, "Women and the People of God," in E. Tamez (ed.), *Through Her Eyes. Women's Theology from Latin America* (Maryknoll, N.Y.: Orbis Books, 1989), pp. 96–117, pp. 106, 107. The next article, T. Cavalcanti's "The Prophetic Ministry of Women in the Hebrew Bible" (pp. 118–39), offers an alternative and much more helpful reading.

his own sexual purity. This means that women are confined in inside spaces in the house or the village."[16]

– And well she remained there, since "The wife was also held responsible for the husband's piety or wickedness. Women in general were believed to be 'gluttonous, eavesdroppers, lazy and jealous,' devoid of intellectual capacity, and living only for self-ornamentation."[17]

In contrast to this monolithic social and religious context emerges a Jesus either untouched by or deliberately rejecting his culture: "As a Jewish rabbi,[18] [Jesus] . . . chose to ignore the traditional Jewish attitudes and instead treated women with compassion and complete acceptance. For his pains he earned the reputation of being the friend of sinners."[19] Thus, "Jesus was a revolutionary [language of "revolution" appears especially in African women's writings.] He never tortured [women], nor segregated them, nor demanded purification rites."[20]

Another critic avers: Jesus was not like the Jews, who "excluded foreigners from [their] ethnic borders in order to retain their purity of blood."[21]

The suggestion that Jesus was the only Jewish man to treat women with compassion is at best ahistorical-apologetic; the connection between "friend of women" and "friend of sinners" is at best overdrawn. The implication that the Jewish system tortured women is

---

[16] H. Kinukawa, *Women and Jesus in Mark. A Japanese Feminist Perspective* (The Bible and Liberation Series; Maryknoll, N.Y.: Orbis Books, 1994), p. 12.

[17] This is but a sample (here citing *Genesis Rabbah*) of the description of Jewish women, from T. Okure, "Women in the Bible," in Fabella and Oduyoye (eds.), *With Passion and Compassion*, pp. 47–59, p. 50.

[18] A frequent tautology.

[19] B. Ekeya, "Woman, For How Long Not?," in King (ed.), *Feminist Theology*, pp. 139–48, p. 145. The same prayer is cited by C. del Prado, "I Sense God in Another Way," in Tamez (ed.), *Through Her Eyes*, pp. 140–9, p. 146, and by T. Okure, "The Will to Arise: Reflections on Luke 8:40–56," in M. A. Oduyoye and M. R. A. Kanyoro (eds.), *The Will to Arise. Women, Tradition, and the Church in Africa* (Maryknoll, N.Y.: Orbis Books, 1992), pp. 221–30, p. 226, who goes on to contextualize Jairus as living in a society where men prayed that the Deity should "'keep thee from daughters' (Rabbinic interpretation of the blessing of Moses, Num. 6:22–27)."

[20] R. N. Edet, "Christianity and African Women's Rituals," in Oduyoye and Kanyoro (eds.), *Will to Arise*, pp. 25–39, p. 37. See also A. Nasimiyu-Wasike, "Polygamy: A Feminist Critique," in *Will to Arise*, pp. 101–18, p. 110, on Jesus who rejected the "Jewish law . . . that took women's inferior status for granted," and idem, "Christology and an African-Woman's Experience," in R. J. Schreiter (ed.), *Faces of Jesus in Africa* (Maryknoll, N.Y.: Orbis, 1991), pp. 70–81, on Jesus' revolutionary message.

[21] Kinukawa, *Women and Jesus*, p. 61.

slanderous. The comments on Jewish particularism ignore the universalistic hopes of Zechariah and Tobit and appear unaware of the numerous conversions of women and men to Judaism in antiquity. The assumption that women had no religious roles (contra the arguments of Brooten, Kraemer, and others), were confined to the home (as if all Jewish homes in the Galilee and Judea, let alone urban Corinth or Athens, had women's quarters, or even more than one room), that women did not appear in public (contrast even the Gospels, which depict women in public frequently, with no one in the text commenting on the anomaly of this freedom), that Jewish men took no personal responsibility for their actions, that *Genesis Rabbah* is legal material, or descriptive of actual society, or a window into pre-70 Judaism, etc., only touch upon the problems of these constructs.

Whether Jesus was a "feminist," let alone whether his "acceptance" of women extended to re-formulations of gender roles or the social system, are at best debated topics. Whether Jesus engaged in a gentile mission, or commanded his disciples to do so, is yet another question.

These popular pronouncements even appear in *Searching the Scriptures*, the pre-eminent feminist collection which explicitly both notes anti-Judaism to be a problem in Christian feminist exegesis and seeks to "protect against Christian anti-Semitism."[22]

In an article on Mark, we read: "The dominant Jewish view of the time was that Gd's holiness must be protected from pollution, impurity, or uncleanness. . . . women were considered less clean than men and constituted a perennial threat of pollution to men. . . . Women were considered dangerously impure."[23] The same collection of adjectives appears in the piece on Matthew: the "inclusive nature of the Basileia" includes "not only those who are sick but also those whom the dominant culture considers unclean or pollutants."[24] The treatment of Luke similarly states: "for most of the women healing means being freed from a constant state of impurity."[25] They appear elsewhere,[26] such that "menstruating women" are described

---

[22] J. Dewey, "Gospel of Mark," in Schüssler Fiorenza (ed.), *Searching the Scriptures, Vol. 2*, pp. 470–509, p. 505.

[23] Dewey, "Mark," pp. 471, 481.

[24] E. Wainwright, "Gospel of Matthew," in Schüssler Fiorenza (ed.), *Searching the Scriptures, Vol. 2*, pp. 635–77, p. 647.

[25] T. Karlsen Seim, "Gospel of Luke," in Schüssler Fiorenza (ed.), *Searching the Scriptures, Vol. 2*, pp. 728–62, p. 728.

[26] For example, "Jewish laws concerning ritual purity were particularly biased against women. Since women were menstruants by nature, they could not be relied

as "discriminated against, degraded, and dehumanized,"[27] as well as, finally, "untouchable."[28] In turn, we read that "Jesus held an alternative Jewish view; instead of understanding contact with the unclean as polluting the pure, Jesus enacted Gd's holiness by ignoring purity boundaries to declare clean what was unclean. Thus Jesus wipes out the discrimination against women that was based on the pervasive purity codes."[29]

"Purity" is never defined.[30] The distinction among "pollution, uncleanness, and impurity" is never explained. Moreover, such "feminist readings" not only associate "pollution, uncleanness, and impurity" with women, they both impose it where the text offers no hint, and they ignore it when it might be relevant to men.

On the one hand, a feminist reading of Matthew describes Peter's mother-in-law as "a possible pollutant, especially if this sickness [her fever] is connected to her time of ritual uncleanness."[31] Extending this negative life for women to daughters, we find a Judaism that despises the birth of girls: "The birth of a daughter is such bad news, because the baby is unwelcome and her mother is subjected

---

upon at all times to be ritually clean. For this reason, they were barred, as a sex, for life for sacred places and ministries in Judaism" (Okure, "Women in the Bible," p. 55). "Jesus wanted to free those who were disinherited, rejected, sinners, pagans, marginalized in any way, including women and children who were not considered very important in Jewish society. . . . By accepting women as they were, including their bodies, considered weak and unclean in their own culture. . . ." So M. C. Bingemer, "Reflections on the Trinity," in Tamez (ed.), *Through Her Eyes*, pp. 56–80, p. 72. Bingemer goes on to list passages in which "Jesus did not shun bodily contact with women."

[27] Kinukawa, *Women and Jesus*, p. 37.

[28] So, for example, from the West, J. Grant, "Becoming Subjects in the Christological Debate," in J. S. Pobee (ed.), *Exploring Afro-Christology* (Frankfurt a. M.: Peter Lang, 1992), pp. 65–83, p. 74 (on Matt. 9:20–22; Mark 5:25–34; Luke 8:43–48). Grant views Jesus as "challeng[ing] the . . . laws of his time regarding women" (p. 76), although she neither cites these "laws" nor recognizes the debates over them in formative Judaism.

[29] Dewey, "Mark," p. 471.

[30] Dewey's lack of understanding of the subject is epitomized by a comment on Mark 7:31–37: "Jesus is portrayed as using spittle to heal a deaf-mute man. Spittle, like blood or a leper's pus, comes out of the body and was therefore unclean" (Dewey, "Mark," p. 485). Spittle is only unclean if its source is unclean. The pus is unclean because it comes from a leper, who is unclean. Blood is unclean if it comes from the genitals (but not, for example, the blood drawn in the act of circumcision) or from a person who is in a state of impurity. Other materials that come from the body—breast milk, tears, urine, feces, sweat, etc.—are only unclean if the person himself or herself is unclean from some other factor, such as just having had sexual intercourse and prior to ritual immersion.

[31] Wainwright, "Matthew," p. 648.

to eighty days of restrictions."[32] We even learn, finally, that Jewish women aren't a part of the covenant. Quoting one of the patrons of liberation theology, Leonardo Boff, yet another writer regards Jesus' relations with women as "not only innovative, but shocking" because women were "not circumcised and hence could not be part of Gd's covenant."[33] Into what, then, were Jewish women born? Into what, then, did female proselytes to Judaism convert?

On the other hand, no commentator ever wonders if, with the exception of lepers, the men whom Jesus heals are "ritually unclean"— from ejaculation, from having buried a corpse, from sitting on a menstruating woman's chair, etc. Nor do they explain what the effects of "uncleanness" are; thus, the reader is left to associate unclean- ness with moral failing, sin, alienation, and dirt rather than see purity legislation as a social system concerned, in Jesus' time, primarily with participation in Temple sacrifice. From what, specifically, new moth- ers are restricted is not described; how they are restricted is not noted; the quite plausible very positive effects of halachic practice on their physical health, social relations, and emotional state are ignored.

In addition to condemnation of anything Jewish, this feminist dis- course denounces Judaism by means of skewed comparative models. The commentary on 1 Thess. 4 in *Searching the Scriptures* notes that the language on self-restraint comes from Paul, "the former Pharisee," whose "argument in vv. 3–5 is loaded with stereotyped Jewish con- tempt of non-Jews in its caricature of pagan licentiousness. By enjoin- ing the former pagans to demonstrate their new Christian identity in accordance with Mosaic rules of purity and superior exclusive- ness, Paul illustrates how comprehensive was the influence of tradi- tional Jewish interpretation on his formative Christian teaching, especially related to gender and sociosexual morality."[34]

---

[32] Kinukawa, *Women and Jesus*, p. 35; see also de Rocchietti, "Women and the People of God," p. 106. Following the work of M. J. Selvidge (*Women, Cult, and Miracle Recital: A Redaction Critical Investigation on Mark 5:24–34* [Lewisburg, PA: Buck- nell University; London: Associated University Presses, 1990], p. 55) Kinukawa con- tinues: "If she attempts to keep the command given to Noah to reproduce (Gen. 9:1), she would be secluded at least eighty days out of every year if she was pregnant, and up to ninety-one days if she was not pregnant" (p. 36). One wonders how Jewish society survived, with all those peasant women removed from the workforce.

[33] Bingemer, "Reflections on the Trinity," p. 71, citing L. Boff, *The Maternal Face of God* (San Francisco, CA: Harper & Row, 1987), p. 81.

[34] L. Fatum, "1 Thessalonians," in Schüssler Fiorenza (ed.), *Searching the Scriptures*, *Vol. 2*, pp. 250–62, p. 258. A. Clark Wire's otherwise astute reading of 1 Corinthians 6 in the same volume (pp. 153–95) blames Judaism for Paul's denunciation of same-

Correct in indicating that Jewish sources of the Graeco-Roman period frequently condemn gentile licentiousness, the comment mis-directs on at least three counts. First, it is by no means clear that the Pharisees specifically cared about pagan licentiousness; their focus was on their fellow Jews. Moreover, the citation conveys the unfor-tunate and unsupported impression that Pharisees were obsessed with sexuality. Second, to delimit Paul's rhetoric to his "Pharisaic back-ground" unnecessarily narrows his cultural influences; Pharisaism, and Paul, both existed within a larger Hellenistic society. Emphasis on Paul's Judaism brackets the fact that "moral values" (however defined) were also a prominent concern in non-Jewish circles of which Paul too was a part. This pattern of negatively portraying Judaism while failing to remark on the universal pervasiveness of patriarchy, is another typical ploy. Even where such arguments have claims to historical accuracy, e.g., on gender differentiation in Judaism, they are incomplete, since the same structure appears throughout antiq-uity.[35] Third, the phrase "stereotyped Jewish contempt of non-Jews" erases those positive relations between Jews and non-Jews, from con-verts to the godfearers to views of righteous gentiles to daily inter-action between Jews and gentiles.

Skewed comparisons are also occasioned by projection of the mod-ern social location into Jewish antiquity.[36] One author writes, "Thus

---

sex practices: "the reference to male homosexuality reflects the more inflammatory aspects of Hellenistic Jewish rhetoric against what they considered Gentile sins (Wis. 19:14–17)" ("1 Corinthians," in Schüssler Fiorenza [ed.], *Searching the Scriptures, Vol. 2*, p. 167). True, Jewish texts of the period are vehemently against same-sex relations. So are non-Jewish texts. To locate Paul's rhetoric only within his Jewish context skews the model; indeed, Paul's comment would more likely have had an impact on the Corinthians if they were familiar with it from the context of their own (gentile) culture.

[35] Kinukawa, *Women and Jesus*, p. 37, again following Selvidge (*Women, Cult*, p. 55), states, "It is very interesting to read that a woman's menstrual cycle was consid-ered a time of cleansing (*katharos*) to the Greeks, while the Jews added a negative prefix and called it unclean (*akathartos, akatharsia*)." For a more comprehensive, salu-tary reading of this language see M. R. D'Angelo's forthcoming study on Mark's haemorrhaging woman.

[36] For example, in her blurb to Kinukawa's *Women and Jesus*, A. Clark Wire writes, "Here we see the remarkable exegetical fruits when an author grafts her agility in [recent] Western interpretation on to roots in an Eastern shame-oriented, patriarchal society." The phenomenon is by no means limited to women, or to feminists. See Chan-Hie Kim, "Reading the Cornelius Story from an Asian-Immigrant Perspective," in F. F. Segovia and M. A. Tolbert (eds.), *Reading from This Place, Vol. 1: Social Location and Biblical Interpretation in the United States* (Minneapolis, MN: Fortress, 1995), pp. 165–74, pp. 172–3: "[M]ost of the mainline U.S. Protestant churches do not seem to realize that these [new immigrants] are the 'gentile' Christians

in our [Japanese] society, just as in first-century Palestine, religious purity codes have contributed to . . . various kinds of segregation."[37] Another avers: "women in India have not come very far from Judaic times," where women were "powerless, nameless, voiceless."[38] Beyond the unsupported stereotype that in "Judaic times" (what times were these? what times are we in now?) women were powerless is the unstated corollary: how far women in India have come from "Vedic times."

This perennial view of a retrograde "Judaic times" is created not only by projection but also by a facile reading of the TaNaK. When sources are cited, usually Lev. 12, 15, and 20, they are typically identified as "Jewish Law" rather than, say, "Torah" or "Scripture." Marcion again comes to mind. Moreover, Levitical materials are assumed to be practiced in particularly rigorous, segregationist ways in the Second Temple period. For example, one critic insists: "Women are unclean not only during their menstrual periods, but they also must be secluded for a week thereafter."[39] Yet no one argues that recalcitrant youths are stoned weekly at the city gates, and no one states where these women were "secluded." (Should we think of those equally hypothetical synagogue balconies?)

---

who do not know and are not willing to accept 'Jewish' laws and practices." The article argues for Peter's, and our, "recognition of multiplicity of our cultures," but in the next sentence it claims that "the Jewish regulations about clean and unclean are not valid, indeed that they contradict the nature of God as the Creator of all living things" (p. 173). Why, I wonder, are only some cultures and cultural practices worthy of respect?

[37] Kinukawa, *Women and Jesus*, pp. 30–1.

[38] A. Gnanadason, "Women's Oppression: A Sinful Situation," in Fabella and Oduyoye (eds.), *With Passion and Compassion*, pp. 69–76, pp. 71, 72. However, Gnanadason also cites Tertullian, Ambrose, John Chrysostom, and John Damascene's misogynistic tendencies.

[39] Kinukawa, *Women and Jesus*, p. 35. An ironic intertext is the observation that "the first Japanese company to market sanitary napkins especially for Japanese women called itself Anne Co., Ltd., and it sold its product under the brand name 'Anne's day' (*Anne no hi*), which quickly became a euphemism for menstruation in Japan." The "Anne" is Anne Frank. See D. G. Goodman and M. Miyazawa, *Jews in the Japanese Mind. The History and Uses of a Cultural Stereotype* (New York: Free Press, 1995), p. 6. See esp. chap. 8, "A Signal Failure. Recrudescent Antisemitism and Japan's 'Spiritual Condition,'" for the denial of anti-Semitism by Japanese intellectuals during the 1980s, when anti-Semitic volumes (e.g., Y. Motohisa's *The Jewish Plot to Control the World*; Y. Kinji's *The Expert Way of Reading the Jewish Protocols*; S. Eisaburo's *The Secret of Jewish Power that Moves the World*; U. Masami's *If You Understand the Jews, You Will Understand the World*, etc.), filled Japanese bookstores, and K. Foumeko's (possibly? unquestionably?) anti-Semitic *Passover* (key passages were excised from English versions) won two prestigious national prizes. This footnote, of course, indicates the problem of stereotyping a culture.

Occasionally, prejudicial and anachronistic citations from the Talmud and Midrashim, or unquestioning readings of secondary sources, appear. The hermeneutics of suspicion tends to be on hold when the subject is formative Judaism. Rather than read the primary sources themselves, place them in historical contexts, explore the problematics of moving from idealistic text to social history, etc., many contemporary feminist studies, some displaying the pressed, desiccated petals of Strack-Billerbeck or, more usually, the citations of others who cited Strack-Billerbeck, continue to repeat the older views.

The favorite passage for locating a patriarchal, purity-obsessed, repressive Jewish system is the account of the haemorrhaging woman, a passage which, although it appears in all three Synoptics, never cites Leviticus, never mentions impurity, never expresses surprise that a bleeding woman would be in public or that Jesus would touch a corpse, never portrays Jesus as abrogating any law. Having elsewhere addressed general studies of Matthew's version, I concentrate here on how explicitly feminist and liberationist women read, indeed celebrate, the pericope.[40]

Teresa Okure notes that for African women readers, Luke 8:40–56 is "a cherished passage." As she summarizes:

> It is treated by M. Kanyoro in *Talitha, qumi!* and by Elizabeth Amoah in *New Eyes for Reading*. Both works emphasize the woman's courage in breaking with crippling cultural taboos imposed on her so as to reach Jesus directly and be fully restored and integrated as a person with full rights in her society.[41]

---

[40] A.-J. Levine, "Discharging Responsibility: Matthean Jesus, Biblical Law, and Hemorrhaging Woman," in D. R. Bauer and M. A. Powell (eds.), *Treasures New and Old. Contributions to Matthean Studies* (SBL Symposium Series, 1; Atlanta, GA: Scholars, 1996), pp. 379–97.

[41] Okure, "Feminist Interpretations," p. 82 (emphasis mine). The same perspective appears in Dewey, "Mark," pp. 481, 505 ("the woman with the hemorrhage challenged Jesus on women's purity issues"). E. Amoah, "The Woman Who Decided to Break the Rules [Reflection, Mk. 5:25–29]," in Pobee and von Wartenberg-Potter (eds.), *New Eyes*, pp. 3–4, p. 3, compares the woman's situation to an Akan tradition (apparently no longer practiced) from Ghana concerning menstrual taboos, and she notes that "added to [the woman's] physical misery were the requirements of the Israelite ceremonial laws about impurities, as stipulated in Leviticus 15:19ff." M. Kanyoro ("Daughter, Arise. Luke 8:40–56," in Oduyoye and Kanyoro [eds.], *Talitha, qumi!*, pp. 54–62) assumes that Levitical Laws governed Second Temple Jewish culture and speaks of the woman's potential to "contaminate others" and "defile Jesus" (p. 57); her "Aids to the Text" section begins by noting that "Faithful Jews . . . believed that uncleanliness was offensive to God's holiness, and that it would separate them from God" (p. 60). Surely not all new mothers or those who prepared corpses saw themselves as so separated (cf. Tobit).

Okure herself hails Jesus, who "touched and allowed himself to be touched by those who were legally classified as unclean, such as the woman with the issue of blood." Therefore, "to continue to exclude women from certain Christian ministries on the basis of outmoded Jewish taboos is to render null and void the liberation that Jesus won for us."[42] I doubt Jewish women, who adhere to the Laws of family purity, would appreciate the classification of their traditional practices as "outmoded taboos." I doubt her opponents would view their own perspectives on women's ordination as "Jewish." Turid Karlsen Seim avers that both the woman with the haemorrhage and Abraham's other daughter, the "bent-over woman" (Luke 13:10–17), are "sick, socially stigmatized, and impure" and the "impure persons were normally regarded as a threat to the collective purity of the people."[43] While Seim cares extensively about ritually unclean women, apparently those attending Luke's synagogue did not. Nor is it clear how the bent-over woman was "impure."

Lieve Troch asserts that the woman in Mark 5:33–34

> breaks through the stigmatization of being an outcast, which led to her full presence in the community. . . . Her vision of life, society, the political, social, and religious position of women surely must have been different from what was allowed to her in the context of a patriarchal design.[44]

Why no one stopped the woman in public, how she made her way to physicians, why not even the disciples caviled against her presence, is never addressed.

Hisako Kinukawa subtitles her chapter on Mark 5:25–34, "Patriarchal Discrimination against Women Reinforced by Religion: The Polluted."[45] Giving several examples of "purity" (especially concerning menstruation and childbirth) coupled with Buddhist, Shinto, and Confucian ideology, she provides no examples regarding formative Judaism. Reading from the perspective of what she perceives to be

---

[42] Okure, "Women in the Bible," p. 55. In "The Will to Arise," p. 222, Okure adds that the woman approached Jesus from behind either because she "was a source of uncleanliness and contamination" [citing Lev. 15:25–30] or because "in Jewish society it was considered indecent for a woman to speak publicly with a man."

[43] Seim, "Luke," pp. 737–8.

[44] L. Troch, "A Method of Conscientization: Feminist Bible Study in the Netherlands," in Schüssler Fiorenza (ed.), *Searching the Scriptures, Vol. 1*, pp. 351–66, pp. 361–2 (emphasis mine).

[45] Kinukawa, *Women and Jesus*, p. 29.

a shame-based position for women in Japan, she claims: "We can feel vividly how brave the hemorrhaging woman was and how revolutionary and liberated Jesus was, all the more so in first-century Palestine where the purity codes were openly enforced" and where "it was never permissible for socially banned persons to come into the crowd and touch anyone, because they contaminate others and break down the integrity of the holy community."[46] [What power all these Jewish women must have had!] For Kinukawa, the woman's "unusually strong desire for recovery points up for us the religious and therefore inevitable social oppression she has to face because of the purity laws."[47] Feeling herself "degraded,"[48] the woman is comparable to the "outcast" people in Japan, who live in segregated villages, must wear certain clothes, are restricted to particular marriage partners, lack family registration, and therefore suffer unbelievable alienation. In turn, Jesus, who "negates the purity laws by ignoring them," "must see her as a person dehumanized by the laws that have been used only to satisfy the honor of men with power."[49]

How laws concerning women affected men in the Gospels is a subject the evangelists do not address. How strong desire indicates social oppression is assumed, not demonstrated. Where the woman's distinct social markings appear cannot be located: if they could, she would not have gotten through Mark's crowd. How lack of reference (i.e., Jesus' "ignoring the laws") indicates an abrogation is neither connected to his injunction that the leper visit a priest nor explained in terms of logic: absence of reference is not the same thing as negation.

Louise Tappa states that the woman "is impure, which from a religious standpoint makes her an outcast," especially since in "Leviticus one can find all kinds of taboos that were in effect during that period." Tappa even explains the mechanism of enforcement: "we must form an idea of Jairus, who in the Jewish community is the one who must make sure that this woman stays where she is. He is a Jewish dignitary and it is precisely his task to make sure that this

---

[46] Kinukawa, *Women and Jesus*, pp. 32, 41.
[47] Kinukawa, *Women and Jesus*, pp. 39–40.
[48] Kinukawa, *Women and Jesus*, p. 35.
[49] Kinukawa, *Women and Jesus*, p. 46. Kinukawa contrasts Jesus' speaking to the women with *Aboth* 1:1 (ca. 250 C.E.), and appeals to L. Swidler's *Women in Judaism* (Metuchen, N.J.: Scarecrow, 1976).

person who is socially dead stays in her place."[50] The confusion of Temple and synagogue, the ahistorical treatment of Leviticus, and the projection of stereotypes only begin to identify the problems with this construction.

Elaine Wainwright is well aware that the history of reception of Matthew has "created a 'politics of otherness' in relation to Judaism."[51] However, this politics is perpetuated in her insistence that the "menstruating woman"[52] is "most likely excluded" from the patriarchal household "because of her condition" of being "ritually unclean, a pollutant."[53] [It becomes difficult to tell from these readings whether the woman is restricted to the home or barred from it.] In turn, the dead child is "introduced as one of the most severe pollutants—a corpse,"[54] such that "each of the females who enters this combined story is encountered as a pollutant, outside the boundaries of ritual cleanliness."[55] Similarly, María Clara Bingemer insists: "As well as breaking the taboo that marginalized women, Jesus redeemed their bodiliness which had been humiliated and proscribed by Jewish law."[56] Once again, do halachically observant Jewish women find their bodiliness humiliated by Jewish law? Do halachically observant Jews leave corpses to rot in the street? Does no one these days read the Book of Tobit?

To observe that purity does not concern dirt, that there is no necessary correlation between purity concerns and fulfilling of *mitzvot* (one is commanded to be fruitful and multiply; sexual intercourse, involving ejaculation, puts both participants in an impure state; it is a *mitzvah* to bury corpses), that the rabbis discuss menstruating women reading Torah, etc., is only a start in redressing these problems.

Unsupported and insupportable historical views of a misogynistic, essentialist, atavistic Judaism lead naturally to theological speculation.

---

[50] L. Tappa, "The Christ-event from the Viewpoint of African Women: A Protestant Perspective," in Fabella and Oduyoye (eds.), *With Passion and Compassion*, pp. 30–4, p. 32.

[51] Wainwright, "Matthew," p. 636.

[52] Wainwright, "Matthew," p. 637. Matthew does not identify the source of the flow.

[53] Wainwright, "Matthew," p. 649.

[54] Wainwright, "Matthew," p. 649.

[55] Wainwright, "Matthew," p. 650. The *Basileia* vision then enables these "most dangerous of pollutant . . . to cross the boundaries that exclude them" (p. 666).

[56] M. C. Bingemer, "Women in the Future of the Theology of Liberation," in King (ed.), *Feminist Theology*, pp. 308–18, p. 314.

The bad history reflected in these numerous citations culminates in a theology that at best can be labelled obscene.

In a World Council of Churches' 1986 collection (the WCC is a major exporter of this sort of drivel) we find:

"Jesus died as a result of the clash between his God [capitalized] and the god [small "g"] of Pharisaic Judaism. . . . Jesus' crucifixion marked the temporal triumph of the patriarchal god of Judaism. . . . But alas, Christianity has fallen back to the patriarchal god of Judaism with even greater zeal. . . . The god of the clan will sanctify any-thing including militarism, war, sexism, apartheid, as long as it serves the interest of the clan."[57] Marcion could not have put it better.

From the same volume: "God who cried out from the cross" was the one "who suffered under the oppressive Jewish tradition."[58] Explaining how and why "the Bible has been used to reinforce the position of inferiority in which society and culture have placed women for centuries," critics lay the blame at the feet of "the Hebrew-Jewish lifestyle,"[59] the "Jewish patriarchal system,"[60] (the expression "Jewish patriarchal system" is a litany in such writings) and the "Jewish back-ground" of Paul.[61]

To a great extent, familiarity with primary sources, with studies of Judaism and women's history, and my own personal interest in the subject of Christian anti-Judaism, allows me to spot these rotten roots. Yet these concerns do not explain why such observation is not being done globally; to name the problem is only to find the blossom; the roots of anti-Jewish readings and the fertilizers that keep them growing also need to be named and removed.

---

[57] L. Kumandjek Tappa, "God in Man's Image," in Pobee and von Wartenberg-Potter (eds.), *New Eyes*, pp. 101–6, p. 102.

[58] Kwok Pui-lan, "God Weeps with Our Pain," in Pobee and von Wartenberg-Potter (eds.), *New Eyes*, pp. 90–5, p. 92.

[59] E. Tamez, "Women's Rereading of the Bible," in King, (ed.), *Feminist Theology*, pp. 190–200, p. 192.

[60] L. Fanusie, "Sexuality and Women in African Culture," in Oduyoye and Kanyoro (eds.), *Will to Arise*, pp. 135–54, p. 140: "The many setbacks faced by women in Christianity are usually rooted in the Scriptures that, for the most part, are a heritage from the Jewish patriarchal system." See also M. Assaad, "Reversing the Natural Order," in Pobee and von Wartenberg-Potter (eds.), *New Eyes*, pp. 25–7, p. 25; reprinted in King, (ed.), *Feminist Theology*, pp. 204–6, p. 204, on "patriarchal Jewish society."

[61] R. Modupe Owanikin, "The Priesthood of Church Women in the Nigerian Context," in Oduyoye and Kanyoro (eds.), *Will to Arise*, pp. 206–19, pp. 210, 215: "Perhaps the lowly status of women in Jewish society was carried over to the early Christian idea of women's roles in religious ceremonies and assemblies," and that

Roots and Fertilizers

In some cases, anti-Jewish readings may be attributed to limited access to sources: for some global locations (including, on occasion, Tennessee, where I live), neither the primary sources nor the latest works on formative Judaism or feminist criticism are available. Interpreters do what they can with what they have.

However, I am not optimistic that entire Judaica libraries would eliminate anti-Jewish re-constructions, any more than volume after volume of feminist criticism necessarily changes the work of many biblical studies specialists. In cases where the author is well aware of the problems of theological anti-Judaism, the negative stereotypes continue. After positively citing Judith Plaskow's work, one commentator asserts:

"*On the other hand*, Third World women as gentiles or pagans are painfully aware of the ethnocentrism, rejection, and disdain of Jews toward the outsiders."[62] The source for such "disdaining" is never cited; I cannot tell if the author is referring to Abraham, Ezra, Hillel, the Baal Shem Tov, or me. Should her reader not yet be convinced of the evils of Judaism, this same author goes on to state that "without blaming the Jews for killing the goddess," we should also "reflect on the circumstances leading to the emergence of monotheism with its predominant androcentric symbolism and the historical implications thereof."[63] How one engages such reflection, especially without blaming Judaism, is not noted, nor does the author indicate that polytheism and female divinities do not themselves necessarily create the good life for women.

Change—social, political, academic, etc.—depends in great measure on personal contact. Studies done apart from work on Judaism

---

Paul's injunction on women [in 1 Cor. 14] could be due to his "Jewish background." Finally, see R. A. James, "The Scope of Women's Participation in the Church," in Oduyoye and Kanyoro (eds.), *Talitha, qumi!*, pp. 173–9, p. 176, on Paul's having "retained certain aspects of Jewish culture [where] . . . women were seen as . . . unclean. . . . Jewish tradition and culture should not continue to be adopted as laws and commandments for today's church women."

[62] Kwok, "Future of Feminist Theology," p. 71 (emphasis mine).

[63] Kwok, "Future of Feminist Theology," p. 71. See also the editors' positive assessment of L. Boff's discussion (*Trinity and Society* [Maryknoll, N.Y.: Orbis Books, 1988], pp. 20–33) of "the political dangers of a-trinitarian monotheism," in S. Brooks Thistlethwaite and M. Potter Engel (eds.), *Constructing Christian Theologies from the Underside* (San Francisco, CA: HarperSanFrancisco, 1990), p. 79.

as well as from contact with Jews also lead to unfortunate catego-
rizations. Just as male readers increasingly recognize sexist presuppositions when confronted with women in their classrooms and
conferences, so too non-Jews may think twice about making pronouncements about how Judaism functions when their audience
and colleagues contain Jews. This is not to say that scholars should
censor their comments; nor is it an assertion that Judaism throughout history has been unfailingly perfect. Rather, it is a plea for historical rigour, precision in language, and recognition of the dangers
of stereotyping.

The acuteness of the problem appeared in my own classroom,
where a graduate student confessed to me after one particularly
difficult semester: "The word for 'Jew' in my [tribal] language means
someone who deceives or betrays; it's taken me a while to get over
that." Social-location based readings need to be aware not only of
the position of the author (according to race, class, ethnicity, etc.),
but also of that author's context and experiences (in a racially or
religiously integrated context, among Christians only, among Roman
Catholics only, etc.).

This observation has a specific academic correlate. Many studies
in Christian origins are developed in theological schools where there
are few courses in formative Judaism, let alone in Mishnaic Hebrew,
or Talmud and Midrash. Even fewer Ph.D. programs in Christian
origins (including my own at Vanderbilt) require students to have
familiarity with Jewish sources (Dead Sea Scrolls, Josephus, Philo,
Apocrypha and Pseudepigrapha, archaeological and epigraphic data,
etc.). The condition is all the worse in the new seminaries arising
in Asia, Africa, and Latin America, where there are fewer Jewish
sources, let alone Jewish people, and where the increasing and entirely
laudable interest in the plight of Palestinian Christians easily serves
to correlate "Judaism" with Israeli hard-liners.[64]

In other cases, the ostensibly feminist-critical hermeneutical ap-

---

[64] The use of "Zionism" is also problematic, cf. such references to the "ruling
class zionist consciousness of the Old Testament" which creates an "ideologically . . .
less liberatory" perspective (I. J. Mosala, "Race, Class and Gender as Hermeneutical
Factors in the African Independent Churches' Appropriation of the Bible," in G. West
and M. W. Dube [eds.], *"Reading With": An Exploration of the Interface between Critical
and Ordinary Readings of the Bible. African Overtures* [*Semeia*, 73; Atlanta, GA: Scholars,
1996], pp. 43–57, p. 52). "Zionism" is not defined (does it imply that people are
entitled to a land, racial superiority, a form of colonialism or a resistance to it,
etc.?); one may suspect negative connotations.

proach exists not just in creative dialogue with and corrective to the historical-critical method but in complete opposition to historical investigation. Historical-critical work[65] is seen as colonial in origin, arbitrary in practice, and irrelevant in the lives of women and men of the believing communities. Such ahistoricism threatens to reify interpretations, to read out of history the roles played by women and those outside the majority groups, and to preserve stereotypes hardly to be celebrated.

The discouraging aspect to all of this is that the new generation of feminist readers is to a great extent perpetuating the older generation's reified, negative view of Judaism. Worse, as women scholars begin to write for their own communities in Asia, Africa, Latin America, Eastern Europe, etc., the weed of anti-Judaism threatens to overrun the new plantings. I do not think we have the luxury of waiting until the final harvest before wheat and chaff are separated.

Anti-Judaism may show up simply because it lies beneath our Western culture; as Cornel West puts it, "Anti-Semitism is as Christian as the New Testament and as American as cherry pie."[66] Yet neither explanation necessarily holds for the international readings. Thus, we are still left to question the sources for the anti-Judaism in global writings. Is it a Western export, is it a scapegoating projection of the problems of contemporary culture coupled with a docetic Christology, is it the remainder of a post-colonial dialectic in which writers have abjected their (Christian) colonizers' own abjected others (i.e., Jews) that had once been used to mediate racist domination,[67] or is it a product of the Bible itself?

From my own social location as a Jewish woman who gives a damn about the effect of readings of the Gospels on scholars and

---

[65] For a helpful commentary on the objectivist basis of historical-critical work, see Kwok, "Racism and Ethnocentrism," pp. 103–4.

[66] C. West, "Forward," in M. Brettschneider (ed.), *The Narrow Bridge. Jewish Views on Multiculturalism* (New Brunswick, N.J.: Rutgers University Press, 1996), pp. xi–xiv, p. xi.

[67] For an analysis of how "Fanon's resolutely masculine self-identifications, articulated through abjectification of femininity and homosexuality [i.e., the masculinist colonizer's abjects] take shape over and against colonialism's castrating representations of black male sexuality," see D. Fuss, *Identification Papers* (London and New York: Routledge, 1995), p. 160. Fanon critiques colonialism but accepts its terms of analysis: the masculine; similarly, these (post-)colonial women critique domination but appear to accept its terms by portraying Christianity as supersessionist and in reformulating and abstracting the condemnation of indigenous ritual into condemnation of "Jewish" practice.

laity (in part because I have myself experienced Christian anti-
Judaism and, worse, because it has attacked my children) and who
is convinced that the Gospels can carry a liberatory message without a strong overlay of anti-Judaism, I find these readings are bad
history and bad theology. I also find that they are not inevitable.

"Reading with" women outside the biblical studies guild tends not
to yield anti-Jewish readings; such negativizing is not, therefore, the
only or "natural" reading of the texts.[68] The absence of anti-Jewish
views in non-Western, non-academic readings may be occasioned by
the women's lack of biblical literacy, but I do not think in cases of
pericopae dealing with women (remarks on, e.g., the haemorrhaging woman, the Syrophoenician or Canaanite woman, divorce pronouncements, Paul) that lack of detailed biblical knowledge is the
cause. These materials do not specifically cite women's roles in Judaism as a negative foil.

The absence I think is rather caused to a great extent by the
women's lack of access to, or interest in, biblical scholarship. In other
words, the problem of anti-Judaism can in great measure be laid at
the feet of "us," the scholars.[69] We Western feminists imbibed anti-
Judaism as the mother's milk of our own academic training; we took
what we were taught in many of our "New Testament" classes and
what we read in mainstream "New Testament scholarship," and
extended the argument to women's concerns. I know this; I have
done it myself.[70] Before (male) scholars such as, especially, E. P.
Sanders[71] detailed in major publications the extent of anti-Jewish
reading, many of us were exposed to no other picture of Jesus' social
context. Then we women, wherever we went, perpetuated the problem. Much of the anti-Judaism named in this paper thus appears to

---

[68] See, for example, A. Verhoeven, "The Concept of Gd: A Feminine Perspective,"
in Tamez (ed.), *Through Her Eyes*, pp. 49–55.

[69] E.g., anti-Judaism never surfaces (nor does Judaism) in, e.g., A. M. Isasi-Díaz
and Y. Tarango, *Hispanic Women. Prophetic Voice in the Church. Toward a Hispanic
Women's Liberation Theology* (San Francisco, CA: Harper & Row, 1988). Although the
questions about Matthew's Gospel formulated by M. W. Dube et al. and addressed
to Batswana women could easily produce anti-Jewish answers ("We frequently
had to push the respondents to address the specificity of Jesus' statement [Matt.
10:5b–6]" [p. 117]; "Is this a story of racism between Canaanites and Israelites?"
[p. 119]), the women interviewed refused this temptation. See Dube's "Readings
of *Semoya*: Batswana Women's Interpretations of Matt. 15:21–28," in *Semeia* 73, pp.
111–29. See also the majority of articles in the exceptionally informative *Talitha,
qumi!*, Oduyoye and Kanyoro (eds.).

[70] Details, and repentance, in my "Hemorrhaging Woman."

[71] See E. P. Sanders, *Paul and Palestinian Judaism* (London: SCM, 1977).

be another colonial product of global symbolic capital, exported along with cured tobacco and DDT. We, the scholars, ship it out explicitly, we fail to stop it when we find it, and we even praise it as a sign of the sophistication and entry into the biblical studies guild of its producers.

As with most toxic exports, the problem existed well before it was named. This lack of notice may have something to do with the marginal place Jews and Judaism hold in feminist biblical criticism; anti-Judaism was not something about which scholars of Christianity or the Church have uniformly cared. As with such dangerous products, even once anti-Judaism was named, it remains ignored even in volumes edited by Western feminists and published by such "enlightened" houses as the WCC, Orbis, and Fortress. To name something "anti-Jewish" comes at a risk, and one not entirely comparable to the naming of something "sexist" or "racist."

– I risk the charge of "playing the Jewish card,"[72] that my concerns are personal, parochial, defensive, and apologetic, rather than historically rigorous and methodologically sophisticated.

– Even if anti-Judaism is acknowledged, it is traditionally discounted as "not as oppressive" as, say, racism, or sexism, or homophobia.[73] In lists of biblical "sins," anti-Judaism and anti-Semitism are—like homophobia and heterosexism—often omitted.[74] Moreover, Jews are not, unless we are also of Asian, African, Native American, or Latin American descent, among those supported by the Society of Biblical Literature's committee on "Underrepresented racial and ethnic minorities."[75]

---

[72] The expression adapts a phrase popularized by some U.S. commentators in their reporting of defense strategies in the trial of O. J. Simpson.

[73] On identity politics, see M. Ackelsberg, "Toward a Multicultural Politics. A Jewish Feminist Perspective," pp. 89–104; E. Torton Beck, "Jews and the Multicultural University Curriculum," pp. 163–77, both in Brettschneider (ed.), *Narrow Bridge*.

[74] Cf. G. West and M. W. Dube's programmatic introduction, "How We Have Come to 'Read With,'" to *Semeia* 73, pp. 7–17, p. 15: "The cry against biblical textual violence, its suppression of diversity—be it gender, race, class, ethnicity, sexual and cultural orientations—and its alignment with global structures of dominance must finally be addressed by those concerned with reading for differences, for liberation, and for both immediate and global social justice."

[75] Jewish women in Asia, Africa, and Latin America typically do not appear in collections of feminist theology, although Muslim women and women practitioners of indigenous religious traditions do. The absence of Israelis is similarly typical. For example, Tolbert and Segovia (eds.), *Reading from This Place, Vols. 1 and 2*, appropriately include a contribution from a Palestinian Christian, but nothing by or mention of Israeli Jews (save as persecutors of those Christians).

– I am not in the appropriate social location to critique anti-Jewish readings that appear in social-location based feminist studies, especially for those studies produced by under-represented racial and ethnic minorities. My critique, any Jewish critique, is "critique from above."

For a North Atlantic woman to argue against another North Atlantic woman is a sign of academic health. On occasion, *ad hominem* arguments appear; as such the less liberatory reading is labelled "anti-feminist" and the writer labelled a lackey of patriarchy. Yet feminist readings in Euro-America are sufficiently strong such that internal critique usually functions, not only civilly, but beneficially. However, for a North Atlantic woman to critique the work of an Asian, African, Australian, or Latin American woman inevitably raises the question: how does one distinguish between scholarly critique and patronizing racism?

This question is the re-framing of the sexist charges of the 1970s and early 1980s: Our critics claimed feminist readings were mushy-minded, unimportant, strained, or simply wrong. We, in turn, accused our critics of sexism and misogyny. Many times, but not always, we were right. Thus, in my disagreements with these new feminist readings, while I believe I am being rigorous, I may instead be racist or blindly apologetic.

Healthy Plots

The best opportunity to answer such questions, and certainly one firmly rooted in feminist method, is to read in community. Thus, I thank formally scholars like Elaine Wainwright, Hisako Kinukawa, Grace Imathiu, and others, who help me confront my own prejudices even as they welcome receiving the concerns of others. Kinukawa has, for example, recently made the extraordinary and most welcome statement: "I am afraid an anti-Jewish interpretation has been unconsciously promulgated by those who have not been exposed to this issue [of Christian feminist anti-Judaism], including myself."[76]

That the Gospels and Paul need not be read by feminists, or women historians and theologians, in an anti-Jewish manner is easily

---

[76] H. Kinukawa, "Looking at the Web: A Political Analysis of Personal Context and its Relationship to Global Context," *Journal of Asian and Asian American Theology* 2 (1997), pp. 51–63, p. 58. I thank Gale Yee for sending me this piece.

demonstrated, and not only by the increasing numbers of articles and books, such as many of the pieces in Elisabeth Schüssler Fiorenza's *Searching the Scriptures, Vols. 1* and *2,* and in the African women's collection, *Talitha, qumi!* Even regarding the haemorrhaging woman, Rosângela Soares de Oliveira's "Feminist Theology in Brazil," Carol J. Schlueter's "Feminist Homiletics: Strategies for Empowerment," Anne Nachisale Musopole's "Sexuality and Religion in a Matriarchal Society," C. Landman's "The Implementation of Biblical Hermeneutics,"[77] and of course the ongoing work on this pericope by Mary Rose D'Angelo[78] offer excellent liberationist messages without the blight of anti-Judaism. They clearly demonstrate that social location can be part of the hermeneutical enterprise without projecting negatives onto Second Temple culture. Critics choose their intertexts, their methods, what to highlight and what not to mention. There is no need to highlight a negative Judaism. Jesus can remain the liberationist Christian feminists want without being removed from his Jewish context.

We are the ones who teach those who will be the next generation's leaders in biblical studies and in ministry; we are the ones who sponsor global conferences, advise publishers, edit the volumes. The problems lay to a great extent at our feet, by commission and omission. The lilies need to be carefully tended, but it's also time to lift the ax. If Christian feminist anti-Judaism continues, more than weeds will be burned.

Lest this paper end on a discouraging note, the following may provide some optimism. At my presentation of an earlier version of this talk to the Catholic Biblical Association,[79] I concluded with the following updating of the well-known song by Gilbert and Sullivan.[80] Most of those in attendance joined the chorus; it is my hope that readers will join as well:

---

[77] R. Soares de Oliveira, "Feminist Theology in Brazil," in Ortega (ed.), *Women's Visions*, pp. 65–76, pp. 65, 75; C. J. Schlueter's "Feminist Homiletics: Strategies for Empowerment," in Ortega, pp. 138–51, p. 143; A. Nachisale Musopole, "Sexuality and Religion in a Matriarchal Society," in Oduyoye and Kanyoro (eds.), *Will to Arise*, pp. 195–205, pp. 203–5; C. Landman, "The Implementation of Biblical Hermeneutics." Paper presented to the Circle of Concerned African Women Theologians, Nairobi, summer 1996. I thank Grace Imathiu for the copy of this paper.

[78] I thank Professor D'Angelo for providing me a copy of the manuscript.

[79] Catholic Biblical Association simultaneous session, summer 1997. My thanks to Gale Yee and Jean-Pierre Ruiz for suggestions and corrections.

[80] Lyrics adapted by Scott F. Gilbert.

The flowers that bloom in the spring (tra-la)
Are lilies and wandering Jews.
They both find it pleasant to sing (tra la)
The joys that commitment can bring (tra la)
From their homes and their fields and their pews.
The differences present can be almost moot.
The flowers spring up from the same wondrous root.
Tra-lalalalala Tra-lalalalala, The flowers that bloom in the spring.
(Chorus: Tra-lalalalala Tra-lalalalala, The flowers that bloom in the spring.)

The flowers that bloom in the spring (tra-la)
Get trampled by well meaning fools.
The anti-Semitic raving (tra la)
Imported by missions took wing (tra la)
Now gets taught as a dogma in schools.
So Africans, Asians, Latinas, don't hate,
This colonial product has hideous weight.
Tra-lalalalala tra-lalalala. The colonial product has weight.
(Chorus: Tra-lalalalala tra-lalalalala Lalalala lala.)

The flowers that bloom in the spring (tra-la)
Are cut up to make a cole slaw.
For some find it useful to sling (tra la)
An obscene theological thing (tra la)
Saying Jews kill the life with their Law.
So please be aware when proclaiming good news
That Jesus was just like a lot of the Jews.
Tra-lalalalala Tra-lalalalala, O Jesus was like many Jews.
(Chorus: Tra-lalalalala Tra-lalalalala, Jesus was like the Jews.)

JESUS AND WOMEN IN FICTION AND FILM

WILLIAM R. TELFORD

Introduction

The Nature, Aims and Relevance of the Topic

The title of this essay is "Jesus and Women in Fiction and Film."
What I intend to do is to examine the way women are portrayed
in relation to Jesus in fiction and film. In particular, I want to focus
on transformative encounters between Jesus and women in representative novels and films, that is, on engagements which emanate in
altered perceptions, new commitments, or even conversion, and which
embody at the same time their own gender ideology. The topic is
a relevant one for a number of reasons. Firstly, fiction and film are
important reflectors of our cultural values. They both mirror and to
some extent influence the way human beings relate to each other.
Secondly, gender issues are not only a recurring item on the agenda
of contemporary literary and film studies, they also constitute a major
cultural concern. It is a matter of considerable importance to us
today how men and women are presented or depicted in the various organs of cultural expression, in art and literature, in broad-
casting and the media, in commerce and advertising, etc., for such
representations have the capacity either to make us slaves to cultural stereotypes or to liberate us from them. Few areas nowadays
remain untouched indeed by feminist concerns or interpretation.

In the area of religion and theology—and this brings me to the
third reason why this subject is relevant—a burning issue for feminist biblical criticism or interpretation[1] has been the representation

---

[1] See P. Joyce, "Feminist Exegesis of the Old Testament. Some Critical Reflections,"
and R. Morgan, "Feminist Theological Interpretation of the New Testament," in
J. M. Soskice (ed.), *After Eve. Women, Ideology and the Christian Tradition* (London: Collins
Marshall Pickering, 1990), pp. 1–9, 10–37 resp.; D. F. Middleton, "Feminist Interpretation," in R. J. Coggins and J. L. Houlden (eds.), *A Dictionary of Biblical Interpretation* (London: SCM; Philadelphia, PA: Trinity Press International, 1990), pp.
231–4; Ph. Trible, "Feminist Hermeneutics and Biblical Studies," in A. Loades (ed.),
Feminist Theology. A Reader (London: SPCK, 1990), pp. 23–9; L. M. Russell (ed.),
Feminist Interpretation of the Bible (Philadelphia, PA: Westminster, 1985).

of women in the Bible, and the effect that the images reflected there have had on Christianity and Western culture.[2] Whether exposing derogatory images of women, highlighting complimentary ones or "offering sympathetic readings of abused women,"[3] feminist approaches have revolutionized the gender-sensitive way that we now regard the Bible. In light of gender issues, feminist theology has sought to re-construct traditional theological doctrines such as Christology[4] or sote-riology,[5] re-defining them in terms of "relational processes," or re-formulating them in categories of "intuitive spirituality," wholeness, self-discovery, affirmation and "mutuality in relation." Treating the Bible as a cultural artefact and not as a religious object, some bib-lical scholars have offered alternative strategies to subvert the gen-der ideology of biblical texts.[6] Some feminist theologians have argued that the sexist nature of the Bible puts in question the very future of Christianity itself in our post-modern age.[7] Yet at the same time, images of biblical women (especially Mary, the mother of Jesus) as well as of Jesus, both traditional and untraditional, have played, and are playing a significant role in the Christianity of the Third World.[8]

While biblical images of Jesus and of women continue to be in-fluential or to arouse debate in religious, theological or academic circles, it cannot be denied that in today's Western secular society the Bible no longer functions, as it once did, as a direct, primary or even significant reference point for gender relations, or as a major influence in reflecting, far less establishing societal norms for male-

---

[2] See A. L. Laffey, *Wives, Harlots and Concubines. The Old Testament in Feminist Perspective* (London: SPCK, 1990); T. Dennis, *Sarah Laughed. Women's Voices in the Old Testament* (London: SPCK, 1994).

[3] Trible, "Feminist Hermeneutics," p. 27.

[4] E.g. J. Hopkins, *Towards a Feminist Christology. Jesus of Nazareth, European Women and the Christological Crisis* (London: SPCK, 1995).

[5] E.g. M. Grey, *Redeeming the Dream. Feminism, Redemption and Christian Tradition* (London: SPCK, 1989).

[6] Cf. e.g. J. Ch. Exum, *Fragmented Women. Feminist (Sub)versions of Biblical Narratives* (JSOT Supplement Series, 163; Sheffield: JSOT, 1993); E. Schüssler Fiorenza, *Bread not Stone. The Challenge of Feminist Biblical Interpretation* (Boston, MA: Beacon, 1984).

[7] See D. Hampson, *After Christianity* (London: SCM, 1996) and *Theology and Feminism* (Oxford: Blackwell, 1990).

[8] Cf. e.g. H. K. Chung, *Struggle To Be the Sun Again* (London: SCM, 1991); R. S. Sugirtharajah, "Jesus Research and Third World Christologies," *Theology* 93 (1990), pp. 387–91; idem, "Wisdom, Q and a Proposal for a Christology," *ExpT* 102 (1990–91), pp. 42–6; idem, "'What Do Men Say Remains of Me?' Current Jesus Research and Third World Christologies," *Asia Journal of Theology* 5 (1991), pp. 331–7.

female relationships. That said, the Bible's prevailing though indirect influence on popular culture should not be underestimated, particularly as it has impacted on literature and film. Indeed, the attention of biblical scholars and theologians is being increasingly drawn nowadays to these areas, so giving us a fourth reason for the relevance of our topic.[9] Cultural images of Jesus have been a subject of investigation, the way a particular age depicts him being an essential key, it has even been suggested, to understanding that age.[10] Reference works on the influence of the Bible on Western literature are now available,[11] and studies of the treatment of Jesus in literature,[12] as well as of biblical women such as Mary Magdalene[13] or Mary, the mother of Jesus, have also emerged.[14]

A similar upsurge of interest is being shown in film.[15] The recent volume edited by C. Marsh and G. W. Ortiz, *Explorations in Theology and Film. Movies and Meaning* (Oxford: Blackwell, 1997) sets out to justify this interest. In my own article in that collection,[16] on the depiction of Jesus in the cinema, I assert:

> [G]iven its popularity, the Christ film is arguably the most significant medium through which popular culture this century has absorbed its

[9] For a review of developments, see W. R. Telford, "The New Testament in Fiction and Film: A Biblical Scholar's Perspective," in J. G. Davies, G. Harvey and W. Watson (eds.), *Words Remembered, Texts Renewed. Essays in Honour of J. F. A. Sawyer* (Sheffield: Sheffield Academic Press, 1995), pp. 360–94.

[10] J. Pelikan, *Jesus through the Centuries. His Place in the History of Culture* (New Haven and London: Yale University Press, 1985). See also J. Pelikan, *Mary through the Centuries* (New Haven and London: Yale University Press, 1996), and S. E. Porter, M. A. Hayes and D. Tombs (eds.), *Images of Christ. Ancient and Modern* (Roehampton Institute London Papers, 2; Sheffield: Sheffield Academic Press, 1997).

[11] Cf. D. L. Jeffrey (ed.), *A Dictionary of Biblical Tradition in English Literature* (Grand Rapids, MI: Eerdmans, 1992).

[12] Cf. e.g. R. Detweiler, "Christ and the Christ Figure in American Fiction," in M. E. Marty and D. G. Peerman (eds.), *New Theology No. 2* (New York: Macmillan, 1965), pp. 297–316; T. Ziolkowski, *Fictional Transfigurations of Jesus* (Princeton, N.J.: Princeton University Press, 1972); W. Hamilton, *A Quest for the Post-Historical Jesus* (London: SCM, 1993).

[13] See S. Haskins *Mary Magdalen* (London: HarperCollins, 1993).

[14] S. Cunneen, *In Search of Mary* (New York: Ballantine, 1996).

[15] Cf. e.g. G. Aichele and T. Pippin (eds.), *The Monstrous and the Unspeakable. The Bible as Fantastic Literature* (Playing the Texts, 1; Sheffield: Sheffield Academic Press, 1997); R. Jewett, *Saint Paul at the Movies: The Apostle's Dialogue with American Culture* (Philadelphia, PA: Westminster John Knox, 1993); C. Marsh and G. W. Ortiz (eds.), *Explorations in Theology and Film. Movies and Meaning* (Oxford: Blackwell, 1997); B. B. Scott, *Hollywood Dreams and Biblical Stories* (Minneapolis, MN: Augsburg Fortress, 1994).

[16] W. R. Telford, "Jesus Christ Movie-Star: The Depiction of Jesus in the Cinema," in Marsh and Ortiz (eds.), *Explorations*, pp. 115–39.

knowledge of the Gospel story and formed its impression of Christianity's founder. It was Cecil B. DeMille's claim that 'probably more people have been told the story of Jesus of Nazareth through *The King of Kings* than through any other single work, except the Bible itself' (Hayne 1960: 258).[17]

If this is so, then it should also be instructive to examine the way that gender relations are configured in this unarguably popular medium. Work of this kind is already under way on the part of biblical scholars, with fruitful results.[18] Such analyses of literature and film have a significant capacity, among other things, to act back on our understanding of the Bible,[19] or to "reverse the hermeneutical flow," to use L. Kreitzer's words.[20]

Issues and Approach

What then are the issues that I want to raise in this essay, and what are the questions I want to address? Firstly, how is Jesus' relationship with women presented in the novels and films under scrutiny? Secondly, to what extent are these images based on the New Testament texts, and to what extent have they been re-worked by novelist, screenwriter or director? Thirdly, how faithful ideologically are our chosen novels and films to their foundation texts, or to what extent do they seek to transcend or subvert them, in light of their contemporary context or agenda? To what extent, to put it another way, are our chosen texts conservative or radical, traditional or subversive, in their interpretation of the biblical text, and in particular in their treatment of women? To what extent are they sensitive to gender issues? Which women tend to be selected, what degree of character development is offered, and how is Jesus' interaction with them depicted? In re-viewing particular transformative encounters,

---

[17] Telford, "Jesus Christ Movie-Star," in Marsh and Ortiz (eds.), *Explorations*, p. 122.

[18] Cf. e.g. A. Bach (ed.), *Biblical Glamour and Hollywood Glitz* (*Semeia*, 74; Atlanta, GA: Scholars, 1996); J. Ch. Exum, *Plotted, Shot, and Painted. Cultural Representations of Biblical Women* (JSOT Supplement Series, 215; Sheffield: Sheffield Academic Press, 1997).

[19] Cf. e.g. D. Jasper, *Readings in the Canon of Scripture. Written for our Learning* (New York: St. Martins, 1995), esp. pp. 68–82.

[20] L. J. Kreitzer, *The New Testament in Fiction and Film. On Reversing the Hermeneutical Flow* (The Biblical Seminar, 17; Sheffield: Sheffield University Press, 1993) and *The Old Testament in Fiction and Film. On Reversing the Hermeneutical Flow* (The Biblical Seminar, 24; Sheffield: Sheffield University Press, 1994).

how are the dynamics of relationship presented? To what extent, for
example, are the women given a voice? Most of us think we know
the answer to these questions, especially where the classic Christ film
is concerned, but it is possible that the genre may have some surprises for us.

The novels I shall refer to are G. Theissen's *The Shadow of the
Galilean: the Quest of the Historical Jesus in Narrative Form* (London: SCM,
1987), N. Kazantzakis' *The Last Temptation* (London: Faber and Faber,
1961) and M. Roberts' *The Wild Girl* (London: Methuen, 1984).[21]
Films commented on will be Cecil B. DeMille's *The King of Kings*
(1927), N. Ray's *King of Kings* (1961), P. Pasolini's *The Gospel According
to St. Matthew* (1964), G. Stevens' *The Greatest Story Ever Told* (1965),
N. Jewison's *Jesus Christ Superstar* (1973), F. Zeffirelli's *Jesus of Nazareth*
(1977), T. Jones' *Monty Python's Life of Brian* (1979), M. Scorsese's *The
Last Temptation of Christ* (1988) and D. Arcand's *Jésus de Montréal*
(1989).[22] In approaching these novels and films, I am very much
aware of the fact that I am neither a literary critic nor a film the-
orist but a biblical scholar. The intricacies of both literary and film
theory I am still in process of mastering![23] In a recently published
article, "The New Testament in Fiction and Film: A Biblical Scholar's
Perspective,"[24] I attempted to suggest some ways in which these literary and film texts could be approached by the biblical scholar,
and I shall be drawing here on some of the ways outlined there.
Three approaches in particular are of value, viz. narrative criticism,
intertextuality, and ideology and social context. We shall be alive, in
other words, to such things as plot, characterization and point of view
in the texts under review, to the relation of these texts to the biblical

---

[21] For a general introduction to these texts, see Telford, "The New Testament
in Fiction and Film," in Davies, Harvey and Watson (eds.), *Words Remembered*, pp.
371–7.

[22] For a general introduction to these films, see Telford, "Jesus Christ Movie-
Star," in Marsh and Ortiz (eds.), *Explorations*, pp. 115–39, and idem, "The New
Testament in Fiction and Film," in Davies, Harvey and Watson (eds.), *Words
Remembered*, pp. 377–83.

[23] In *Biblical Epics. Sacred Narrative in the Hollywood Cinema* (Manchester: Manchester
University Press, 1993), B. Babington and P. W. Evans enter into some discussion
of the subject (pp. 1–24), as does the first part of Marsh and Ortiz (eds.), *Explorations*.
A useful, but far more technical book is J. Monaco's *How to Read a Film. The Art,
Technology, Language, History, and Theory of Film and Media* (Oxford and New York:
Oxford University Press, 1981). See the bibliography there.

[24] Telford, "The New Testament in Fiction and Film," in Davies, Harvey and
Watson (eds.), *Words Remembered*, pp. 360–94.

text, and to the relation of our chosen texts to their contemporary context (with regard to their underlying concerns or subtext).

Representations of Jesus and Women in the Bible

Women in the Bible

Most of us are familiar with the general picture portrayed by the Bible concerning the role and status of women.[25] Consider the following summary statements from the article "Woman" in *The Interpreter's Dictionary of the Bible* (1962). On the Bible and women in general, the author writes:

> The function and status of woman in the Bible are strongly influenced by the patriarchal form of family life which prevailed. Woman's principal function is performed in her role as wife and mother. In this connection she makes her sexuality available to her husband for his pleasure and for reproductive purposes. As a mother she sustains a relationship to children which involves their care and nurture. In her wider relationships which extend beyond the family, she takes part in the economic and social life of the community and in its political and even military affairs. She shares also in the religious life of her contemporaries, both in the home and in the tribe, city, or national community of worship. . . . [In sum, however, the author states] Woman's position in the Bible is largely that of subordination to her father or her husband.[26]

Women in the New Testament

The evidence presented specifically by the New Testament is more ambiguous. On the New Testament and women, the *IDB* article goes on to state:

> While not differing radically from the concept which the OT presents, the view of woman in the NT reflects the influence of the Christian

---

[25] For scholarly overviews, see O. J. Baab, "Woman," in G. A. Buttrick (ed.), *The Interpreter's Dictionary of the Bible* (New York and Nashville, TN: Abingdon, 1976), pp. 864–7; D. M. Scholer, "Women," in J. B. Green, S. McKnight, and I. H. Marshall (eds.), *Dictionary of Jesus and the Gospels* (Downers Grove, IL: InterVarsity, 1992), pp. 880–7; Ph. Trible, "Woman in the OT" and "Woman in the NT," in K. Crim (ed.), *The Interpreter's Dictionary of the Bible, Supplementary Volume* (Nashville, TN: Abingdon, 1976), pp. 963–6, 966–8 resp.

[26] Baab, "Woman," in *IDB*, pp. 864, 865.

as well as the Jewish community. . . . Accepting the biblical view of woman's subordination to man, the writers of the NT stressed the duty of modesty, submission, and piety.[27]

After reviewing a number of well-known "negative" passages (1 Cor. 14:34–36; 1 Tim. 2:12, 14–15; 5:2) the author concludes that "in theory at least, woman was expected to exhibit chiefly the domestic virtues as a demonstration of her piety and faith. In actual practice, her leadership and influence extended to the life of the entire Christian community, as the NT itself reveals."[28] This picture has been supported by some feminist writers. Contributing to a later article in the Supplementary Volume of the *IDB*, Ph. Trible writes:

> Contrary to the position of subordination in which woman generally lived in first-century Mediterranean culture, the position they discovered in the early Christian communities was one of acceptance and, particularly in the earliest decades, equality. Women were seen as equal to men and participated in every level of church activity. In the later NT church the equality was compromised and stabilized at a point where they still received warm acceptance but were again placed in subordinate roles.[29]

This view was shared by E. Schüssler Fiorenza in her ground-breaking book, *In Memory of Her* (1983).[30] Cosmopolitan in its social mix and outlook the early church offered equal opportunities to women, some of whom were active as rich patrons and prominent as leaders. Paul shared this egalitarian vision but, in light of practical circumstances, modified it, so laying the basis for the patriarchalism which followed.

Women in the Gospels

The image of women in the Gospels is more ambiguous still, and has been the subject of lively scholarly debate.[31] One begins by noting

---

[27] Baab, "Woman," in *IDB*, p. 867.
[28] Baab, "Woman," in *IDB*, p. 867.
[29] Trible, "Woman in the NT," in *IDB(S)*, p. 966.
[30] E. Schüssler Fiorenza, *In Memory of Her. A Feminist Theological Reconstruction of Christian Origins* (London: SCM, 1983). See also idem, "Missionaries, Apostles, Coworkers. Romans 16 and the Reconstruction of Women's Early Christian History," in Loades (ed.), *Feminist Theology*, pp. 57–71; A. Cameron, "Women in Early Christian Interpretation," in Coggins and Houlden (eds.), *Dictionary of Biblical Interpretation*, pp. 729–31.
[31] For a review of recent discussion on Mark, see W. R. Telford, *The Theology of the Gospel of Mark* (New Testament Theology; Cambridge: Cambridge University

that many of the women who appear in the Jesus story are anonymous, e.g. the woman with the haemorrhage (Mark 5:25–34 parr), the Syrophoenician woman (Mark 7:24–30 par), the woman who anoints Jesus' head (Mark 14:3–9; Matt. 26:6–13), the woman who anoints Jesus' feet (Luke 7:36–50; John 12:1–8, Mary of Bethany) or the woman taken in adultery (John 7:53–8:11).[32] Those who are specifically named fall principally into two classes, according to O. J. Baab: those who were healed by him, and those who followed and watched over him.[33] Among those named are Joanna, Mary, mother of Jesus, Mary Magdalene, and Mary and Martha of Bethany. Joanna is identified as the wife of Chuza, Herod's steward (Luke 8:3) and, apart from being named by Luke as among the women who reported Jesus' resurrection (24:10), is given no characterization or function other than that of a follower and supporter. Although Mary, mother of Jesus, is of obvious importance in the history of Christianity, her narrative role in the Gospels is essentially a minor one.[34] She figures at the beginning and end of his life, in the birth and infancy narratives (Matt. 1–2; Luke 1–2), at the cross (John 19:25–27) and—if she is to be equated with Mary, the mother of James (and Joses)—the resurrection (Mark 16:1; cf. Mark 15:40 and 47 with 6:3), and in-between only at the wedding at Cana (John 2:1–11) and in paying Jesus a visit in order to restrain him (Mark 3:21, 31–35 par).[35]

Press, 1999; idem, *Mark* (New Testament Guides; Sheffield: Sheffield Academic Press, 1995), p. 111; idem (ed.), *The Interpretation of Mark* (Issues in Religion and Theology; Edinburgh: T&T Clark, 1995), p. 12; on John, see I. R. Kitzberger, "'How Can This Be?' (John 3:9). A Feminist-Theological Re-Reading of the Gospel of John," in F. F. Segovia (ed.), *"What is John?" Volume II: Literary and Social Readings of the Fourth Gospel* (SBL Symposium Series, 7; Atlanta, GA: Scholars, 1998), pp. 19–41; idem, "Mary of Bethany and Mary of Magdala—Two Female Characters in the Johannine Passion Narrative. A Feminist, Narrative-Critical Reader-Response," *NTS* 41 (1995), pp. 564–86; idem, "Love and Footwashing: John 13.1–20 and Luke 7.36–50 Read Intertextually," *Biblical Interpretation* 2 (1994), pp. 191–206; J. M. Lieu, "The Mother of the Son in the Fourth Gospel," *JBL* 117 (1998), pp. 61–77.

[32] This passage is omitted by most of our ancient textual authorities for the Gospel of John. Although beloved as a story, it appears to have been a stray tradition, undoubtedly secondary, which has found its way into our manuscript tradition at various points (e.g. after John 7:36 or 21:25 or Luke 21:38).

[33] See Baab, "Woman," in *IDB*, p. 867. The two are not necessarily mutually exclusive, of course (cf. e.g. Luke 8:1–3).

[34] See D. L. Jeffrey, "Mary, Mother of Jesus," in Jeffrey (ed.), *Dictionary of Biblical Tradition*, pp. 489–95.

[35] For a sharp comment on this last passage, see E. Moltmann-Wendel, *The Women around Jesus* (London: SCM, 1982), p. 65.

Mary Magdalene's narrative presence is also relatively slight.[36] She is mentioned among Jesus' followers in Luke 8:2, as having been healed "of evil spirits and infirmities" and as one "from whom seven devils had gone out," and in the passion and resurrection narratives as having witnessed the crucifixion (Mark 15:40–41; Matt. 27:56; John 19:25) and the burial (Mark 15:42–47; Matt. 27:61). She visits the empty tomb (Mark 16:1; Matt. 28:1) and receives a post-resurrection appearance either along with the other women (Matt. 28:9–10) or on her own (John 20:11–18). The narrative roles of Mary and Martha of Bethany are also relatively inconsequential. Mary is described as the sister of Martha (John 11:2; 12:3) and of Lazarus, whom Jesus raises from the dead (John 11:1–46), and she is identified as the one who anoints Jesus' feet (John 12:1–8). The two sisters are played off against each other by Luke (Luke 10:38–42), with Mary being commended by Jesus for preferring contemplation of Jesus' teaching over the domestic round pre-occupying Martha.[37] It is worth reminding ourselves at this point that nowhere is there any specific NT identification of Mary of Bethany with Mary Magdalene, or of Mary Magdalene with the woman who anointed Jesus' feet (Luke 7:36–50). Consequently, there is no biblical warrant for the traditional image of Mary Magdalene as the prostitute or repentant sinner. The theological difference between the two "anointing" stories is also worth noting, that of Jesus' head by the anonymous woman in Mark 14:3–9 being a prophetic act pre-figuring his salvific death, and that of his feet by the woman in Luke 7:36–50 being an act of love and contrition. What subsequent tradition has made of these named women is well-known, and is summed up conveniently by E. Moltmann-Wendel:

> A long accepted view of the Bible, which is mostly hostile to women, has given form to a history of the tradition which has made a deep mark on human consciousness. Women are associated with sexuality and sin (Mary Magdalene), cooking and housekeeping (Martha), and motherhood (Mary). Women in the Bible are not allowed any beauty, independence or originality of their own, and are made to fulfil the function of providing whatever image of womanhood Christianity may desire.[38]

---

[36] See M. Hannay, "Mary Magdalene," in Jeffrey (ed.), *Dictionary of Biblical Tradition*, p. 486.

[37] See D. L. Jeffrey, "Martha," in Jeffrey (ed.), *Dictionary of Biblical Tradition*, pp. 489–95.

[38] Moltmann-Wendel, *Women around Jesus*, p. 8. Elsewhere, she quotes the refrain (p. 21):
Martha and Mary in one life.
Make up the perfect vicar's wife.

Jesus and Women

One component in the popular estimation of the role and status of women in the New Testament concerns the relation of Jesus to women. Here, like many others, E. Moltmann-Wendel makes of Jesus a notable exception to what is often now reckoned as the Bible's overall disparagement of women:

> Psychoanalytical research has demonstrated that Jesus was the only man not dominated by the *animus*; Hanna Wolff calls him 'the integrated man', i.e. a man who integrated and brought to maturity the masculine and feminine attitudes which are to be found in any human being. As a result of this he was capable of entering into a more absolute partnership with women.[39]

Others have expressed similar judgements. According to P. Avis, "Jesus himself ignored and subverted Jewish conventions regarding contact with women. He treated them with respect and affection and without condescension."[40] A more cautious judgement is expressed by D. Hampson:

> That Jesus was personally kind to women there is no reason to doubt. That he freed people to be themselves and to be present for others is the undeniable witness of the texts. But that he had a feminist analysis of society is something for which there is no evidence. To contend under these circumstances that Jesus was a feminist, or that he spoke out for women, must imply a very low estimate of what being a feminist (or speaking out for women) might mean.[41]

It is not my purpose here to enter into a debate on the patriarchal nature of the Bible, to assess the relative weight to be given to the positive and negative evaluations of women that are to be found in it, or even to second-guess Jesus' own self-consciousness with regard to this issue. In citing some of these representative attitudes and opinions, I want merely to set the context for what follows.

---

[39] Moltmann-Wendel, *Women around Jesus*, p. 3. See also idem, *A Land Flowing with Milk and Honey* (London: SCM, 1985), pp. 79–80.
[40] P. Avis, *Eros and the Sacred* (London: SPCK, 1989), p. 105.
[41] Hampson, *Theology and Feminism*, pp. 89–90.

Representations of Jesus and Women in Fiction

G. Theissen, *The Shadow of the Galilean: The Quest of the Historical Jesus in Narrative Form* (London: SCM, 1987)

Our first representation of Jesus and women in fiction, G. Theissen's *The Shadow of the Galilean* (1987) is a historical novel by a respected New Testament scholar which aims to document, through the experiences of its leading character, a series of transformative encounters between Jesus and others. At first sight the choice of this novel seems inappropriate for our purposes, at least where narrative voice and characters are concerned. The first-person narrator, Andreas, a wealthy grain merchant enlisted by the Romans to obtain information on Jesus, is masculine. Jesus himself does not appear. Instead, the reader is presented with various pictures of him from the point of view of diverse groups (Pharisees, Sadducees, Essenes, Zealots, Romans, etc.) and individuals. These include Baruch, an ex-communicated Essene whom Andreas rescues in the wilderness; Chuza, Herod Antipas' steward, and his wife, Joanna; Tholomaeus, a poor farmer from Nazareth, and his wife, Susanna; Barabbas, a friend of Andreas and a Zealot; Mattathias and Hannah of Capernaum, parents of another Zealot and their ailing daughter Miriam, and Kostabar, a tax-collector who has replaced Levi (Matthew) at the toll-gate near Bethsaida. Most of the main characters, therefore, are fictional (including at least two of these four women), and where named Gospel women are concerned, Mary Magdalene, Mary, mother of Jesus, and Mary and Martha of Bethany are not included.

Nevertheless, the Jesus constructed by the reader out of the reactions of the various characters to him is a compelling one, from a historical point of view, at least, if not from a literary one.[42] To Andreas, he is a philosopher, a poet and, above all, a prophet of an oppressed people, a defender of the poor and weak. To Barabbas, he is revolutionary "who wants to take the gentle way,"[43] a man who "wants change and peace at the same time."[44] To Joanna, he is a teacher bringing about "a revolution in values, a take-over of upper-class attitudes by the lower classes," someone claiming "for little people," as Theissen himself explains in a letter to the fictitious

---

[42] For discussion, see Hamilton, *Post-Historical Jesus*, pp. 139–46.
[43] Theissen, *Shadow*, p. 89.
[44] Theissen, *Shadow*, p. 91.

Dr Kratzinger, "the attitudes and modes of behaviour of the upper classes, e.g. freedom from material care for those without possessions, wisdom for the unlearned."[45] It is the presence of Joanna in the narrative, indeed the characterization she receives, and the report of her transformative encounter with Jesus, which gives the novel not only a contemporary dimension but also some relevance for our topic.

Joanna, the beautiful, young wife of Andreas' former business partner, Chuza, is first introduced to the reader in chapter 6 when she intervenes robustly in a conversation between the two men on the subject of Pilate's recent atrocities in Jerusalem and Herod Antipas' execution of John the Baptist. Taking the part of Herodias against those who were blaming her for the Baptist's death, and stoutly defending Herodias' rights in the matter of divorce, she goes on to inform Andreas that she herself had met Jesus and had been attracted by his teaching on this subject (cf. Mark 10:11–12, "Here at least the two sides have equal rights").[46] Andreas' second meeting with Joanna takes place in chapter 13, where he questions her on Jesus in private only to learn that she has since become a secret follower and supporter. Embarrassed, angered and ultimately made rebellious by her husband's subsequent disparagement of the Galilean, his supporters and the "little people" who follow him, her passionate defence of Jesus for his desire "to cure the little people of their superstitious mistrust of themselves" leads to the revelation that she too has become a disciple.

Theissen's development of the character of Joanna, and in particular the dialogue he invents for her in relation to Chuza and Andreas, illustrates his own observation that "the conversations in this book reflect scholarly discussion more accurately than learned articles."[47] In keeping with other characters in the book, Joanna speaks from a clear ideological position. It is obvious to the reader that she speaks for women and represents feminist concerns. Criticized for cultural anachronism (one reviewer, for example, has questioned his assumption that in first century Palestine a man might have a long private conversation with a woman in the absence of her husband),[48]

---

[45] Theissen, *Shadow*, p. 127.
[46] Theissen, *Shadow*, p. 53.
[47] Theissen, *Shadow*, p. 55.
[48] J. H. Neyrey, "Review of G. Theissen, *The Shadow of the Galilean*," *CBQ* 50 (1988), pp. 548–9, esp. p. 549.

and for making his characters subordinate to modern ideology, Theissen's treatment of Joanna is nevertheless worthy of note. By allowing her a voice (however stilted) in which to articulate her trans- formative encounter, he shows himself sensitive to present-day con- cerns as well as contemporary readings of the New Testament.

N. Kazantzakis, The Last Temptation (London: Faber and Faber, 1961)

Our second representation of Jesus and women in fiction, N. Kazant- zakis' *The Last Temptation* (1961), offers a much more controversial treatment of Jesus and his relationships with the women around him, particularly Mary Magdalene and Mary, the mother of Jesus. The characterization of Jesus himself is interesting, unconventional and powerful.[49] When compared with the Jesus of the Gospels, Kazant- zakis' Jesus is a truly human figure, one tormented by God (sym- bolized throughout the novel by the vulture which buries its claws into his head) and struggling with his divine destiny. He is para- lysed with guilt.[50] He confesses himself (and is regarded by others as) a coward. He has been prone to fear since childhood.[51] The hero of *The Last Temptation* is a man at war with his own neurotic, obsessive and masochistic tendencies and one seeking to resolve these conflicts in an act of self-destruction. He whips himself every evening,[52] has persecutory hallucinations,[53] is obsessed with crucifixion,[54] and plans his own death.[55] Though frequently vicious to himself, he is tender to animals and plants.[56] In matters of politics, he preaches love rather than violence,[57] wishing (as lamb) to free the soul from sin rather than (as lion) to free Israel from the Romans.[58] This lat- ter way is the way of Judas who, as Jesus' *alter ego*, represents one of the temptations that he must resist.

The other temptation is that presented by the women in his life. He is obsessed with Mary Magdalene, for whom he is consumed with desire, to whom he wishes to be married, and by whom he

---

[49] For discussion, see Hamilton, *Post-Historical Jesus*, pp. 205–9.
[50] Kazantzakis, *Last Temptation*, pp. 19, 94, 95.
[51] Kazantzakis, *Last Temptation*, pp. 21, 30, 96, 131, 151.
[52] Kazantzakis, *Last Temptation*, pp. 19, 86.
[53] Kazantzakis, *Last Temptation*, pp. 31, 32, 35, 74, 164, 311, 452, 465.
[54] Kazantzakis, *Last Temptation*, pp. 37, 56.
[55] Kazantzakis, *Last Temptation*, pp. 332, 389, 421, 431.
[56] Kazantzakis, *Last Temptation*, pp. 74, 132, 162, 221, 242.
[57] Kazantzakis, *Last Temptation*, pp. 195, 198, 202.
[58] Kazantzakis, *Last Temptation*, pp. 208–9, 254–5, 303, 337, 395–6, 412.

wants to have children.[59] Even while escaping from her to an Essene monastery, he is reminded (by an old woman) that "God is found not in monasteries but in the homes of men! Wherever you find husband and wife, that's where you find God; wherever children and petty cares and cooking and arguments and reconciliations, that's where God is too."[60] This domestic temptation is represented also by his mother against whom he wishes to rebel.[61] When compared with the Christ of the Gospels, Kazantzakis' Christ is not simply the divine Son of God, carrying out his father's will, the wish that he should redeem the world. He is also the human son of Mary, resisting his mother's will, her desire that he should marry, settle down and raise a family.[62] It is his conquering of the "flesh" by "spirit," however, the victory that he achieves over the way of Judas and the way of Mary, his renunciation in particular of the "last temptation" which the devil offers on the cross—the pleasures of the body, sex, procreation, home, wife, family, domestic bliss, and happy longevity, all mediated through the figures of Mary Magdalene, Mary and Martha—which ensures in the end the accomplishment of his divine mission.

Ultimately heroic as Kazantzakis' presentation of Jesus is, his treatment of women is more problematic. Apart from a Christ figure in psychological tension with the female sex,[63] there would be some discomfort nowadays with the novel's sole depiction of women as objects of sexual desire or as models of domesticity. Judas aside, the significant others in Jesus' life are Mary, *the mother*, and Mary Magdalene, *the whore*. In developing the biblical Mary Magdalene, Kazantzakis has built upon the post-biblical tradition of her as the "great sinner," the prostitute, the temptress. Identified furthermore with the woman taken in adultery, she is saved from stoning by Jesus and becomes his follower, although "[i]t was not Magdalene he had lifted from the ground, but the soul of man—and he was its bridegroom."[64] But this is not the transformative encounter around which the plot revolves, however, nor where its personal dynamics are centred. A much ear-

---

[59] Kazantzakis, *Last Temptation*, pp. 32, 33, 87, 95, 96, 99, 150, 263–4, 303, 360.
[60] Kazantzakis, *Last Temptation*, p. 77.
[61] Kazantzakis, *Last Temptation*, p. 151.
[62] Kazantzakis, *Last Temptation*, pp. 69, 174.
[63] While there are some hints of homosexuality (cf. e.g. pp. 211, 400) a major emphasis of the novel is on Jesus' genuine heterosexual feelings for Mary Magdalene.
[64] Kazantzakis, *Last Temptation*, p. 337.

lier encounter had taken place between them in childhood,[65] a physical experience of intimacy which had involved both of them and which had first awakened their desire for each other. Neither had forgotten this experience. For Mary it was a "sweetness" and a "sweetness ... which I've been seeking ever since from man to man; but I have not found it."[66] For Jesus it was something that explained her descent into prostitution, and for which he blamed himself.[67] As a result he wishes to save her, paying an unsuccessful visit to her brothel to beg her forgiveness before departing to the desert to escape her and discover his destiny.[68] Escape from the flesh, however, proves difficult, for the "saving" of Magdalene is to confront him again as a diabolical temptation.[69] Even after her spiritual submission to him as a follower, there are secretly observed signs of physical affection between them ("All he [Matthew] could do was watch the rabbi's severe afflicted face and his hand, which ever so often skimmed Magdalene's hair").[70] In the end, he is able to marry her only in a devil-inspired dream, before she is murdered by Saul of Tarsus, and his diabolical imaginings on the cross turn to love, physical union and procreation with Mary of Bethany and her sister Martha.[71]

Kazantzakis' treatment of Mary, the mother of Jesus, is another significant element in the novel. This mother's feelings for her son, however, hardly represent conventional piety. "She had been so unfortunate in her life, unfortunate in her husband, unfortunate in her son. She had been widowed before she married, was a mother without possessing a child; and now she was growing older."[72] Mary has seen her son, as a carpenter and maker of crosses, help crucify another woman's son, a Zealot, and, like Jesus, has been stung by the mother's words ("'[M]y curse upon you, Son of the Carpenter. As you crucified another, may you be crucified yourself! ... And you, Mary, may you feel the pain that I have felt!'").[73] Mary's plans for Jesus do not represent a reverent submission to the divine will.

---

[65] Kazantzakis, *Last Temptation*, pp. 99, 150.
[66] Kazantzakis, *Last Temptation*, p. 99.
[67] Kazantzakis, *Last Temptation*, pp. 19, 95, 150.
[68] Kazantzakis, *Last Temptation*, pp. 85–102.
[69] Kazantzakis, *Last Temptation*, pp. 263–4.
[70] Kazantzakis, *Last Temptation*, p. 360.
[71] Kazantzakis, *Last Temptation*, pp. 462ff.
[72] Kazantzakis, *Last Temptation*, p. 36.
[73] Kazantzakis, *Last Temptation*, p. 57.

> The woman loved by God heard and shook her head, unconsoled. 'I don't want my son to be a saint,' she murmured. 'I want him to be a man like all the rest. I want him to marry and give me grandchildren. That's God's way. Let him build troughs, cradles, ploughs and household utensils as his father used to do, and not crosses to crucify human beings'.[74]

For Jesus, then, his mother is an object of hostility as well as of love.[75] She, perhaps, is the shade who pursues him throughout the book, to whom he bids farewell on the cross, and to whom by his death he is reconciled.[76] But since "[t]here is only one woman in the world," as the angel reminds him,[77] "one, with innumerable faces," then the shade could also be the Zealot's mother, or Mary Magdalene, or any woman. Kazantzakis' characterization of Mary, mother of Jesus, then, is undoubtedly striking and even subversive, although it could be seen to echo some elements of tension in the Gospel's portrayal of Jesus' relationship with his mother. In other respects, however, it could be interpreted as transgressive. Women are given a voice, but that voice is the voice of temptation.

M. Roberts, The Wild Girl (London: Methuen, 1984)

The same cannot be said for our third representation of Jesus and women in fiction, M. Roberts' The Wild Girl (1984). Written as a fifth Gospel, it offers an account of Jesus' teaching and Mary's relationship with him.[78] The entire novel indeed can be said to be a record of her transformative encounter with Jesus. Like Theissen's novel, it is written in the first person narrator form, only this time the narrative voice is feminine, with Mary herself as the narrator. Mary relates her first meeting with Jesus in which he "directed a beam of affection" at her that pierced her.

> I looked at the man who was speaking. He seemed to me quite ugly, with a lined face and a big nose, a slightly hunched back. Then I became aware of his energy that poured from his eyes and his wide mouth, from the set of his long limbs. His gestures disconcerted me at first, and I realized why: he had the grace of a woman.[79]

---

74 Kazantzakis, Last Temptation, pp. 174, 69.
75 Kazantzakis, Last Temptation, p. 151.
76 Kazantzakis, Last Temptation, pp. 72, 84, 164, 311, 452, 465.
77 Kazantzakis, Last Temptation, p. 476.
78 For a critique, see Haskins, Mary Magdalen, pp. 385–6.
79 Roberts, Wild Girl, pp. 33–4.

Before long she has come under the spell of this charismatic figure, whose gestures she describes as "utterly feminine,"[80] whose disciples hung on his every word,[81] and who "talked a great deal, on themes such as justice and the rights of the poor, and the love of the Most High whom he called our Father and Mother."[82] Jesus establishes an egalitarian movement whose male and female followers practise "an ethic of licence very different from the reserved ways we were used to in Bethany."[83] Among the women who become his followers are: Mary, the mother of Jesus, Mary, her sister, and Mary Magdalene, who is distinguished from among the three Marys—as she herself relates with some satisfaction—as "the companion of the Saviour, in recognition of the special love that Jesus and I had for one another. It was a sweet title to my ears, very different to those I had previously borne, or had awarded myself: the slut, the bad sister, the exile, the profligate."[84]

In developing the character of Mary Magdalene, Roberts draws on a considerable range of biblical and post-biblical images, both positive and negative, and this is what makes the novel rich and compelling. On the morning of the third day after Jesus entombment, Mary has a nightmare in which she herself visits "the kingdom of the fallen," and is summoned to identify herself before its Master:

> I am Mary, I cried out: the lover of the Lord. . . .
> I am Mary, I cried even louder: Mary the free woman, Mary the traveller, Mary the singer of songs, Mary the healer and the layer-out of the dead, Mary the sister of Martha and the friend of the mother of Jesus, Mary the disciple and the apostle, she who is sworn to spread the word of the Saviour to those who know him not.[85]

The reader is frequently presented with striking accounts of Mary's vivid dreams and visions. Her dream of the origin of the world subverts the traditional creation story of Adam and Eve ("Both were of great beauty, with black skins that shone like the most precious jet or ebony") by offering an alternative myth in which God's feminine part, Sophia-Wisdom, gives birth to a son, Ignorance, and a daughter, Zoe-Eve; the latter is sent "as an instructor to raise up Adam,

---

[80] Roberts, *Wild Girl*, p. 34.
[81] Roberts, *Wild Girl*, chap. 5.
[82] Roberts, *Wild Girl*, p. 37.
[83] Roberts, *Wild Girl*, p. 50.
[84] Roberts, *Wild Girl*, p. 49.
[85] Roberts, *Wild Girl*, p. 100.

in whom there was no waking soul, and to inspire him;" and the children of Ignorance spread the fiction that she was created out his rib.[86] Her address to the male disciples after the resurrection brings a revelation of the risen Christ's words which announce that "the man and the woman within us have become separated and exiled from each other," that "Christ came to repair the separation and to reunite the two" and that "[w]e have lost the knowledge of the Mother."[87] In another yet more powerful dream of judgement, an unusual twist is given to the classic theory of atonement when Jesus himself is presented as the anti-Christ, and appears in the dock for mankind's crimes against women.[88]

Roberts' depiction of the relationship between Jesus and Mary is an equally bold and uncompromising one. Mary becomes Jesus' lover, and describes (at times with naiveté) the sexual relationship that develops between them ("He held me against him and I smelt his sweat and his hot skin. His tongue gently exploring my mouth was one of the sweetest and sharpest pleasures I have ever known").[89] She describes Jesus as her husband[90] and unites with him, after his resurrection, in the ritual of the bridal chamber.[91] Their intimacy extends to the sharing of personal details, with Jesus telling her of his past life and loves, of his family, of the "slowly dawning sense of his mission, the relief of his mother when finally he told her, and the support she was able to offer him."[92] It also allows emotional exchanges. Jesus gets angry with Mary who warns him against going to Jerusalem.[93] Present nevertheless at the Last Supper,[94] she is later to comfort him in Gethsemane before the soldiers tear him from her arms.[95] Their physical intimacy offends Peter ("Why do you love her more than any of us? Simon Peter burst out, his face red with anger: you know what she's been. It's not right"),[96] leading Jesus to defend her:

---

[86] Roberts, *Wild Girl*, pp. 77–82.
[87] Roberts, *Wild Girl*, pp. 110–11.
[88] Roberts, *Wild Girl*, p. 173.
[89] Roberts, *Wild Girl*, p. 41.
[90] Roberts, *Wild Girl*, pp. 95, 96.
[91] Roberts, *Wild Girl*, chap. 8.
[92] Roberts, *Wild Girl*, p. 44.
[93] Roberts, *Wild Girl*, p. 86.
[94] Roberts, *Wild Girl*, pp. 87–91.
[95] Roberts, *Wild Girl*, pp. 91–3.
[96] Roberts, *Wild Girl*, p. 58.

I am willing to accept the witness of women, he said: and so should you be. I am willing to learn from a woman's vision of the truth. . . . That is what I meant by destroying the works of femaleness. I have come to destroy the works of maleness too.[97]

Although not as profound, or even as well-written as Kazantzakis' *The Last Temptation*, Roberts' novel presents the informed reader with a rich amalgam of intertextual references, a number of which I have commented on elsewhere.[98] Roberts' Mary Magdalene combines the canonical Mary Magdalene (cf. Mark 15:40, 47; 16:1–8 parr; Luke 8:2; John 20:1–18) with Mary of Bethany, the sister of Lazarus and Martha (John 11:1–46; 12:1–8; cf. Luke 10:38–42). Later Christian tradition has supplied further traits: "the great sinner" (her seven demons as the seven deadly sins); the sensual woman (her demonic possession due supremely to sexual obsession); the fallen maiden rescued from moral depravity; the apostle to the apostles; the first missionary preacher sent to France (Provence), and so on.[99] Gnostic texts in particular have suggested some of the more radical elements: the lover, companion, and friend of Jesus; the rival to the male disciples and especially Peter, and the receiver of divine revelations. At a number of points, Roberts has exercised her literary prerogative in adding to or altering the biblical or apocryphal texts or in developing the characterization. Trained as a concubine (*hetaira*) by Sibylla,[100] for example, Mary Magdalene has a gift for song,[101] as well as for magic.[102] Although possessed, her demons are merely figurative ones (restlessness, pride, loneliness).[103] This then is a sympathetic as well as a contemporary approach to the subject of Jesus and women. The ideology pervading the text is clearly and consistently feminist. The novel echoes the work of some of the feminist biblical scholars reviewed above, and expresses in narrative form many of the emphases and concerns of feminist theology. In giving Mary her own voice, and emphasizing the mutuality of the relation between herself and Jesus, it presents, where all three novels are concerned, the most dynamic picture of the transformative encounter.

---

[97] Roberts, *Wild Girl*, p. 61.
[98] Telford, "The New Testament in Fiction and Film," in Davies, Harvey and Watson (eds.), *Words Remembered*, pp. 375–7.
[99] See Moltmann-Wendel, *Women around Jesus*, pp. 61–90.
[100] Roberts, *Wild Girl*, chap. 1.
[101] Roberts, *Wild Girl*, p. 13.
[102] Roberts, *Wild Girl*, pp. 39–41.
[103] Roberts, *Wild Girl*, pp. 14, 85.

Representations of Jesus and Women in Film

Representations of Jesus in the Christ Film

Some reference has already been made to recent literature on religion, theology and film, but within this field there has been considerable interest in representations of Jesus.[104] A variety of celluloid Christs have appeared since the dawn of the cinema, treatments of which were analysed in my article in *Explorations in Theology and Film*. Where the classic Christ film is concerned, I outlined there seven master-images or types which, to avoid repetition, may here be summarized as follows:

1. The *patriarchal* Christ (cf. Henry Byron Warner, or H. B. Warner, as he is invariably known, in Cecil B. DeMille's *The King of Kings*, 1927).

2. The *adolescent* Christ (cf. Jeffrey Hunter in N. Ray's *King of Kings*, 1961).

3. The *pacific* Christ (cf. again Jeffrey Hunter in N. Ray's *King of Kings*, 1961, and Robert Powell in F. Zeffirelli's *Jesus of Nazareth*, 1977).

4. The *subversive* Christ (cf. Enrique Irazoqui in P. Pasolini's *The Gospel According to St. Matthew*, 1964).

5. The *mystical* Christ (cf. Max von Sydow in G. Stevens' *The Greatest Story Ever Told*, 1965).

6. The *musical* Christ (cf. Ted Neely in N. Jewison's *Jesus Christ Superstar*, 1973, and Victor Garbor in D. Greene's *Godspell*, 1973).

7. The *human* Christ (cf. Willem Dafoe in M. Scorsese's *The Last Temptation of Christ*, 1988).

Presently we shall examine some encounters between these Christ-figures and the women who appear in such films.

---

[104] In addition to those already mentioned, see T. Aitken, "The Passion on Film," *The Tablet* (1998), pp. 473–4; Channel Four, *Jesus Christ Movie-Star* (documentary shown April 20, 1992); G. E. Forshey, *American Religious and Biblical Spectaculars* (Westport, CT: Praeger, 1992); D. Graham, "Christ Imagery in Recent Film: A Saviour from Celluloid?," in Porter, Hayes and Tombs (eds.), *Images of Christ*, pp. 306–14; N. P. Hurley, "Cinematic Transformations of Jesus," in J. R. May and M. S. Bird (eds.), *Religion in Film* (Knoxville, TN: University of Tennessee Press, 1981) pp. 61–78; R. Kinnard and T. Davis, *Divine Images. A History of Jesus on the Screen* (New York: Citadel 1992); P. Malone, *Movie Christs and Antichrists* (New York: Crossroad, 1990); G. Ortiz, "Jesus at the Movies: Cinematic Representation of the Christ-Figure," *The Month* (1994), pp. 491–7; J. O. Thompson, "Jesus as Moving Image. The Question of Movement," in Porter, Hayes and Tombs (eds.), *Images of Christ*, pp. 290–304.

Representations of Women in the Christ Film

Because of the relatively insignificant role played by women in the Gospels, film directors have had some difficulty in drawing upon them for characterization and plot. In the classic Christ film, it is not surprising that it is the four previously named women, Mary, mother of Jesus, Mary Magdalene, and Mary and Martha of Bethany who receive the greatest narrative development, especially the first two. Salome, of course, is another figure beloved of film directors,[105] but because she does not appear on screen together with Jesus, I have omitted her. Likewise, there are certain key Gospel passages which are popularly reproduced again and again: the birth story, the anointing of Jesus' feet, the woman taken in adultery, the women at the cross and at the tomb. Interestingly, as in Christian art, no Christ film, as far as I am aware, offers us the anointing of Jesus' head—the Markan and Matthean version—although some, e.g. F. Zeffirelli's *Jesus of Nazareth* (1977), adumbrate it.[106] In general, where the depiction of women in these scenes is concerned, the treatment is for the most part traditional and conservative.

Mary, Mother of Jesus

"Nowhere," according to Babington and Evans in their discussion of women in the Christ film, "is the conservative thrust of the films more evident than in the reiterated depiction of the iconic Mother, an absolute of asexual purity and self-sacrifice."[107] This is clearly seen in Cecil B. DeMille's *The King of Kings* (1927), where, in the second sequence, we are introduced to Mary (Dorothy Cummings), seated at her loom, surrounded by doves, chaste and nun-like in her appearance, modest, gentle and passive in her demeanour, maternal in her actions (she is later to introduce the little blind girl to Jesus, and to accompany and befriend the chastened Mary Magdalene). The doves are apt. A symbol of chastity in ancient Greece, the dove represents a number of things in the Bible, among them purity, gentleness, love, simplicity, longing, guilelessness and innocence,[108] all qualities

---

[105] See A. Bach, "Calling the Shots. Directing Salome's Dance of Death," in Bach (ed.), *Biblical Glamour*, pp. 103–26. Some of my own favourite exchanges are those between the young Salome (Brigid Bazlen) and John the Baptist (Robert Ryan) in N. Ray's *King of Kings* (1961).

[106] For comment, see Moltmann-Wendel, *Women around Jesus*, pp. 100–1.

[107] Babington and Evans, *Biblical Epics*, p. 108.

[108] G. F. Hasel, "Dove," in G. W. Bromiley (ed.), *The International Standard Bible*

adhering to the conventional cinematic mother of Jesus. A symbol of the Spirit and hence of spirituality, the dove is associated not only with the baptism of Jesus (Mark 1:10 parr, esp. Luke 3:22), but also in connection with Mary and Jesus together, at their purification, being the offering of the poor for the redemption of the firstborn (Luke 2:24). Mary's association with the loom is also worth commenting on. Spinning and weaving are not often mentioned in the Bible,[109] nor does the loom figure in connection with Mary in the Gospels. Nevertheless, spinning is given as the task of the industrious house-wife (Prov. 31:19), and one tradition mentioned by Origen (although attributed to Celsus' antagonistic Jewish source) claims that Mary was "a poor country woman who earned her living by spinning."[110]

The loom re-appears in other Christ films, in N. Ray's *King of Kings* (1961), for example, or in G. Stevens' *The Greatest Story Ever Told* (1965). The former occurrence is an interesting one. It features in the scene where Jesus visits his mother prior to his departure to Jerusalem, along with his disciples, to face the growing opposition there to him. Introduced by the narrator's voice-over, this scene shows the two spending some time together, he engaged in carpen-try (the making of a chair), she in spinning. Stylistically, as elsewhere in Ray's film, the scene is striking with regard to its use of colour. One's first impression, indeed, in seeing this film, is of its sense of style, its aesthetic look, its painterly quality. The costumes are immac-ulate, and the colours well-defined, especially the solid blocks of blue, brown, white and red. Mary is dressed in black over dark red, and fringed with white, and Jesus in rust-red on top of white. The cam-era gives a close-up of the yarns in Mary's basket, their colours reflecting the palette used in the film itself. Where characterization is concerned, the adolescent Jesus, played by Jeffrey Hunter, offers a sharp contrast to H. B. Warner's patriarchal Jesus in the 1927

Encyclopedia (Grand Rapids, MI: Eerdmans, 1979), pp. 987–9; E. W. G. Masterman, "Dove," in F. C. Grant and H. H. Rowley (eds.), *Dictionary of the Bible* (Edinburgh: T&T Clark, 1965), p. 221; J. L. McKenzie, "Dove," in J. L. McKenzie (ed.), *Dictionary of the Bible* (London: Geoffrey Chapman, 1966), p. 203.

[109] D. Irvin, "Spin; Spindle," in Bromiley (ed.), *International Standard Bible Encyclopedia*, pp. 597–9; J. L. McKenzie, "Spinning," and "Weaving," in McKenzie (ed.), *Dictionary of the Bible*, pp. 840 and pp. 925–6 resp.

[110] Origen, *Contra Celsum*, 1:28, transl. H. Chadwick (ed.), *Origen: Contra Celsum* (Cambridge: Cambridge University Press, 1965), p. 28. Cited in J. Stevenson, *A New Eusebius: Documents Illustrative of the History of the Church to A.D. 337* (London: SPCK, 1968), p. 138.

version. The part of Mary is played by Siobhan McKenna, which gives *The King of Kings'* earlier pious characterization of the mother of Jesus an added Irish Catholic dimension.[111] As with *The King of Kings* (1927), her accepting and nurturing relationship with Mary Magdalene is earlier emphasized when she receives a visit from the latter and repeats her son's parable of the lost sheep to the enquiring woman. Jesus' visit to his mother is also an invented one, and it introduces a further element of the mother-son relationship not highlighted in DeMille's earlier more passive presentation of Mary. With knowing fatalism at Jesus' decision to postpone his work ("the chair," she declares, "will never be mended") and go to Jerusalem, she nevertheless announces her firm intention to accompany him ("I am going with you!").

If Jesus' fictional visit to his mother in *King of Kings* re-inforces their traditional relationship, her canonical visit to him (cf. Matt. 12:46–50 par) in Pasolini's *The Gospel According to St. Matthew* (1964) tilts in a more subversive direction. Filmed in black and white, the screenplay follows the text of Matthew closely, with the arrival of mother and brothers and Jesus' words about his true family interrupting a series of teachings delivered by him from an elevated battlemented walkway above the crowds. Pasolini's camera-work is active, rough and intimate, with frequent, lingering, facial close-ups, either of Jesus, whose animated persona is in sharp contrast to the silent and awe-struck stares of the crowds, or of Mary, whose beatific expressions reflect, and even sublimate, the passion displayed in her son's vehement utterances. The Jesus portrayed in this film is an angry, subversive Christ, a Christ of the people. Grim, unsmiling, ascetic, disconcerting, Enrique Irazoqui's Jesus, though somewhat distant and detached, displays a far wider range of emotions than previous celluloid Christs, and gives to the role a refreshing urgency and vitality. In line with Pasolini's neo-realism, Mary is initially depicted in the film as an adolescent girl (Margherita Caruso). Subsequently, as in this scene (Jesus' "re-definition" of the family), she appears as an aged peasant woman, played in this case by the director's own mother, Susanna Pasolini.

Jesus' rejection of his mother is particularly striking here, given

---

[111] Babington and Evans, *Biblical Epics*, p. 108. One might contrast here the more subversive use of Sinead O'Connor for the Virgin Mary in Neil Jordan's recent *The Butcher Boy* (1997).

that it so seldom features in the Christ film. The notice intimating
the arrival of his mother and his brothers is given twice, the first
time immediately before Jesus utters the saying about the house
vacated by one unclean spirit only to be re-occupied by seven others
(Matt. 12:43–45), the second where one would expect it, that is, immediately before Jesus' words concerning his true family.[112] Framed
by this notice, the seven spirits saying is given added significance,
therefore (especially "I will go back to my own dwelling"), serving,
as it does, in this context, to increase the harshness of Jesus' words.
Moreover, there is no warmth in Jesus' expression, especially when
he looks at Mary, and asks rhetorically, "Who is a mother, who are
brethren, to me?" Here Mary lowers eyes that are dignified and full
of calm resignation. At the words "If anyone does the will of my
Father in heaven, he is my brother, and sister, and mother," the
camera turns to her in a final close-up. Her face lined with sorrow,
these same eyes touched by pathos, she responds to her son's rejection only with love. She is smiling.

Such subversion is mild, however, when compared with *Monty
Python's Life of Brian* (1979). Not a Christ film, but a merciless par-
ody of the conventions employed in such, this is the antidote to the
pathos induced by two thousand years' worth of dying Christ/suffer-
ing Madonna artistic representations. With a career paralleling that
of his biblical counterpart, the infant Brian is visited (erroneously)
by the three wise men, learns in time that he is actually the son of
a Roman soldier, Naughtius Maximus, joins the politically-correct
People's Front of Judaea (or is it the Judaean People's Front?) under
their leader Reg, falls in love with the fellow-enlistee Judith, is mistaken for the Messiah, witnesses the interrogation of his mother by
the crowd (in respect of her virginity) and is visited on the cross *in
extremis* by the two women in his life. The one is upbeat and appre-
ciative of his sacrifice. "Terrific, great! Reg has explained it all to
me. I think it is great what you are doing! Thank you, Brian. I'll
never forget you," says Judith, and departs.

A very different reaction is given by the other. "So there you are!
I might have known it would end up like this. Just think of all the

---

[112] Note, however, that these words, although present in the Markan text (3:32),
are absent from a number of the major Matthean textual witnesses. Matthew's version of Mark 3:31–35, it should also be observed, is less harsh than that of Mark,
omitting, as it does, the damning introductory notice of Mark 3:21 that his family
regarded him as mad.

love and affection I have wasted on you. Well, if that's how you treat your poor old mother in the autumn years of her life, all I can say is, go ahead, be crucified. See if I care!," says the mother of Jesus, and departs. Easy to laugh at, and therefore to dismiss, *Monty Python's Life of Brian* (1979) nevertheless offers us an actualization of the tension between Jesus and his mother which is merely hinted at in the biblical account (Mark 3:21; John 2:4). It can also be seen as representing in cinematic terms that alternative tradition regarding Jesus and his mother which was mentioned already in connection with Origen's *Contra Celsum*, and which, in naming him Jesus ben Panthera, likewise attributes to him a less than divine paternity. The passage from Origen is worth quoting in full:

> 28 After this he [Celsus] represents the Jew [his alleged interlocutor] as having a conversation with Jesus himself and refuting him on many charges, as he thinks: first, because "he fabricated the story of his birth from a virgin; and he reproaches him because he came from a Jewish village and from a poor country woman who earned her living by spinning". He says that "she was driven out by her husband, who was a carpenter by trade, as she was convicted of adultery". Then he says that "after she had been driven out by her husband and while she was wandering about in a disgraceful way she secretly gave birth to Jesus".

> 32 Let us return, however, to the words put into the mouth of the Jew, where "the mother of Jesus" is described as having been "turned out by the carpenter who was betrothed to her, as she had been convicted of adultery and had a child by a certain soldier named Panthera".[113]

Mary Magdalene

Such an approach to the relationship between Jesus and his mother can only be taken, however, in a spoof. Mary, the mother of Jesus, allows little room for unconventional embellishment. For that reason, the most prominent female character in the classic Christ film, as in the novel, and the one most subject to character if not to narrative development, has been Mary Magdalene. In sharp contrast to Mary, mother of Jesus, Mary Magdalene has offered screen-writers and directors an opportunity to exhibit the erotic. The biblical image

---

[113] Origen, *Contra Celsum*, 1:28, 32, transl. H. Chadwick (ed.), *Origen: Contra Celsum*, pp. 28, 31. Cited in Stevenson, *New Eusebius*, pp. 138–9.

of Mary, as we have noted, is essentially that of the healed follower, the first witness to the resurrection, and therefore, in a sense, the first apostle.[114] In contrast, the cinematic Mary Magdalene draws on an image of Mary Magdalene which is not biblical, yet has become the dominant one in Western art and literature, viz. Mary as the prostitute and repentant sinner (cf. e.g. Cecil B. DeMille's *The King of Kings*, N. Jewison's *Jesus Christ Superstar*, F. Zeffirelli's *Jesus of Nazareth*, M. Scorsese's *The Last Temptation of Christ*). The image came about when Mary Magdalene was identified by the Church Fathers with the woman who anointed Jesus' feet (Luke 7:36–50),[115] an identification that today draws cries of anguish from feminist writers.[116] The word "magdalen" itself has come to mean a repentant prostitute or unwed mother. Her use of ointment in the story led in turn to her becoming the patron saint of the perfume industry in the Middle Ages.[117] In D. Arcand's *Jésus de Montréal* (1989), Mary Magdalene is represented allegorically by Mireille, a model who is first seen exploiting her body in a perfume commercial,[118] as well as (but to a lesser extent) by Constance, a priest's lover. In a number of the Christ films, Mary Magdalene is identified with the woman taken in adultery (cf. e.g. N. Ray's *King of Kings*, G. Stevens, *The Greatest Story Ever Told*).

Other more positive images of Mary Magdalene, one observes, tend to be ignored, e.g. the traditional but again non-biblical image of her as a model for the contemplative life, an image which arose when Mary Magdalene was equated both with the Johannine Mary of Bethany (John 11:1–46; 12:1–8) and with the Lukan Mary (cf. Luke 10:38–42, which does not mention Bethany), and when Luke 10:42 ("Mary has chosen the good portion, and it shall not be taken away from her") was consequently applied to her. It is this image, of Mary as the contemplative and the visionary, which is prominent in the apocryphal Gospels, in particular in the Gnostic texts previously referred to. There, she is not only given a physical relationship with Jesus, as we have seen, but also receives revelations and visions from Jesus, which put her into rivalry with the male disciples. It was

---

[114] Moltmann-Wendel, *Women around Jesus*, pp. 72, 75.
[115] Hannay, "Mary Magdalene," in Jeffrey (ed.), *Dictionary of Biblical Tradition*, p. 486.
[116] Moltmann-Wendel, *Women around Jesus*, pp. 64, 84.
[117] Moltmann-Wendel, *Women around Jesus*, p. 87.
[118] See Haskins, *Mary Magdalen*, p. 375; J. Schaberg, "Fast Forwarding to the Magdalene," in Bach (ed.), *Biblical Glamour*, pp. 33–45, esp. p. 37, n. 10.

this aspect of the Magdalene which effectively ended when her identification with Mary of Bethany was challenged (by Calvin) at the Reformation,[119] and it is these elements of the Magdalene image (the contemplative and the visionary, as well as the competitive and the erotic) which have not, on the whole, been exploited by screen-writers and film directors as they were, for example, by M. Roberts in *The Wild Girl*.

Yet this is not the full story. Some subversive elements of this kind do appear in the Christ film. Physical contact between Mary Magdalene and Jesus is offered in *Jesus Christ Superstar* (1973) and a sexual rela-tionship in *The Last Temptation of Christ* (1988). In Stevens' *The Greatest Story Ever Told* (1965), Mary Magdalene is shown sitting in the com-pany of the men as Jesus discourses with them. In a number of films, Mary Magdalene's visit to the tomb (as in Stevens' *The Greatest Story Ever Told*) and her encounter with the risen Jesus (as in Ray's *King of Kings*) is given special emphasis. Mary's *disbelieved* message is given particular prominence, for example, in Zeffirelli's *Jesus of Nazareth* (1977). In the celebrated ending to Ray's *King of Kings* (1961), when the "shadow of the Galilean" falls over the nets abandoned by his disciples on the shore to form a cross, Mary Magdalene is shown in close-up among the male disciples when they receive their great commission.[120]

Subtleties in the nature of the relationship between Jesus and Mary Magdalene can also be observed when one reviews a number of these Christ films. The most famous transformative encounter between Jesus and Mary Magdalene is the exorcism scene in Cecil B. DeMille's *The King of Kings* (1927). This was the first full-length, silent Hollywood epic on the life of Jesus as seen from the perspective of Mary Magdalene, its screenplay being the result of DeMille's collaboration with script-writer Jeanie McPherson.[121] Combining sex and piety, the film presents Mary as a rich courtesan, whose lover Judas has been snatched out of her clutches by the carpenter from Nazareth. The

---

[119] Hannay, "Mary Magdalene," in Jeffrey (ed.), *Dictionary of Biblical Tradition*, p. 487.

[120] Babington and Evans, *Biblical Epics*, pp. 108–9.

[121] In view of the prominence given to Mary Magdalene, but the patriarchal nature of the resulting product, it is interesting to speculate on the nature of this collaboration. For some revealing comments, see D. Hayne (ed.). *The Autobiography of Cecil B. DeMille* (London: W. H. Allen, 1960), p. 255, esp. n. 1. See also L. Francke, *Script Girls: Women Screenwriters in Hollywood* (London: British Film Institute Publishing, 1994).

encounter between them is carefully prepared and takes place in the third sequence. Mary arrives at the house where Jesus is to be found in her zebra-drawn chariot. "Where is this vagabond carpenter," she asks, and to Judas, "Where is this Man who holdeth thee from Mary Magdalene?" The two meet and Mary is discomfited by his knowing gaze. He drives out the demons in her (viz. lust, greed, pride, gluttony, indolence, envy, anger) with the words of Matt. 8:3 ("Be thou clean!"). "He doth cleanse her of the seven deadly sins," Peter cries (cf. Luke 8:2). "Blessed are the pure in heart," says Jesus (Matt. 5:8), and the scene ends.

The style of this sequence is representative of the film as a whole, with its medium, close-up and point of view shots, which do much to humanize the biblical characters, with its employment of biblical quotations (Authorised Version) as captions which function as an unspoken commentary on the actions (Jesus' words "Be thou clean," Matt. 8:3, are actually those to the man with leprosy!), and with its use of traditional Christian hymns ("Blessed are the pure in heart," as here) to achieve a heightened emotional charge. In iconic counterpoint to Mary, the mother of Jesus, Mary Magdalene, as played by Jacqueline Logan, is youthful, brazen, sensual, aggressively sexual, oozing a mixture of self-assurance and eroticism. Alongside her, H. B. Warner's Jesus, in line with DeMille's conception of him,[122] is both tender and virile, a mature, majestic, ethereal, composed, and essentially controlled figure. With such an extravagant depiction of Mary, we have almost reached the apogee of the "Mary as whore" tradition, and the post-biblical identification of her seven demons (Luke 8:2) with the seven deadly sins is an added flourish. It is Warner's spirituality, and not his masculinity, however, which responds to the sensual woman confronting him.

Babington and Evans, in their discussion of this sequence, note that it "accords with DeMille's reputation for indulging the erotic under cover of the pietistic," but add, "to agree that DeMille is the master of such contradictory effects—the pleasures of the Magdalene's haughty libido, gleaming flesh and daringly fetishistic costumes, followed by her submission to the patriarchal gaze of Christ—is not

---

[122] See Hayne (ed.), *Cecil B. DeMille*, p. 253. "H. B. Warner perfectly understood the conception of Christ that I wanted to portray. All my life I have wondered how many people have been turned away from Christianity by the effeminate, sanctimonious, machine-made Christs of second-rate so-called art, which used to be thought good enough for Sunday schools."

to exhaust the interest of what is so uninhibitedly given."[123] What we have here is an unrestrained acting out of the important cultural tension between religion and sexuality, a conflict which the Christ film did not adequately engage until Scorsese's *The Last Temptation of Christ* (1988). Mary represents not only woman in her guise as sexual temptress but also in her role as usurper of male power and authority. She is brash, confident, sure both of herself and of her influence over men. "The intertitle [in the first sequence]," Babington and Evans note, "emphasises the double aspect of her transgressions: 'The beautiful courtesan MARY OF MAGDALA, laughed alike at God and Man.'"[124] The exorcism scene represents, then, the taming of this dangerous quality, and its sublimation to the power of the patriarchal Jesus. "Mary," they suggest, "is acting out but an extreme version of the 'new' woman, more than half celebrated in DeMille's comedies but here seen dangerously as, to use the title of one of his films near in date to *The King of Kings, The Godless Girl* (1928). Powerful, wealthy, contemptuous of family and marriage, she is a fascinating minatory vision of the female not just removed from the male order but exercising control over men."[125]

The process of Mary's domestication is made painfully obvious in the body language. After her exorcism, Magdalene adopts a passive, submissive pose. "Looking down at her body and, perceiving it to be immodestly exposed, she rearranges the dark cloak she is wearing into a nunnish robe that imitates the clothing and headdress of Mary the Mother standing nearby, and then kneels at the Saviour's feet."[126] Her conversion from activity to passivity, from domination to submission, from sensuality to modesty is not complete, however, for traces of her former self (and eroticism) are retained, not only in three later invented incidents (her enthusiastic support for Jesus' coronation, and her attempts to prevent both the bribing of the crowd and the piercing of Jesus' side) but also in her dress (the continuing exposure of her arms and hair).[127]

A more conventional, indeed muted, treatment is offered of Jesus' relationship with Mary Magdalene in G. Stevens' *The Greatest Story Ever Told* (1965). Their encounter takes place in Capernaum, with

---

[123] Babington and Evans, *Biblical Epics*, p. 113.
[124] Babington and Evans, *Biblical Epics*, p. 115.
[125] Babington and Evans, *Biblical Epics*, p. 115.
[126] Babington and Evans, *Biblical Epics*, p. 115.
[127] Babington and Evans, *Biblical Epics*, p. 117.

the viewer being introduced to her through the familiar story of the woman taken in adultery. As with Ray's *King of Kings* (1961), Stevens' film too has a decidedly aesthetic feel to it. The settings as well as the colours are striking. In place of Ray's predilection for a range of solid colours, however, Stevens preferred a more limited number, many of his characters being dressed, as in this scene, in plain white, grey or black, neutral colours which blend in more naturally with the background. A surrealistic touch is given at the beginning of the scene by the presence of the devil (Donald Pleasence), dressed in dark grey rags.

In traditional fashion, Jesus (Max von Sydow) is presented as a defender of the woman. With his straight, black hair and beard, and Swedish accent, von Sydow's Byzantine Jesus conveys a spiritual and unearthly quality. Jesus' nobility of character, firmness of purpose, certainty of mind, and sadness of spirit are also conveyed well by him. With his strange, otherworldly and ascetic demeanour, the actor brings us a mystical Christ in sharp contrast to the energetic and driven figure of Pasolini. The characterization of the woman (Joanna Dunham) is far less satisfactory. Clearly colour-coded, she is dressed in scarlet, and, as so often in the Christ film, she is given no voice other than to utter her name, Mary of Magdala. With the silence of the crowds as a backdrop, their encounter generates no more dynamism or reciprocity than that between a scared rabbit rescued by a motorist from the glare of headlights. Intertextually, too, the scene is curious for it represents a multiple conflation: the anonymous woman caught *flagrante delicto* (John 7:53–8:11) linked with the canonical Mary Magdalene, combined in turn with Luke's "sinner" (Luke 7:36–50), to produce a Mary of Magdala who is not only an adulteress but is also a prostitute![128]

If Stevens' *The Greatest Story Ever Told* (1965) hardly broke new ground where Jesus' relationship with women is concerned, N. Jewison's *Jesus Christ Superstar* (1973) certainly did. One particular sequence illustrates this well. Jesus and his youthful band of followers have taken refuge in a cave prior to the events of Holy Week. The women, particularly Mary Magdalene, are seeing to his needs, but Judas is critical of the relationship between them. At first viewing, the sequence appears dated, and with a black Judas (Carl Anderson) as the lonely outsider it would perhaps even be consid-

---

[128] See Schaberg, "Fast Forwarding," in Bach (ed.), *Biblical Glamour*, p. 37, n. 10.

ered politically incorrect nowadays. Indeed all the film's characters (Jesus, the disciples, the Jewish authorities, Mary, Judas) can clearly be seen to be rehearsing the rhetoric and counter-rhetoric of the youth revolution of the late sixties and early seventies. Conventionally, however, Jesus (Ted Neely) is not only dressed in white, but bathed in white light. Traditionally, too, he acts as Mary's defender, with Mary (Yvonne Elliman) at times appearing quite child-like. Her face is seen in close-up, for example, at child's height, alongside Jesus' white garment, when Judas issues his rebuke:

> Yes I can understand that she amuses, but to let her kiss you, stroke your hair, that's hardly in your line. It's not that I object to her profession, but she doesn't fit in well with what you teach and say. It doesn't help us if you're inconsistent. They only need a small excuse to put us all away.

Mary's characterization clearly draws on Luke 7:36–50, a passage which is called to mind when Mary washes Jesus' feet and Judas objects (cf. also John 12:1–8) in a manner reminiscent of Simon the Pharisee, "It seems to me a strange thing, mystifying, that a man like you can waste his time on women of her kind" (cf. Luke 7:39, "If this man were a prophet he would know who is touching him and what kind of woman she is—that she is a sinner"). Other less conventional elements, however, are invoked. Judas' more specific objection to their physical intimacy ("to let her kiss you, stroke your hair") recalls the Gnostic version of their relationship previously referred to (cf. e.g. *The Gospel of Philip* 63:32–64:5).[129] Where gender relations are concerned, one notes indeed a considerable advance in the depiction of Jesus' relation to women. Not only is Mary Magdalene a more important character in this Christ film (cf. e.g. other key sequences such as the incomparably beautiful, "I don't know how to love him"), but her physical relationship to Jesus is here explored in a dramatically new way. "Let me try to cool down your face a bit," says Mary, mopping his brow in a manner that is hardly perfunctory. E. Moltmann-Wendel sees dramatized here what she calls the "helpless therapy of the world by women:"

---

[129] See E. Hennecke and W. Schneemelcher (eds.), *New Testament Apocrypha I* (London: SCM, 1963), p. 277; E. Pagels, *The Gnostic Gospels* (London: Weidenfeld and Nicholson, 1979), p. 64; J. M. Robinson (ed.), *The Nag Hammadi Library in English. Fourth Revised Edition* (Leiden: Brill, 1996), p. 148.

> The women surround Jesus like nurses, and while Mary Madgalene
> speaks hypnotically to him, to make him relax, to close his eyes, to
> think of nothing and to let the world be the world, the others mut-
> ter in confirmation, as though in a refrain, 'Ev'rythings alright yes
> ev'rythings alright yes ev'rythings alright'.[130]

The film also offers us a more animated, a more energetic, a more
contemporary Jesus whose own needs arc emphasized in relation to
Mary. "She always tries to give me what I need just here and now,"
says Jesus of her. After Judas' attack on her, Jesus responds initially
by stroking Mary's face. Then he rises to his feet to defend her, and
advancing aggressively towards a retreating Judas sings, "Who are
you to criticize her? Who are you to despise her? Leave her, leave
her, let her be now, leave her, leave her, she's with me now, if your
slate is clean, then you can throw stones, if your slate is not, then
leave her alone."

A solid return to a more conservative Christ and a more traditional Mary Magdalene is to be seen in F. Zeffirelli's *Jesus of Nazareth*
(1977). With its colourful costumes and realistic settings (filmed in
North Africa), this is "an immaculate conception," a Bible-stories-
brought-alive production with little creative interpretation. The script
(by Anthony Burgess and others) follows that of the Gospels, and
because of its leisurely pace, it has time to fill in the gaps and iron
out the creases in the biblical narrative in respect of character and
motivation. Notwithstanding, the scene where Mary Magdalene bursts
into Simon the Pharisee's house and anoints Jesus' feet with her tears
is disappointing. The part of Jesus in this film is played by Robert
Powell, and the strength of the performance is its depiction of the
power, clarity, wit and idealism of Jesus' teaching. Powell's Jesus
comes over as a dignified and articulate pacifist, who, although per-
ceptive, is strangely out of tune with the political and religious currents of his day. His Jesus is a monumental Christ certain of his
divine status and without a hint of self-doubt. There is very little
scepticism in this presentation, a believing ideology, a subtext of faith,
pervading the script. This comes out in Jesus' interaction with Mary
Magdalene. A close-up of his face, as she kisses his feet, registers
mild shock, a sense of compassion, but no vulnerability. Dressed, as
usual, in deep scarlet, Mary Magdalene is played by Anne Bancroft,

---

[130] Moltmann-Wendel, *Women around Jesus*, pp. 89–90.

whose unforgettable performance as Dustin Hoffman's nemesis, the cynical Mrs Robinson, in Mike Nichols' *The Graduate* (1967), is one that gives added poignancy to her role as the ageing prostitute here.

Although the scene is introduced with Simon the Pharisee's question, "But who is my neighbour?" (cf. the parable of the Good Samaritan), its dependence on Luke 7:36–50 is strong. As in this passage, the woman (here identified with Mary) is carrying an alabaster pot. Jesus' speech in Luke 7 is also repeated here with the exception of the parable of the two debtors. The Jewish authorities in black scrutinize her with patriarchal disapproval, and Simon's vocal remonstration, "Rabbi, you know what kind of a woman this is," voices the silent objection that is raised in Luke 7:39. The guests' discomfiture with Jesus' pronouncement of forgiveness is amplified, however, from Mark 2:7 ("Only God can forgive sins, no man"). And when Jesus takes Mary's head in his hands and pronounces "Your faith has saved you, go *and sin no more*," these words (italicized) are borrowed not from Luke 7:50, but again from the story of the woman taken in adultery (John 8:11). Incongruously, the address "daughter" is added to Jesus' words "Your sins are forgiven" (cf. Mark 5:34, where Jesus addresses the woman with the haemorrhage in the same fashion) as is the justification "because of the greatness of your love" (in Luke 7:47 these words are spoken to Simon, one notes, not the woman, "her sins . . . are forgiven, for she loved much"). The scene ends with Jesus' instruction, "Daughter, take this ointment, *keep it for my burial*; go in peace" (cf. Mark 14:3–9 and par Matt., where, however, it is *the woman's initiative* which is described, where she anoints Jesus' *head*, not his feet, as a *prophetic* action anticipating his death). Not only is the (Markan and Matthean) anointing woman's role as *agent* taken from her, but Mary Magdalene, who is identified with her, is also given no voice. Consider this recent feminist reaction:

> Her scene at the house of Simon the Pharisee I find very difficult to watch. . . . She enters screaming at those who would keep her out, but then utters a long, embarrassing series of wordless sighs and whimpers, as she grovels at Jesus' feet, refused a discourse. . . . She moves from representing somebody's idea of the force and danger of female sexuality and male fear of it, to representing sexuality tamed. Jesus' acceptance and forgiveness brings her under control, under his protection. In contrast to 'the Last Temptation', where her sexuality threatens to draw Jesus away from his goal, and where she must die at least

in his dream, Jesus here is invulnerable to her, does not desire or fear her, smugly calls her 'daughter' in spite of the difference in the actors' ages.[131]

Appearing in a later scene, when Jesus is taken down from the cross, Mary, this time in a black, nun-like habit like the other women, again kisses his feet. It is only in her final dramatic exit (after visiting the empty tomb, and reporting to the disciples behind locked doors), in what Schaberg claims is Mary Magdalene's only self-defence in the history of interpretation, that she recovers her voice.[132] Disbelieved by the male disciples when she claims to have seen the risen Jesus, she angrily exclaims, "Was his death a fantasy? Why should he not appear to me?" Then, coldly and deliberately, she declares, "He told me to tell you, and I have done so," before slamming the door and departing.

Of all the representations of Jesus and Mary Magdalene in the classic Christ film, that of M. Scorsese (and his script-writer P. Schrader) in *The Last Temptation of Christ* is perhaps the most challenging, and the most contemporary. The film is based on the book by N. Kazantzakis, which we have discussed already, but Scorsese and Schrader bring further dimensions to it. Their treatment of Jesus' visit to Mary Magdalene's brothel is particularly innovative. After waiting all day to see her, Jesus approaches Mary after her last client has gone. Inspired by Pasolini, Scorsese uses a very mobile and intimate camera, which frequently captures the turbulence of its central character, played here by Willem Dafoe. One is struck by the stillness of this scene, however, and the absence of sound, except for the vaguely oriental music at the beginning. The intimacy is enhanced by a lack of any others in the scene, as well as by the subjective camera-work. There is a prolonged view, from Jesus' perspective, of the naked Magdalene, from behind, as he furtively approaches her, a shot whose subjectivity surpasses that of the topless girl on whom the camera lingers as he approaches Mary's house. Jesus' eyes are fixed on Mary, a gaze which is normally reversed in the classic Christ film.

Scorsese offers us here a massively unmonumental Christ, a human Jesus, open and vulnerable, seeking something from Mary, and not *vice versa*. If Cecil B. DeMille's *The King of Kings* (1927) gave us a Christ who encounters the "new" woman (albeit of the twenties and

[131] Schaberg, "Fast Forwarding," in Bach (ed.), *Biblical Glamour*, p. 39.
[132] Schaberg, "Fast Forwarding," in Bach (ed.), *Biblical Glamour*, pp. 41–2.

thirties!), Scorsese's *The Last Temptation of Christ* (1988) gives us a Mary Magdalene who encounters the "new" man (of the eighties and nineties). His actions as well as language are uncharacteristic. This is a penitent Jesus who asks for forgiveness. "'What are you doing here?,' says Mary. 'I want you to forgive me,' says Jesus. 'I've done too many bad things. I'm going to the desert, and I need you to forgive me . . . before I go,'" he says almost in a whisper. Although he is a Jesus with a mission to save the world ("'Look, Mary. Look at this [surveying the brothel]. God can change this, God can save your soul'"), he is a saviour who is vulnerable to sexual temptation. At one point, Mary turns from rejecting him to seducing him. "'You want to save my soul? This is what you have in mind [gradually exposing her body]. You know that. You're the same as all the others although you can't admit it. You're pitiful. I hate you. Here's my body. Save it. Save it [she places his hand on her stomach].'" When Jesus rejects her advance violently, and turns away, she calls out to him in rebuff, questioning his manhood. This is also a Jesus with a past relationship with the Mary he wishes to save. As Jesus is about to leave he turns to her, reminding her of their childhood experience. "'Mary, don't you remember?' 'No, I don't remember. Why should I? Nothing has changed. Say the truth.'"

If the Jesus of this transformative encounter is given untraditional words and actions, then Mary too is given a voice, as well as a distinct personality. She is allowed to challenge Jesus. "'Oh I see. You sit out there all day with the others, and then you come in here with your head down saying 'Forgive me!' Forgive me! It's not that easy. Just because you need forgiveness, don't ask me to do it.'" She is even permitted to emote against God when told that he can save her soul. "'He already broke my heart. He took you away from me. And I hate both of you,'" she replies. Barbara Hershey, who plays the part of Mary Magdalene in the film, and who first put the novel in Scorsese's hands, speaks of the part as follows:

> The thing that fascinates me about Mary Magdalene is that she represents all aspects of womanhood: she's a whore and a victim, a complete primal animal, and then she's reborn and becomes virginal and sisterlike. She evolves through all phases of womanhood, so it was a wonderful role in that way . . . I felt that I was put on earth to play this part.[133]

---

[133] *Gratia* Schaberg, "Fast Forwarding," in Bach (ed.), *Biblical Glamour*, p. 35, citing Lemos: 126, 124.

As with Kazantzakis' novel, Scorsese's film has attracted a great deal of controversy,[134] especially from fundamentalists who have objected to its depiction of Jesus. As one critic has observed, however, "[t]he use of females throughout to signify only motherhood and temptation (of the male) suggests that if anyone should be objecting to this film, it is women of all denominations rather than fundamentalists of both sexes."[135] It is not that there is none of the reciprocity, the mutuality, the equality in relationship that feminists have called for in depictions of gender relations. As Babington and Evans remark:

> The limitation of the film's portrait of women is less disdain for female sexuality (Barbara Hershey's Magdalene hardly represents that), more an inability to figure women as other than sexual, as female *and* spiritual. . . . So even though celebrated as sexual being, like the other women, she is ultimately portrayed as biological trap for the hero, the male never correspondingly representing the same threat for the spiritual woman.[136]

A final sequence worthy of comment is from D. Arcand's *Jésus de Montréal* (1989), a French-Canadian film about actors who get drawn into a passion play and whose real-life experiences, especially that of the Jesus character, begin to reflect that of the Gospel story. At one point Daniel Colombe (Lothaire Bluteau), the actor playing Jesus, accompanies Mireille (Catherine Wilkening), the model (and Mary Magdalene surrogate), to an audition for a television commercial. When she is asked to remove not only her jeans but her top, Daniel objects. Intertextually, the scene takes its cue from the Cleansing of the Temple (Mark 11:15–19 par). "Can we have the big scene another day? We've got work to do," says the hard-bitten female audition head. "You [motioning to Daniel] sit at the back, and you [to Mireille] show us your tits or you go home, OK?" "I'll make a scene," says Daniel, and before the shocked eyes of the hitherto leering executives, proceeds to overturn the table with the refreshments, and then a camera. Jerzy, the audition head's male colleague, ushers them out with embarrassment. The unstoppable Daniel then overturns a table with a TV monitor, and when the audition head declares

---

[134] See Telford, "Jesus Christ Movie-Star," in Marsh and Ortiz (eds.), *Explorations*, pp. 136–7; idem, "The New Testament in Fiction and Film," in Davies, Harvey and Watson (eds.), *Words Remembered*, pp. 378–81.

[135] J. Rosenbaum, "Raging Messiah. The Last Temptation of Christ," *Sight and Sound* 57 (1988), pp. 281–2, esp. p. 281.

[136] Babington and Evans, *Biblical Epics*, p. 166.

"An actor's tantrum!," he strikes her. The scene eventually becomes humorous when Jerzy, attempting to reassure his clients in the lobby ("It often happens on a shoot. I'll handle him"), is confronted by the charging Daniel, wielding an electrical cord, and all are made to beat a hasty retreat from the building, with Daniel's "Bastards!" ringing in their ears.

Here then we have the usual defence of the woman by the Christ figure, but with obvious contemporary developments. Absent is the passivity associated with the Magdalene figure. Though Daniel leaps to defend her, she has already been robustly self-protective. He asks her not to expose herself, and she replies "I don't mind. . . . I'm used to it." "You're worth more than that," he says. "How would you know?," she replies with pain and sadness. "Let's go," he says. At the end of the scene Mireille (still without her jeans), follows Daniel outside, pins him against the wall and in an intense mutual close-up declares, "I love you, you madman!" She kisses him on the cheek (which is all he offers her) and looks lovingly at him. He remains serious and inscrutable. In this naturalistic interchange we have come a long way from Cecil B. DeMille's *The King of Kings*!

Conclusion

In this essay, we have examined actualizations of biblical texts in fiction and film which embody the relationship between Jesus and women. We have commented on the relation of these texts to the biblical (and apocryphal) texts on which they are based, and have sought to throw light on the dynamics of the transformative encounters reflected in them, and on the gender ideology underlying them. Where intertextual relations are concerned, we have noted the favouring, in general, of the canonical texts over the apocryphal ones, the fondness of script-writers and directors in particular for certain key Gospel passages (e.g. the anointing of Jesus' feet, the woman taken in adultery), and their avoidance of others (e.g. the anointing of Jesus' head), and the frequent conflation of characters and settings. Where specific characterization is concerned—for example, with Mary Magdalene—there has been a tendency to draw on the post-biblical "great sinner" or "prostitute" tradition, and to ignore the more radical tradition (of Mary as contemplative and visionary, as consort of Jesus and rival of the apostles) represented in the Gnostic texts.

M. Roberts' *The Wild Girl* (1984) represents a prominent exception.

As for the treatment of Jesus and women, narrative development and characterization was found to be greater in the novels under scrutiny than in the Christ films, as we would expect. Gender-sensitivity was expressed through the character of Joanna in G. Theissen's *The Shadow of the Galilean* (1987). In N. Kazantzakis' *The Last Temptation* (1961), however, despite its other radical elements, women were treated as objects of sexual desire or as icons of domesticity. Although women were given a voice, it was the voice of temptation. In M. Roberts' *The Wild Girl* (1984), Mary Magdalene, on the other hand, is given not only a voice as a character, but also as the narrator who, in this case, represents the implied (as well as the real) author's ideological point of view. The Christ films were found to be more conservative and more traditional than the novels we have reviewed. Although we drew attention to the different ways Christ has been depicted on screen, a major tendency in many of the transformative encounters between Jesus and women in these films is for Jesus to be given a strong, masculine presence and a commanding albeit compassionate voice, and for the women with whom he interacts to be given a submissive presence and virtually no voice at all. The depiction of Mary, mother of Jesus, in particular tends to be both conservative and traditional. Characterization, if not narrative development, is more considerable in the case of Mary Magdalene, although conservative treatments occur in G. Stevens' *The Greatest Story Ever Told* (1965) and F. Zeffirelli's *Jesus of Nazareth* (1977). Her bold, over-the-top treatment in DeMille's *The King of Kings* is followed nevertheless by her domestication.

This traditional pattern has been subverted in the Christ films, however, on more than one occasion. We have noted, for example, the mildly subversive treatment of Mary, mother of Jesus, in P. Pasolini's *The Gospel According to St. Matthew* (1964) and the boldly subversive one in *Monty Python's Life of Brian* (1979). Subversive elements in the depiction of Mary Magdalene have also been observed in both novels and films. Her physical contact with Jesus was noted in N. Jewison's *Jesus Christ Superstar* (1973), and her sexual relationship in N. Kazantzakis' *The Last Temptation* (1961), M. Roberts' *The Wild Girl* (1984) and M. Scorsese's *The Last Temptation of Christ* (1988). Furthermore, an increased interaction and a more dynamic or mutual relationship between Jesus and Mary Magdalene was observed in M. Roberts' *The Wild Girl* (1984), N. Kazantzakis' *The Last Temptation* (1961), N. Jewison's

Jesus Christ Superstar (1973), M. Scorsese's *The Last Temptation of Christ* (1988) and D. Arcand's *Jésus de Montréal* (1989).

Commenting on the Hollywood Christ film, Babington and Evans state: "These films are complex negotiations between the original texts and later cultural moments marked by female demands for autonomy and by an instability in the meanings of masculinity and femininity."[137] This essay may be said to bear out this conclusion in respect of the literary and filmic texts that we have considered. The limitations under which novelists, script-writers and directors have operated in their depiction of Jesus and women should also be borne in mind: the largely negative depiction of women in the Bible over-all, and the (at least) ambiguous one represented in the New Testament and particular in the Gospels; the limited characterization and nar-rative role of women in the Gospels; the practical demands of the screenplay (where the Christ film is concerned) in terms of the need for condensation, economy of scene, etc.; the nature of the Christ figure, the religious dimension surrounding him, the ever-present threat of censorship, and so on. What is clear is that if the Christ novel or Christ film is to have a future, then it must seek to por-tray the transformative encounter between Jesus and women in ways that take into account the dynamics of interpersonal relationship as understood in a post-Christian and now post-feminist world, and give due weight to the contemporary values of mutuality and reciprocity in gender relations.

---

[137] Babington and Evans, *Biblical Epics*, pp. 107–8.

INDEX OF NAMES

INDEX OF SUBJECTS

INDEX OF SCRIPTURE AND OTHER
ANCIENT SOURCES

NEW TESTAMENT

HEBREW BIBLE

Ancient Jewish Literature

Apocrypha

Pseudepigrapha

GRAECO-ROMAN LITERATURE

EARLY CHRISTIAN LITERATURE

(Apocrypha)